Screen Ages

Screen Ages is a valuable guide for students exploring the complex and vibrant history of US cinema and how this film culture has grown, changed, and developed.

Covering key periods from across American cinema history, John Alberti explores the social, technological, and political forces that have shaped cinematic output and the varied impacts of cinema on US society.

Each chapter has a series of illuminating key features, including:

- "Now playing," focusing on films as cinematic events, from *The Birth of a Nation* to *Gone with the Wind* to *Titanic,* to place the reader in the social context of those viewing the films for the first time.
- "In development," exploring changing genres, from the melodrama to contemporary superhero movies.
- "The names above and below the title," portraying the impact and legacy of central figures, including Florence Lawrence, Orson Welles, and Wes Anderson.
- Case studies, analyzing key elements of films and film culture in more depth.
- Glossary terms featured throughout the text, to aid non-specialist students and expand the reader's understanding of changing screen cultures.

Screen Ages illustrates how the history of US cinema has always been and continues to be one of multiple screens, audiences, venues, and markets. It is an essential text for all those wanting to understand the power of American cinema throughout history and the challenges for its future.

The book is also supported by a companion website (www.routledge.com/cw/alberti), featuring additional case studies, an interactive blog, a quiz bank for each chapter, and an online chapter, "Screen ages today," that will be updated to discuss the latest developments in American cinema.

John Alberti is Director of Graduate Studies and Director of Cinema Studies in the Department of English at Northern Kentucky University, USA. His previous books included *The Working Life: Readings on Work, Labor, and Career, Leaving Springfield: The Simpsons and the Possibilities of Oppositional Culture*, and *The Canon in the Classroom: Pedagogical Implications of Canon Revision in American Literature.*

Screen Ages

A Survey of American Cinema

John Alberti

Routledge
Taylor & Francis Group

LONDON AND NEW YORK

First published 2015
by Routledge
2 Park Square, Milton Park, Abingdon, Oxon OX14 4RN

and by Routledge
711 Third Avenue, New York, NY 10017

Routledge is an imprint of the Taylor & Francis Group, an informa business

British Library Cataloguing in Publication Data
A catalogue record for this book is available from the British Library

Library of Congress Cataloging in Publication Data
Alberti, John.
Screen ages : a survey of American cinema / John Alberti.
pages cm
1. Motion pictures--United States--History. 2. Motion picture industry--United States--History.
I. Title.
PN1993.5.U6A825 2014
791.430973--dc23
2014014904

ISBN: 978-0-415-53551-9 (hbk)
ISBN: 978-0-415-53552-6 (pbk)
ISBN: 978-1-315-76310-1 (ebk)

Typeset in 9/12 Sabon LT Pro
by Fakenham Prepress Solutions, Fakenham, Norfolk NR21 8NN

Printed and bound in the United States of America by Sheridan Books, Inc. (a Sheridan Group Company).

To my mother, Eleanor Alberti, who gave me the gift of her own love and joy for the movies.

Contents

Figures

Chapter 3

Chapter 4

Chapter 5

Chapter 6

Chapter 7

Chapter 8

Acknowledgments

Although this book technically has my name on the cover, it is really the result of the wisdom, scholarship, encouragement, and friendship of so many people over the years who have guided and influenced my life-long study and love of the movies. If anything in this book provides a fresh insight, sparks a new perspective, or enriches your own screen experiences, credit goes to these people who have taught me so much; any errors or mistakes are mine alone.

I owe my deepest thanks and gratitude towards my two editors at Routledge. Natalie Foster was the person who invited me to submit a proposal for what would become *Screen Ages* and guided me through the process of developing the structure and focus of the book. We have had wonderful conversations at the annual Society for Cinema and Media Studies conference about the movies, culture, and publishing. When Natalie became a senior editor, I was lucky enough to begin working with Niall Kennedy, who has been exemplary in every regard in the tricky but necessary process of moving an author along toward completion. In our communications, both over the phone and by email, he has provided support, expert critical acumen, creative suggestions, and most of all genuine understanding and enthusiasm for the project. I have been privileged to collaborate with many good editors, but I can't imagine a better one to work with than Niall.

I also feel especially lucky to have been offered a teaching position at Northern Kentucky University over twenty years ago, a school that has allowed me to develop and flourish as both an instructor and a writer, and this book would have been impossible without the support of so many people on campus. A university sabbatical provided the time and resources to work on the initial proposal for this book, and during the writing process both of my department chairs (and friends) Dr. Jonathan Cullick and Dr. Emily Detmer-Goebel have given their wholehearted support to the project. Special thanks are due to Ms. Marcia Johnson, the media specialist in Steely Library, who has provided me with access to dozens of movies from the entire range of American movie history. Our library has an exceptional media collection for a university of our kind, and much of the credit belongs to her.

Friends and faculty associated with our Cinema Studies minor and fellow cinephiles across campus have acted as both sounding boards and sources of inspiration while I have worked on this book, including Andrea Gazzaniga, Andy Miller, Steven Leigh, Caryn Connelly, Tamara O'Callaghan, Rudy Garns, Matt Bennett, Kristin Hornsby, Ali Godel, Paule Ellis, Chris Strobel, Sara Drabik, Jimmie Manning, Allen Ellis, Eric Chatterjee, and Angie Hesson. It has also been my privilege to work with a number of gifted cinema students, both undergraduate and graduate, who have also helped shape my thinking about the study and especially teaching of American cinema, including Rich Shivener, Amy Fugazzi, Robert Myers, Jennifer Whalen, and Austin Lee Brown. As always, special thanks to Dr. Tom Zaniello, the Dean of Cinema Studies at NKU, without whose achievements little of my own work would have been possible.

As I have developed my work in Cinema Studies, I have found support and friendship in a group of scholars across the country and around the world from whom I continue to learn much about the movies and about the joys of a supportive academic community. My thanks to Kelli Marshall, Brad Riddell, Suzanne Diamond, Cindy Miller, Karen Randell, Karen Ritzenhoff, Clémentine Darling, and Tiel Lundy. Many thanks as well to Tim and Margaret Swallow, who have run Cincinnati World Cinema for over a decade and have become fast friends and provided many opportunities to both enjoy and lecture about world cinema.

The work of the writer, of course, finally amounts to hours, days, and weeks in front of a computer, and my favorite composing place has been the local coffee house on our campus, which has combined solitude and society in just the right measure. My thanks to Angie, Brittany, Brenda, and the rest of the wonderful staff for their friendship and the many gallons of hot tea that fueled the composition process.

Finally, none of this would have been possible without the love and support of my partner Kristin Dietsche and daughter (and recipient of the movie fan gene) Martha Dietsche-Alberti, who are my favorite movie companions and most perceptive collaborators.

Introduction: Hollywood in the screen ages

Now playing

Movies in the twenty-first century

What does "going to the movies" mean in the twenty-first century? Consider the following three examples, each involving an Academy Award Best Picture nominee from 2009:

- In early 2010, a couple of hundred people – families, groups of teenagers, couples on dates, college students – all gather in a multiplex theater to watch *Avatar* (James Cameron) in IMAX 3D. The venue features "stadium-style" seating, meaning the theater has a steep rise and patrons climb stairs to reach their seats. Every seat rocks gently and comes with a full backrest and cup holder. As people enter, a series of commercials and movie previews are playing (in 2D) on the massive 72 by 52.8 foot screen. As the previews of coming attractions begin, the audience is instructed to put on their large 3D glasses. As the movie begins, the soundtrack thunders from speakers located behind the screen and along the sides of the theater. As James Cameron's massively constructed 3D computer-generated images seem to immerse the viewers in the visual world of the movie, the audience may feel as if they are on an amusement park ride. Indeed, many amusement parks not only feature rides based on popular movies, such as the "Harry Potter and the Forbidden Journey" ride at Universal Studios Orlando or the upcoming Avatar ride being built just down the road at Disney World, but many of these rides use much of the same technology – computer-generated images, large screens, digital surround sound, even the actors from the movies – to create similar immersive experiences. Such experiences, whether at the IMAX 3D movie

Fig 0.1
Zoë Saldana as the Na'vi warrior Neytiri, a mixture of live action and computer-generated imagery, in James Cameron's blockbuster *Avatar*.

or on the theme park ride, do not come cheap, however. The moviegoers in that suburban multiplex may have paid $15 or more for their tickets. Add to that the price of movie concessions, and a person could spend well over $20 for this screen experience.

- Later that year but just a few miles away, a couple of friends – recent college graduates with a love of the movies – settle down on an apartment sofa in front of a modest nineteen-inch flat screen TV to watch *Precious: Based on the Novel by Sapphire* (Lee Daniels). Unlike *Avatar*, which features an allegorical fantasy involving a conflict between humans and intelligent, blue, cat-like creatures, called the Na'vi, on the imaginary planet of Pandora, *Precious* is a gritty melodrama set in a poor Harlem neighborhood that tells the story of a lonely, abused African American teenager with the ironic nickname of "Precious." The movie is not in 3D, and it inspired no amusement park rides, although it did spark much critical discussion, ranging from praise that a low budget drama about a poor black girl created so much viewer interest to concerns that the movie might also reinforce stereotyped images about black urban life. In any case, these two friends are not watching the movie in a large theater, nor are they playing a DVD. Instead, they are streaming the movie via Netflix through a home video game system. Their screen experience involved no advance planning or even a trip outside, and the monthly Netflix subscription costs less than a night at the IMAX movie. Using their game controller, they scrolled through the movies available for instant viewing and settled on *Precious*. Within less than a minute, they were watching the movie, although on a screen some fifty times smaller and considerably closer than in the IMAX theater. The sound is provided by two small speakers in the flat screen unit, and the friends periodically pause the movie to take phone calls, get snacks, or take bathroom breaks. Unlike the dark of the movie theater, they sit in a lighted room, and the flat screen is just one visible feature of the cluttered apartment.

- A vacationing family speeds down an Interstate in a minivan. The four children, aged four to eleven, ride in the back, but even after an hour on the road they are still sitting quietly. That's because they are all absorbed in watching a Blu-ray copy of the computer-animated feature *Up* (Pete Docter and Bob Peterson) playing on a seven-inch screen attached to the ceiling just behind the front seats. To give their parents a break, the children listen to the movie via headphones. *Up* has become a family favorite; the children have seen the movie many

Fig 0.2
Gabourey Sidibe portrays the abused teenager Claireece "Precious" Jones in Lee Daniels' *Precious*.

Fig 0.3
A dreamlike image of a
house lifted into the sky
by thousands of children's
balloons in the Pixar
company's *Up*. Over the
last 20 years, Pixar's use
of computer animation has
revolutionized the feature-
length cartoon movie.

times, but on many different screens. They first saw the movie in 3D on a large multiplex screen not unlike the *Avatar* viewers above. When the movie became available on disc, it entered the regular rotation on the family's Blu-ray player, screening on a flat screen television larger than the one the two friends above are using to watch *Precious*. And sometimes the eleven-year-old watches *Up* on a laptop computer while lying in bed. Not only have they watched the movie several times, but they also enjoy the "extra" features included on the disc, including two animated shorts, one telling the back story of Dug, the talking (by way of a special electronic collar) dog who befriends the main characters, and a mini-documentary on a research trip the moviemakers took to Venezuela to help create the visual look of the movie.

What do these three different kinds of contemporary movie experience tell us? For one, that the single term "movie" really encompasses a broad and diverse range of viewing experiences. Just consider the case of screen size. In the examples above, the screens range from the dramatic fifty-foot-high screen of the IMAX multiplex, creating the literally "larger than life" images we have long associated with the movies, to the decidedly "smaller than life" minivan ceiling screen. And even these two examples do not define the limits of screen size. We can watch movies on small screens embedded in the backs of airline seats, on iPods, and on smart phones, or we can watch movies projected on the side of a downtown building as part of a summer festival.

Sometimes, as in the *Avatar* example, we watch movies in the dark, surrounded by dozens of others, the soundtrack of the movie the loudest noise in the room (depending on the chattiness of the people sitting next to you). Sometimes we watch movies by ourselves or with only one or two other people in our living rooms, which may or may not be darkened, with all the sounds of the household and the outside world mixing in. The two friends watching *Precious* above very likely chatted with each other about the movie as they watched. Sometimes we watch movies on the move, in a car or on a plane, being jostled by turbulence or bumps in the road, facing the distractions of the scenery going by, or the flight attendant bringing us a snack. And many college students follow the pattern of the 11-year-old *Up* fan and watch movies on their personal computers, relaxing in bed after a long day of studies and work.

Given how different these viewing experiences are, we can see that talking about the movies, even talking about a single movie, is more complex – and more interesting – than we might first suppose. After all, watching *Avatar* in 3D on a giant screen is a very different experience from watching a 2D version on an iPad. We might still say that we are watching the "same" movie in both cases, but just think about the different reactions you might expect from a viewer who has only seen *Avatar* on the IMAX screen and another who has only seen it via DVD on a small, picture tube television set inherited from a grandparent. And if you have seen *Avatar* on multiple screens, consider the differences in your own screen experiences. Were you overwhelmed by the scope and visual density of the big screen experience? When the main character Jake's avatar goes flying on the dragon-like Toruk creature, did you even become a bit dizzy as the camera swooped and turned in mid-air? On the other hand, though, while you still might be impressed by the visual imagination of the movie and the excitement of the Toruk sequences on a much smaller screen, you probably weren't as viscerally affected. In fact, the small screen experience may have given you more of a chance to focus on the dialogue and the interpersonal relationships among the characters, causing you to think more carefully about the ethics of Jake's actions in the movie.

The screen ages: The myth of Hollywood's "Golden Age"

Given the variety of possible screen experiences today, which one represents the "best" way to see a movie? It's easy to think that this diversity of movie experiences must be unique to the present day. After all, just consider all the recent historical and technological developments that have changed the ways we experience movies:

- the rise of the Internet in the 1990s creating competition (and new screening venues) for the movies
- the invention of the first VCRs, and now DVD, Blu-ray, and digital streaming, greatly expanding the number of movies we can access and giving us the ability to watch movies when we want as many times as we want
- the expansion of digital technologies that not only allows us to watch movies on our portable electronic devices but even to make them ourselves.

At the same time, you are probably familiar with people expressing nostalgia for the "good old days" when "going to the movies" seemed simpler and less complicated. Accompanying this nostalgia is a desire to define the "true" movie experience, the way watching movies is "supposed" to be. The past always has a way of seeming more stable and understandable than the chaotic, unpredictable present. The writing of history (including this textbook) turns the past into stories, narratives with protagonists and antagonists, main conflicts and (seemingly) inevitable conclusions. In our present lives, however, we not only never know what is going to happen next, we are not sure if we are even paying attention to the right developments.

If you happened to be born after 1990, you have probably heard some version of this nostalgia: "Back when I was young, everything was simpler. We didn't have computers or the Internet, we didn't have cable television. If we wanted to watch a movie, we went to the local movie theater." If (like me), you were born (well) before 1990, you may well have offered such an opinion yourself. These historical observations are often accompanied by moral and aesthetic judgments as well:

"People today have a shortened attention span and need constant stimulation"; "Movies were better in the past." Even though people have been saying that "things were better in the old days" for as long as there have been people, the idea persists that the past was, if not better, than at least more understandable than the present.

The study of American movie history has been particularly susceptible to the idea of a "Golden Age," a mythical time in the long ago past when movies were supposedly at their height, in terms of artistic quality, cultural importance, and financial health. Along with this idea of a Golden Age comes a kind of golden ideal of what a "real" movie is. As we will see throughout *Screen Ages*, however, just what this ideal is has actually differed quite dramatically over the one hundred plus years of American moviemaking, but the idea of an ideal continues to influence the way many of us think about the movies. And whatever that ideal might be, many of us are sure that the way we watch movies nowadays isn't it, as expressed in this comment from *New York Times* movie critic Manohla Dargis: "I try to resist whining about the good old days – though here I do need to point out that film as film is on the verge of extinction even if cinema is not – but the mainstream media pay even less mind to serious cinema than it did."[1]

The most common candidate for the Golden Age of American movies, and the one most prominently featured in most textbooks and histories, is what is called the "Studio System," the period in the 1930s and 1940s when a group of five major studios – operating under a mass production factory model – dominated movie production in the United States. The point of adopting a factory model had been to provide stability, uniformity, and predictability to a notoriously volatile, hyper-competitive industry. In our collective imagination, we often think of this as the era of "classic" Hollywood, a time of glamorous movie stars, lavish productions, and spectacular movie palaces. As a result, it's tempting to think of the history of American movies as one of rise and fall (a recurring cultural trope for thinking about historical narratives), a building up from the first experiments with capturing movement on film to the heights of 1940s Hollywood, followed by a gradual disintegration into the confusing world of the present. As contemporary students of American cinema, we latecomers to the party can feel that we missed out on the most thrilling and fascinating era of moviemaking and have to settle for the mostly mediocre, but occasionally interesting, creations of a movie culture whose best days are behind it.

But we can just as easily look at the apparent stability of the Studios Era as an anomaly, an exception to the more chaotic norm of American movie history. After all, the time period we will study in Chapter 4, "The studios era: Dominance and diversity in the Golden Age of Hollywood, 1929–1948," lasted barely twenty years, accounting for less than 20 percent of the history of American movies. And just how "stable" was this Golden Age after all? Born out of the combination of the advent of the sound era and the economic catastrophe of the Great Depression, the Studios Era witnessed a constant struggle among the major studios to maintain market dominance against each other as well as the proliferation of smaller studios, all the while dealing with the continuing threat of government censorship and the shifting economic climate of the Depression and the global crisis of World War II. Creative artists such as writers, directors, and actors rankled against having to sign exclusive studio contracts that limited their personal and professional options and forced them to work on projects assigned by studio executives. Movie industry workers of all kinds, from stage crews to camera operators to writers, struggled to establish unions and guilds that would protect their economic rights and interests.

For the movie fans in the Studios Era, the over 17,000 movie theaters in operation during the 1940s represented their own diversity of screen experiences, ranging from the 6,000 plus seats at New York's Radio City Music Hall to small town theaters with a capacity of only a couple of hundred or so. The movies these fans had access to varied greatly as well: while a cinematic extravaganza like *Gone With the Wind* might have officially premiered in December of 1939, most Americans had to wait a year or more for the movie to make its way through the movie distribution system to their own home town theaters on screens much smaller than the big city movie palaces. What is more, these viewers were experiencing the movie only after it had already become part of a larger national conversation. In fact, for most movie fans living outside large metropolitan areas, still a sizable percentage of the American public in the 1940s, they were more likely to hear a radio version of a new movie (often with the stars of the movie reprising their roles) before they could actually see it.

So which model best represents the mainstream of American movie history? The three examples of watching movies in the twenty-first century that open this chapter, or the myth of the Golden Age of Hollywood? Writers, scholars, and teachers of American cinema have long wrestled with questions like this as they try to come up with a coherent story of the history of movies in the United States, one unified enough to provide clarity and understanding yet open enough to recognize the complexity and diversity of that history. In short, how do you define a "mainstream" Hollywood tradition while also taking into account the immense and vibrant variety of movie culture in America?

It is this question that both motivates *Screen Ages: A Survey of American Cinema* and explains its title. *Screen Ages* is a chronological survey of American movie history that takes contemporary movie culture – the culture in which we all live and which first nurtured in us a love for the movies – as a baseline for exploring how that culture has evolved and developed from the late nineteenth century to the present. The title *Screen Ages: A Survey of American Cinema* refers to the defining reality of movies today: that our experience of the movies takes place on multiple screens in multiple venues involving multiple audiences, from the large screens in a suburban multiplex to television screens to the small screens of personal computers and smart phones. Rather than seeing this multiplicity and diversity as something wholly new or as a radical departure from previous eras in American movie history, the focus on the idea of **screens** signals the defining principle of this book: that the history of American movies – from its beginnings in vaudeville theaters, tent shows, and Kinetoscope parlors through the movie palaces, small town theaters and church basements of the 1940s to the Imax screens, Blu-ray discs, and streaming videos of the 2010s – has always been one of diversity and variety, of multiple screens, audiences, venues, and markets.

The same movie on different screens: The event-centered approach to movie history

As our three opening examples of the diversity of contemporary movie watching suggest, our ability to watch the "same" movie on such different screens in such different contexts raises the question of whether we are really watching the "same" movie after all in these cases. On the one hand, whether we watch *Up* in 3D or "2"D, in a multiplex or on an iPhone, the balloons still float off with the house every time we watch it, Dug the dog remains obsessed with squirrels, and the opening prologue to the movie (a beautiful tribute to the art of silent filmmaking) probably still makes you cry.

On the other hand, we will just as often recommend a specific kind of viewing experience as the "right" way to watch a particular movie: "You've got to see *Avatar* in 3D!" or "Watch *Inception* on DVD so you can go back over the confusing parts." Similarly, we all know that different types of movies work differently depending on the viewing situations. Comedies, for example, are often funnier when we watch them with a responsive audience around us than if we are all alone. At other times, a restless audience can distract us from really getting into a quiet, slow-moving movie. And as any teacher or student can tell you, watching a movie as a class requirement is a different experience from choosing a film on your own.

The fact that no two viewing experiences are ever the same (no more than any two reading experiences of a novel or two listening experiences of a song) speaks to the pleasure, excitement, intellectual stimulation, even frustration and exasperation that make the arts such an indispensible part of what it means to be human. It's why we can watch a favorite movie over and over again, each new viewing a unique mixture of the familiar and new. The formal structures of the movie may remain the same, but our screening technology, the places and situations in which we view the movie, and, most important, our very selves constantly change and develop. In *Screen Ages*, we will explore the constantly evolving nature of American movie culture and American movie viewing experiences.

We can call this focus on the experience of watching movies an **event-centered approach**, a way of looking at movies that brings with it several important benefits for the introductory study of American cinema history:

- It helps us recognize and take into account the diversity of movie audiences and moviemakers and their equal diversity of responses, attitudes, and opinions.
- It reminds us that history is always about change, uncertainty, conflict, including our efforts to study and make sense of history.
- Maybe most important, it helps us connect the present to the past, to use our own experiences as contemporary movie fans to explore the experiences of earlier generations of movie goers.

Contemporary arguments over whether the glory days of the movies have passed or whether the best is yet to come, whether movies represent the best or the worst in American culture, even whether movies have long to survive, have all been a part of American movie culture from the beginning. In Chapter 3, for example, we will focus on the troubled and notorious history of D. W. Griffith's *The Birth of a Nation*, a movie that was both enormously popular and enormously hated, one that divided audiences from the moment it premiered in 1915 at Clune's Auditorium in Los Angeles. In using enormous craft and skill to tell a story that justified and even celebrated the racism and violence of the Ku Klux Klan, Griffith's movie forced its viewers to confront fundamental questions of how we understand the relationship between art and morality, the significance of American slavery and racism, even the question of whether a movie can be dangerous or harmful to watch. The history of *A Birth of a Nation* is both a story of the choices made by moviemakers in constructing their cinematic text as well as the history of how specific viewers and groups of viewers experienced and reacted to that text. However we individually judge Griffith's movie, it has become an inescapable part of American movie history, one that can't be avoided and one that continues to demand our ethical judgment and engagement.

As we consider both important individual movies as well as the larger overall patterns of development in American movie history, we will be guided by a series of questions you may be familiar with as the "Five Ws (and One H)" from your writing or journalism class:

- **Who?**
- **What?**
- **Where?**
- **When?**
- **Why?**
- **How?**

Journalists view these questions as a guide to gathering complete information. In *Screen Ages*, we will use these questions as a guide to thinking about movies as events, as specific moments and experiences in the lives of individual moviegoers and in the cultural history of America. For any movie event, we can ask:

- **Who** is watching?
- **What** are they watching?
- **Where** are they watching?
- **When** are they watching?
- **Why** are they watching?
- **How** are they watching?

As an example of just how useful these questions can be, consider this case history about a difficult situation involving Steven Spielberg's 1994 dramatic movie about the Holocaust, *Schindler's List*.

Case Study 0.1: *Schindler's List* and Castlemont High School

Fig 0.4
Liam Neeson as Oskar Schindler, a German factory owner who managed to save the lives of hundreds of Jews during the Holocaust in Steven Spielberg's *Schindler's List*. The media controversy over the reactions of some high-school students to the movie made dramatically clear how much the context in which we watch a movie profoundly shapes our experience of it.

How important is it to consider the specific context and details of a screen experience? In 1994, the controversy and media furor following the expulsion of a class of 69 Oakland, California high-school students from a theater screening of Steven Spielberg's Academy-award winning movie about the Holocaust – *Schindler's List* – illustrates how our understanding and reaction to any movie varies tremendously based on all the factors involved in the screening experience, from our expectations about what we are going to see, our familiarity with the subject matter, whom we are with, even the mood we are in on a given day.

In this case, some high-school students in an Oakland movie theater were heard laughing at events on the screen such as the shooting of a Jewish woman by a Nazi soldier. This behavior so shocked the theater manager – who couldn't imagine how anyone could laugh at such a serious film about one of the most tragic episodes in human history – that he expelled all of the students. The story quickly made the national and even international news media, and the shock and outrage spread. The controversy became even more heated – and even more complicated – by the fact that the students, who were mainly African American and Latino and attended an economically deprived high school, had been taken to *Schindler's List* as part of a holiday field trip commemorating Martin Luther King, Jr. Day.

Why had some of these students laughed? How could any decent person think a movie about the Holocaust was funny? As the story made its way through the media life cycle – including a visit to the school by Steven Spielberg, who felt the students had gotten a bad rap – these questions persisted. Conversations with the students involved as well as a more careful discussion and debate of the situation among educators and scholars began to tease out how important the issue of the screen context was, how this controversy said more about how complex the movie-watching experience can be than about whether these young people lacked compassion or courtesy. Some students, for example, were almost completely unfamiliar with the Holocaust and World War II and whether the movie was fiction or not. Others were excited about a day away from school with their friends (and anticipating a trip to a roller rink after the movie), not the prime situation for viewing such a serious movie. And while some students laughed, others were undoubtedly interested in the movie.

How do all these multiple variables of the movie-watching experience – the demographic background of the students; the context for a trip to the movies; familiarity with the history of the Holocaust; the ambiguous status of *Schindler's List* as education and/or entertainment – influence our understanding and reaction to what happened in that Oakland movie theater in 1994? What other factors might we take into consideration as well? If you are interested, you might do your own further research to explore how the questions of Who, What, Where, When, Why, and How can help us appreciate how many factors are at play in any screen experience.

The structure of *Screen Ages*

Every chapter of *Screen Ages* will follow the same general format:

- **Now playing:** A collection of three case studies featuring movies that evoke the diversity of that age's screen experiences. For example, Chapter 5, "Theaters, drive-ins, and living rooms: Changing screens, changing movies, 1949–1966," starts by looking at the gala premiere of the epic blockbuster *The Ten Commandments* (Cecil B. DeMille 1956) at New York city's 1,700-seat Criterion Theatre, an old-fashioned, big city movie palace; a showing of the low budget teen musical *Beach Party* (William Asher 1963) at a suburban drive-in theater; and a (very) small screen television episode of *Alfred Hitchcock Presents* produced by that most famous of Hollywood directors. These dramatically different screen experiences illustrate the increasing diversity of what "going to the movies" meant in the 1950s, preparing us for the next section of the chapter, where we will consider some of the most influential stories of why these developments occurred.

- **Screen ages:** An introduction to some of the most influential historical narratives about the key people and developments – technological, economic, social, and artistic – that shaped the movie-going experience of that era. The emphasis on screen *ages* reminds us that no one story can capture the variety and complexity of any historical period. As in our discussion of the "myth of Hollywood's 'Golden Age'" above, "The screen ages" section will consider the significance of these different historical narratives – both those seen as "mainstream" and as "alternative" – and what they tell us about how our understanding of Hollywood's history affects the ways we understand our contemporary screen age.

- **In development:** Focusing on the history of the formal dimension of movies, "In development" introduces the concept of movie "genres" – types and categories of movies such as the romantic comedy, the action movie, or the musical – and traces how some of the most significant movie genres have evolved over time. Just as different types of movies rely on different types of characters, we will also look at genres of movie identities and how they have changed over time as well in relation to larger social developments, whether in terms of gender, race, ethnicity, social class, or sexuality. For example, just as the role of women has changed dramatically in the United States from the late nineteenth century to now, the types and genres of male and female characters in the movies have changed as well, in ways that reflect the hopes, anxieties, and debates that marked those social changes. From the dashing swashbucklers played by Douglas Fairbanks and the "America's Sweetheart" image embodied by Mary Pickford in the silent age, to the hard-boiled heroes and the dangerous femme fatales of 1940s film noir, to the nerdy losers and tough-as-nails female action heroes of today, American movies have created and played with different "genres" of what it means to be a man or a woman, male or female, sometimes reinforcing old stereotypes, sometimes breaking traditional boundaries.

- **The names above and below the title:** Every chapter of *Screen Ages* ends with another set of case studies – "The names above and below the title" – highlighting significant individuals who made a mark during that period of American movie history. From legendary filmmakers such as Orson Welles and the groundbreaking female director Dorothy Arzner in the 1930s and 1940s, to contemporary innovators such as Kathryn Bigelow and Quentin Tarantino, "The names above and below the title" reminds us both that American movie history is the result of the actions and ambitions of specific people in specific places and times and that who gets to make movies has always been a story of inclusion and exclusion, of those who want to maintain the status quo and those who want to widen the possibility of who can shape the history of American movies.

This case study approach to the study of screen ages also provides room for you to take part in the writing of that history. Throughout the print text and on the *Screen Ages* website, there will be opportunities for you to practice researching and writing about more case histories, more examples of the diversity of stories that make up the story of the different screen experiences that have always defined movie going in

America. Just as every new viewing experience of a movie represents a new version of that movie, so too every new student of movie history represents a new revision of that history, a new way of understanding and relating to the stories of how our own diverse experiences of the movies came to be. Rather than an ending, whether happy or sad, *Screen Ages* is meant to be a beginning, an opening scene for the story of your own exploration of American movie history, a history we can shape as much as it shapes us.

Note

1   Manohla Dargis and A. O. Scott, "Changing Science of Movie-ology," *The New York Times*, January 20, 2012; http://www.nytimes.com/2012/01/22/movies/j-hoberman-talks-about-village-voice-and-film-culture.html?_r=0

CHAPTER 1

Beginnings: Multiple cinemas, multiple audiences, 1895–1907

Now playing

Vitascope debuts at Koster and Bial's Music Hall, New York City, April 23, 1896

The playbill at Koster and Bial's Music Hall on that Thursday night in spring 1896 was typical for a variety show of the period. A mix of music and theatrical performances featuring "Great Foreign Stars" – most notably the British singer and actor Albert Chevalier, who entertained the crowd with comic and sentimental songs as well as dramatic stories and humorous anecdotes – the line-up at Koster and Bial's represented one of the dominant forms of popular entertainment at the turn of twentieth-century America. But there was a new addition to the playbill that night: the premiere of the latest innovation from the workshops of Thomas Edison, already the most famous inventor in America and a symbol of technological innovation and progress. Two strange machines, each with two turret-like lenses and covered in velvet to match the lush upholstery of the theater, were set up in the balcony.

Fig 1.1
Edison's Great Marvel.
Source: Library of Congress.

As show time approached, a screen lowered from above, surrounded by a gilt frame. A reporter from the *New York Times* tells what happened next:

> When the hall was darkened last night a buzzing and roaring were heard in the turret, and an unusually bright light fell upon the screen. Then came into view two precious blonde young persons of the variety stage, in pink and blue dresses, doing the umbrella dance with commendable celerity. Their motions were all clearly defined. When they vanished, a view of an angry surf breaking on a sandy beach near a stone pier amazed the spectators.[1]

A year before this performance, Americans had been introduced to the marvel of "moving pictures" through individual "peep show" viewers such as the Mutoscope and Edison's own Kinetoscope, screen experiences limited to a single person at a time. Now, however, that solitary experience could be a social one, brightly lit on a large screen.

The short (very short – less than a minute each) films projected that evening displayed the same variety of "actualities" – brief glimpses of everyday scenes such as a busy city street, firemen at work, or a picturesque natural setting – that viewers had come to expect from the peep show viewers, along with the dancers described above, a comic boxing match, a scene from a popular stage play, and the "view of an angry surf breaking on a sandy beach near a stone pier" – "Rough Sea at Dover" by the pioneering British cinematographer Birt Acres. And if the *Times* reporter is to be believed, the Vitascope was a big hit:

> For the spectator's imagination filled the atmosphere with electricity, as sparks crackled around the swiftly moving, lifelike figures. So enthusiastic was the appreciation of the crowd long before this extraordinary exhibition was finished that vociferous cheering was heard. There were loud calls for Mr. Edison, but he made no response.

Fig 1.2
Thomas Edison with a prototype of his Vitascope projector. Source: Boyer/ Getty Images.

Before either the single viewer peep show machines or the first projectors appeared shortly before the turn of the twentieth century, audiences had never seen movies before. They had, however, been enjoying projected photographic images for almost half a century, mainly in the form of the "stereopticon," or magic lantern, a device already familiar to vaudeville audiences that involved projecting photographs onto the same screens that now featured motion pictures. In fact, many stereopticon projectionists had developed various techniques for creating the illusion of movement on screen: moving images forward and back, superimposing multiple pictures, and other special effects. But nothing compared to the level of detail, excitement, and realism of the "Rough Seas at Dover," whether viewed on the small screen of the peephole viewer or the big screen in at Koster and Bial's Music Hall.

A day at a Mutoscope peep show, St Louis, Missouri, 1900

The sign on the front of the building advertised the price of the attraction: "1¢." Inside, patrons found rows of tall machines, each featuring a round, clamshell-shaped device with an eye viewer and a crank on the front. For their penny, customers would peer into the machine and turn the crank. Four years after the commercial introduction of projected moving pictures, the peepshow business was still going strong. Unlike projected movies, which were still usually shown as part of a variety show such as the one at Koster and Bial's, where admission could cost a dollar or more (at a time when the average American income was still less than $500 a year), peep show machines were an entertainment option well within the budget of most people. The subject matter of most peep show movies resembled the line-up described in the newspaper story above. Some, however, contained more provocative (at least by the standards of the time) images: modern dancers, boxing matches (prize fighting was still illegal in all fifty states at the turn of the century), even the suggestion of peering through a keyhole at a woman changing her clothes.

Mutoscope/ Kinetoscope Two of the main competing versions of individual viewing machines in the early ages of cinema. The Edison Company's Kinetoscope used the same technology as later movie projectors by shining a light source through a moving strip of film. The Mutoscope, marketed by the American Mutoscope Company (later American Biograph), used flipbook technology based on a series of photographs attached to a rotating drum.

Fig 1.3
A Mutoscope parlor at the corner of Olive and Leonard in Saint Louis shortly after the turn of the twentieth century. Source: Missouri History Museum.

The machines in this St. Louis storefront parlor were Mutoscopes, single-viewer moving picture devices built by the American Biograph Company to compete with the Edison Company's single-viewer Kinetoscope. While the Kinetoscope used the basic technology that would form the basis of movie projection until the digital age – an electric motor pulling a length of perforated film in front of a light bulb – the Mutoscope relied on a more ancient technology for creating the illusion of movement: the flipbook. The crank turned a wheel with dozens of stiff paper cards attached, each featuring a single photograph. As the machine flipped through each individual picture, viewers would have an experience of moving pictures. Although flipbooks were first sold as novelties in the mid-nineteenth century, the phenomenon of flipbook animation had been known for much longer. Even today, it remains a popular type of "do-it-yourself" moviemaking, as many a bored student with a textbook and a pen can attest. Just draw a series of simple pictures in the top corner of succeeding pages in the book, changing the position of each picture just slightly, and then ruffle the pages with your thumb. Instantly, you have your own version of the Mutoscope, and your own mini-movie.

The peep show machine challenges our contemporary ideas about what the experience of "going to the movies" means. There is no darkened theater, and while the viewing experience takes place in public, it is also extremely private, with each person at his or her own individual machine. The very name "peep show" that became attached to these machines stressed the potentially illicit quality of the experience, especially as flipbook machines later in the century increasingly lured viewers with the promise of "forbidden" images (a promise that – to escape local censorship laws – often proved greatly exaggerated).

Fig 1.4
The flip cards of the Mutoscope machine relied on older moving picture technology. Source: Science & Society Picture Library/Getty Images.

***The Great Train Robbery* plays at the Nickelodeon theater, Pittsburgh, 1905**

Pittsburgh's Nickelodeon theater, opened in 1904 by two local showmen and entrepreneurs, John P. Harris and his brother-in-law Harry Davis, represented the beginning of a new screen age in American movie history. For one thing, the Nickelodeon theater was devoted solely to the showing of moving pictures, one of the first of its kind in US movie history. In fact, for many years Harris and Davis' theater was even thought to be the first all-movie theater in the country, and while that particular claim has come into dispute, the nickelodeon still represents an important evolution in American movie history.

The name of Harris and Davis' theater–the "Nickelodeon" – was also the generic name given to the thousands of all-movie theaters that began to appear across the country at that time, a reference to their usual admission price of 5¢. Much less expensive than the vaudeville theaters, the nickelodeons attracted patrons from a broad spectrum of American society, including many working-class and immigrant viewers who hadn't been able to afford projected moving pictures before.

Nickelodeons spread rapidly. By 1908, there were some 8,000 nickelodeons in the United States, and close to 14,000 less than a decade later. The arrival of the Nickelodeons signaled the growth of the movies into a major mass medium, no longer just one feature among many at a vaudeville show or an individual peep show attraction but a significant popular art form of its own, one that would contribute to the decline of the variety show circuits from which it arose.

The moving picture those patrons were paying a nickel to see that day in Pittsburgh – *The Great Train Robbery* – represented an even greater evolution in the screen experience of the movies. From the early actualities lasting less than a minute

Fig 1.5
The Waco Theatre in New York City was typical of the early storefront nickelodeon theaters. Source: The Kobal Collection.

Fig 1.6
The dramatic concluding shot (or depending on the whims of the local projectionist, the opening shot) of *The Great Train Robbery*, featuring one of the stars of the movie, Justus D. Barnes.

that defined the early screen age in America, the moviegoers in Pittsburgh watched a twelve-minute fictional narrative about a group of desperadoes who hijack a train. When locals learn of the crime, an exciting chase on horseback ensues, ending with a shootout in the woods and the recovery of the money. In what has become an iconic scene in American movie history, the movie concludes with one of its stars, Justus D. Barnes, pointing and shooting his gun directly at the movie audience.

The Great Train Robbery had been a sensation since its premier in 1903. Appearing less than ten years after the first Vitascope screening at Koster and Bial's theater, the ambition and innovation of *The Great Train Robbery* is impressive, a testament as much to the increasing sophistication of early movie audiences as early moviemakers. *The Great Train Robbery* continued to play in nickelodeons across the country and in theaters around the world for years after its premiere. In this movie, we can recognize the basic components of movie narrative that would dominate how Hollywood would tell stories on screen up to the present.

Screen ages

The invention of "the movies"

The story of how the movies began in the United States is really (at least) two stories. One is of technology and business, the invention of the mechanical devices and marketing practices that made "moving pictures" possible. The other, inseparable from the first, is social and cultural: the creation of the very idea of "the movies," a blanket term we use to cover a wide variety of filmed subject matter and an equally wide variety of screen experiences and responses. Nowadays, the idea of "going to the movies" is such a normal part of everyday life that we rarely think twice about it. At the very beginnings of American cinema, however, there were literally no "movies" (the term "movie" likely entered the vocabulary after 1905 or so). The first decade of moving pictures in the United States was a period of dynamic change and experimentation, as what we now think of as "the movies" formed out of a wide variety of screen experiences.

Beginnings: Pre-cinema

As visual creatures, we have always experimented with forms of visual representation and projection, from ancient cave paintings that could only be viewed by firelight (the play of light and shadow on the walls creating the illusion of movement) to woven tapestries that told visual stories in sequential order, from painted theatrical backdrops showing far off vistas or distant empires to the use of perspective to create the sense of depth and distance in landscape paintings. One of the foundational stories of Western philosophy – Plato's "Allegory of the Cave," from his work *The Republic*, written almost 2,400 years ago – is based on a kind of movie experience. A group of chained prisoners sits in a dark cave. Their only ideas of reality come from watching the shadows projected on the cave wall by people walking in front of a fire behind them.

If many of Plato's concerns about the slippery connection between illusion and reality have remained a part of our cultural thinking about the arts, we likewise continue to share a fascination with how artists are able to create their imaginary realities, to imitate nature, an ability that Plato's student Aristotle argued was essential to human beings. And the art that Plato chose to feature in his allegory is a form of shadow puppetry, a screen experience as old as humanity itself.

Photography and nineteenth-century screen shows

By the mid-nineteenth century, projected images featuring apparatuses like the magic lantern and the stereopticon were a staple of popular entertainment and a focus of scientific interest in the United States. Their development coincided with the invention of photography, the key technological precursor to the movies. Just as we use the single term "the movies" to cover a wide array of different screening and exhibition practices, "photography," especially in its early years, refers to just as broad a range of experiments in lens development, chemistry, and mechanics. The earliest photographs actually suggested the opposite of "motion" pictures: they involved long exposure times and required the subjects, whether people, animals, or things, to remain perfectly still sometimes for minutes on end.

Magic lantern/ stereopticon A device for projecting photographs using glass slides, a light source, and lenses that became a popular form of entertainment in the nineteenth century. Some skilled projectionists created the impression of movement by rapidly switching between slides.

Fig 1.7
This late nineteenth-century magic lantern allowed the operator to project two separate images at once, allowing for various effects such as the impression of depth and even movement.

We tend to think of photography as allowing us for the first time to capture "the way things really look," not just the shadows that Plato warned us about, but the truth is actually somewhere in between. You might think of an early photograph as a kind of shadow, an impression of light that left its traces on the chemically embedded glass plates used by the first photographers. Even more significant, for both science and the movies, photography not only captured what our eyes could see, but what they couldn't see as well: a bolt of lightning, caught mid strike; images of insect anatomy and human cells much too small to be perceived by the naked eye; a race horse in mid stride.

Eadweard Muybridge and the first movies

In fact, one of the first and most important developments leading to the invention of the movies involved using photography to answer an old question that could never be answered with the naked eye: Does a galloping horse ever lift all four legs off the ground at the same time? In 1872, Leland Stanford – a wealthy businessman, former California governor, and horse racing enthusiast – hired the nature photographer Eadweard Muybridge to settle the question by taking pictures of Stanford's racehorse, Sallie Gardner, at Stanford's Palo Alto ranch.

Muybridge's photographs did prove that a running horse does indeed leave the ground with every stride. Muybridge continued his photographic experiments using multiple cameras to record different natural movements. He even invented an early kind of projector called the "zoopraxiscope" that allowed audiences to watch the images of animals in motion and people engaged in various activities, from walking down the stairs, playing sports, to dancing. Many of his human models (including himself) were photographed in the nude or wearing only light clothing, all in the name of scientific accuracy.

Fig 1.8
Eadweard Muybridge's groundbreaking studies of human and animal motion played a crucial role in the transition from photography to moving pictures. Source: The Kobal Collection.

Although we have no reason to doubt the sincerity of Muybridge's scientific ambitions, that didn't stop him from including artistic and even provocative flourishes in his work. This is especially true in his photographs of women, whose nudity is combined with poses, attitudes, and actions that at the same time reflected dominant nineteenth-century ideas of "femininity" and "modesty," such as a mother comforting a child, or a woman turning away in fright.

The beginnings of mass media in nineteenth-century America

As the three examples in "Now playing" demonstrate, the movies emerged out of an already highly evolved, complex, lucrative, and diverse culture of popular entertainment experiences in nineteenth-century America. Fueled by many sources – the rapid development and expansion of transportation and communication technology that accompanied the growing territorial ambitions of the United States; the explosion in size of cities and urban culture; continuing patterns of immigration; the rise of public education – the first truly mass media had begun to appear in America. From the vast numbers of locally based newspapers and literary societies, national magazines such as *Harper's* and *Godey's Lady's Book* emerged at mid-century, creating the possibility for writers to become household names across the country and around the world. Novelists such as Charles Dickens and Harriett Beecher Stowe became international celebrities as a result and were mobbed wherever they went on tour.

In the first half of the nineteenth century, variety defined both the options and styles of local popular entertainment in America. Traveling performance troupes would stage programs that featured jokes, stories, folk songs, a few scenes from Shakespeare, a demonstration of acrobatics, perhaps a sales pitch for a miracle elixir or cure all. Minstrel shows featuring white performers in blackface revealed the simultaneous fascination with and racial animosity toward African Americans and African American culture among white identifying audiences in a country whose economy depended on slave labor. Circuses, "dime museums" featuring curiosities and fakes, burlesque and saloon shows that promised the thrill of illicit entertainment; these various forms of entertainment and diversion began to be organized into their own mass medium: the regional and national networks of staged entertainment known as "vaudeville."

These networks, known as "circuits," developed business relationships among chains of theaters across the country to schedule regular programs of entertainment that featured some of the first national performing stars. These variety shows also included screen experiences such as magic lantern and stereopticon shows that built off the growing fascination with photography and the promise of motion pictures. This infrastructure of theaters across the country would prove crucial to the development of the movies, and vaudeville likewise provided many of the performers, directors, and producers who worked in the early movie industry.

The development of forms of entertainment that operated on a national rather than a local scale created tensions between the local and the national, between the extraordinary diversity of American culture and the idea of a unified national identity, that not only informed the beginnings of the movies in the United States but remains a defining feature of America in the twenty-first century as well. Contemporary debates about immigration policy, for example, remain as contentious today as they were at the turn of the twentieth century. As the movies grew out of the screen curiosities of nineteenth-century traveling shows and the vaudeville circuit

Vaudeville A type of live variety show popular in the United States from the mid 1800s until the 1930s.

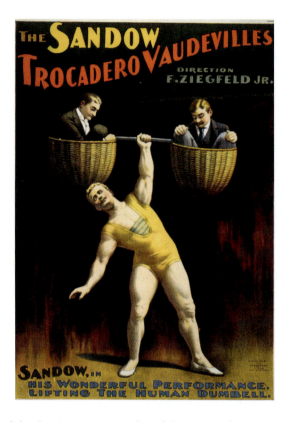

Fig 1.9
A 1894 poster for the traveling vaudeville show featuring the strongman Eugene Sandow and produced by the legendary vaudeville showman Florenz Ziegfeld. Sandow's celebrity led Thomas Edison to make him the subject of one of the earliest short Kinetoscope movies. Source: Library of Congress.

to become one of the dominant mass media of the twentieth century, these powerful visual imaginings of American life played a central role in the shaping of the ideas of not only Americans but people around the world about the meaning of the United States.

The movies begin in America

The very simple question of "who invented the movies" is really impossible to answer, because it refers to more than just a technological question of building a particular kind of camera or projector. Inventing the movies also involved the development of an entire social structure, a kind of cultural experience that did not emerge all at once in any place or at any time. The invention of the movies and of American cinema in particular can't be traced to a single source. It was an international project, one where ideas were borrowed (and sometimes stolen) freely, and where lines of influence crossed lines of language, culture, and nationality.

Sensing the potential that lay in the prospect of moving pictures, in 1888 Thomas Edison filed a "caveat" – a description of his company's intention to develop a new invention – with the US Patent Office that stated, "I am experimenting upon an instrument which does for the Eye what the phonograph does for the Ear, which is the recording and reproduction of things in motion."[2] The man Edison put in charge of the research effort to develop this new technology was William Kennedy Laurie (W.K.L.) Dickson, a young Scottish immigrant working as a photographer and inventor for Edison. The result was the Kinetoscope, which made its "official" debut in 1893 at the Brooklyn Institute of Arts and Sciences, where the viewers watched a short film called *Blacksmith Scene*.

Fig 1.10
A short film of blacksmiths at work, one of the earliest movies made by the Edison studios. Source: *Edison: The Invention of the Movies*, Kino, http:// www.kinolorber.com/ edison/.

Fig 1.11
Another staged early Edison movie filmed at the "Black Maria" studio, this one purporting to show a barber at work.

Fig 1.12
Edison Kinetoscopic Record of a Sneeze. Source: Library of Congress.

Dickson meanwhile had designed what might be considered the first movie studio, a wood and tar paper building at the Edison Laboratories in Orange, NJ, that employees called the "Black Maria" because of its ungainly resemblance to the police wagons called by the same name. In the Black Maria, Dickson and others began filming a variety of short subjects, ranging from the everyday – including the blacksmith scene and a man being shaved by a barber – to famous vaudeville performers.

Just how wide a variety is indicated by the second movie ever copyrighted by the Edison studios (records of the first have been lost), *Edison Kinetoscopic Record of a Sneeze*, more popularly known as *Fred Ott's Sneeze*. The film is just what the title suggests: Edison employee Fred Ott sneezing on camera.

Watching *Fred Ott's Sneeze* often baffles contemporary audiences. Was this really considered entertaining by turn-of-the-century audiences? Who would pay to watch a man sneeze? The short answer would be to point out that the film was never intended for commercial distribution to Kinetoscope parlors. It was commissioned by *Harper's Weekly* magazine for an article on the new invention, and frames from the film were printed in the issue. But perhaps the more important point remains how unsettled and experimental early American film culture was. The fact that the *Harper's* article featured the example of a sneeze caught on film illustrates the uncertainty over just what kind of invention the Kinetoscope – and moving pictures in general – was and how seriously, or not, to take it.

The Kinetoscope business really began in earnest in 1894. For the next year peep show parlors and arcades spread across the United States as viewers were intrigued by the novelty of moving pictures. From the beginning, spectacle and action – including sex and violence – were mainstays of moving picture screen experiences. At the Edison Company, Dickson and others were kept busy filling the demand for new short films, and their choice of subject matter reflected the popular culture of the late nineteenth century. Boxing matches, exotic dancers, Wild West shows – all were a part of the early Kinetoscope experience. Cock fights, dog fights, and other brutal and controversial activities made their way into the peep shows. These early movies were created by men for a largely male audience, but the private nature of the Kinetoscope meant that almost anyone with the money could take part in this first movie screen age.

By the end of 1895, however, the novelty was wearing off the Kinetoscope. These very short films, watched in random order on individual viewers, could no longer rely on the amazement of viewers who were already becoming more sophisticated and more demanding in their expectations. Audiences began returning to vaudeville and variety shows, and the race to create the next important screen experience – moving pictures projected on a large screen – was on.

Competition and diversity: Taking control of events

With the Vitascope projection system, the Edison Company hoped to dominate the new era of projected moving pictures in America, but competitors quickly developed their own systems. These competing companies, such as American Vitagraph, the Selig Polyscope Company, and the Lubin Manufacturing Company, also quickly began creating their own moving pictures. Perhaps the most important of these competitors was the company that developed the Mutoscope, the Kinetoscope's main rival in the peep show business, the American Mutoscope and Biograph Company (later called simply the Biograph Company). Among the company's founders was W.K.L. Dickson, the man who had led the development of motion picture technology for Edison.

The proliferation of competing moving picture companies motivated early filmmakers to expand their offerings beyond the actualities and vaudeville performers featured on the program at Koster and Bial's Music Hall. In searching for new screen experiences to present to their viewers, these movie pioneers began to explore the creative possibilities for moving pictures. Companies like Biograph and American Vitagraph began sending camera crews around the country and the world to film exotic scenery and historical events.

This early period of the American moving picture industry proved extremely volatile, as audiences at first flocked to new screen experiences like the peep show viewer or projected movies and just as quickly became bored with seeing the same short films and subjects over and over again. Theater and arcade owners had quickly realized how this new art form could combine popularity with profitability, allowing anyone with the necessary capital and connections to enter show business without having to hire and retain live performers or maintain a theater.

Early motion picture audiences began to expect and demand novelty and change; they wanted to see a new slate of films almost every day. And since early motion pictures, whether made for the individual viewer or for projection, were rarely more than a minute or two long, the need for new material was constant and growing. Different studios banked on different strategies to meet this demand. The Edison Company, for example, had a greater focus on actualities and scenes from "real life." The Biograph Company, on the other hand, featured more experiments with using moving pictures to tell scripted stories, and Biograph began to outstrip even the Edison Company in terms of the quantity and variety of productions.

For the early moving picture studios, survival and success meant not only coming up with new movie experiences to maintain public interest, but also controlling and managing these experiences as a way of guaranteeing a predictable and lucrative business model. On the one hand, continuous innovation and experimentation could feed the public curiosity for ever new and different screen experiences. On the other hand, all of this change and invention brought with it anxiety and unpredictability about profit and loss from one year to the next. These conflicting motives – the desire to always offer new and exciting screen experiences versus the equal if not greater desire to establish steady and predictable sources of revenue – defines one of the central conflicts in the history of the commercial, market-based movie industry, one as true at the beginning of American movies as it is today in the world of digital technology, globalized capitalism, and the Internet.

For Edison, the rapid growth of the moving picture industry and of moving picture production companies posed both an opportunity and a threat. His company quickly moved to make sure that no matter how successful any other production company might be, they would still have to pay Edison for the right to use the movie-making technology he had patented. At the same time, the sheer number of new companies made it difficult for the Edison Company to police the new industry, and the flood of new movies into the market challenged his monopoly status and his company's ability to control the future development of moving pictures.

The result was that the early American movie business was dominated by a blizzard of lawsuits and court cases. Many exhibitors turned to imported European movies to supply the demand that was impeded in the American market by battles over patent rights. Foreign movies – especially the movies produced by the Pathé Freres Studio and the great special effects pioneer Georges Méliès – soon became a major part of the American movie market, further influencing local tastes and expectations about what movies could be.

Even many supposedly "new" productions were simply thinly disguised remakes of popular hits. The Lubin Company, for example, made its own *The Great Train Robbery* shortly after the Porter original became a popular success for the Edison Company. Not that the Edison Company shied away from this practice, either. Its laboriously titled *How a French Nobleman Got a Wife through the "New York Herald" Personal Columns* from 1904 was a thinly disguised copy of American Biograph's hit *Personal*, a comedy in the increasingly popular "chase movie" genre involving an impoverished French aristocrat newly arrived in New York who

Fig 1.13
Personal/Seven Chances/ The Bachelor in triptych form: American Biograph's *Personal* (left), an imitation of the Edison Company's chase movie *How a French Nobleman Got a Wife*, was an early example of a staple of Hollywood moviemaking: endlessly remaking a popular hit. Buster Keaton's classic silent comedy *Seven Chances* (1925) and the more recent movie *The Bachelor* (Gary Sinyor 1999) with Chris O'Donnell and Renée Zellweger are both remakes of that early Edison film.

The Motion Picture Patents Company An organization founded by the Edison Company in 1908 in an effort to establish monopoly control over the American movie industry by controlling the patents for the technology involved in movie production. The MPPC eventually included all the major film production companies of the early years of American cinema but was increasingly challenged by the proliferation of independent movie companies (see below) in the nickelodeon era. A successful antitrust case against the MPPC led to its disintegration in 1918.

advertises for a bride in the "personal" section of the newspaper and names a date and time to meet likely candidates. Hoping to marry a rich American heiress, he instead finds himself surrounded by dozens of working-class women, each hoping to marry a rich European. The heart of the movie, a frantic chase, follows, as the women chase the hapless immigrant across fields and over fences until he is finally captured by a fast runner armed with a gun.

The movie played on stereotypes and concerns about European immigrants, class issues, gender, and the turbulent social environment of the cities. Not to be outdone, the Lubin Company also issued their own *Personal* copy, *Meet Me at the Fountain*. This practice of remaking popular movies would become a standard practice in the movie business. The great silent comedian Buster Keaton would issue his own remake of *Personal* as *Seven Chances* in 1925, and New Line Cinema would release *The Bachelor* with Chris O'Donnell and Renée Zellweger, a further remake of *Seven Chances*, in 1999, showing the durability of a genre and theme from 1904 to the present.

Controlling the movies: Edison and the Motion Picture Patents Company

By 1907, American Biograph and the Edison Company had emerged as the two dominant movie production companies, with Selig, Lubin, and American Vitagraph forming a vibrant second tier. Hoping to take control of the volatile early movie industry, Edison and his main competitors created the **Motion Picture Patents Company** (with the exception of Biograph, which eventually joined after tense negotiations the following year). Members gained exclusive rights to use the vital movie equipment covered by Edison's patents. What's more, the Eastman Kodak Company, the biggest manufacturer of movie film, also joined the MPPC, selling only to fellow MPPC members. The MPPC created its own rental and distribution system, setting standard prices for exhibitors who wanted to show its movies, and it enforced its contractual dominance just as thoroughly – and often just as brutally – as Edison had.

The MPPC was the first motion picture cartel in American movie history, an attempt to locate control of the movie business in a small group of companies who could then dominate the production and distribution – and as a result, shape the meaning and development – of the movies. In so doing, these companies were following the example of other turn-of-the-century industries such as oil, mining, and railroads by forming what was called a trust, a virtual monopoly that would become the focus of reform efforts throughout the **Progressive Era** in American history. Throughout the screen ages of American cinema, we will see efforts by other groups of businesses to take similar control of the movies, from the studio system of the 1920s through the 1940s to the corporate mergers of the 1960s through the 1980s to the globalized media conglomerates today. In each case, we will see how business

Fig 1.14
Members of the Motion Picture Patents Company (MPPC) including Thomas Edison, seated nearest the camera.

decisions are also artistic and social decisions, and we will also see how none of these efforts have ever been completely successful at controlling the events of movie history.

In development

The invention of "the movies" and the first narrative genres

Film historians refer to the early period of commercial moving pictures – both the peep shows and the first projected movie – as the "novelty" years, an early experimental phase when the very fact of motion was enough to attract and intrigue paying customers, regardless of the subject matter. But as we all know from our current experience of living in an era of rapidly changing communications technology, novelty wears off quickly, and the same was true of these early days of American cinema. Audiences quickly began to demand more innovative and interesting uses of this exciting new technology, and early filmmakers themselves were eagerly pushing the boundaries – both formal and technological – of what moving pictures could do and be.

By the time the first nickelodeons appeared, movie fans (and they were fans, not just curiosity seekers) knew what they liked, and they went to the nickelodeons with very specific expectations about what they wanted to see: mainly, fictional narratives featuring identifiable characters and familiar situations. If many of the movies shown at Koster and Bial's in 1896 seem odd to contemporary eyes, we can readily recognize the genres or types of these later nickelodeon movies. In this section, we will take a look at the development of the earliest genres or types of American movies, genres that not only influenced the definition of what we now think of as the "movies" but that continue to define our screen experiences and expectations to the present day.

The Progressive Era
The period in American history between the 1890s and 1920s featuring efforts by politicians and social reformers to curb the power of increasingly large and monopolistic corporations. These reforms were also concerned with the impact of large-scale immigration and urbanization as well, featuring a mix of radical reform and condescending paternalism.

Actualities and the documentary tradition

For the Edison Company, moving pictures seemed less like an art form and more like a new kind of journalism and history, the type of screen experiences we associate today with the documentary. Of course, Edison was not wrong to connect moving pictures with news and information. In addition to actual documentary movies, the use of film and later video has become central to the news industry, even more so in the Internet age. There were significant cultural and commercial reasons to stress this "educational" dimension of the new medium as well, as various institutions of social authority, from religious groups and schools to government and social improvement organizations, began to raise concerns about the moral impact of moving pictures. Emphasizing the documentary aspect of moving pictures – even if what was being documented was sensational or controversial – promised to lend them a kind of social respectability.

The pioneering French filmmakers the Lumiére brothers coined a term for these "real life" moving pictures: "actualités," or "actualities" in English. In this early screen age, moviemakers turned to an increasingly wide and diverse range of subjects to hold the attention of the first movie audiences, from dramatic news events such as scenes of devastation from the 1900 Galveston, Texas hurricane to the ridiculous or comical, such as a movie of cats boxing. Actualities remain a mainstay of the age of YouTube and Vimeo (with actualities of amusing cats an enduringly popular subgenre). In fact, most of the surviving actualities from early American cinema can be found on these sites, offered both as historical curiosities and objects of continuing interest. And boxing was not just popular when it involved cats; actual prizefighting and other sporting events also proved popular subjects for early movies.

Fig 1.15
The Edison Company filmed these scenes of devastation following the 1900 Galveston, Texas hurricane, an early example of how actualities served as a powerful new form of journalism.

Fig 1.16
Not all actualities were so serious. One of the earliest movies filmed at Edison's Black Maria studio featured "Professor" Henry Welton's trained cats, the first of what has proved to be an enduringly popular subject.

Case study 1.1: From Kinetoscopes to YouTube

The first screen experiences in American movie history were incredibly brief, ranging from only a few seconds to little more than a minute, and these experiences featured a wide range of subjects from the serious to the silly, the picturesque to the shocking. In our own digital screen age, the appearance of video sharing sites like YouTube and Vimeo, the popularity of animated GIFs, and the creation of the six-second video on Vine suggest that the attractions of the early peep shows have come back again a century later. Every day, millions around the world find themselves drawn to these short screen experiences, experiences that likewise reflect a wide range of subject matter and purposes.

In looking at these early screen experiences, we have begun identifying emerging genres or types of peep show movies, such as actualities, that would later evolve into the longer narrative forms of the Nickelodeon era. As participants in another new screen age of short screen experiences, try your own hand at categorizing what we find on these various video sites. You might start by examining how the sites themselves and the creators of the videos on them are already trying to organize and describe them, from broad categories such as "Education" and "Sports" to user-generated hashtags. How do we think future scholars and researchers will define and interpret our current screen age of short videos? What do and don't they share in common with the short films of the first screen age (many of which themselves are available on these sites)?

As any experienced Internet user knows, however, even when a moving picture claims to be true, there is probably more there than meets the eye. A healthy skepticism is a necessity when surfing the web, but the need for such skepticism is nothing new in American movie history. Even though actualities were supposed to show us reality the way it "actually" was, this claim proved to be quite complicated, especially when we think of images – whether moving or still – as forms of storytelling and persuasion. Most of the Edison Company's early actualities, for example, were staged and filmed in their New Jersey studios, regardless of where they claimed to be set, including the barbershop scene seen above as well as the boxing match.

The powerful impact of actualities as a new form of journalism led movie companies to send film crews on location to places like Havana Bay in Cuba, where the mysterious explosion aboard the naval warship the *USS Maine* was being used by political leaders and newspaper owners like William Randolph Hearst to justify war against Spain. The goal of early American moviemakers, however, was not necessarily to create a faithful record of current events but to provide exciting and interesting screen experiences for audiences. If shooting on location proved too expensive or dangerous, movie companies were not above passing off staged scenes of news events as genuine, as when the Edison Company released an actuality entitled "Capture of Boer Battery by the British" in 1900 supposedly showing an exciting military charge from the civil war in South Africa. In truth, the whole scene had been staged and photographed at their studios in West Orange, New Jersey.

As actualities progressed from brief snippets of single actions to the representation of complex historical events, whether boxing matches, wars, or presidential elections, filmmakers found themselves experimenting with movies as a way of telling stories in a new, visual way, one drawn from the older tradition of the magic lantern and the emerging parallel medium of the comic strip. The desire to create exciting stories

Fig 1.17
The Edison Company's "Capture of Boer Battery by the British" claimed to show a crucial battle in the war between the British army and Boer settlers in South Africa, but the film was actually shot in New Jersey.

blurred the lines between reality and fantasy, fiction and non-fiction, and led to the creation of the first movie genres in American cinema, many a direct development of these early actualities.

From actuality to melodrama: *The Life of an American Fireman*

An early movie hit, *The Life of an American Fireman* (1902) demonstrates how an exciting and popular subject for early movie actualities – firefighters on their way to battle a blaze – evolved into a form of storytelling that would prove an equally popular narrative genre throughout the history of American movies: the rescue melodrama. *The Life of an American Fireman* was the work of the Edison Company's Edwin S. Porter, the same man who would be responsible for *The Great Train Robbery* just the next year. In creating his six-minute movie, Porter mixed previously shot actuality footage of the Newark, New Jersey fire department responding to an alarm with an invented story about the rescue of a young mother and her child from the second floor of a burning building. The movie starts with an interior scene of a fire chief dozing at his desk dreaming about a young woman (who appears in an oval above his head – an early example of "special effects") putting a young child to bed.

A close-up of a hand pulling a fire alarm box on a city street leads to scenes of firemen waking up, quickly dressing, and rushing through the streets of the city in their horse-drawn fire engines, state-of-the-art firefighting technology in 1904. In the burning building, a young woman gestures wildly out of her bedroom window. A firefighter knocks down the door at the right of the set, enters the room, and takes first the woman and then her child out the window at the back. We then move to the exterior of the house again, where we see the same actions repeated, only this time from the outside: a firefighter rushes into the building; a ladder is put up to the second floor window; the firefighter brings first the woman and then her child out of the room. Rescue complete, the movie ends.

The Life of an American Fireman builds on the powerful mix of curiosity and fear that viewers associated with fire by placing exciting images of firefighters and fire engines at work within a narrative that provides meaning and context for those images. Even at this early stage in American movie history, *The Life of an American Fireman* reveals that viewers had already become familiar with an array of new cinematic storytelling techniques, such as making connections between edits

Fig 1.18
The Life of an American Fireman: the Newark, New Jersey fire department cooperated with Edwin S. Porter in this early and influential example of narrative filmmaking.

to understand that the interior of the smoky bedroom was the same house that the firefighters had just pulled up to.

Did early moviegoers consider *The Life of an American Fireman* fiction or non-fiction? An actuality or a story film? The promotional materials from the Edison studios suggest that the distinction between true and false, fiction and non-fiction was both significant and also ambiguous as early filmmakers developed the narrative potential of the moving watching experience:

> Almost the entire fire department of the large city of Newark N.J., was placed at our disposal and we show countless pieces of apparatus, engines, hook-and-ladders, horse towers, horse carriages, etc., rushing down a broad street at top speed, the horses straining every nerve and evidently eager to make a record run. Great clouds of smoke pour from the stacks of the engines as they pass our camera, thus giving an impression of genuineness to the entire series.[3]

In the simple phrase "an impression of genuineness," the Edison Company shows that it was less concerned with insisting on the truth of the story than on the effect the movie had on the audience. That we are watching "actual" firefighters is clearly meant to appeal to moviegoers – and as contemporary viewers, we can't help but be fascinated by the glimpse into the unpaved streets of 1902 Newark and the steam-driven fire equipment that represented the state-of-the-art firefighting technology of the time – but Porter and others were learning that audiences didn't mind that other scenes – such as the rescue scenes – were obviously staged. As viewers, we imaginatively knit these different components together into a unified and emotionally engaging experience, one informed by our personal and cultural backgrounds, our familiarity with storytelling on the stage and on the page, and for those early moviegoers, by a rapidly growing understanding of the language of the movies, a language developing in response to the concerns and experiences of turn-of-the-century America.

Turn-of-the-century genres of gender: Muscle men and dancing girls

What does it mean to look like a man or a woman? This question has always been central to visual culture, including our day-to-day decisions about what to wear and how to behave. Stores still divide clothing into "men's" and "women's" sections (although we see more and more overlap between the two), and every morning each of us takes on the duties of a movie costumer, picking out just the right clothes and accessories to create the "character" we will inhabit for the rest of the day. But where do we get our ideas about how we should dress, about what constitutes a "normal" look for a man or a woman, or what counts as unusual or even defiant? And once we have decided on our external appearances, what influences the ways we walk, talk, and interact with others, our "style" of being? How do we learn about what counts as typically "masculine" or "feminine" behavior?

The idea of the "typical" has been especially important in the visual arts: theater, painting, photography, and, of course, the movies. Characters in the visual arts always operate as *both* typical and unique, as both familiar and one of a kind. So in *Romeo and Juliet* the title characters are both highly specific individuals – Romeo Montague and Juliet Capulet – and familiar types: the impetuous young man, the naive and innocent ingénue. The history of American movies is at the same time the history of highly original characters – Charles Foster Kane, Princess Leia, Bruce Wayne – and the history of repeated character types – the cowboy, the girl next door, the femme fatale.

This interplay of the individual and the typical involves all the varied aspects of our identities, including race, age, ethnicity, sexuality, social class, etc., and all are important in the history of American cinema, but none is more so than gender.

Our ideas and ideals about gender and genres of gender are always changing, and the beginnings of American movies occurred at a particularly significant transition point in terms of gender. Rapidly increasing urbanization meant new ways of life for millions of Americans changing from country to city life. For many young women, cities represented new challenges but also opportunities for a social and economic independence that was impossible in their previous lives. Many immigrant families depended on the labor of women and girls, often in unsafe and unhealthy sweatshop factories, for their very survival. Across Europe and the United States, movements for women's rights, and most specifically the right to vote, were gaining momentum. At the same time, men found themselves divided between those involved in physically intensive factory and manual labor and those who were becoming more affluent "white collar" workers, part of the new corporate culture that was reshaping the American economy.

Consider these images of men and women from early Edison moving pictures created for the Kinetoscope parlor. From one perspective, we can see these two images as reinforcing the idea that typical men and women are very different from each other. *Annabelle Serpentine Dance* emphasizes grace and delicacy, with Annabelle Whitford encased in flowing skirts, while *Sandow* focuses on size and strength. Yet both images are intensely physical, and both feature displays of the body that pushed the boundaries of turn-of-the-century convention and propriety. Both were meant to be seen as beautiful, and both were also seen as slightly scandalous. If social commentators could not decide whether these new forms of mass visual entertainment should be celebrated or condemned, no one could deny their popularity, and this very popularity only made the debate over the influence moving pictures were having on changing social values even more heated.

As these early moving pictures became part of the screen experience we call "going to the movies," these questions and controversies about gender would continue. They would also parallel the role of gender within the movie business as well, as production would become increasingly dominated by men over the next several decades while at the same time the rise of the female movie star would give at least some women a fame and cultural influence that would challenge ideas about what it meant to be a man or a woman.

Fig 1.19
This early movie *Serpentine Dance* of the popular vaudeville performer Annabelle Whitford was considered somewhat scandalous.

Fig 1.20
Along with other short films like *Serpentine Dance*, images like these of Eugene Sandow demonstrated how early screen experiences could shape cultural expectations and ideas about masculine and feminine gender genres.

Case study 1.2: An early movie scandal: "The Kiss"

Fig 1.21
May Irwin and John Rice recreate the kiss from their popular stage hit *The Widow Jones*.

In 1896, the Edison Company filmed two popular vaudevillians of the day, May Irwin and John Rice, performing a celebrated scene from their stage play *The Widow Jones*, a kiss. The film itself is a little over fifteen seconds long, and much of the time is spent in Rice's elaborate preparations for the kiss, mainly involving his mustache. The two both face each other and the audience, making the kiss visible but also rendering the whole process a bit awkward. The scene is hardly shocking to contemporary audiences, but "The Kiss" (one title given the film) became an early movie controversy – and, not surprisingly, one of the most popular short movies of 1896. Some newspapers called for the movie to be banned. The Chicago journalist Herbert Stone argued that "[m]anifested to gargantuan proportions and repeated three times over, it is absolutely disgusting. Such things call for police interference."

What was it about "The Kiss" – and most specifically, the experience of watching a kiss in close-up on a movie screen, a scene that has become a fixture of the movies – that so excited and alarmed audiences? First, speculate on your own about why you think "The Kiss" was so shocking. Where do you think your own ideas – about history, about American culture, about censorship and the movies – came from?

Follow up your speculation by doing research into both historical reactions to "The Kiss" found in magazines and newspapers from the turn of the century and what contemporary scholars today say about Edison's short film. Stone's reaction to "The Kiss" represents one of the earliest calls for movie censorship. What do you think Stone was concerned about? How did others at the time, including the Edison Company, respond to opinions like Stone's?

The names above and below the title

Thomas Edison and the cult(ure) of invention

In 1881, when he turned his attention to the challenge of moving pictures, Thomas Alva Edison was 41 years old, already one of the most famous men in America, credited as the inventor of the phonograph and the electric light bulb and considered the personification of technological progress and innovation. In truth, while Edison was a skilled inventor, his success and fame owed as much to his business and promotional skills as his technical accomplishments. A classic nineteenth-century entrepreneur, Edison combined a keen instinct for ideas that would catch the public imagination, the organizational and management skills that allowed him to assemble teams of talented researchers who could turn these ideas into reality, and the marketing acumen to exploit the emerging mass media in order to advertise and publicize his work. In these ways, Edison is the forebear of such contemporary figures as the late Steve Jobs of Apple computers and Bill Gates of Microsoft, men whose main creativity lay in their abilities to make the innovative work of others accessible to a larger public, a description that equally fits the studio owners who we will see emerge from the tumult of this early period in American movie history.

It's not surprising that much of the Edison Company's work focused on communications technologies, from the telegraph to the phonograph to motion pictures, given how adept Edison was at using mass communications to promote his business and himself. Indeed, the mythic image that still persists of Edison as the master inventor, the solitary genius who almost singlehandedly created the modern world of electric lights, recorded music, and moving pictures, is perhaps one of Edison's most significant inventions, one that fits into the emerging early-twentieth-century ideology of American ingenuity and innovation. This heroic myth, while making for a great story, can obscure the even more fascinating reality of the world of early cinema, a world of multiple screen experiments and multiple possibilities for the development of these various moving picture inventions into the cultural medium we came to call "the movies."

Fig 1.22
Thomas Alva Edison. Source: Edison/The Kobal Collection.

Fig 1.23
Alice Guy-Blaché.

Less heroic perhaps but probably even more significant, Edison was even more concerned with cornering the market on the technologies his company developed as he was with creating a new art form. The Edison Company aggressively enforced its patent rights, challenging the ability of the dozens of other innovators who were equally involved in the development of the movies to compete with Edison. In his efforts to organize, control, and dominate the emerging business of the movies in America, Edison set a pattern that would repeat throughout the history of American cinema, down to the massive media conglomerates of our current screen age.

Alice Guy-Blaché and women in film

Alice Guy-Blaché may be the most important early filmmaker that most people have never heard of. While an increasing number of movie scholars agree that her contributions to the development of motion pictures in both France and the United States rival and predate those of D. W. Griffith (profiled in Chapter 2), for years Alice Guy-Blaché's name almost disappeared from the standard narratives about movie history. There are many reasons for this shameful neglect, and one of them stems from our own tendency to mistakenly assume that before the 1960s women were largely absent from the worlds of business and professional achievement. It is also the case that the history of movies in America has been a history of gender inequality, with women still grossly underrepresented in the ranks of movie directors.

Women, however, were very active and played major roles in the early history of American cinema, not just as actors but also as producers, directors, and even studio heads. Filmmakers such as Cleo Madison, Ida May Park, and Lois Weber (also profiled in Chapter 2) directed hundreds of movies during the silent era, and no early film pioneer was more important than Alice Guy-Blaché.

Guy-Blaché was born Alice Guy in Paris in 1873. In 1894, she was working as a secretary for the French movie pioneer Léon Gaumont. The early movie business – before movies became "the movies" – was still a wide open place, where

Fig 1.24
A scene from Alice Guy-Blaché's first short film *La Fée aux Choux* (*The Cabbage Fairy*) from 1896, one of the first narrative movies ever made.

the production process had not yet developed the strict division of labor between directors, camera operators, writers, set designers, crew members, and on-screen talent that would come to dominate the motion picture industry. Though only twenty-three years old, Guy-Blaché saw an artistic potential in moving pictures. Working up her courage, in 1896 she asked Gaumont if she might try her hand at moviemaking, and he agreed – as long as she confined her filmmaking to her lunch hours and didn't neglect her secretarial work.

That first movie by Guy-Blaché – *La Fée aux Choux* (*The Cabbage Fairy*) – was about a minute long and was based on a folk tale for children explaining that babies were brought by fairies to a cabbage patch, a variation on the stork story. The movie featured a fanciful set of large, painted cabbage plants and a fairy dressed in a flowing gown complete with wings who produces one wiggling baby after another from behind the plants. It's a simple story, but a story nonetheless. In fact, *The Cabbage Fairy* stands as one of the first narrative movies in the history of cinema, and with it Guy-Blaché became the first woman filmmaker. Recognizing her talent and imagination, Gaumont soon had Guy-Blaché creating dozens of short films, and by 1906, at age thirty-three, Guy-Blaché was not only Gaumont's most important director but his head of production. Over the course of her career, from 1896 to 1920 when she made her final movie, Guy-Blaché would personally direct some 350 movies and be responsible for the production of twice that number.

In addition to being a crucial innovator in the development of movies as narratives, Guy-Blaché also was a leading pioneer in the use of special effects and color tinting, and even conducted some of the earliest experiments in the use of synchronized sound in movies. Her 1906 movie *La Vie du Christ* (*The Birth, the Life, and the Death of Christ*), a thirty-three minute epic featuring a cast of over 300, demonstrated the breadth of Guy-Blaché's ambition and vision. A sensation in both France and the United States, *The Birth, the Life, and the Death of Christ* inspired the imaginations of filmmakers on both sides of the Atlantic to rethink the artistic possibilities of the new medium, two years before Griffith even made his first short movie.

In 1907, Guy-Blaché married fellow filmmaker Herbert Blaché, and the two emigrated to the United States, where they initially worked in Gaumont's American division. Three years later, Alice Guy-Blaché became a studio head when she and

Herbert started their own studio, the Solax Company. Eventually locating in Fort Lee, New Jersey, a hub of the American movie industry before the great migration to California, Solax became one of the largest and most successful American studios, and Guy-Blaché continued to direct her own movies while supervising the production of hundreds of others, all while raising two children. Solax's fortunes began to decline, however, as more and more film production moved to Hollywood, and Guy-Blaché's marriage began to fall apart as well. Herbert Blaché left his family in 1918 and relocated to California; the two officially divorced in 1922.

Guy-Blaché directed what was to be her final film, *Tarnished Reputations*, in 1920, when she almost lost her life to a flu epidemic. Her divorce in 1922 forced her to sell the remainder of her studio and declare bankruptcy. She returned briefly to France and tried to revive her film career, but by the 1920s gender segregation had become solidified in the movie industry, and even a filmmaker of the stature of Alice Guy-Blaché was no longer able to direct movies. She returned to the United States and lived in New Jersey until her death in 1968 at age 95. This giant of the early cinema, whose accomplishments and influence we are only just beginning to appreciate, seemed to vanish from movie history, in part owing to the physical fragility of her early movies, most of which are lost forever, but more so to the growing sexism of the movie industry that accompanied the equally growing financial and cultural influence of the movies. For contemporary students new to the study of the screen ages of the United States, the career and movies of Alice Guy-Blaché and other early women filmmakers represent an exciting area of discovery and recovery.

Edwin S. Porter and the artisanal screen age

At the beginning of the movies in America, there were no "directors" or "cinematographers," no "set designers" or "movie stars." The idea of movie production as involving an extensive division of labor and hyper-specialization is

Fig 1.25
Edwin S. Porter. Source:
The Kobal Collection.

reflected in both the guild and union structure of mainstream American moviemaking as well as the myriad technical categories of the Academy Awards. The men and women involved in those early days of moving pictures were making up the new medium of "the movies" as they went along, and none could have predicted the size and scope of the movie industry that grew out of their early experiments.

As a result, one of the most influential and important early movie directors never thought of himself as a "director" or even primarily as an artist. Edwin S. Porter, like his famous early employer Thomas Edison, his colleague W.K.L. Dickson, and many other film pioneers around the world, was a technician turned artist, a man with an interest in electricity and mechanics who was also attracted to the idea of showmanship and entertainment. Both early moving pictures and still photography required complex technological, mechanical, and chemical expertise, true art forms of the industrial age. As with Eadweard Muybridge, these early experimenters did not necessarily differentiate between the technological and the artistic, between science and entertainment. Today, a person can become a successful movie director without being able to build or repair a movie camera, but the early cinema involved jacks-of-all-trades, people who moved from the workbench to the studio and back again.

After working as a telegraph operator and a US Navy electrician in his early twenties, Porter went into the brand new movie exhibition business in 1896, traveling throughout North and South America as a projectionist, gaining familiarity with a wide variety of early screen experiences, learning what different audiences responded to and found compelling and entertaining. Porter brought this utterly unique expertise with him when he went to work for Edison in 1899, where he was put in charge of production at a time when being in charge of production meant really being in charge.

Porter would find stories, cast and direct actors, operate the camera, and put the final film together. What films there were typically lasted less than a minute each, and as we have seen they were usually shown as part of a larger live vaudeville program. In these early days of American cinema, there was no standard operating practice.

Fig 1.26
A bank robber shoots a passenger fleeing towards the camera in Edwin S. Porter's *The Great Train Robbery*.

Everyone involved in the early movie industry automatically became an "innovator," and every new film was an "experimental" film. Porter soon recognized that this new form of visual communication needed to change if it was going to flourish. As he told a *New York Times* reporter near the end of his life, "I felt there was nothing wrong with the screen itself, but that the public was becoming tired of the short, single-scene type of newsreel film … I came to the conclusion that a picture telling a story in continuity form might draw the customers back to the theatres, and set to work in this direction."[4] And set to work he did.

In movies ranging from *Life of an American Fireman* through to his triumph in *The Great Train Robbery*, Porter introduced or invented most of the key innovations that were to become the basic components of cinematic storytelling: crosscutting (switching back and forth between simultaneously occurring story elements) and the use of parallel narratives; continuity editing (assembling individual shots into a seamless whole); special effects such as rear-screen projection and split screens; even the core idea of the "shot" (the space between when the camera starts and when it stops) as the key element of moviemaking. Which of these elements did he himself invent and which did he borrow from the work of other early filmmakers? Such questions are extremely difficult to answer, not the least because it seems that such distinctions were not all that important to Porter himself.

Porter's work – and particularly the widespread success of *The Great American Train Robbery* – led to the explosion of the movie industry in the nickelodeon era and laid the foundation for the studio system, but Porter himself chafed at the increasingly specialized and factory-based model of film production. Porter finally left Edison in 1909 to help start Rex Studios, where he could still work in the more holistic style he preferred. He later worked as a "director" for the Famous Players Film Studio (the forerunner of Paramount Studios) for a couple of years, but movie production was no longer a friendly place for a technician and tinkerer such as Porter. He made his last movie in 1915, and spent the rest of his life in technical

Fig 1.27
This shoot-out between the robbers (foreground) and the posse pursuing them in *The Great Train Robbery* places the audience in the middle of the action. Note the evidence of hand-coloring, an early form of adding color to the screen experience of the movies.

pursuits, first as president of a projector company and later as an inventor and salesman. When he died in 1941 in New York City, film buffs mourned the passing of a crucial pioneer in the film industry, but the rest of the general public took little notice.

We might say that filmmakers like Edwin S. Porter were products of the early "artisanal" phase of American movie history, a time when a small group of experimenters made "handcrafted" films that expressed their own interests and curiosities, all in a spirit of innovation and the search for the screen experiences that would capture the imagination of the new movie audiences. As we will discuss in Chapter 8, the current digital revolution in visual culture perhaps represents another "artisanal" age, as anyone with a smart phone and iMovie on her computer can make a movie and post it online, for an audience of millions or just a few friends. Social media sites such as YouTube and Vimeo house thousands of new experiments in digital moviemaking, ranging from the fascinating to the ridiculous, the tedious to the surprising. What will the culture of digital moviemaking look like in twenty years? Which of the various screen experiences will come to define a mainstream, and which an avant-garde? The answers to these questions are probably as unknowable – and intriguing – to us as the development of the screen ages of the twentieth century were to these first American filmmakers.

Notes

1   "Edison's Vitascope Cheered," *The New York Times,* April 24, 1896.
2   Robinson, David, *From Peep Show To Palace: The Birth of American Film.* New York: Columbia University Press, 1996, p. 23.
3   Musser, Charles, *Before the Nickelodeon: Edwin S. Porter and the Edison Manufacturing Company.* Berkeley: University of California Press, 1991, p. 217.
4   Goodman, Ezra, "Turn Back the Clock: Reminiscences of Edwin S. Porter, or the History of the Motion Picture," *The New York Times*, June 2, 1940.

Explore further

Gunning, Tom, "The Cinema of Attraction: Early Film, Its Spectator and the Avant-Garde." *Wide Angle* 8.3–4 (1986): 63–70.

May, Lary, *Screening Out the Past: The Birth of Mass Culture and the Motion Picture Industry.* Chicago: University of Chicago Press, 1983.

Musser, Charles, *Before the Nickelodeon: Edwin S. Porter and the Edison Manufacturing Company.* Berkeley: University of California Press, 1991.

—— *The Emergence of Cinema: The American Screen to 1907.* Berkeley: University of California Press, 1994.

Robinson, David, *From Peep Show To Palace: The Birth of American Film.* New York: Columbia University Press, 1996.

Sklar, Robert, *Movie-Made America: A Cultural History of American Movies.* New York: Vintage Books, 1994.

Slide, Anthony, *Early American Cinema.* Metuchen, NJ: Scarecrow Press, 1994.

Stokes, Melvyn and Richard Maltby (eds.), *American Movie Audiences: From the Turn of the Century to the Early Sound Era.* London: BFI Publishing, 1999.

CHAPTER 2

Becoming "the movies": The nickelodeon age, 1908–1915

Joseph Medill Patterson reports on "The Nickelodeons," *Saturday Evening Post*, November 23, 1907

In this eternal struggle for more self-consciousness, the moving-picture machine, uncouth instrument though it be, has enlisted itself on especial behalf of the least enlightened, those who are below the reach even of the yellow journals. For although in the prosperous vaudeville houses the machine is but a toy, a "chaser," in the nickelodeons it is the central, absorbing fact, which strengthens, widens, vivifies subjective life; which teaches living other than living through the senses alone. Already, perhaps, touching him at the psychological moment, it has awakened to his first, groping, necessary discontent the spirit of an artist of the future, who otherwise would have remained mute and motionless.

Joseph Medill Patterson, "The Nickelodeons"[1]

As **nickelodeons** – theaters devoted exclusively to showing moving pictures – spread rapidly throughout the US, the screen experience of sitting in a darkened room with dozens of others, friends and strangers alike, to watch glowing images on a screen reached millions of Americans in every corner of the country. This runaway success also brought with it increased scrutiny. For the first time, the movies were more than just a novelty; they were a bona fide mass medium. As with any suddenly popular fad, authority figures of various types, from elected officials to members of the clergy, from business groups to political reformers, began to ask questions about whether the nickelodeons – and the "movies," as moving pictures were increasingly called – were a good or bad thing for the country.

This mix of curiosity and concern led the prominent American journalist Joseph Medill Patterson to publish his own overview, titled simply "The Nickelodeons," in the Thanksgiving edition of the *Saturday Evening Post* in 1907. We can read Patterson's article, with its mix of statistics and social analysis, as a reaction to the fascination and anxiety provoked by the rise of the nickelodeons. At the beginning, he pictures the typical nickelodeon as a modest affair, quickly put together to take advantage of the new craze for moving pictures:

Nickelodeons Small movie theaters popular from 1905 through 1915 that typically showed a rotating series of short films. The term "nickelodeon" refers to the common admission price of five cents.

The nickelodeon is usually a tiny theatre, containing 199 seats, giving from twelve to eighteen performances a day, seven days a week. Its walls are painted red. The seats are ordinary kitchen chairs, not fastened … The spectatorium is one story high, twenty-five feet wide and about seventy feet deep. Last year or the year before it was probably a second-hand clothier's, a pawnshop or cigar store. Now, the counter has been ripped out, there is a ticket-seller's booth where the show-window was, an automatic musical barker somewhere up in the air thunders its noise down on the passersby, and the little store has been converted into a theatrelet.

Humble though he portrays the nickelodeon to be, Patterson not only stresses how popular they have become, but how they are attracting new groups of people beyond those who typically frequented the music halls and vaudeville theaters of turn-of-the-century America:

The nickelodeon is tapping an entirely new stratum of people, is developing into theatregoers a section of population that formerly knew and cared little about the drama as a fact in life … Incredible as it may seem, over two million people on the average attend the nickelodeons **every day of the year**, and a third of these are children. (*emphasis his*)

For many of Patterson's readers, the idea of so many different people all coming together in a darkened room to watch movies featuring an equally wide variety of subject matters, from boxing matches to chase scenes to recreations of news events to melodramas and slapstick comedies, raised concerns that have stayed with the movies ever since: Are the movies "good" or "bad" for us? Do they represent a new form of artistic expression to be nurtured and developed, or a powerful influence that demands regulation and oversight? And just who belonged to this "entirely new stratum of people" that Patterson refers to?

Los Angeles nickelodeon showing of *Kid Auto Races at Venice*, 1914

When the patrons in a Los Angeles nickelodeon theater on a spring day in 1914 looked over their programs, they would have seen an assortment of movies listed, mostly single reel features of around ten or twelve minutes each. If one of those titles happened to be *Kid Auto Races at Venice* featuring Charlie Chaplin, the name of the star would probably have meant little to them, but they would almost certainly have recognized the name of the studio – Keystone – that released the movie. The creation of the actor/director Mack Sennett, Keystone had become world famous for its slapstick comedies, funny movies full of outrageous sight gags and physical humor, epitomized by the series of "Keystone Kops" movies. These short films featured a group of hapless policemen usually involved in the wild pursuit of a criminal, chases that always involved destruction and mayhem.

Whether those moviegoers in 1914 realized it at the time or not, *Kid Auto Races at Venice* exemplified several important developments in American cinema in the period between 1908 and 1915, none more significant than the name of the movie itself. The "Venice" of the title was Venice, California, a seaside neighborhood in Los Angeles famous for its series of canals. Los Angeles, meanwhile, had become increasingly famous over the last four years as the home of the American movie industry, as studio after studio left the East coast for the sunshine, fair weather, and (at the time) cheap real estate of southern California. The name of the neighborhood nestled between downtown Los Angeles and the Santa Monica mountains to the north where some of the first studios set up shop – Hollywood – soon became a synonym for American moviemaking and movie culture itself.

From 1910 to the present day, southern Californian locations have stood in for cities and countrysides around the world (and sometimes from out of this world). *Kid Auto Races at Venice* represented a common practice of the time, as Keystone studios took advantage of a local children's event as the backdrop for a short comic feature. For Los Angeles audiences, the movie had the added attraction of seeing their hometown on the movie screen; for audiences across the country, the movie offered a chance to broaden their horizons and glimpse a new and interesting locale, a selling point that moving pictures inherited from the tradition of magic lantern shows and illustrated lectures.

Finally, *Kid Auto Races at Venice* provided American moviegoers with a glimpse of a performer who would shortly become one of the most influential early moviemakers and one of the most famous people in the world: Charlie Chaplin in his role as the Little Tramp. A seasoned British music hall performer, Chaplin had been signed by Keystone and sent out with director Henry Lehrman and cameraman Frank Williams to improvise some comic scenes during the race. During the six minutes of the film, we see the actual race spectators – including an LA policeman – react to Chaplin's antics as well as to the presence of the movie camera, sometimes watching the races, sometimes Chaplin, and sometimes looking right at the movie audience. Just as audaciously, Chaplin also occasionally mugs for the camera,

Fig 2.2
One of the first appearances of Charlie Chaplin as the Little Tramp in *Kid Auto Races at Venice*; a later version of the character would become known around the world. Source: The Kobal Collection.

Fig 2.3

The ornate interior of the Knickerbocker Theatre where *Cabiria* made its debut in 1914, a far cry from the storefront nickelodeon. Source: Cinema Treasures website, http://cinematreasures. org/theaters/39953/ photos/59599.

breaking the "fourth wall" and seeming to acknowledge the fact that he is, in fact, appearing in a movie about appearing in a movie. This casual confusion of the distinction between fiction and reality (the Little Tramp character "pretends" to interfere with the races by actually interfering with the races, at one point barely jumping out of the way of one of the cars) demonstrates just how sophisticated moviegoers in 1914 had become about the process of making movies.

Cabiria premieres at the Knickerbocker Theatre, New York City, June 1, 1914

"To-day no one is above 'the movies.'"[2] So wrote the New York playwright and cultural critic Channing Pollock in 1914 with a mix of resignation and concern. After initially dismissing the new art form as appealing to "the most primitive instincts" of its audiences, Pollock had to confront the fact that moving pictures had become a central part of American life. And the screen experiences of his day were not just limited to the storefront nickelodeon. The motivating occasion for Pollock's article was the American debut of an epic movie from Italy: *Cabiria*, a story set in ancient Rome during the third century BCE. Clocking in at over two hours, this multireel production featured lavish sets, spectacular scenes of destruction and warfare, and a cast of hundreds. The appearance and audience experience of movies

Fig 2.4
The spectacular eruption of Mount Etna from *Cabiria*, an example of a new epic vision for the movie screen experience.

like *Cabiria* helped change expectations about what a movie could be for both audiences and cultural critics alike.

Unlike the short films that made up the usual rotating nickelodeon program, movies like Cabiria were presented as special events that deserved a special setting. Instead of presenting themselves as an alternative form of entertainment to the vaudeville variety show, these longer movies from abroad such as Alice Guy-Blaché's *La vie du Christ* (*The Life of Christ*) in 1906 modeled their viewing experience on the dramatic theater, where audiences would spend an entire evening watching a single play, thus also challenging the monopolistic business model of the Motion Picture Patents Company, which dictated that a movie should never be longer than one reel (15 minutes).

The screen experience of *Cabiria* represented the most extensive effort yet to both reproduce and excel the experience of live theater. The movie made its American debut not at a crowded nickelodeon but at a Broadway theater: the Knickerbocker. The movie was accompanied by a score written especially for it, performed by a live orchestra. In its visual size and scope, however, *Cabiria* offered a screen experience that directly challenged the limitations of even the most expensive live production. Cloaked in the cultural status of providing a window into ancient history, *Cabiria*'s depictions of an erupting Mount Etna and children being offered as human sacrifices in the vast Temple of Moloch offered as much excitement and sensation as any nickelodeon show, on a scale beyond the scope of live theater.

Just seven years after Joseph Medill Patterson felt the need to explain the new phenomenon of the nickelodeon to his white, middle-class readers, screen experiences such as *Cabiria* were achieving new heights of social acceptance. President Woodrow Wilson even staged an outdoor screening of *Cabiria* at the White House. American filmmakers like D. W. Griffith, inspired by the ambition of these movies, began campaigning to make their own multireel screen experiences, in spite of the reluctance of many movie producers to change their model for making – and selling – movies. As we will see in Chapter 3, the move towards greater ambition and spectacle in American screen experiences would be impossible to resist, and the era of the Hollywood blockbuster would begin.

Screen ages

A new medium for a new America

If the period from the 1890s to the birth of the nickelodeon in 1908 was a screen age of explosive growth and development in the history of American cinema, the next decade saw equally dramatic changes in the kinds of screen experiences available to early moviegoers. In the storefront nickelodeons spreading across the country, patrons would pay a nickel to watch a variety of single reel films, each no more than fifteen minutes long, with the entire program usually lasting about an hour or so. Slapstick comedies, melodramas, westerns, chase movies, actualities; the slate of moving pictures would typically change daily.

For the urban, working-class audiences who made up the majority of nickelodeon patrons, the moving pictures were an inexpensive and entertaining way to spend a lunch hour or to relax after work. In some ways, the contemporary screen experience of an evening spent surfing the Internet – moving from watching a funny web video to checking out a breaking news story to catching up on an episode of a favorite television show – evokes the variety and eclectic nature of the nickelodeon.

However, by the end of the nickelodeon era in the mid-1910s, more and more theaters specialized in what came to be called "feature films," multiple reel movies of one or two hours, a viewing experience much closer to what most of us think of as "going to the movies." Rather than a quick place to stop in during a busy day for some welcome entertainment, the **feature film** experience focused more on the moving picture as an event, much like a play or a symphony, with a set starting time.

Feature film A multiple reel movie that told an extended narrative beyond the fifteen-minute limitation of the single reel movies popular in the nickelodeons. This term has remained to this day to refer to the standard Hollywood movie.

Rather than screening for only a day in any one theater, movies like the Italian epic *Cabiria* or D. W. Griffith's *Judith of Bethulia* (1914) would play for weeks and even months at a time. Movies like these also traded on the cultural prestige associated with more formal theatrical experiences, as well as subject material taken from the Bible, history, and literature, to appeal more to affluent, middle-class audiences.

The screen age from 1908 to 1915 saw the movies develop a kind of split identity as they become a dominant and influential medium. On the one hand, movies were seen as an inexpensive, lively, often sensational and exploitive kind of entertainment, one especially appealing to broad swaths of the population who had rarely had access to mass media before. On the other hand, moviemakers and exhibitors aspired to promote the movies as a serious new art, one that might take its place among the fine arts and – not coincidentally – attract a more affluent and socially influential part of the population.

This uncertain social status played itself out in the name of the new medium itself. Some of the producers and exhibitors anxious about the cultural status of their new business worried that the growing popularity of the term "movies" would never do if they wanted to be taken seriously by the established cultural gatekeepers, insisting instead on what they saw as the more dignified "motion pictures." This debate continues to this day: consider, for example, how many colleges and universities offer "Film Studies" or "Cinema Studies" courses as compared with "Movie Studies."

This split identity for the movies reflected the dramatic developments that were transforming turn-of-the-century America as quickly as the nickelodeons were growing in popularity: the massive influx of immigrants from southern and eastern Europe (on the east coast) and Asia (on the west coast); the increasing size and influence of corporations; the rapid industrialization and urbanization of America; and the explosive growth of technological development, of which the movies were a primary example. The accessibility of the nickelodeons was attracting a more diverse and socially mixed audience than previous types of popular entertainment. Movies, less than a decade old, were emerging as a democratizing force in American culture. Their visual storytelling helped overcome barriers of language and culture in a multicultural society; the modest admission price and continuous daily program made the nickelodeon available across lines of income and social class.

Not everyone saw these changes as positive. Many of Patterson's white, middle-class readers were anxious about what these demographic changes meant for their traditional ideas about what "America" and "American" meant, ideas rooted both in tradition and in prejudices about race, ethnicity, and social class. Like Patterson, some expressed this anxiety as concern about the effect of the movies on what he called the "lower classes."

These anxieties also reflected fears his readers had about themselves. Indeed, although Patterson describes the nickelodeon as mostly a phenomenon of what he calls "the slums," we also know that the nickelodeons attracted a wide clientele, from the prosperous to the poor, from city dwellers to rural residents. In fact, many nickelodeon operators were eager to attract a more affluent customer base with more money to spend. In any case, however, the arguments about the social impact of the movies were here to stay.

Growing demand and the rise of the independents

The explosive growth of the nickelodeons created an equally explosive demand for new movies. In order to survive in an increasingly competitive market, exhibitors needed to change their programs every day. By the nickelodeon era, this demand was met by "exchanges" – businesses that purchased movies from production companies that then rented these movies to exhibitors. Some of these exchanges, however, were actually owned by the production companies; in particular, the General Film Company, created by the MPPC to monopolize distribution as well as production, a fact that contributed to the antitrust lawsuit eventually brought against the MPPC by the government. Even though the distribution and exhibitions businesses were uncertain and volatile, they were also potentially extremely lucrative, and much easier to get into than the production business. The popularity and demand for the movie experience continued to outstrip the abilities of the MPPC to supply the market, a situation ripe for newcomers to enter the field.

In spite of the efforts by the MPPC to control the movie industry, the growing popularity of movies in the nickelodeon age attracted more and more people into the business. Nickelodeons presented a particular opportunity for immigrants looking to secure a place in American society; in particular, Jewish immigrants who had fled persecution in Europe began to open chains of these new, affordable theaters that appealed to working-class urban audiences that they knew particularly well. This new group of movie pioneers, men like Carl Laemmle, William Fox, Adolph Zukor, Marcus Loew, and Jack Warner and his brothers, would themselves go on to form the companies – Universal, Fox, Paramount, Warner Brothers, MGM – that would dominate the American movie industry in the studio periods and whose names still define American cinema today.

The movies go west

Several factors contributed to the westward migration of movie production at the beginning of the 1910s. The legal battle between the MPPC and the independents was one. Eager to avoid harassment from the MPPC, some independent production companies began to abandon New York and New Jersey and explored other parts of the country where they could produce movies far from the reach (so they hoped) of the MPPC.

The independents Any of a group of movie production companies not a part of the Motion Picture Patents Company. Some of these independents, such as the Independent Moving Pictures Company – later Universal Pictures – and Famous Players Film Company – later Paramount Pictures – eventually became some of the dominant companies in the studios age. The term "independent" has remained a part of the Hollywood lexicon to refer to various movie productions in some way outside "mainstream" Hollywood moviemaking.

Fig 2.5
The independent film company Nestor's studio at the corner of Gower and Sunset in 1913, believed to be the first studio actually located in Hollywood. Source: Los Angeles Public Library Photo Collection.

In 1910, Biograph sent its most important director, D. W. Griffith, to southern California in order to assess the suitability of Los Angeles as a studio location. The immediate result was the first "Hollywood" movie – *In Old California* – but the success Griffith found in California was just part of a steady migration of film production to the west coast. Southern California, with its mild climate, year-round sunshine, and geographic variety – from seacoasts to mountains to deserts to lush hillsides – expanded the opportunities for filmmakers to experiment with and develop the craft of moviemaking. While the dozens of studios that were built across the area provided indoor facilities similar to what filmmakers had known in the east, the lure of outdoor and location shooting began to liberate the camera from the confines of the studio set. The striking scenic panoramas that soon became a staple of the westerns changed the visual imaginations and expectations of moviemakers and moviegoers alike.

By 1915, California had become the center of the American movie industry, a position it holds to the present day. At the same time, other forces had begun to erode the MPPC cartel. Independents made the transition to multiple reel movies much more quickly than the MPPC companies, and these longer screen experiences began proving popular with audiences. New, larger, and more opulent movie theaters, such as the Mark Strand in New York, were eclipsing the nickelodeons in defining the screen experience that more and more people associated with "going to the movies" and ushering in the age of the "movie palace." Rather than relying on the exhibition strategy of the nickelodeons, showing multiple short films that changed on a daily basis, the model upon which the MPPC was built, these new theaters emphasized longer features that ran for weeks, even months at a time.

Meanwhile, the original patents issued to Edison for the moviemaking technology developed by his company began to expire, Eastman Kodak began selling film to independents, and finally in 1915, the US government ruled against the MPPC as an illegal monopoly. The group limped along appealing this decision for a few years, but by 1918 the MPPC was finished. The screen age of the major Hollywood studios had begun, a story we will continue in the next chapter.

In focus: Early censorship and the question of who goes to the movies
On Christmas Eve, 1908, at the height of the nickelodeon era, New York City mayor George McClellan suddenly revoked the licenses of every moving picture theater in

the city, closing them all. The main reason given in the mayor's statement had to do with public safety; namely, the danger of fire. But the conclusion of the mayor's proclamation – along with its release on Christmas Eve – reveals that more than just physical safety was on the mayor's mind:

> Because of the serious opposition presented by the rectors and pastors of practically all the Christian denominations in the city, and because of the further objections of the Society for the Prevention of Cruelty to Children and the Society for the Prevention of Crime, I have decided that licenses for moving-picture shows shall only be issued hereafter on the written agreement that the licensee will not operate the same on Sundays. And I do further declare that I will revoke any of the moving-picture show licenses on evidence that pictures have been exhibited by the licensees which tend to degrade or injure the morals of the community.[3]

It's clear that fire can degrade or injure the bodily health of nickelodeon patrons, but the question of whether watching a moving picture can "degrade or injure the morals" of the audience is much more open to debate. And how exactly would the closing of movie theaters protect children and prevent crime? In Mayor McClellan's order, we can see evidence of a longstanding argument in American cultural history over censorship, over whether certain ideas, works of art, or other forms of public expression represent a threat to the moral or spiritual health of the community, and, just as important, who gets to decide what does or doesn't count as such a threat, and who gets to define just what we might mean by "the public good."

As Patterson's article suggests, these early arguments over the effect of moving pictures in the United States were really arguments about American culture; specifically, how we define that culture and who gets to participate in it. Many of the early advocates of movie censorship identified with a vision of the United States as a primarily Protestant, Anglo-Saxon country, and they saw the rapid influx of people

Fig 2.6
This cartoon from *Punch* magazine in 1910 expresses concerns that the movies were leading children astray from the lessons they should be learning in church. Fears such as these led to early censorship efforts directed at the movies. Source: Library of Congress.

from Catholic and Jewish areas of southern and eastern Europe – as well as the increasing numbers of Asian immigrants from China and Japan – as a threat to their understanding of America. More than any other public entertainment to that point, the reach of the movies quickly extended to even the most remote communities.

The increasing demand for movies meant hundreds of films were being quickly produced by an almost equally large number of filmmakers, in spite of the efforts of the MPPC to control the movie industry. The movies quickly became an attractive path to prosperity and cultural prominence to many immigrants and children of immigrants, particularly Jewish people fleeing European persecution, looking to find their place in American society. Ultimately, this infusion of new perspectives and experiences would help fuel the rich development of American culture in the coming century, but to many critics of moving pictures, this newness represented a disturbing challenge to their notions about what America was.

The National Board of Censorship and the Mutual case

Alarmed by Mayor McClellan's order, the successful New York nickelodeon owner Marcus Loew and other members of the Motion Picture Patents Company teamed with the social activists at the People's Institute to create the National Board of Censorship in 1908. The industry idea was to avoid government censorship – and more theater closures – through self-censorship, a strategy we will see repeated again and again during the history of American movies. The National Board of Censorship (the name was later softened to the National Board of Review in 1915) advised the members of the MPPC and reviewed their movies, offering their approval of movies they felt suitable for public distribution.

In spite of these efforts, however, the National Board did not stem the many local efforts to censor movies that were spreading across the country. Eventually, these developments culminated in what is known as the "**Mutual case,**" the US Supreme Court case of *Mutual Film Corporation v. Industrial Commission of Ohio* in 1915, which challenged the state of Ohio's movie censorship law as a violation of Mutual's First Amendment rights to free speech. The state of Ohio insisted instead that movies were a business, not a form of speech or a part of the press, and that they could therefore be regulated like any other business.

The US Supreme Court agreed with the state of Ohio, ruling that movies were no more entitled to free speech protection than "the theater, the circus and all other shows and spectacles." In effect, the court ruled that governments were free to censor the movies and any other form of public entertainment. The decision that movies

Mutual case Refers to the landmark 1915 legal case of *Mutual Film Corporation v. Industrial Commission of Ohio,* in which Mutual challenged the ability of the Industrial Commission to censor movies, claiming such censorship violated its First Amendment right of free speech. The US Supreme Court ruled, however, that movies were a business, not a form of speech, and thus could be regulated and censored by the government. The court later overruled its decision in 1952, granting movies free speech protections.

Fig 2.7
Not everyone agreed that the movie industry required censorship oversight. This cartoon from 1914 makes the case that adults should not be limited in their screen experiences to only those also appropriate for children, an argument that continues throughout American movie history.

IS THE HAND OF OFFICIAL CENSORSHIP FINALLY TO BLOT OUT ALL THAT IS INTERESTING
IN THE PHOTOPLAY, FOR THE BENEFIT OF THE CHILDREN?

were not protected by the First Amendment would eventually be overturned in 1952, but until then the ruling dramatically shaped the history of movie regulation and censorship over the next several decades. Just as significant, the language of the ruling reflected the worldview of Mayor McClellan and many other early censors: that it was the responsibility of those considered educated and respectable to monitor and regulate what the "people at the bottom" were watching:

> They [moving pictures] may be used for evil, and against that possibility the statue was enacted. Their power of amusement and, it may be, education, the audiences they assemble, not of women alone nor of men alone, but together, not of adults only, but of children, make them the more insidious in corruption … Besides, there are some things which should not have pictorial representation in public places and to all audiences.[4]

The fear that not just "women alone" nor "men alone" but women and men "together" were going to the movies; that children were often in attendance – these meant to the members of the Supreme Court that movies could not be trusted. More significant, they feared that "all audiences" could not be trusted to judge what they saw on their own. This would not be the first time that the diversity of viewing experiences that make up what we call "the movies" would be a source of concern, and in many ways these early forms of censorship would set the pattern for arguments over the course of American movie history about who should be able to see what and when.

In development

Comedies, westerns, and melodramas: The genres of the nickelodeon age

The popularity of the nickelodeons represented another decisive development in the screen experiences of early moviegoers: the preference for story films such as *The Great Train Robbery*. Actualities of everyday life or exotic scenes from around the world might have been enough when moving pictures were still a novelty, but more and more audiences were looking for narratives that provided meaning and significance for the images on the screen.

Early movie narratives reflected the experiences, concerns, and fascinations of turn-of-the-century America, as rapid urbanization, mass immigration, technological expansion, and the growth of monopoly capitalism were changing social experience so quickly that only "motion" pictures could adequately express the sense millions of Americans had of a world constantly being reinvented around them. Itself a product of the same technological revolution that was producing the automobile and the airplane, the movies and the stories they told became a focal point for the hopes and fears of a country wrestling with questions of tradition and progress, wealth and poverty, democracy and imperialism.

As Joseph Medill Patterson's article on the nickelodeon craze revealed, the explosion of movie popularity in the middle of the first decade of the twentieth century meant an exciting new world of visual and entertainment experiences for some, a potentially disruptive social force for others. For many working-class and immigrant audiences as well as for isolated rural viewers, the nickelodeons represented a more open and democratic source of excitement, information, and social activity. For the more affluent readership Patterson addressed, these same aspects of the nickelodeon were a source of concern as the America they thought they knew was changing, and thanks to the movies they could see these changes literally right before their eyes. What would be the effect of these new screen experiences on audiences who for many of Patterson's readers seemed unfamiliar and even frightening?

For the makers of movies in the nickelodeon era, providing screen experiences that satisfied all of these often contradictory impulses created their greatest challenge as businessmen in search of the greatest profits. They wanted to maintain a steady output of the kinds of movies that would keep audiences returning again and again to the nickelodeons. At the same time, they were interested in attracting audiences who could both afford higher ticket prices and influence public opinion about the social role of the movies, especially as the first efforts at movie censorship began. It is in this context that a number of different genres emerged as particularly popular, each of which reflected these different attitudes and concerns about the role of the movies in the nickelodeon screen age.

The western

For many contemporary students, the historical popularity of the western can seem puzzling (in my courses, it's usually the genre students are least interested in). But although far fewer westerns are made today than other genres, their influence remains widespread. *Star Wars*, for example, is essentially a space western, especially in its scenes set on the desert planet of Tatooine and in the modified cowboy costume worn by Han Solo. A war movie like *The Hurt Locker* uses the landscape of Iraq to draw on the tradition of cowboy warriors dealing with an insurgent native population. Action adventure movies, martial arts movies; all draw on the tradition of the American western.

For turn-of-the-century American audiences, the idea of the "Wild West" formed a major part of the public imagination, especially in the increasingly urbanized and industrialized eastern part of the country. The image of the cowboy – a rugged individualist doing battle with both the primal forces of nature and with "wild savages" – acquired mythic power as a symbol of American strength and resolve, even if the real lives of actual cowboys were much less romantic. For Americans who had only known city or small town rural life, for the millions of new Americans arriving every year from around the world, the idea of the Wild West promised adventure, freedom, and excitement.

But westerns have always stood for more than just exciting adventure stories involving cowboys, horses, ten-gallon hats, and revolvers. They helped shape and express in powerful visual narrative form feelings and beliefs about the history of US expansion and the treatment of native peoples, about the conflict between rural and urban ways of life, about the tensions between freedom and community, about the very meaning of America itself.

Many westerns shared the same unreflecting and even racist belief in the rightness of western expansion held by many white Americans. At the same time, these movies also offered viewers complex and even contradictory experiences that spoke to more ambivalent and troubled reactions towards the violence, ambition, and brutality that marked the history of the West, even as this violence, ambition, and brutality was often essential to the visual excitement of the genre.

D. W. Griffith's *The Red Man's View* (1909), for example, depicts a tribe of Kiowa Indians (all portrayed by non-Indian actors, a practice that became the norm

Fig 2.8
Actors portraying Kiowa
Indians displaced from
their homes in D. W.
Griffith's *The Red Man's
View* (1909).

in Hollywood westerns) forced off their land by a group of gun-toting white men described as "the conquerors" by the title cards. The minimalist plot concerns a young Indian woman, played by Lottie Pickford, the sister of the movie star Mary Pickford, forced to remain with "the conquerors" as their slave, until a young warrior bargains for her return after the death of the tribe's chief on their forced march. On the one hand, the movie offers a sympathetic view of how native peoples had been mistreated at the hands of white "conquerors"; on the other hand, the fate of the tribe in *The Red Man's View* also seems inevitable, the result of a noble but "primitive" people giving way before a more selfish and violent but also stronger and triumphant white civilization.

It's interesting and useful to think about how different audiences at the time might have responded to a movie such as *The Red Man's View*. To viewers who shared Griffith's white middle-class background, the movie may have prompted feelings of admiration and pity for the tragic fate of a "vanishing" people, one they saw as no longer representing a threat to their understanding of America. For many immigrant audiences, however, this movie about a group of people forced to leave their native land to seek a haven somewhere else, all under the threatening and watchful eye of "the conquerors," *The Red Man's View* could be seen as a cautionary tale about their new lives in a land ruled by gangs of men with six shooters, a perspective that would equally resonate with the cultural experience of many African American moviegoers.

Slapstick comedy

Comedy has always been a staple of American cinema from its earliest days and remains one of the most popular film experiences to this day. Comedy thrives on violating the rules of proper social behavior, on making fun of what is considered serious, important, and at times even sacred, and for these reasons the artistic and cultural reputation of comedy has always been uncertain. This ambivalent cultural status of the comedy is especially true when it comes to **slapstick** or physical comedy. Pratfalls, mishaps, collisions, accidents; slapstick comedy deals with bodies moving in space, the most elemental and universal quality of human experience, and as a result slapstick comedy reaches across lines of culture, education, and social position.

The early Edison short, *What Demoralized the Barber Shop* (1904), demonstrates how slapstick comedy toys with ideas of propriety in ways that could both attract audiences and raise concerns among those who questioned the moral fitness of the

Slapstick A form of
movie and stage comedy
that relies on physical
mishaps and violence.

Fig 2.9
The sight of two pairs of legs causes havoc in *What Demoralized the Barber Shop*, an early slapstick comedy.

movies. The premise of the movie is simple. A group of men are gathered in a barber shop, one getting a shave on the right hand side of the shot, another a shoeshine on the left. The open doorway in the center of the back wall shows steps leading up, supposedly to the street outside. Suddenly, two pairs of women's legs appear at the top of the stairs, clad in stockings and visible from the calf down underneath skirts. We never see any more of the women than this, but the appearance of the legs is enough to send the men into a frenzy of comic action, including the barber, who is so distracted he begins pummeling his poor customer with a ridiculously large razor, while the other men fall over each other with excitement.

As silly as this short movie seems, it still appeals to a wide range of viewer attitudes and emotions related to larger trends and issues in American society. Most obvious is the comic use of sexual excitement and the suggestion of voyeurism that was part of both the appeal of and concern over peep shows in particular and the movies in general. The movie is keyed to a primarily male audience, offering both laughs and thrills, but the movies also allowed women the opportunity to experience men's culture, a source of anxiety for those who fretted over the changing role of women in turn-of-the-century America. These anxieties are equally captured in the urban setting of the movie and the implication that city women are less modest and more provocative than their rural counterparts. In fact, many critics argue that the original viewers of *What Demoralized the Barber Shop* would assume that the legs belonged to prostitutes, an interpretation suggested by the way the women seem to be deliberately exposing their calves to passersby.

Slapstick comedy thus offered a screen experience where all sorts of social rules and norms could be violated, all under the guise of harmless fun. While we might sympathize with a movie that challenged what we might see as repressive rules about gender and sexuality, other early comedies regularly exploited racial stereotypes (such as the many so-called comedies featuring black characters eating watermelon and fried chicken). Growing concerns about the possibility of movie censorship, discussed in the "In focus" section above, slowed the production of slapstick comedies in the early nickelodeon period, but the genre came roaring back after 1910, especially with the rise of Keystone Studios described in the "Now playing" section.

Case study 2.1: The problem of slapstick

As we discussed, slapstick comedy thrives on rule breaking: rules of social behavior, of artistic decorum, sometimes even rules of the physical universe. Slapstick comedy has also presented a problem to those constructing narratives about American movie history. Always a popular form of screen experience, slapstick can seem as out of keeping with a desire for cultural and artistic respectability. Rather than focusing on developing coherent storylines with consistent character development, slapstick seems to delight in the sight gag and the pratfall, more interested in producing the emotional reaction of laughter than the moral education associated with "uplift" movies.

This contrast – between creating complex narratives and providing visual excitement – has become a recurring argument about what makes a movie a movie, and especially what makes a movie a "good" movie. So is slapstick just a guilty pleasure, or does it express qualities central to the cinematic experience? Explore your own reactions to slapstick by watching and writing about the classic Mack Sennett Keystone Kops movie, *Love, Speed, and Thrills,* from 1915. Featuring Sennett slapstick stars Mack Swain and Chester Conklin, *Love, Speed, and Thrills* ostensibly tells a crazy story about a hunting accident that leads to a kidnapping, but this storyline really provides an excuse for the kind of chase sequence – in this case, on foot, horseback, a motorcycle with sidecar, and even a boat – that was at the heart of many Keystone Kop movies.

As you watch the movie, pay special attention to what you find exciting, strange, or even puzzling about it. Why do you think movies like this and slapstick in general have proved such problems in our understanding of the importance and impact of American movies? In their disregard for the formal unity of narrative construction, their simultaneous defiance of and capitulation to the laws of gravity, and their tweaking of social decorum and authority, slapstick comedies can even be seen as a kind of experimental filmmaking. How does this way of thinking change how we might view slapstick? Develop your exploration by reading samples of how film critics at the time reacted to slapstick, how later historians and critics have dealt with the era, and what some of the most current histories of the movies say about early slapstick.

Fig 2.10
Energy, movement, and irreverence: the Keystone Kops in full pursuit from *Love, Speed, and Thrills.*

Gender genres: The New Woman

Anxieties over the upending of conventional gender roles found particular expression in the idea of the "New Woman," a genre of gender that offered an exciting progressive ideal for some, an anxiety-producing erosion of traditional values for others. Educated and independent-minded, affluent and assertive, the New Woman developed out of the nineteenth-century struggle for women's rights and the changing economic and social conditions that were challenging the Victorian idea that women were best suited only for the domestic occupations of wife, mother, and homemaker. Even though poor and working-class women had always been a part of the labor force since the beginning of the industrial revolution in the early nineteenth century, the dominant ideologies of the time still insisted on the ideal that "a women's place was in the home." The emergence of the gender genre of the New Woman revealed, however, the growing instability of these traditional views, and visual culture was quick to respond, in ways both supportive and exploitive.

The New Woman became a focal point for all sorts of conflicting and contradictory hopes, anxieties, and fears about the changing meaning of gender in the first decade of the twentieth century in the United States, and the development of the movies, with their powerful expression of new visual genres of gender identity, drew on these powerful social, cultural, and emotional currents. To take one example, D. W. Griffith's *The Girl and Her Trust* from 1907 plays with the gender genre of the New Woman to tell a story that can at the same time be seen as challenging and reinforcing traditional gender roles.

The "girl" of the title is actually a young woman named Grace (played by Dorothy Bernard) who is working as a telegraph operator at a remote railroad station. Grace is depicted as independent, assertive, and intelligent; as the title indicates, she not only has a job, but a job with some skill and responsibility: her "trust." The dramatic conflict in the story stems from this responsibility, as a pair of wandering men plans to steal the payroll she is entrusted with. When she realizes the danger she is in, Grace locks herself in her office and manages to send an urgent SOS telegraph alerting her fellow employee and would-be suitor Jack. When the robbers initially try to break in, she stalls them by cleverly lodging a bullet in the keyhole and then firing it by placing a pair of scissors against the bullet and hitting it with a hammer.

Fig 2.11
This stereo image from 1907, titled "The New Woman – Wash Day," comically expresses conservative anxieties that new roles for women would result in an upending of traditional gender roles, here indicated visually through the suggestion of cross-dressing. Such visual conventions would influence the early movies as well. Source: Library of Congress.

Fig 2.12
All in a day's work: Grace and Jack enjoy a sandwich after successfully foiling the robbery.

When the robbers try to flee with the locked payroll box on a railroad hand car, Grace chases after them and tries to fight them for it; as the title card says, "She Risks Her Life for Her Trust." For audiences at the time, Grace's heroism would elicit admiration, concern, and even some confusion, as a young woman actively takes on an aggressive and physically violent role that would normally be associated with a man.

A railway chase ensues, with Jack's locomotive finally overtaking the hand car, allowing him to rescue Grace. Rather than ending on an image of a grateful Grace falling into Jack's arms, however, *The Girl and Her Trust* reinforces Grace's New Woman character, as she and Jack ride back to headquarters seated on the front of the train, sharing the sandwich he had brought that day for lunch. Grace and Jack seem to remain equals at the end, co-workers as much as lovers. That Griffith assumed such a story would be attractive to audiences in 1912 demonstrates both the significance of changing ideas of gender and the power of the movies in creating concrete visual narratives embodying these ideas.

The names above and below the title

Florence Lawrence and the invention of the "movie star"

Stars – featured performers whose fame and name recognition made them powerful box office draws – were a standard feature of live theater and vaudeville at the turn of the twentieth century, their names prominently displayed on advertising posters. In the early years of the moving picture industry, however, movies almost never listed the names of actors. There were two main reasons for this practice. For one, many stage actors who found work in early movies weren't sure they wanted to be associated with this new medium, one that lacked the prestige and status of "serious" live theater. More important, though, was the desire of studio owners to build customer loyalty to the studio brand name rather than to individual performers. Having movie actors become as famous as some theater performers would give these actors economic leverage with the studios. Just as theatrical stars demanded higher salaries and control over the productions in which they appeared, the fear was that moving picture stars would do the same (and they would prove to be right).

The story of Florence Lawrence, often described as the first "movie star," illustrates how the development of movie star culture changed the early movie industry, provided a way for actors and especially women actors to gain artistic and commercial influence, and posed risks for both stars and studios. Born in 1886 in Canada to a theatrical family, Lawrence moved as a child to the United States.

Fig 2.13
Florence Lawrence, one of the first movie stars. Source: IMP/
The Kobal Collection.

Fig 2.14
Florence Lawrence (standing) in D. W. Griffith's *The Song
of the Shirt* from 1908.

When she was twenty years old, she moved with her mother to New York City to
pursue a career as an actor, finally becoming a full-time performer for D. W. Griffith
at Biograph Studios. Over the course of her career, Lawrence appeared in over 300
movies, and her years at Biograph saw the explosive growth in her popularity with
movie audiences, all clamoring to know the true identity of the "Biograph" girl. She
became one of the highest paid actors in the movie business, but Biograph refused to
put her name in film credits or on movie posters.

The growing moviegoing public would not be denied, however. Despite the
deliberate efforts of early studios to conceal the names and identities of the actors
appearing in their movies, early movie fans began to recognize the faces and styles of
their favorite performers. If the movie studios would not release the names of these
actors, the fans began to provide their own.

They referred to the "Biograph Girl," or the "Vitagraph Girl," linking performers
to the studios in whose movies they appeared. This early fan practice indicates that
from the beginning, moviegoers were not just passive witnesses to the development
of American movie culture, but active participants who helped shape that culture,
not just through buying tickets but also by forming fan clubs, writing letters to local
papers and movie trade publications, and even aspiring to provide stories and scripts
for future movies.

Carl Laemmle, the president of the Independent Moving Picture Company (or
"IMP"), decided that promoting the names of his actors would provide an edge
over those companies that belonged to the dominant MPPC. Even though it meant
that his most popular actors would gain their own power and influence, Laemmle
felt that the risk was worth the payoff that would result from fans eager to see their
favorite "stars," and he signed Lawrence as one of the first "movie stars."

For Lawrence and some other early actors, the new status of "movie star" not
only brought fame and money but power as well. In 1912, when she was only 26,

Fig 2.15
The development of the movie star also resulted in the appearance of fan magazines. Here is Florence Lawrence on the cover of *Photoplay* in 1914.

Lawrence and her husband Henry Solter successfully lobbied Laemmle to create the Victor Film Company, where the two had complete artistic control of their productions. Laemmle bought out the company the following year to become a part of his new Universal Studios, an outgrowth of IMP, but a pattern had been created. Mary Pickford, who went on to become one of the biggest stars of early Hollywood, had succeeded Lawrence as the Biograph girl. In 1919, along with fellow stars Douglas Fairbanks (who became her husband), Charlie Chaplin, and the director D. W. Griffith, Pickford founded United Artists studios.

For contemporary moviegoers, it is hard to imagine American movies without movie stars. The place and the influence of the movie star would change over the course of American movie history, but movie stardom and celebrity have remained a significant part of movie culture and the way we interact with movies. They have also contributed to the mythology and legends of Hollywood, and the story of Florence Lawrence can be read as an early version of the "tragic star" story, often told as a cautionary tale about the dangers of fame and fortune. At the height of her stardom in 1914, she was seriously injured in a stage fire, leading to her divorce from Solter, and ill health effectively kept her away from acting for seven years. When she tried to return to stardom in 1921, she had been away from the screen for too long and public attention had focused on other actors. Although she acted periodically in the following years, she suffered a series of personal and financial reversals and was diagnosed with a rare bone disease that left her in severe chronic pain. She finally took her own life in 1938 at age 52.

The "tragic star" story might lead us to read Lawrence's biography as a moral lesson about the price paid by ambitious women, a story that would be applied to later stars such as Marilyn Monroe and Judy Garland. But it's important to keep in mind that the "tragic star" story is itself a product of movie culture, a kind of legend that is as much its own genre as the western or the musical. In truth, there was nothing inevitable about the tragic end to Lawrence's life, and there were many other contributing factors besides her loss of stardom. We can equally understand hers as a story of how an intelligent, talented, and ambitious woman achieved one of the most successful careers in the early history of American movies.

D. W. Griffith

There is no more famous nor more polarizing figure in the history of early American cinema than D. W. Griffith. Praised by many as the director who did the most to transform the movies into a legitimate art form, he would also create arguably the most controversial and notorious movie in American film history, *The Birth of a*

Fig 2.16
D. W. Griffith. Source:
United Artists / The Kobal
Collection.

Nation (which we will explore further in the "Now playing" section of Chapter 3). While publicity during his career and even some later historians credited Griffith with inventing most of the key filmmaking techniques – crosscutting scenes between parallel lines of action; creating individual scenes out of a variety of close-up, medium, and long shots; the use of point-of-view shots and a moving camera – the reality is that while Griffith may not have been the first to use some or even all of these techniques, few of his contemporaries showed his ambition and skill in adopting these new techniques. Most important, he consistently used these innovations not just for novelty's sake, but also in the service of creating a richer and more emotionally exciting screen experience for early movie audiences. An artist who was also an expert at sensation and spectacle, a high-minded moralist who trafficked in stereotypes and racism, Griffith's early career exemplifies both the promise and many of the contradictions that defined the development of American movie culture.

These contradictions begin with his biography. A man who would achieve fame as a master of the art form most associated with the twentieth-century culture of technology and progress, David Wark Griffith was very much a product of nineteenth-century Victorian America. He was born in 1875 on a farm just outside Louisville, Kentucky, his father a former colonel in the Confederate Army during the Civil War. His family soon fell on hard times, moving from their farm to Louisville where their dire economic circumstances forced Griffith to leave school at a young age and enter the workforce. A sympathy for those victimized by economic circumstances beyond their control would become a theme in Griffith's films, especially *A Corner in Wheat* from 1909. At the same time, an equal sympathy for white southerners whose way of life had been destroyed by the disastrous war to preserve slavery – a sympathy that gained wide acceptance among many white Americans north and south in the late nineteenth century – would contribute to what we see as the most problematic and offensive aspects of Griffith's work.

These two aspects of Griffith – his skill at developing the storytelling capabilities

Fig 2.17
A scene from D. W. Griffith's *A Corner in Wheat*, based on a short story by Frank Norris, shows the impact of speculation in the wheat market on food prices for the poor.

of the movies along with an ability to play to the hopes, fears, anxieties, and prejudices of conservative, white, middle-class audiences – made him the perfect filmmaker to create screen experiences that would answer the movie industry's increasing desire for cultural respectability. This effort to raise the cultural profile of the movies in the nickelodeon screen age – known generally as the "uplift" movement – was fed by a combination of concern over the growing threat of movie censorship and the economic recognition that attracting more affluent audiences could mean greater profits.

These nickelodeon-era entrepreneurs, particularly members of the Jewish American community, keen to the anti-Semitism and anti-immigrant sentiments of turn-of-the-century American culture, began to appreciate that what brought audiences to the movies was not technology but the quality of the screen experiences waiting for them in the theaters. Newcomers to the movie business like Adolf Zukor, who would go on to found Paramount Pictures, were especially keen to raise the prestige of the movies so that they would be seen as the cultural equal of the Broadway stage.

This is the environment that Griffith entered as a filmmaker, and he was uniquely positioned to take advantage of the opportunity. While Griffith's Victorian sensibilities were not in tune with the urban working-class and immigrant audiences found at many nickelodeons, they almost exactly matched those of Patterson's readers, including a guilty desire for adventure and excitement, a desire that these audiences often projected onto the "lower orders" at the urban nickelodeons. Any filmmakers who could create screen experiences that would provide audiences with both sensational excitement and the feeling that this excitement was all in the name of moral and cultural "uplift" could not only possibly quell the threat of censorship but also greatly expand the market – and profits – of the movie business.

Two of Griffith's landmark films – *Enoch Arden* (1911) and *The Musketeers of Pig Alley* (1912) – exemplify these two strands. *Enoch Arden* is a melodrama based on a literary source: a poem by Alfred, Lord Tennyson that tells the story of a love triangle involving a young woman named Annie Lee and the two friends who love her. One suitor is a man of property, but Annie's heart belongs to the poor but honest fisherman Enoch Arden, whom she marries and starts a family with. Threatened with destitution, Enoch agrees to ship out on a merchant vessel to earn money for his family, only to be shipwrecked on a desert island. Even though her husband seems to have disappeared from the face of the Earth, Annie remains faithful to him for years until she finally gives up hope and marries the wealthier friend. Enoch is finally rescued and returns to his hometown, but when he discovers that Annie has happily remarried, he keeps his return a secret and dies alone.

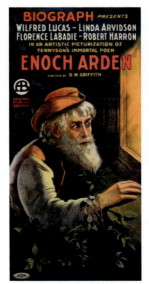

Fig 2.18
The poster for D. W.
Griffith's *Enoch Arden*
emphasizes its literary
source material.

Fig 2.19
Returning home after years stranded on a desert island,
Enoch spies on the happy home life of his remarried wife
Annie.

It doesn't take much thought to realize that a poem is a curious source text for
a movie. While a few intertitles in Griffith's film contain brief snatches of the poet's
actual words, the movie really just borrows the story from Tennyson (who himself
had been given the story by a friend). Instead, Griffith's movie hopes that the positive
cultural status of poetry – and poetry by Tennyson in particular – will attach itself to
his film by association. The poster for *Enoch Arden* makes this strategy clear when
it describes the movie as "an artistic picturization of Tennyson's immortal poem." In
1911, the idea that movies could be either "artistic" or "immortal" was still a novel
concept to many Americans. The idea of movie reviewing was in its infancy, but a
movie like *Enoch Arden*, with its picturesque location shooting, its innovative use of
crosscutting, and most of all Griffith's aspirations for his movie to be regarded in the
same context as the poetry of Tennyson, was part of a self-conscious movement to
frame movies as a positive and even influential force in American society.

If Griffith's *Enoch Arden* offered many moviegoers an opportunity to expand their
educational horizons through an experience of "serious literature," his *Musketeers of
Pig Alley* followed the tradition of the actuality by immersing the viewers in Griffith's
view of the teeming streets of New York's Lower East Side. One of the earliest
gangster movies, *Musketeers of Pig Alley* focuses on two groups of city dwellers. The
first, a poor but honest musician and his wife (played by the great silent film actor
Lillian Gish) struggle to make ends meet in their tiny apartment. The second are the
"musketeers," members of street gangs embodied in the character of the Snapper
Kid, a swaggering young man who both accosts the wife and robs the musician of
his meager earnings.

The Musketeers of Pig Alley presents itself as both a kind of sociological
travelogue/exposé of inner-city slum life, along the lines of the photojournalist Jacob
Riis' *How the Other Half Lives*, and an exciting crime story. For the more affluent
audiences, the movie could tap into the reformist concerns expressed in Patterson's
article, play off prejudices about life in poor immigrant communities, and offer the
illicit excitement of the crime movie. For rural audiences, *The Musketeers of Pig
Alley* could both confirm fears about the "decadent" city and appeal to curiosities

Fig 2.20
An example of Griffith's innovative use of the close-up and focus to create a dynamic sense of depth in a flat screen image. The street criminal Snapper Kid (Elmer Booth) slowly walks toward the camera prior to the big shoot out in *The Musketeers of Pig Alley*.

Fig 2.21
Lois Weber. Source: The Kobal Collection.

about just how "bad" those cities were. And for urban moviegoers, Griffith's movie validated their own lives and experiences while raising questions about how the movies could define those experiences – either for good or ill – to a larger national audience.

Both of these early Griffith films express the deep contradictions that defined Griffith's career and the emerging cultural status of the movies in America. In films like *The Musketeers of Pig Alley* and *A Corner in Wheat* (1909), he expressed a progressive interest in the plight of urban and rural workers in what he saw as an exploitive economic situation. At the same time, his Victorian sensibilities and prejudices would both motivate his desire for movies to achieve a kind of middle-class artistic respectability while also betraying a condescending and, as we will see in the next chapter in regards to *Birth of a Nation*, racist understanding of emerging multicultural America.

Lois Weber: Lost pioneer of early cinema

> When the history of the dramatic early development of motion pictures is written, Lois Weber will occupy a unique position. Associated with the work from its infancy, she set a high pace in its growth, for not only is she a producer of some of the most interesting and notable productions we have had, but she writes her own stories and continuity, selects her cast, directs the pictures, plans to the minutest detail all the scenic effects, and, finally, cuts and assembles the film. Few men have assumed such a responsibility.[5]

When Aline Carter wrote these words in the fan magazine *Motion Picture* in 1921, Lois Weber had already written and directed well over 100 movies in ten years. When her ambitious and controversial movie *Hypocrites* became a hit in 1915,

Uplift movement An
effort by movie studios
in the early 1910s to
appeal to more affluent
audiences and avoid
censorship pressures by
trying to raise the cultural
status and respectability
of the movies, often
by creating screen
experiences based on
prestigious literary or
theatrical works, religious
and historical stories,
or other supposedly
"uplifting" sources.

Weber was firmly established as one of the most famous filmmakers in America. Weber's movies were influential examples of the same **uplift movement** that interested D. W. Griffith, and her position as a woman director who understood both the older world of Victorian morality and the emerging modern world of the New Woman allowed her to create movies in the second decade of the twentieth century that spoke to the values, concerns, and anxieties of a broad cross-section of moviegoers, both working-class audiences and members of the middle class who were suspicious of the movies. She was also an innovative stylist who used split screen, close-ups, double-exposures, crosscutting between plot lines, and other techniques praised in the work of her contemporary Griffith. So why is this important filmmaker still waiting to receive the recognition she deserves?

Case study 2.2: Telling stories with pictures: Lois Weber's *Suspense*

As the title to this chapter suggests, one of the most important questions cinema historians continue to explore and debate in this screen age centers on the idea of "becoming the movies." How did the dizzying variety of screen experiences and experiments in the early years of commercial cinema develop into a set of dominant ideas about what makes a movie a "movie"? How were other kinds of screen experiences absorbed into these dominant practices, and what alternative forms of screen experiences have persisted?

As we have also seen, one crucial version of this larger question has to do with how early moviemakers and movie watchers developed strategies and techniques for telling stories with images, some borrowed from the theater and earlier forms of visual storytelling, some coming from the possibilities and potentials of the new moving picture technology. Explore some of these different experiments and innovations by closely examining your screen experience of Lois Weber's aptly titled *Suspense* (1913).

The theme and plot of *Suspense* were common for the nickelodeon era: a young wife (played by Weber herself) left home alone with her baby when her husband goes to work is menaced by a passing homeless man. A phone call of distress to the husband precipitates a desperate chase home, where he saves his wife and baby at the last minute. But in telling this familiar story, Weber employs a fascinating array of formal techniques and strategies, including split-screen, the use of mirrors, off-balance point-of-view shots, and rapid editing to evoke the emotion expressed in the title of the movie. As you watch and rewatch this ten-minute movie, list and describe what you see as the most unusual or creative storytelling techniques you see Weber using. Why do you find them so effective? Which seem most and least "modern" and why? Expand your case study by reading how different film scholars, critics, and historians have described this early action movie. What do they see as most significant and innovative, and how do their reactions and analyses compare with your own?

Fig 2.22
Weber's imaginative use
of a three-way split-screen
shot in *Suspense* (Weber
herself is in the upper
right).

The answer to this question includes many causes, such as the fact that only about twenty or so of her movies have survived to the present day, but the main reason has to do with how the history of women behind the camera in early American film, from writers to producers to directors, became obscured as the Hollywood movie industry became more conservative in terms of gender roles during the 1920s. Exploring and understanding the screen experiences of the nickelodeon era, an era when the movies became a true mass medium and also began to gain a wider cultural acceptance, means understanding the crucial role that women filmmakers like Lois Weber played in the development of American cinema.

Like Griffith, Weber was born into a Victorian, middle-class white American family in the last quarter of the nineteenth century. In her late teens and early twenties, Weber alternated between a career as a concert pianist and evangelical work in rescue missions before moving to New York in pursuit of a career as an actor. She eventually entered the movie business in 1908, first as a writer and then as a producer and director. Weber became the first American woman to direct a feature-length movie – an adaptation of Shakespeare's *The Merchant of Venice* – and she acquired a reputation as a serious director of uplift movies focused on controversial social issues of particular interest to women, including the emerging issue of birth control in movies like *Where Are My Children?* and *The Hand That Rocks the Cradle*.

Weber created screen experiences combining visual interest and excitement, suspenseful narratives, and a missionary commitment to educate and "improve" audiences, experiences that allowed people who might otherwise feel guilty about indulging in the movies to feel they were taking part in something cultivated and proper. There is no better example of Weber's artistic skill, sense of moral purpose, and willingness to challenge conventional propriety than her 1915 hit *Hypocrites*.

Less a single narrative than a series of vignettes that works as a kind of cinematic essay, *Hypocrites* features a double structure, one part focused on the futile efforts of a contemporary Protestant minister to convince his parishioners that they were leading lives of moral hypocrisy, the other on a kind of allegory involving a medieval monk (played by the same actor, Courtenay Foote, as the minister) who pursues the image of Truth, eventually creating a statue to her that brings the wrath of the hypocritical community down upon him. Along the way, we see examples of contemporary forms of moral failure, from adultery to greed.

Hypocrites features as much technical and formal experimentation and innovation as any movie by Griffith. It was the allegorical depiction of Truth, however, that provoked the greatest controversy over *Hypocrites*, because Truth was portrayed as a naked young woman (the actor Margaret Edwards). Many twenty-first century viewers might be surprised by the presence of nudity in early movies, but the truth

Fig 2.23
Margaret Edwards as naked Truth and Courtenay Foote as the minister/Gabriel the monk in *Hypocrites*.

is nudity had complicated meanings in the visual culture of early-twentieth-century America. On the one hand, it represented the violation of cultural norms and an appeal to sex and voyeurism; on the other, nudity was associated with the classical tradition of Greek and Roman sculpture as well as the history of European fine art. For some Americans, an appreciation for "artistic" representations of nudity was a mark of cultural sophistication and a rejection of the more puritanical strains in American culture.

In using a naked woman to portray the exalted ideal of Truth, Weber's movie appealed to this more culturally valued position, as signified by the classical statue of Truth that the monk creates. In most parts of the country, the movie garnered positive reviews, and local community leaders and members of the clergy were invited to special screenings meant to insure their endorsement. Still, the censorship board in the state of Ohio felt very differently, and the movie was banned there. The mayor of Boston only allowed the film to be shown if special prints of the movie were made that "clothed" Truth. One of Weber's most popular films, it paved the way for a career that made her one of the most important filmmakers in the early screen ages of American movies.

Weber's fame peaked in 1921 with the release of *The Blot*, considered by many to be her greatest movie, a protest against the meager salaries of college faculty members but also an examination of the effects of class differences on family life. Hollywood and America were changing around her, however. The emergence of the studio system made life harder and harder for independent movie companies like Weber's. She chafed under the increasing micromanagement of the moviemaking process within the studio system, with every detail of movie production subject to the approval of studio management. She made a few more movies, but her career in the movie business dwindled over the rest of the 1920s and was essentially over by 1934. She died from a chronic ulcer condition in 1939.

The decline of Weber's career speaks to several developments that accompanied the emergence of the American movie industry as a dominant mass medium in the mid-1910s, including the increasingly corporate and hierarchical organization of moviemaking that began to define film production in the late 1910s and the 1920s. As we enter the great screen age of American silent cinema in the next chapter, we will see how the power and influence of "Hollywood" would grow both nationally and around the world. At the same time, for visionary pioneers like Weber in general and women filmmakers in particular, the new screen age also represented a loss of opportunity and access. This tension – between Hollywood as a big business and the movies as cultural expression – would become a central source of debate and criticism that continues into our own screen age.

Notes

1   Patterson, Joseph Medill, "The Nickelodeons," *Saturday Evening Post*,
    November 23, 1907, pp. 10–11.
2   "Even Channing Pollock Writes About 'the Movies'," *The Green Book
    Magazine*, September, 1914, p. 495.
3   Quoted in Grieveson, Lee, *Policing Cinema: Movies and Censorship in Early-
    Twentieth-Century America*. Berkeley: University of California Press, 2004, p.
    96.
4   *Mutual Film Corporation v. Industrial Commission of Ohio*, 236 U.S. 230,
    Supreme Court of the United States, 1915.
5   Carter, Aline, "The Muse of the Reel," *Motion Picture Magazine,* 21, number
    2 (March 1921): 62. Quoted in Anthony Slide, *Lois Weber: The Director Who
    Lost Her Way in History*, Westport, CT: Greenwood Press, 1996, p. 6.

Explore further

Abel, Richard, *Americanizing the Movies and "Movie-Mad" Audiences, 1910–1914*.
    Berkeley: University of California Press, 2006.
Bowser, Eileen, *The Transformation of Cinema: 1907–1915*. Berkeley: University of
    California Press, 1994.
Brownlow, Kevin, *Behind the Mask of Innocence: Sex, Violence, Crime: Films of
    Social Conscience in the Silent Era*. Berkeley: University of California Press, 1992.
Fuller, Kathryn H., *At the Picture Show: Small-Town Audiences and the Creation of
    Movie Fan Culture*. Charlottesville: University Press of Virginia, 2001.
Gabler, Neal, *An Empire of Their Own: How the Jews Invented Hollywood*. New
    York: Crown Publishers, 1988.
Grieveson, Lee, *Policing Cinema: Movies and Censorship in Early-Twentieth-Century
    America*. Berkeley: University of California Press, 2004.
Hallett, Hilary A., *Go West, Young Women!: The Rise of Early Hollywood*.
    Berkeley: University of California Press, 2013.
Hansen, Miriam, *Babel And Babylon: Spectatorship in American Silent Film*.
    Cambridge, MA/London: Harvard University Press, 1991.
Keil, Charlie, *Early American Cinema in Transition: Story, Style, and Filmmaking,
    1907–1913*. Madison: University of Wisconsin Press, 2001.
Moore, Paul S., *Now Playing: Early Moviegoing and the Regulation of Fun*. Albany:
    State University of New York Press, 2008.
Slide, Anthony, *Early Women Directors*. New York: Da Capo Press, 1984.
—— *Lois Weber: The Director Who Lost Her Way in History*, Westport, CT:
    Greenwood Press, 1996.
Smith, Andrew Brodie, *Shooting Cowboys and Indians: Silent Western Films,
    American Culture, and the Birth of Hollywood*. Boulder: University Press of
    Colorado, 2003.
Uricchio, William and Roberta E. Pearson, *Reframing Culture: The Case of the
    Vitagraph Quality Films*. Princeton, NJ: Princeton University Press, 1993.

CHAPTER 3

Movie palaces, corner theaters, and tent shows: The silent era and the first Hollywood, 1915–1928

Now playing

The premiere of *The Clansman*, later *The Birth of a Nation*, at Clune's Auditorium, Los Angeles, February 8, 1915

Few films in American movie history were as eagerly anticipated as was D. W. Griffith's *The Clansman* in early 1915. Reported to be the most expensive and ambitious feature film ever, *The Clansman* was also based on a controversial source: a novel of the same name by the minister and writer Thomas Dixon, Jr., part of a trilogy of novels defending the idea of white supremacy in general and the heroism of the notorious Ku Klux Klan in particular. The recently formed civil rights organization the National Association for the Advancement of Colored People (NAACP) organized protests against Griffith's new movie, and prominent social reformers such as Jane Addams condemned the movie's racist depictions of black Americans. It was in this atmosphere that over 2,000 southern Californians filed into Clune's Auditorium, a massive theater turned movie palace (and a future home of the Los Angeles Philharmonic Orchestra) on a Monday evening in February.

That audience was in for an extreme screen experience. A full orchestra performed a score written specifically for the almost three-hour film. The movie told a story about the Civil War and the rise of the Ku Klux Klan by focusing on the destinies of two white families, the southern Camerons and the northern Stonemans. Along the way, Griffith's film depicted panoramic battle scenes, images of massive devastation, even the assassination of Abraham Lincoln. At the heart of the movie was a melodramatic romance that dealt with issues of race and sexuality and reinforced the idea popularized by certain historians and politicians (and, in the case of college professor turned president Woodrow Wilson, a historian politician) that the division between the north and south, between the Union and the Confederacy, could be healed by white citizens north and south uniting against the "threat" of African Americans.

Each family suffers terrible losses, as the abolitionist Stoneman's daughter Elsie (played by Lillian Gish) falls in love with the eldest Cameron son, Ben (Henry B. Walthall). It is part two that contains some of the most controversial scenes in the movie, when Ben Cameron forms the Ku Klux Klan as a way of defending the

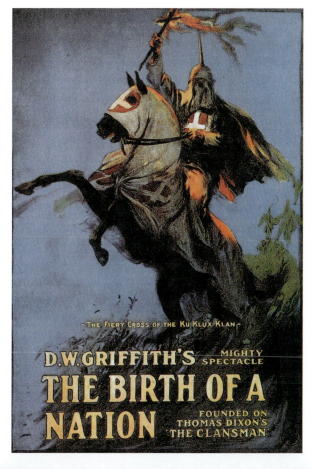

Fig 3.2
An iconic image from *The
Clansman/The Birth of a
Nation*: the southerner
Ben Cameron (Henry B.
Walthall) leads a doomed
charge against Union
lines, concluding with
this dramatic shot of his
thrusting the Confederate
flag into the cannon's
mouth.

"white race" against the supposed tyranny and – most crucially – sexual danger posed by the free black population. We see Ben's younger sister Flora flee from the threat of rape at the hands of a black soldier – played, as were many of the "black" characters in the movie, by a white actor (Walter Long) in blackface make-up – finally leaping to her death from a cliff to avoid what the movie clearly intimates is a fate worse than death.

Later, at the movie's climax, the Camerons find themselves trapped inside a cabin besieged by "black" soldiers. Dr. Cameron (Spottiswoode Aiken) is about to bash in his daughter's head with a pistol to "save" her when the Klan rides in triumphantly to the rescue, saving the Camerons and then, the next day, preventing black voters from going to the polls. The movie ends with dual marriages between the Stoneman and Cameron children and the image of Christ, with an intertitle posing the rhetorical question, "Dare we dream of a golden day when the bestial War shall rule no more? But instead – the gentle Prince in the Hall of Brotherly Love in the City of Peace."

The white audience at Clune's auditorium was transfixed by what they saw. Griffith used an astonishing array of cinematic techniques – crosscutting during ride-to-the-rescue scenes; mixing epic battlefield images with close-ups of the characters involved; using hundreds of extras in monumental set pieces – to create a powerful emotional experience and appeal to his audience's deeply held anxieties, fears, and prejudices about race, sexuality, and contemporary American life. The spectators roared with approval as Klan members, dressed in elaborate regalia, save the white south – and by implication white America – from the supposed dangers posed by an integrated multiracial and multiethnic society. At the end of the movie, the audience leapt to its feet and demanded the appearance of Griffith, who took the stage and accepted the crowd's adulation.

Fig 3.3
The perceived threat to racial purity is at the heart of *The Clansman/The Birth of a Nation*. Here the patriarch Dr. Cameron (Spottiswoode Aiken) prepares to beat his daughter to death to "save" her from the black(face) soldiers outside.

The Clansman played for months and months at Clune's, and its popularity swept the nation. Eventually renamed *The Birth of a Nation*, the movie became the first real blockbuster hit in American movie history, both at the box office and in the opinion of most (white) movie critics, who hailed Griffith's film as a triumph of movie art; indeed, as the first real "work of art" created by an American moviemaker. Controversial from before its premiere to the present day, *The Birth of a Nation* has always posed problems for film historians and critics. Some have tried to separate the technical and artistic achievement of Griffith from the racist "content" of the movie (German filmmaker Leni Reifenstahl's equally artistically ambitious tribute to Adolf Hitler, *The Triumph of the Will* from 1935, provides a similar case study).

In fact, *The Birth of a Nation* remains so controversial that contemporary teachers of American movie history still debate whether or not to show the movie in a course like the one you are currently taking. It's a question all of us who teach film must confront. Whatever choice an individual instructor ultimately makes, the decision-making process always involves thinking about the *experience* of watching *The Birth of a Nation*, of who our students are, where we are teaching, of what reactions we might expect or what reactions might take us by surprise. As every year passes, the decision must be revisited again and again, as each new generation of movie fans and students brings with them new sets of shared experiences, new historical perspectives, new attitudes and values. And one thing is for sure: whether an instructor does or does not choose to show *The Birth of a Nation*, there will be students who disagree with that decision, with reasons just as valid as those used by their teachers.

Case study 3.1: To screen or not to screen – the problem of *The Birth of a Nation*

As we have noted, D. W. Griffith's *The Birth of a Nation* presents a special problem for teachers of American film history. There's no denying the cultural impact of the movie when it premiered in 1915, setting box office records and influencing a generation of filmmakers around the world. This cultural impact, though, is bound up with the movie's endorsement of white supremacy and its stereotyped representation of African Americans. As a student of the screen ages of American cinema, how would you approach the question of whether and/or how to teach *The Birth of a Nation*?

To begin your exploration, consider the issues of context and purpose. Where would you be teaching (or not teaching) *The Birth of a Nation*? Who would be the students? What are the learning goals for the class, as understood both by the teacher and the members of the class? What are the previous screen experiences that students and teachers bring with them to the class? What different understandings and perspectives on American history, especially the history of race, slavery, abolition, and the struggle for civil rights, do people have? What ideas or impressions do students have about the United States in 1915? About the silent era in cinema? What are the assumptions about how movies affect their viewers and the larger culture?

All of these questions speak to the diversity of screen experiences represented by any one movie, especially a movie as fraught and complicated as *The Birth of a Nation*. After writing some beginning thoughts, ideas, and opinions, expand your consideration by reading further in how the movie has been discussed and argued about over the years, beginning with contemporary reviews from a range of critics at the time the movie premiered and continuing with samples of scholarly and pedagogical opinions over the years since. Remember that your goal in this case study is to make a recommendation about how to deal with *The Birth of a Nation* (should we show it or not?), but that there is no such thing as a definitive answer. In focusing on the problem of *The Birth of a Nation*, however, we can gain insight into other cinema-related controversies over the years as well as the rich complexity of any screen experience.

A typical silent bill at a small-town movie theater, 1920

Just how would you describe a "typical" movie experience in the early twenty-first century? Enjoying a 3D movie from a plush stadium-style seat in a twenty-theater multiplex? Watching Netflix on your iPad while relaxing on your bed? Picking out your favorite scenes from a Blu-ray disc to watch multiple times? We sometimes think this diversity of viewing experiences is unique to the digital age, but the truth is that movie watching was just as diverse in the silent era as it is now.

It might surprise some, for instance, that in the supposedly "silent era" many theaters highlighted the musical experience of going to the movies. Moviegoers expected music before and during the films, performed by singers, piano players, small combos, all the way up to full orchestras in the biggest movie palaces. Some prestige productions such as *The Birth of a Nation* came with musical scores and instructions created specifically for the movie; for most other screenings, musicians and band leaders would rely on a stock assortment of musical themes and light classical music to create the right emotional tone for different scenes, from exciting chases to sentimental romantic moments. For many local theaters, having a lavish Wurlitzer organ was a particular point of pride (they would even list how much they paid for the instruments in their advertising).

Sound effects produced in-house likewise grew in prevalence and importance, from simple effects such as firing off blanks and slamming doors to the recreation of thunder and howling wind. And of course the audience continued to play a role in the sonic experience of the movies. Rules and customs regarding proper behavior in the movie theater continued to evolve, and there was great variation across the country in a just how vocally interactive an audience could be while the movie screened. Commentators at the time would complain, for example, about viewers who insisted on reading all the intertitles out loud. Still, reviews of the period regularly offered enthusiastic expressions of approval from movie audiences as proof of the success of a film, including cheers, applause, and shouts of encouragement.

One surprising aspect of screen experiences in the silent era from a contemporary perspective is the lack of standardization from one performance to the next. Although motorized movie cameras had been invented in the early 1910s, many movies were still made with hand-cranked cameras and shown on hand-cranked projectors. With the coming of sound at the end of the 1920s, it became essential that movies be filmed and projected at exactly the same speed, but in the silent era there was no such uniformity. Cameramen might aim for a consistent speed of 16 feet per second, but actual filming speeds varied considerably.

If the filming of movies lacked uniformity, even greater liberties were taken in exhibition. Exhibitors thought nothing of cutting whole scenes out of movies,

Fig 3.4
The Strand Theatre in
Salisbury, North Carolina
continued to feature both
live performers and movies
into the 1920s. Note the
reference to "Black Face
Comedians" as a regular
part of American popular
culture in the silent era.

either to mollify local censors, meet the time demands of their exhibition schedule, or simply to "improve" the movie. Even more disconcerting, projectionists would change the speeds at which movies were shown, again sometimes to meet time demands (for example, making a ninety-minute movie fit an eighty-minute slot), sometimes to try to heighten the experience of the movie by making a comic sequence play even faster.

As a result, what we understand as a single "movie" from the silent era varies considerably. Today, movies will be issued in "director's cut" or "unrated" versions, containing extra scenes or (as in the famous case of Ridley Scott's *Blade Runner*) completely different endings and plot lines. These multiple versions raise questions about which is the "real" movie experience. In the silent era, such ambiguity was par for the course. Directors, producers, exhibitors, and audiences of the time understood the movies as experiences that varied in meaning and intensity from performance to performance, just as with different live performances of the "same" play. The tension between the ghostly permanence of the cinematic image and the radical variability of any single screen experience defines the fascination that the history of American movies continues to hold for us.

Case study 3.2: "Silent" movies? The role of sound in the silent era

As we have seen, screen experiences in the supposedly "silent" screen age were anything but silent, as virtually all movie exhibitions included sound effects and music of some kind, all produced in-house at the local movie theater. The impact of sound on screen experiences presents a tantalizing mystery for students and scholars of these early screen ages in American cinema. What was it really like to watch a movie in the silent era, when a single movie might be accompanied by a single piano player in one venue, an organist in another, a small band in a third?

Explore how sound affects our experience of silent cinema by comparing and contrasting how watching the "same" movie with different soundtracks changes that experience. As surviving prints of silent cinema have been transferred at first to videotape and more recently to DVD, Blu-ray, and other forms of digital storage, archivists and distributors have used different approaches to deal with the issue of sound. For those movies that had actual musical scores written for them, those scores can be included with the film. For other movies, companies and organizations working in silent film restoration have hired contemporary composers and musicians to create all new scores for silent cinema. Sometimes these scores try to evoke the musical styles of the late 1910s and 1920s; in other cases, musicians use twenty-first-century styles to complement the emotional tenor of the movie. When the Kino Lorber company issued their DVD/Blu-ray of Buster Keaton's classic *The General* in 2008, for example, the discs included the option of three different modern scores for the movie. Many other silent movies can be found on disc or online at YouTube and other streaming sites, featuring differing soundtracks.

Choose a silent film from this screen age that now exists with multiple scores. As you watch and compare these different versions of the "same" movie, pay close attention to some of the following questions: What kind of mood or tone does each musical score try to create? To what extent does the music seem to remind you that the movie is from an earlier historical period? Does the movie exist with a really modern soundtrack? How do these different musical scores affect your screen experience of the movie? Focus in particular on an important key scene and write a detailed analysis of how the music and visuals interact to create different impressions on the viewer. To provide greater context for your exploration, try to locate reviews from when the movie first appeared that include references to the music. What can we infer about how viewers at the time reacted to the music accompanying the movie? What seemed to be their expectations for the relation of music to visuals? How has your lifetime of experience watching movies with soundtracks affected your reaction to the differing soundtracks accompanying these "silent" movies?

A screening of *The Jazz Singer* at the Garrick Theatre, downtown Chicago, December 1927

The patrons making their way to the impressive Garrick Theatre in Chicago's downtown loop had reason to believe they were in for a special occasion. The movie playing this night – Warner Brothers' *The Jazz Singer*, featuring the vaudeville and radio star Al Jolson – had already been the subject of a major publicity push by the studio and had, if newspaper reports were to be believed, already become a sensation after its Broadway premiere in New York two months earlier.

Of course, even people with only a passing familiarity with the history of
American cinema know why *The Jazz Singer* became one of the most famous movies
of all time: it is credited as the movie that launched the sound era in American film.
Jolson's signature catchphrase – "You ain't seen nothing yet" – one of the few lines
of actual dialogue in the movie, has become legendary. It is true that after the success
of *The Jazz Singer*, the move towards sound in Hollywood movies was rapid (though
not instantaneous) and decisive. By 1930, sound movies became the norm, and the
phrase "silent movie" was invented to refer to the era that was coming to an end.

Sound movies had been a goal from the beginning of movies in America. In
the 1920s, a number of competing systems – from the sound-on-film "Phonofilm"
system to the Warner Brothers's sound-on-disk "Vitaphone" system – were featured
in various experiments and exhibitions. Just one year earlier, Warner Brothers had
premiered *Don Juan*, a three-hour epic starring the enormously popular Broadway
and movie star John Barrymore that boasted a fully recorded symphonic soundtrack
along with various sound effects.

If many members of the audience in the Garrick Theatre waiting for *The Jazz
Singer* had likely already experienced one of these sound experiments, why has
The Jazz Singer become so associated with the beginning of sound movies? From
a business perspective, the success of *The Jazz Singer* did help demonstrate the
economic viability of sound movies. Another answer stems from those few words
spoken by Jolson as well as the story *The Jazz Singer* tells. Jolson's colloquial "You
ain't seen nothing yet," delivered in the accent and cadence of the Russian Jewish
immigrant communities in which he was raised, introduced the variety of American
speech into the movies, a variety connected to the ethnic, racial, and cultural
diversity of the country, a diversity that has been central to the screen experience of
American movies.

In spite of the focus on *The Jazz Singer* as one of the first sound movies, what
probably makes the biggest impression on the contemporary viewer of *The Jazz
Singer* is the fact that in the movie Jolson regularly performs in blackface, a legacy
of the minstrel tradition in which "white" performers put on black make-up in
imitation of African American singers. No less shocking to modern eyes than D. W.
Griffith's endorsement of the Ku Klux Klan, the popularity of blackface performance
in nineteenth- and early-twentieth-century American popular culture expresses both
the rigid lines of discrimination and oppression that defined American society and
the profound cultural influence and impact of African American culture.

Fig 3.5
One of the most famous
and troubling images from
The Jazz Singer: Al Jolson
in blackface performing
"Mammy" at the
conclusion of the movie.

As we have seen, the history of movies in America is inextricably linked to the changing demographics of American society in the twentieth century, and screen experiences revolving around narratives of race, ethnicity, sexuality, and gender played a central role in the development of the American political and cultural imagination. *The Jazz Singer* tells a story of immigration and assimilation, the desire to join what was often a less than welcoming American society while also maintaining a sense of cultural pride and identity. Jolson's character of Jacob Rabinowitz is the son of an immigrant Jewish cantor who changes his name to "Jack Robin" to pursue a career as a vaudeville performer, much to the distress of his traditionally-minded parents.

The use of blackface served as a further disguise for both Jack Robin and Al Jolson, each doubly hidden behind their new names and black makeup. Blackface became a means of gaining acceptance in an American society marked by open anti-Semitism. At the same time, embracing the racist tradition of blackface provided another way of belonging to American culture by endorsing the racial divisions that defined that society; ironically, wearing blackface became a way of identifying as a "white" American. Jolson's musical performances are at the same time cruel parodies of black musical styles and expressions of Jolson's (and his character's) genuine love of African American music.

The connection between the advent of sound and a narrative centered around ideas of identity, race, and ethnicity emphasizes the powerful ways that the movies reflect and influence how we see and, after *The Jazz Singer*, hear America on screen. Jolson's blackface performing style was just as much about the auditory as the visual, as he built his career on his vocal imitations, invocations, and exaggerations of a variety of American speech types and styles, both those marked as black and white, urban and rural, bourgeois and working class. At the end of the silent era, the sound of these American voices would further transform the screen experiences of American cinema.

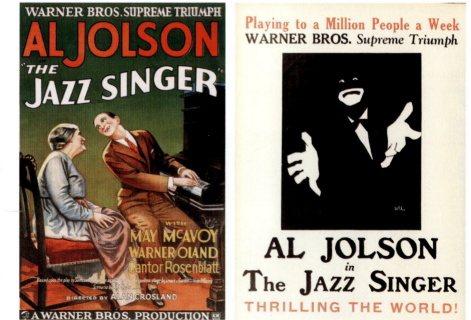

Fig 3.6
Two movie ads from 1927, two different views of *The Jazz Singer*. The poster on the left features Jolson as Jacob Rabinowitz playing to his mother, played by Eugenie Besserer, and emphasizes more traditional ideas of family loyalty. The ad on the right reflects the stylized art deco style of the 1920s in emphasizing both the use of blackface and the idea of the movie as modern and up-to-date. Sources: The Kobal Collection and *Motion Picture News*, 1928.

Screen ages

In the silent era: Liberation and repression

In the screen age from *The Birth of a Nation to The Jazz Singer*, the word "Hollywood" came to stand for not just for the mainstream American movie industry but also for a whole complex and contradictory collection of ideas, feelings, and fantasies. Hollywood worked as both a noun and an adjective, a place where movies were made as well as a kind of attitude, a display of glamor, beauty, and excess that inspired admiration and repulsion. For many Americans, and for many people around the world, the single word "Hollywood" evoked what they saw as the best and the worst aspects of American society.

That the single word "Hollywood" could provoke such contradictory concerns and reactions speaks to the volatility and upheaval of American society during the era when movies became the dominant form of mass media. Just as *The Birth of a Nation* premiered, Europe became engulfed in World War I, a global catastrophe killing over 16 million people. The war dramatically slowed the major European movie industries; the French film industry, in particular, forever lost its role as a significant player in the American film industry. The disruption caused by the war provided a competitive advantage for American movies on the international market.

With its entry into the war in 1917, the United States also felt the trauma of modern mass warfare as well over 100,000 American soldiers lost their lives. The war proved as divisive domestically as had the earlier Spanish American war. Supporters saw the war as further evidence of the growing economic and military importance of the United States, part of its evolution into a world power, a power reflected in the equally growing international cultural influence of Hollywood movies. Opponents condemned the war on many fronts, describing it as a conflict among the wealthy and powerful that had nothing to do with the lives of the ordinary citizens who would do most of the fighting.

At the same time, the US labor movement was organizing for the rights of working people against the entrenched and powerful business interests, a situation that made many government officials nervous about the whole subject matter of revolution. The confluence of World War I and the Russian Revolution in 1917 resulted in a concerted effort by the US government to investigate and prosecute suspected radicals and subversives, culminating in the notorious Palmer Raids (named after Attorney General A. Mitchell Palmer) of 1919 and 1920, an effort that would be repeated after World War II in the anti-Communist crusades led by Senator Joseph McCarthy and the House Un-American Activities Committee.

For the Hollywood film industry, already under suspicion as a negative influence on American society, these political conflicts made the treatment of such issues both attractive and fraught with difficulty, as in D. W. Griffith's *Orphans of the Storm* from 1921, an epic two-and-a-half hour melodrama about the French Revolution. A screen experience in the tradition of *The Birth of a Nation*, *Orphans of the Storm* again promised to bring history to vivid life as a cast of hundreds enacted the storming of the Bastille and the Reign of Terror. Emotionally, the movie hinged on the story of twin sisters Henriette and Louise, played by the acting sisters Lillian and Dorothy Gish, who travel to Paris on the eve of revolution hoping to find a cure for Louise's blindness. The sisters are soon separated, and their lives become intertwined with the progress of the revolution in a plot involving Louise's true identity as the lost child of a noble woman, an ill-starred romance between Henriette and a young aristocrat, and the threat of execution by guillotine.

Fig 3.7
The acting sisters Lillian
(left) and Dorothy Gish
play stepsisters separated
by revolution in D. W.
Griffith's *Orphans of the
Storm*.

In telling a story set against the backdrop of revolution, Griffith walked a
tightrope when it came to explaining the politics of his movie. On the one hand,
the intertitle cards clearly express sympathy for the plight of the oppressed people
and the justice of overthrowing a corrupt aristocracy. On the other hand, Griffith is
also worried about appearing to express sympathy for the Russian Revolution. An
introductory intertitle makes explicit what he hoped would be the "lesson" of the
movie:

> The lesson – the French Revolution RIGHTLY overthrew a BAD government.
> But we in America should be careful lest we with a GOOD government
> mistake fanatics for leaders and exchange our decent law and order for
> Anarchy and Bolshevism.

Of course, whether this is the lesson individual viewers took away from the movie is
another question.

These two impulses – the attraction of revolutionary new freedoms associated
with modernity and the fear of the changes represented by these new freedoms –
marked both American culture and the American film industry in the silent era. On
the one hand, many of us are familiar with the idea of the "Roaring Twenties," a
time when all sorts of challenges were being mounted to what were seen as restrictive
social and moral codes, challenges reflected in and popularized by the growing
culture of mass media represented by movies and radio. Hollywood contributed to
the rise of celebrity culture, a part of modern society that continues to this day, as
movie stars such as Mary Pickford, Douglas Fairbanks, Rudolph Valentino, and
countless others became "idols." Fans obsessively followed the personal lives of
the stars in fan magazines, gossip columns, and in the newsreels, just as they began
following the lives of radio celebrities and sports stars.

Nationally, women finally acquired the right to vote with the passage of the
Nineteenth Amendment in 1920, and within the movie industry women likewise
continued to command an influence and importance they were still restricted from
enjoying in other professions, although by the end of the silent era this influence,
especially in terms of the producing, writing, and directing of movies, began to
shrink as Hollywood developed ever more conservative management styles in synch
with the larger corporate world. Lois Weber continued to be an important American
filmmaker through the late 1910s and early 1920s, and screenwriters such as Frances
Marion and June Mathis were major figures in the business, commanding large
salaries and shaping the film careers of stars such as Mary Pickford and Rudolph
Valentino.

Fig 3.8
Frances Marion was one of the most important and influential screenwriters of the silent era. Source: The Kobal Collection.

The 1920s was also the age of **Prohibition** following the passage of the Eighteenth Amendment in 1919 that forbid the manufacture and sale of alcoholic beverages in the United States. No other historical development so captures the tension between modernity and tradition, between competing visions of what America is and should be than the political and social conflicts that defined the Prohibition era. Those in favor of Prohibition included evangelical Protestant organizations, social reformers, and even the Ku Klux Klan. They saw alcohol use and abuse as a moral issue, a social health crisis, and a symbol of immigration associated with the influx of Catholics and Jews. Those opposed ranged from immigrant organizations to civil libertarians to millionaires who wanted to get rid of the federal income tax (a result of the Sixteenth Amendment in 1913) that had helped pave the way for Prohibition by easing the federal government's dependence on liquor taxes.

Prohibition The period in American history from the passage of the Eighteenth Amendment to the Constitution in 1919 forbidding the manufacture and sale of alcoholic beverages in the United States to its overturning by the Twenty-Third Amendment in 1933.

The business of the movies: The rise of the studio system and vertical integration

The silent screen age in American movies from 1915 to 1927 saw the mainstream movie business pattern itself more and more after corporate models of mass production, in part due to the influence of the Wall Street investors who became increasingly interested in investing in what they realized was an extremely lucrative – if volatile – entertainment business. For the American film industry in 1915, this meant the development of what is known as the structure of vertical integration.

As we have seen, the American film business has always been a complex network of many different kinds of businesses, from production to distribution to exhibition. Most movie fans have focused mainly on the work of movie producers, directors, and production companies, the people who write, direct, and create the cultural texts we call "movies." In the late 1910s and the early 1920s, the largest movie

Vertical integration The strategy of incorporating all aspects of the movie business, from production to distribution to exhibition, within a single company. Vertical integration was the central process in establishing the Hollywood studio system of the late 1920s through the end of World War II.

studios began combining these three aspects of moviemaking into a single operation. Companies like Adolph Zukor's Famous Players-Lasky Corporation and Marcus Loew's Metro Pictures began buying smaller studios and strings of theaters across the country, creating the powerhouse studios Paramount and Metro Goldwyn Mayer.

This incorporation of production, distribution, and exhibition into one single company is what is meant by vertical integration. The move to vertical integration accelerated the process of turning studios into movie factories, using the same assembly line practices that had revolutionized the automobile industry. Studios began signing everyone involved in making movies, from actors to carpenters, to long-term contracts, assigning them to projects as the studios saw fit. For the workers involved in making movies, there were potentially ominous aspects to these developments. While some studio contracts offered job security, many involved in film production feared the loss of creative independence and experimentation as business pressures demanded increasing predictability and uniformity.

Counter-reactions to vertical integration: Star power

While the major studios continued to acquire more control over the movie industry, movie stars also began to exercise the power and influence that came with celebrity. In the silent screen age, all the dominant studios recognized the marketing power of featuring "name" stars and directors in their movies. In terms of the screen experiences of audiences, their reactions to images of favorite movie stars were inseparable from their reactions to the characters they played. When fans watched a movie like *The Poor Little Rich Girl* (Maurice Tourneur 1917), a melodrama about a wealthy young girl named Gwen who is ignored by those around her, they saw both Gwen and the silent movie superstar who portrayed her, Mary Pickford (profiled in "Names above and below the title").

While the character of Gwen may have been new to most of them, they most likely already had an emotional relationship with the celebrity image of Pickford, dubbed "America's sweetheart" by the press. Pickford's image suggested both innocence and mischief, beauty and strength. Though small in size, "Little Mary" (another favorite nickname) represented an energetic and lively resilience, a model of American pluck and optimism, qualities that became a part of every role she played, whether comic or tragic. Movie executives knew the name and picture of Pickford was enough to ensure an audience for almost any movie, and they were all anxious to have her make pictures for them.

Stars such as Pickford, Lillian and Dorothy Gish, Gloria Swanson, and Theda Bara, Douglas Fairbanks, Charlie Chaplin, and Rudolph Valentino, western stars such as Tom Mix and William S. Hart; all became familiar not just in America but around the world, and they would become the objects of fierce bidding wars among competing studios.

These stars knew that celebrity was both powerful but often short-lived, and they resisted giving control over their lives and careers to studio executives. Power struggles between movie stars and studios became a regular part of mainstream American cinema, one that continues to this day. Increasingly, star actors and even star directors began to use their power and influence to achieve vertical integration over their own careers, becoming movie producers and distributors of their own.

The most famous example of these efforts in the silent screen era was the formation of the United Artists Corporation in 1919. Four of the biggest, most recognizable figures in American movies – Mary Pickford, her soon-to-be husband

Fig 3.9
One of the biggest stars of the silent era, Lillian Gish appeared in many of D. W. Griffith's most popular and influential movies, as in this scene from *Broken Blossoms* (1919). In another example of the widespread use of ethnic and racial stereotyping in the silent era, Gish appears opposite Richard Barthelmess, a white actor portraying a Chinese immigrant.

Fig 3.10
Two silent movie superstars, Gloria Swanson and Rudolph Valentino, appear together in the romantic melodrama *Beyond the Rocks* (Sam Wood 1922). Valentino's tragic death at age 31 in 1926 led to a national outpouring of grief.

Fig 3.11
Douglas Fairbanks in *The Thief of Bagdad* (Raoul Walsh 1924). Known for his athleticism, Fairbanks was one of the most popular action stars of his day, the epitome of the swashbuckling hero.

Fig 3.12
The founders of United Artists, from left Douglas Fairbanks, Mary Pickford, Charlie Chaplin, and D. W. Griffith. Source: The Kobal Collection.

Douglas Fairbanks, Charlie Chaplin, and D. W. Griffith (the western film star William S. Hart was originally involved but dropped out) – banded together to form their own studio, United Artists. The more established studios originally scoffed at the project, but they feared that if United Artists proved successful, it would threaten their efforts to establish a monopoly over the movie industry. While United Artists was never as successful as the founders hoped, the name and idea behind United Artists have proved resilient, and the model they established of allowing individual performers to create their own independent productions would become dominant after the end of the studios system following World War II.

Liberation and repression II: Celebrity, scandal, and censorship

The explosion of fan culture and celebrity gossip may seem an exclusive phenomenon of the Internet age, but the silent screen age of the late 1910s and 1920s also witnessed the rapid growth of a large, lively, and powerful fan culture in the form of dozens of fan magazines such as *Photoplay* and *Motion Picture Magazine*. Both studios and actors recognized the value of celebrity, and both became increasingly concerned with maintaining a positive public image.

If the 1920s marked the development of the mass celebrity culture that still defines entertainment media today, they likewise marked the development of another equally enduring feature of celebrity: the scandal. Concerns about Hollywood immorality and the possibly pernicious influence of the movies on American culture came to a head with the murder trial of one of the silent screen's most popular and beloved comedians, Roscoe Arbuckle, known professionally as "Fatty." In spite of his rotund appearance, Arbuckle was an agile and gifted physical comedian, a major star in his own right and the mentor to both Charlie Chaplin and Buster Keaton. At the time of the scandal in 1921 that would destroy his career and lead to the next major effort by the movie industry at self-censorship, Arbuckle was one of the most highly paid stars in the world.

Fig 3.13
Roscoe (Fatty) Arbuckle (on the left), here with his friend and protégé Buster Keaton in his self-directed western parody *Out West* (1918), was one of the most popular comic stars in Hollywood at the time of the scandal that wrecked his career.

Fig 3.14
The actor Virginia Rappe in the comic short *His Musical Sneeze* (Jack White 1919).

The Arbuckle scandal resulted from a party that the star and two of his friends held over the Labor Day weekend in 1921 at the St. Francis Hotel in San Francisco. A young actress named Virginia Rappe became ill at the party. The hotel doctor initially diagnosed the problem as intoxication, but two days after the party Rappe entered the hospital where she died the next day from an infection caused by a ruptured bladder. How Rappe sustained this injury would become a subject of dispute to this day and the focus of the scandal. For Matthew Brady, the local District Attorney, Rappe's death combined with Arbuckle's fame proved irresistible, and he charged the comedian with murdering Rappe during the course of a drunken orgy.

The press, especially the newspapers owned by William Randolph Hearst, were just as eager to capitalize on the chance to increase sales, and their coverage of the case fed increasingly lurid and sensational speculation and rumors about just what had happened in the St. Francis Hotel. The unfortunate Rappe became either a symbol of lost innocence or a cautionary tale about the dangers of sexual freedom. While many Arbuckle fans loyally defended their favorite star, the press – as well as the flimsy case constructed by the DA – portrayed him as a grotesque predator, an image that played off of prejudices and stereotypes related to his weight. Condemnations of Arbuckle went hand in hand with condemnations of Hollywood as the source of everything wrong with American society, and studio owners became more and more concerned that the Arbuckle scandal was accelerating the prospect of government censorship of movies.

In the end, the case against Arbuckle was weak and built on suspect testimony and hearsay. The consensus today is that Arbuckle was not guilty, a verdict the jurors in the third trial (the first two ended with deadlocked juries) finally affirmed. The Arbuckle scandal was not the only one that made studios nervous. The accidental poisoning death of the actress Olive Thomas, wife of Mary Pickford's brother Jack, the murder of director William Desmond Taylor, the mysterious death of movie pioneer Thomas Ince, and the fatal drug addiction of handsome screen star Wallace Reid all added fuel to negative media depictions of the movie industry.

The MPPDA and self-censorship

Hollywood reacted to the scandals by creating the Motion Picture Producers and Distributors of America (MPPDA) in 1922 and hiring the Postmaster General of the United States, Will H. Hays, to be its president. The Motion Picture Producers and Distributors of America was created specifically to enhance the image of the movies, and the choice of Will Hays, a conservative politician and a leader of the Republican Party, was meant to align the movies with an older, Protestant, affluent, and Anglo-Saxon idea of America.

Hays' job was two-fold: on the one hand, to monitor the production and content of Hollywood movies and to intervene with local boards of censor and various religious and other community groups to forestall objections or other efforts at censorship. These efforts at mollifying local censors often relied on the very glamor and glitz of the movie industry that was a cause of suspicion of Hollywood, as Hays would introduce local officials to movie stars and arrange for studio tours. The result was more or less successful, but there was considerable confusion as well as to what was and wasn't allowed as part of the screen experiences of the silent age, a confusion that would lead to the creation of the Production Code at the beginning of the sound era.

Motion Picture Producers and Distributors of America (MPPDA) A trade organization created by the Hollywood movie industry in 1922 to promote the image and interests of the movies, especially in the light of several major scandals, such as the Roscoe (Fatty) Arbuckle trial, which brought the threat of increased government censorship. Under founding MPPDA president Will Hays, the organization eventually developed the set of self-censoring guidelines that would form the motion picture Production Code. After World War II, the organization changed its name to the Motion Picture Association of America, which continues to this day.

Fig 3.15
Will Hays (second from the right), the first president of the Motion Picture Producers and Distributors of America, on the set of *The Exquisite Sinner* (Josef Von Sternberg and Phil Rosen 1926) in 1925 with (from left) Irving Thalberg, co-head of production at Metro Goldwyn Mayer studios, studio head Louis B. Mayer, and the other co-head of production Harry Rapf. Source: The Kobal Collection.

Fig 3.16
An editorial cartoon by Cy Hungerford that appeared in the *Pittsburgh Post-Gazette* in 1922 shows Will Hayes coming to the rescue of a movie industry drowning in scandal, including the Arbuckle case.

Screen experiences such as *The Birth of a Nation* and *The Jazz Singer* encapsulate these conflicting and conflicted reactions to the power of this still relatively new art form, reactions we still experience today watching these two landmarks of the first era when movies became a dominant part of American and world culture. If we are disturbed by the racism that operates as a central theme of *The Birth of a Nation*, it is because the power of the screen experience that Griffith created forces us to acknowledge that racism as a disturbing truth about American history, even if Griffith's own intention may have been otherwise. If *The Jazz Singer* (along with countless other movies of the period) uses blackface and stereotyped expressions of African American culture so casually, we are again confronted by aspects of American culture that the screen experience of the movie – including its history as a "landmark" film in American cinema history – makes unavoidable. These aspects of their screen experiences do not "excuse" these movies, but they also underscore the fact that all screen experiences – all experiences of art – are complex, fascinating, and yes, often disturbing.

In development

Melodrama

The term "melodrama" has a long and complicated history in the worlds of theater, opera, and literature. Within cinema history, filmmakers, critics, scholars, and viewers have tended to point to certain features that characterize the melodrama: a focus on personal conflict, often involving thwarted romance or the threat of danger; a set of familiar character types that can be clearly divided into "good" and "bad"; and an emphasis on creating a strong emotional response on the part of the viewers.

This definition seems broad enough to include most Hollywood movies, then and now, and that's part of the point. The power of moving images to provoke powerful emotions has been central to the screen experience since the first Kinetoscope films. At the same time, the way that a culture defines and understands "emotions" – from an essential aspect of the human experience that binds us together in spite of social differences to dangerous, primal feelings that threaten to overwhelm reason and logic – has been central to our understanding of the value and purpose of art and entertainment. The use of quickly recognizable character types was especially useful in silent American cinema, allowing audiences to quickly understand without extensive explanations and regardless of demographic backgrounds. And the focus on "good versus evil" – along with the potentially unstable and ambiguous definitions of that distinction, allowed movie narratives to draw on the deeply held values of the moviegoers.

Movies like the Mary Pickford vehicle *Stella Maris* (Marshall Nielan 1918) or *The Jazz Singer* define the melodrama in the silent era. *Stella Maris* tells the story of two young girls – the wealthy but disabled Stella Maris, and the poor orphan, Unity Blake – whose paths cross in the person of a journalist named John Risca. A family friend of the Maris', Risca is unhappily married to Louise at the beginning of the movie, a woman whose alcoholism has made her violent and sadistic. She adopts Unity not as a daughter but as a domestic servant, and after she nearly beats Unity to death, Louise is sent to prison.

John then adopts Unity, and over the next three years (the length of Louise's sentence), both Unity and Stella mature and fall in love with Risca. Meanwhile,

Melodrama A broad type of dramatic narrative that often involves placing characters in extreme peril, from the physical to the psychological, and that often seeks to provoke a strong emotional response from the audience. Many Hollywood melodramas have focused heavily on personal and romantic relationships and have featured strong women characters, leading to an association (and even a stereotype) of melodramas as "women's pictures."

Fig 3.17
Mary Pickford played
the roles of both Stella,
the wealthy invalid, and
Unity, the poor abused
orphan, in *Stella Maris*.
Here they appear together
in a processed shot.

surgery restores Stella's ability to walk, and although her aunt and uncle had sought
to shield her from the harsh realities of the world, she finds out that John is already
married after Louise is released from prison. Stella contemplates suicide, and when
the simple but noble Unity finds out, she murders Louise and then takes her own life
so that Stella and John will be free to marry.

Stella Maris was a tour de force for Pickford, who plays both Stella and Unity,
and the power of her performance along with the beauty of Marshall Nielan's
direction gives the movie an emotional power that had audiences weeping in spite
of the far-fetched plot. In *Stella Maris*, the characters of Stella and John are clearly
meant to be seen as good and virtuous, and their future happiness is thwarted by
John's "bad" wife Louise. The character of Unity Blake is at first presented as a
mischievous troublemaker, but we recognize her virtue over the course of the story.
Her sacrifice in shooting Louise before taking her own life provides a complex and
even contradictory wish fulfillment for the audience. While murder is wrong, the
death of Louise does solve the major problem for Stella and John, and thus they can
benefit from murder while we can still see them as unscathed from any moral blame,
especially when Unity punishes herself.

In *The Jazz Singer*, the hero is torn between conflicting goods: wanting to please
his mother and honor his ethnic heritage, or fulfilling his artistic ambitions (and
achieving love and marriage as well). Again, his conflict is expressed through his two
names, Jakie Rabinowitz/Jack Robin. The mortal illness of his father forces Jakie/
Jack to make a choice, and he leaves his Broadway premiere to sing in his father's
place at the synagogue. The virtue of his choice reconciles all the people he loves
in his life to his dual nature as both cantor and jazz singer, and he is rewarded by
having his cake and eating it, too, becoming a Broadway star after all.

As we have seen, even an epic such as *The Clansmen/The Birth of a Nation*, a
movie ostensibly about events on a grand historical scale, from the Civil War to
the assassination of Abraham Lincoln to, at the end of the movie, the history of
humanity itself, presents events through a melodrama involving two families, and
the fate of the divided nation is condensed into the thwarted romance between Ben
Cameron and Elsie Stoneman. Griffith uses the power of this melodramatic romance
plot to convince audiences to identify Ben as the hero, in spite of his involvement
with the Klan and his efforts to defend slavery.

It's a pattern that will be repeated throughout American movie history, and by
Griffith himself in his next movie, the even more epic *Intolerance*, which purports
to trace the history of the concept of intolerance from ancient Babylonia to

contemporary America. He does so by weaving together four melodramatic stories from four different time periods, concluding in the modern period with characters identified only as "The Boy" and "The Dear One," names that openly admit how familiar Griffith knew his viewers would be with the basic structure of melodrama. From epic Douglas Fairbanks' adventures such as *The Thief of Bagdad* to *Robin Hood* to *Gone with the Wind*, *The Ten Commandments,* to *Forrest Gump*, *Saving Private Ryan* and *The Dark Knight*, the elements of melodrama provide personal emotional connections to larger than life stories.

Even in the screen ages of early Hollywood, melodrama often acquired a bad name. For those critical of the genre, melodrama was manipulative and unrealistic. The emphasis on emotional intensity was seen as contrary to intellectual engagement. Perhaps most controversially, melodrama was seen as a "women's genre" because of this focus on emotions, family life, romance, and the lives of female protagonists. In recent years, feminist movie critics have challenged this gender-based bias, pointing out that assessments of "realism" depend on who gets to define what we mean by "reality," and that the neat distinction between emotions and logic, the head and the heart, is itself not based in "reality" but is itself a particular cultural construct, one not coincidentally used historically to justify the subordinate status of women. Melodrama remains a contested critical term to this day in discussing our screen experiences.

Movies as art/art movies

As we saw in the last chapter, as movies became a central and influential part of American cultural life in the silent era, Hollywood began to see the value in promoting the idea of movies as an art form, both as a way of resisting censorship pressures and as attracting a broader and more affluent audience. Of course, this emphasis on movies as art seemed in conflict with the organization of studios into movie factories, a conflict the movie industry has wrestled with to this day. Nevertheless, in the silent age a group of directors emerged whose work did not always achieve commercial popularity but who were seen as advancing the artistic potential of the movies in ways that lent prestige and respectability to the industry. As a result, they were able to create screen experiences that stretched audience expectations about what it meant to go to the movies. Two in particular – Erich Von Stroheim and F. W. Murnau – exemplify the promise and paradox of mainstream Hollywood's artistic ambitions.

Erich Von Stroheim

Perhaps no director more self-consciously and even notoriously embodied the image of the director-as-great-artist than Erich Von Stroheim. D. W. Griffith was clearly the most famous American director of the silent age, but it is Von Stroheim's persona, with his dictatorial reputation on the set and the pretensions to aristocracy suggested both by his name and his dress (especially his habit of wearing a monocle), that defined the stereotype of the arrogant movie director. His directorial career also came to define another equally influential stereotype: the uncontrollable genius so stymied by the small-mindedness of studio executives that he never is able to achieve his full potential. This image of the director as misunderstood artist would surface again and again in histories of American movies, from Orson Welles to Francis Ford Coppola.

The movie he is most remembered for as a filmmaker – and one of the first examples of a film project that was seen as an expensive disaster at the time only to

Fig 3.18
The director Erich Von Stroheim. Source: The Kobal Collection.

be revered later as a masterpiece of American cinema (again, presaging such movies as *The Magnificent Ambersons* and *Apocalypse Now*) was *Greed* (1924), Von Stroheim's adaptation of Frank Norris' novel *McTeague*. Norris' turn-of-the-century novel is a prime example of literary naturalism, a kind of hyperrealism that tried to depict human life as subject to the same impulses – sex, food, the survival instinct – that defined the natural world. In his movie, Von Stroheim sought to create a similar screen experience, arguing that after the horrors of World War I audiences were ready for movies that frankly depicted the human condition in all its physical reality and tragedy.

Von Stroheim insisted that *Greed* be filmed on location, and he eschewed the use of artificial sets. The movie is set mainly in working-class San Francisco and tells the story of a struggling gold miner named John McTeague (Gibson Gowland) who learns the trade of dentistry and sets up shop in San Francisco, marrying Trina (ZaSu Pitts), the cousin of his good friend Marcus Schouler (Jean Hersholt). The apparent windfall of winning the lottery instead leads to family strife and McTeague murdering Trina. The story ends in the bleak expanse of Death Valley, where Schouler, bent on revenge, pursues McTeague. Schouler catches up with McTeague in Death Valley, and their subsequent fight ends with McTeague handcuffed to Schouler's corpse, lost in the middle of the desert with no horse and no water.

Studio executives at the Goldwyn Company, where Von Stroheim was under contract, were concerned about several aspects of the production, including the unrelenting tragedy of the story, cost overruns, and the length of the movie. Von Stroheim shot over eighty hours worth of film during production and spent a year in the initial editing process, much longer than most Hollywood productions. His first cut of *Greed* was over ten hours long, and subsequent struggles with MGM eventually resulted in the release of a two-hour plus version.

Fig 3.19
The bleak ending to Erich Von Stroheim's *Greed* shot on location in Death Valley. McTeague has defeated and killed his one-time friend Marcus Schouler after a confrontation in the middle of the desert, only to realize that his being handcuffed to Schouler's corpse means he too is doomed.

The film was a flop at the box office and with many movie critics, but among a select group of movie lovers and filmmakers it began to acquire a reputation as one of the most innovative and original movies of the silent era. Its critical status has only grown over the years, and *Greed* now regularly appears on lists of the most important movies ever made. What was so distinctive about the screen experience of *Greed*? In the biggest sense, it is those very qualities that made the movie so controversial in the first place: the attention to visual detail in every scene, the use of authentic locations, including the starkness of Death Valley, its length and ambition. *Greed* defies the expectations of audiences familiar with a more conventional story arc, whether comic or tragic. Neither McTeague nor any of the other characters function like a hero, and the ending likewise offers neither resolution nor redemption. Instead, Von Stroheim's movie tries to immerse its viewers in an intensive experience meant to challenge our understanding of human behavior and the idea that truth and justice will always ultimately prevail. In presenting audiences with such rich and detailed imagery, *Greed* in effect argues that it presents a more accurate view of human society than other films.

F. W. Murnau

When the Fox Company brought the German filmmaker Friedrich Wilhelm (F. W.) Murnau to Hollywood in 1926, he was already one of the most celebrated movie directors in the world. If Von Stroheim struggled with studio executives who wanted him to make movies that were less artistically ambitious and more commercially successful, Murnau from the beginning was seen as bringing prestige to American movies. More specifically, Murnau represented the tradition of Expressionist filmmaking that had come to define post-war German cinema, and America moviemakers were eager to learn from him.

Expressionism provided viewers with dream-like, visually surprising screen experiences. Expressionist filmmakers experimented with the approach of having the external world – the world we can see with our eyes and that can be recorded on film – express the internal, psychological world. As a result, these movies were

Expressionism An artistic movement strongly associated with Germany in the first decades of the twentieth century that experimented with using external visual details to express internal psychological conflict. In movies, the films of German directors such as F. W. Murnau and Fritz Lang, both of whom would emigrate to the United States, featured exaggerated, distorted sets and dramatic uses of deep shadows to create disturbing and powerful screen experiences. The large-scale immigration of German expressionist directors and cinematographers into Hollywood during the 1920s and 1930s, particularly after the rise of the Nazi Party, had a significant influence on American cinema, especially in genres such as the gangster movie and film noir (see Chapter 4).

Fig 3.20
The director F. W. Murnau (seated center, with the bow tie) on the set of *Sunrise*. Source: Fox Films / The Kobal Collection.

less interested in whether they looked like everyday reality and more in using visual details to create strong emotional reactions in viewers. Even the subject matter of these films was more concerned with mood than "realism." Murnau's first major success as a director in Germany, *Nosferatu* (1922), was the first great vampire movie and one of the most influential horror movies ever made, although a lawsuit brought by the family of Bram Stoker, author of the novel *Dracula*, almost resulted in having all copies of the movie destroyed. The movie featured the off-balance camera angles as well as the striking use of light and shadow that defined Expressionism. The main character of Nosferatu himself featured grotesque and elongated fingers, nose, and face.

When Murnau came to Fox with a contract to make three movies, he set to work on the movie that would establish him as a giant of American cinema as well, *Sunrise* (also called *Sunrise: A Song of Two Humans*). The reference to the movie as a "song" rather than a "story" in the full title connects *Sunrise* to Murnau's other movies in aiming to provide a screen experience that was more about mood and feeling than narrative and plot. *Sunrise* does have a plot – even a melodramatic plot involving a love triangle. A poor farmer (George O'Brien) meets a "Woman from the City" (Margaret Livingstone) who persuades him to murder his wife and join her in the city. Unable to carry out his plan, he still terrifies his wife, who herself flees for her safety to the big city, where he follows her. In the city, she overcomes her horror and the two renew their love for each other as they wander through the bright lights and attractions of the metropolis.

This plot summary makes *Sunrise* sound like a frantic chase movie, but the movie's fame and influence derive from the beauty of its style. Fox allowed Murnau to construct elaborate sets for *Sunrise*, including the big city. *Sunrise* presents the city as both a place of confusion and as a wonderland, and Murnau uses exaggerated

Fig 3.21
The image of the city carnival from F. W. Murnau's *Sunrise* combines realism and fantasy to express a sense of wonder and hope for the two main characters.

proportions to suggest the magical effect of the city on the couple. Set designers built the city using diminishing perspective to create illusions of size and distance. The movie also used complex tracking shots throughout, particularly in the Man's meeting with the Woman from the City in the marsh (another studio set), where the cameraman was suspended from a track in the ceiling to follow the couple as they made their way to each other. *Sunrise* was also the first movie to feature a complete musical soundtrack using the Fox Movietone system.

The set of *Sunrise* became a kind of pilgrimage site for Hollywood filmmakers anxious for the opportunity to see Murnau at work. When the movie premiered in November 1927, it was more of a critical than financial success. What *Sunrise* did do is influence a generation of American filmmakers and establish an identity for the screen experience of the "art" movie in the final years of the silent screen age. That the Hollywood movie industry consciously thought in terms of the art movie as its own kind of genre is reflected in the first Academy Awards ceremony, where there were initially two Best Picture categories: Outstanding Picture (given to the war movie *Wings*, which featured fighter plane sequences shot in flight) and the Unique and Artistic Production category, which was given to *Sunrise*. The Unique and Artistic Production category was dropped the next year, but its initial presence showed the importance to Hollywood of establishing the idea of movies as art.

Genres of gender: The girl next door, the vamp, and the flapper
Consider the three images of silent movie stars in Figure 3.22. What differences can you see in these three versions of how the movies represented women? In Mary Pickford, we see the image of the "girl next door," a throwback to Victorian ideals

Fig 3.22
Mary Pickford in *The Poor Little Rich Girl* (Maurice Tourneur 1917); Theda Bara in *Cleopatra* (J. Gordon Edwards 1917) (Source: Fox Films/Witzel/The Kobal Collection); Clara Bow in *It* (Clarence G. Badger 1927).

of modesty and delicacy. Pickford sometimes played literal "girl" characters until she was thirty, and her long curls were her visual trademark. As we have also noted, though, while one part of Pickford's image may have been girlish and innocent, her characters were also feisty, physical, and assertive, offering audiences a mixed screen experience that spoke to a complicated fantasy ideal, both delicate and strong, old-fashioned and modern.

In the same year (1917) that audiences flocked to watch Pickford in *The Poor Little Rich Girl*, they were also drawn to one of the biggest Hollywood productions of that time, *Cleopatra*, starring Theda Bara in the title role. Bara specialized in the gender genre of the vamp (derived from "vampire"), a sexually powerful, even dangerous woman who uses her sexuality to seduce and overpower men. Bara is often credited as American cinema's first sex symbol, and she made over forty movies before essentially retiring in 1926.

The contrast in the two images is striking, almost literally black and white. Pickford is dressed as a boy, striking childlike poses before a mirror. Bara is dressed provocatively, with dark hair and dark eye makeup. Publicity for *Cleopatra* emphasized Bara's "exotic" appearance, meaning something vaguely foreign and not completely white. A whole new biography was constructed for her, claiming she was born in Egypt of French and Italian parents, even though in reality she was the daughter of middle-class Jewish immigrants in Cincinnati. Even the meaning of her screen name was wrapped in mystery, with the studio floating the rumor that it was an anagram of "Arab death." And Bara's image is far more explicitly revealing than Pickford's. Her gender genre mixed fear and desire, excitement over her character's openly aggressive sexuality, and concern over how this sexuality would disrupt conventional society.

If the vamp represented an exaggerated version of fears generated by the changing roles of women, the flapper figure became a symbol of the 1920s, an image of a freer, wilder young woman who embraced the excitement of the Jazz Age. The flapper was the girl next door turned vamp, a transformation that was sometimes pictured as the source of comedy, at others the stuff of tragedy. No actor of the silent era embodied these contradictions more than Clara Bow, who became one of the most popular stars of the 1920s. Known as the "It" girl after *It* (1927), one of her most popular movies, Bow's characters alternated between the seductive and the playful. Unlike Pickford, Bow wore her hair in the most modern styles, including the short, easy-to-care-for bob that became a symbol of the flapper. The term "flapper" was popularized by the 1920 comedy *The Flapper* (Alan Crosland), written by Frances Marion and starring Olive Thomas. Unlike the layered, complicated, and restrictive dresses of the Victorian era, flappers were associated with a more androgynous style, wearing looser dresses and short hair that facilitated easy movement and jazz dancing. The flapper was another evolution of the New Woman of early cinema, and actors like Bow, Thomas, Jean Harlow, Louise Brooks, and Norma Talmadge symbolized the image. While the Great Depression put an end to the playfulness and excess associated with the flapper, the reaction against restrictive genres of women's identity will continue to reappear in American movie history.

The names above and below the title

Mary Pickford

Mary Pickford, also known as America's sweetheart – one of her many nicknames – was actually Canadian, born in Toronto in 1892. Pickford and her siblings Jack and Lottie, who also became movie actors, were raised by her single mother Charlotte. The family struggled financially until a stage manager who was boarding with them suggested that the children could make money in the theater. In spite of the popularity of the theater, acting was still seen by many at the turn of the century as a suspect profession, especially for girls and women. Pickford's own career, as well as that of other early women stars, was in part responsible for establishing the legitimacy of acting as a profession for women, not to mention the larger idea of the career woman.

Like her lifelong friend Lillian Gish, Pickford helped develop acting for the screen as a craft distinct from the more demonstrative styles associated with stage acting of the day. Working with D. W. Griffith, Pickford brought a more naturalistic approach to silent film acting, taking advantage of the increasing use of close-ups to signal complex emotional reactions through subtle changes of facial expression.

Pickford went on to become a giant of the silent screen, starring in over fifty pictures before retiring in 1933 at age forty-one when sound was remaking the movie industry. As significant as the size of her stardom, however, was how she took

Fig 3.23
Mary Pickford in 1918, one of the most famous people in the world and one of the most powerful in silent Hollywood. Source: The Kobal Collection.

control of and used her stardom to shape the artistic direction of her career and the role of the movie star in the movie business. When she signed with Adolph Zukor and the Famous Players studio (later Paramount) in 1916, she was given complete control over her films as well as an astronomical salary. Pickford realized that being able to oversee the production of her movies was vital for maintaining the quality her fans had come to expect, helping her to maintain financial success and artistic fulfillment.

When her contract with Paramount ended, the studio actually offered to pay Pickford to leave the movie business altogether rather than sign with a competitor. She instead signed with First National Pictures, a company formed by a consortium of independent theaters hoping to counter the increasing power of studios such as Paramount. But Pickford's boldest move in using her star power to gain independence from the vertical integration and hierarchical structure of the studios was in joining with D. W. Griffith, Charlie Chaplin, and her soon-to-be husband Douglas Fairbanks in forming the United Artists studio in 1919. Although the company was an equal partnership, Pickford was recognized as one of the most active participants and the keenest business mind in putting the plan together.

During Pickford's career, only Charlie Chaplin rivaled her in terms of fame and popularity, and since her retirement it is difficult to find another star, male or female, no matter how renowned, who could compare with how she dominated the silent film industry. Very few could compare in terms of the sheer range of characters she portrayed as well. She took advantage of the formative years of the early screen ages of American cinema to create a flexible persona that opened opportunities for rethinking the role of women in the entertainment industry and American culture in general. Although her gender genre of "the girl next door" seemed old-fashioned, it was really also like nothing that had come before. In many ways, the gender genres for women that followed her in the silent film screen age, including the vamp and the flapper, limited the ways the lives of women could be represented on screen by defining them primarily in terms of their sexuality and sexual appeal. Pickford played both young women and mature adult women, her characters both sexually naive and sexually playful. She even successfully played male roles on screen, and cross-dressing was a recurring plot device in her movies. Pickford lived a long life, most of it out of the public eye after her retirement. Small in stature, this giant of early American cinema died in Los Angeles in 1979. She was eighty-seven years old.

Oscar Micheaux and black cinema

The United States in the first three quarters of the twentieth century was a country strictly divided by race, both by law and by social practice. Throughout the southern states, Jim Crow laws enforced racial segregation and oppression, denying black Americans their civil rights and forbidding them from fully participating in American life. Public places of all kinds, including nickelodeons and movie theaters, featured separate "white" and "colored" entrances, seating areas, and accommodations, when African Americans weren't barred from entrance altogether. In the rest of the country, including California, such segregation was usually not enforced by law, and while there were more examples of racial integration and comparatively greater opportunity for African Americans, local custom and practice still maintained a racial separation and hierarchy.

In the silent era, an African American tradition of moviemaking slowly began to emerge, offering screen experiences that challenged those major studio productions,

from *The Birth of a Nation* to *The Jazz Singer*, that played off of the stereotypes and prejudices associated with the construction of racial identity in America. Frustrated at the racist portrayals and casting of black characters in mainstream movies, some African American artists and entrepreneurs undertook the difficult challenge of creating movies that would feature far broader and more complex and diverse screen experiences of black life in America. Oscar Micheaux, an ambitious and restless young man who had left his family's Illinois farm to try his hand at business, farming, and novel writing, would emerge as one of the most significant and successful early black filmmakers. Over his thirty-year career, Micheaux would produce and direct almost forty movies, all outside the mainstream Hollywood system. His movies addressed issues of race and racism in ways that mainstream Hollywood films would avoid, and also in some cases acted as counter-experiences to the representation of race in those movies.

His second movie, for example, *Within Our Gates* from 1920, has been seen as a cinematic response to *The Birth of a Nation*. Rather than Griffith's depiction of two white families, one southern and one northern, reunited in the face of the threat of black sexual violence, Micheaux's movie shows that the real violence was directed by white communities against black Americans, and that the threat of sexual exploitation was part of the racial oppression of African American women. The main character, Sylvia Landry, played by black screen pioneer Evelyn Jarvis, was the result of a union between a wealthy white southern man and a poor local woman. Adopted and raised by a black family, Sylvia works to raise money in the north for a school to educate rural black children in the south. Along the way, the movie features the brutal lynching of Sylvia's family by a white mob, and the film ends with her marriage to a prominent African American social activist.

Other black-owned movie companies appeared and disappeared in the silent era, such as Lincoln Motion Pictures and the Foster Photoplay Company. Meanwhile, other white-owned companies, such as Norman Studios in Florida, began making movies aimed at African American audiences. Even the mainstream studios recognized the economic potential of the black film market and created a separate group of "race movies." The advent of sound along with the Great Depression finished off many black-owned companies, although Micheaux kept his company going until 1948, when he left the movie business to return to writing. He died of heart failure in 1951. The portrayal of African Americans in the movies and the history of black filmmaking points to the central issue of how the movies have represented the racial and ethnic diversity of American society, a question we will continue to return to in *Screen Ages*.

Three giants of silent comedy: Charlie Chaplin, Buster Keaton, Harold Lloyd

Ask most people to name an important personality from the silent screen ages of American movies, and chances are they will name a comedian. There is no greater evidence of the importance of comedy to film history than the fact that three of the most enduring and influential filmmakers of the silent screen age were comedians: Charlie Chaplin, Buster Keaton, and Harold Lloyd. While comedy is often regarded as an escapist genre, the comedies of all three of these comic filmmakers were rooted in the social and economic experiences of their audiences. All three based their comedies on the turbulent economic times of the late 1910s and the 1920s: the promise (or fantasy) of overnight riches; a widening gap between rich and poor; an increasingly competitive society based on the accumulation of material wealth; an era of rapid technological change and development that evoked both wonder and anxiety. The screen experiences provided by these great silent comedians drew laughter from the mixed emotions the fast-changing modern world created in audiences.

Charlie Chaplin

Charlie Chaplin is often seen as the warmest and most sentimental of the "Big Three" of silent comedy, but his movies, both shorts and feature films, just as often contain the starkest representations of poverty and the wide gap between the haves and have-nots of any silent filmmaker. His "Little Tramp" figure became one of the most beloved characters in the world, an anachronistic cartoon figure that everyone could identify with and root for. Although he was often homeless and on the verge of starvation, the Little Tramp always maintained the manners and habits of an old-fashioned gentleman. With his out-of-date bowler hat and cane and his too-small formal clothing, Chaplin's trademark character was an outsider in every world he tried to inhabit. This juxtaposition of the personal eccentricity and even self-delusion of the Little Tramp with the coldness and cruelty of the larger world allowed Chaplin to portray extremes of poverty and danger while maintaining an air of comic fantasy. No matter the peril, we know that the Little Tramp will survive and even triumph, bowler hat intact.

Fig 3.25
Charlie Chaplin sitting down to a meal of boiled boot in *The Gold Rush* with another silent comedy star, Mack Swain.

With the dawn of the 1920s, Chaplin turned to making the feature films that would ensure his place in American movie history. These full-length movies demonstrate Chaplin's ambition to create comic movies with varied emotional landscapes and complex character development. He described *The Gold Rush* (1925), for example, as a "dramatic comedy," and he embeds slapstick sequences within a larger narrative arc that invites viewers to emotionally invest in the characters on screen. Both *City Lights* (1931) and *Modern Times* (1936) – each made after the advent of sound but told in a "silent" style – feature similar stories showing the Little Tramp as out of place in the modern industrial metropolis, finding common cause with destitute young women – a blind flower girl in *City Lights*, a homeless orphan in *Modern Times*. In *City Lights*, the Tramp survives the vicissitudes of the arbitrary whims of the wealthy, the difficulty of earning a living, and even jail to amass the money to pay for the operation that restores the flower girl's sight. In *Modern Times*, the Tramp and the orphan never succeed in achieving their dream of creating a middle-class home of their own. Instead, at movie's end they are still destitute, walking down a road away from the camera, although the Tramp maintains his usual hopefulness. It marked Chaplin's last appearance as the Tramp on screen.

Buster Keaton

In his films, Joseph "Buster" Keaton also created a distinct persona, one that like the Little Tramp set his character apart from everyone else in his films. Unlike Chaplin's Tramp, Keaton's character inhabited a wide range of social roles, from the poor film projectionist in *Sherlock, Jr.* (1924) to a stockbroker in *Seven Chances* (1925) to a Civil-War-era train engineer in his masterpiece *The General* (1926). While every part of the Little Tramp's costume was part of his iconic identity, Keaton was known by primarily two features: his porkpie hat and his deadpan facial expression. His comedies were marked by his acrobatic and death-defying stunt work and a cosmic sense of the absurdity of human ambition and effort.

If Chaplin aspired to engage his audiences emotionally, evoking both laughter and tears, Keaton kept his character at more of a distance. Instead, his movies have become influential for the ways they made audiences aware of the movies as the movies. Keaton played with the formal and technological possibilities of the movies to create screen experiences that were sometimes harder for his audiences to read in terms of their emotional focus. Never as beloved or as widely popular in his time as Chaplin was, Keaton has become especially revered among comedians and filmmakers for his astonishingly creative experiments in movie comedy.

If Chaplin successfully combined tragedy and comedy, Keaton's movies provided more surreal and absurdist experiences for his audiences. His screen persona was

Fig 3.26
One of Buster Keaton's trademark deadpan reaction shots from *The General*.

constantly buffeted about by powerful structures that dwarfed his puny efforts, whether those structures were social institutions and traditions or even the laws of physics themselves. Like comic versions of the literary naturalism that Erich Von Stroheim evoked in *Greed*, Keaton's movies emphasize the smallness and fragility of the individual against the implacable forces of the universe. Yet his character remains remarkably resilient and persistent no matter how great a battering he takes, while the perpetual deadpan expression he wore that earned him the nickname of "The Great Stone Face" left his interior emotional life a mystery.

Critical consensus over the years now recognizes *The General* as Keaton's most important achievement, but audiences at the time were more puzzled by the movie. An epic comedy adventure set during the Civil War, *The General* features Keaton as Johnnie Gray, a young railroad engineer in the South who desires to enlist in the Confederate Army not out of ideological or political conviction but to impress his fiancée. When he is rejected because the Army believes his work as a civilian train engineer is too valuable to risk, he is mistakenly rejected as a coward by his fiancée and her family. When his train, *The General*, is hijacked by Union forces with his fiancée on board, Johnnie seizes the opportunity to prove his heroism and gives chase on another locomotive, creating in essence a railroad chase movie.

The General was shot on location in Oregon and is in its way Keaton's response to the self-seriousness of movies such as *The Clansmen/The Birth of a Nation* (Keaton enjoyed tweaking the emerging cliches and mannerisms of other popular movies, as in the crime movie parody in *Sherlock, Jr.* and his detailed and hilarious lampooning of the westerns of William S. Hart in *The Frozen North*). The tracking shots of the locomotives at full steam, Keaton's acrobatics in leaping and climbing all over the moving train, and the epic sweep of the movie, including a sequence showing a Union train plunging into a river canyon after Johnny has successfully sabotaged a bridge, have caused scholars and filmmakers to label *The General* one of the most important movie comedies ever made. As time went by, Keaton's mixing of genres in *The General* came to seem more and more innovative and forward-looking, but in the 1920s Keaton's relentless formal experimentation provided screen experiences that were exciting in their originality but that also challenged audience expectations. While Chaplin could rely on the affection and sympathy viewers felt for the Little Tramp to bring them along in his own innovative films, the deadpan expression of Keaton's "Stone Face" character resisted such audience identification.

Harold Lloyd

Both Charlie Chaplin and Buster Keaton played outsiders of different types. Chaplin's Little Tramp was an economic and social outsider, always poor, always out of step with the competitive, money-driven world he found around him. More by personality and temperament than social position, Keaton's characters were misfits, never changing expression even as the world churned in chaos around them. Harold Lloyd's classic comic character, however, known as "Glasses" because of his trademark eyewear, often began as an outsider in his movies, but an outsider who wanted in.

While both Chaplin and Keaton followed the clowning tradition of creating distinctively costumed characters who stood out from the crowd around them, Lloyd's character looked like a contemporary member of 1920s American society. His character represented the striver, the ardent believer in the American dream who worked tirelessly to make his way up the ladder of economic success. The

Fig 3.27
His character always on the edge of chaos, Harold Lloyd dangles perilously from a clock face in his most famous movie, *Safety Last!*

comedy in Lloyd's films often derives from his character's trying too hard, being too willing to conform to the demands and dictates of those in power around him. Lloyd's comedies reflect the power of the American dream in the hypercompetitive environment of 1920s America, the idea that with hard work, anyone can achieve money and status, a dream that many in his audiences wanted to believe in. That his character's pursuit of that dream often highlighted how much chance and dumb luck mattered more than hard work and determination also spoke to his audience's fear that the American dream might really be a fantasy, a fear easier to face when expressed in the comic experience of a Harold Lloyd comedy.

Lloyd's most famous and iconic movie, *Safety Last!* (1923), takes the idea that only a thin line separates reaching one's dreams or experiencing total defeat and makes it the heart of our screen experience of the movie, as Lloyd's character of "The Boy" literally teeters between life and death as he scales the outside of a twelve-story building as part of a publicity stunt for the department store where he works as a humble clerk. Once again, Lloyd plays the striver, a young man from a small town looking to make it in the big city so he can marry his sweetheart. While The Boy's dogged persistence ultimately seems to win the day in *Safety Last!*, the plot of the movie as well as the constant jeopardy The Boy finds himself in makes us question whether hard work or dumb luck really determines his fate. In spite of his dedication and punctuality, The Boy can't seem to get anywhere in his job.

The climbing sequence in *Safety Last!* has become legendary in the annals of silent comedy. Lloyd boasted that no photographic tricks were used, and he carefully guarded information about how the sequence was filmed. We know now that Lloyd and co-directors Sam Taylor and Fred Newmeyer created the illusion of height in the movie using a number of different approaches, including building a set on the roof of a tall building. Still, the stunts that Lloyd performs in *Safety Last!* were breathtakingly dangerous, as he clings to the side of the building, battling a series of comic obstacles, from pigeons to swinging windows to a rogue volleyball net. The stunts are all the more remarkable considering that Lloyd had lost the thumb and forefinger of his right hand in an accident in the late 1910s.

The image of Lloyd hanging from the building's clock face has become one of the most famous in movie history, both for its sheer daring and for its symbolic richness. All of the great silent film comedians built on the attraction and ambivalence audiences felt about the experience of living in a world, like our own, where technology was rapidly expanding and changing everyday life in ways both exciting and confusing. They all recognized that movies, the most technologically complex of art forms in the early twentieth century, were uniquely suited to expressing this technological uncertainty. As Lloyd clung for dear life to the clock face, the audiences watching him found themselves both laughing and gasping, both thrilled and terrified, finding an emotional expression for their own mixed feelings about the changing modern world around them.

Explore further

Altman, Rick, *Silent Film Sound*. New York: Columbia University Press, 2004.

Bachman, Gregg and Thomas J. Slater (eds.), *American Silent Film: Discovering Marginalized Voices*. Carbondale: Southern Illinois University Press, 2002.

Basinger, Jeanine, *Silent Stars*. New York: Alfred A. Knopf, 2000.

Beauchamp, Cari, *Without Lying Down: Frances Marion and the Powerful Women of Early Hollywood*. New York: Scribner, 1997.

Bernardi, Daniel (ed.), *The Birth of Whiteness: Race and the Emergence of U.S. Cinema*. New Brunswick, NJ: Rutgers University Press, 1996.

Bilton, Alan, *Silent Film Comedy and American Culture*. New York: Palgrave Macmillan, 2013.

Bogle, Donald, *Bright Boulevards, Bold Dreams: The Story of Black Hollywood*. New York: One World Ballantine Books, 2006.

—— *Toms, Coons, Mulattoes, Mammies, and Bucks: An Interpretive History of Blacks in American Films*. New York: Continuum, 2003.

Chadwick, Bruce, *The Reel Civil War: Mythmaking in American Film*. New York: Alfred A. Knopf, 2001.

Cohen, Paula Marantz, *Silent Film and the Triumph of the American Myth*. Oxford and New York: Oxford University Press, 2001.

Cooper, Mark Garrett, *Love Rules: Silent Hollywood and the Rise of the Managerial Class*. Minneapolis: University of Minnesota Press, 2003.

Everson, William K., *American Silent Film*. New York: Da Capo Press, 1998.

Francke, Lizzie, *Script Girls: Women Screenwriters in Hollywood*. London: British Film Institute, 1994.

Gaines, Jane M., *Fire and Desire: Mixed-Race Movies in the Silent Era*. Chicago: University of Chicago Press, 2001.

Karnick, Kristine Brunovska and Henry Jenkins (eds.), *Classical Hollywood Comedy*. London and New York: Routledge, 1995.

Koszarski, Richard, *An Evening's Entertainment: The Age of the Silent Feature Picture, 1915–1928*. Berkeley: University of California Press, 1994.

Lang, Robert (ed.), *The Birth of a Nation: D.W. Griffith, Director*. Brunswick, NJ: Rutgers University Press, 1994.

MacCann, Richard Dyer, *The Silent Screen*. Lanham, MD: Scarecrow Press, 1997.

Menefee, David W., *The First Female Stars: Women of the Silent Era*. Westport, CT: Praeger, 2004.

CHAPTER 4

The studios era: Dominance and diversity in the Golden Age of Hollywood, 1929–1948

Now playing

A pre-Code screening of *The Public Enemy* at the Strand Theatre, New York, 1931

Before the main feature began at the Mark Strand Theatre, a movie palace on Broadway in New York City, the assembled audience watched a puppet show. In the words of a *New York Times* review, they saw "a brief stage tableau, with sinuous green lighting, which shows a puppet gangster shooting another puppet gangster in the back."[1] What followed was a screening of *The Public Enemy* starring James Cagney and directed by William Wellman, the latest in a series of gangster movies mainly put out by Warner Brothers studios focused on the criminal activities and crime bosses that flourished during Prohibition.

The Public Enemy followed the same pattern as other early sound gangster films such as *Little Caesar* (LeRoy 1931) and *Scarface* (Hawks 1932) in showing the rise and fall of a crime boss loosely based on the careers of such notorious real-life personalities as Al Capone, Bugs Moran, and Frank Nitti. In *The Public Enemy*, Cagney portrays Tom Powers, a working-class kid who along with his lifelong friend Matt Doyle (Edward Woods) moves from petty theft as a child to being a major gang enforcer. With the money he makes from his violent and dangerous work, Tom is able to buy expensive clothes for himself and provide for his naive but doting mother, but in the end, a gang war results in Tom's kidnap and murder by a rival gang.

Why were gangster movies so popular at the end of the 1920s and in the first part of the 1930s? One big reason was the public fascination with organized crime, especially the sensationalized treatment of bootlegging and bootleggers in the news media during the Prohibition era, a fascination that has remained a part of American popular culture and the movies. But another was the advent of sound. Gangster movies were made for sound. The squeal of car tires; the rat-a-tat of machine guns; the slap of skin on skin in a fistfight; the wail of police sirens: gangster movies brought a new level of audio excitement to the screen experience.

Most of all, though, it was the talk. More than any other genre, gangster films reveled in the diversity and creativity of American speech, especially the speech of

Fig 4.1
James Cagney and Jean
Harlow in *Public Enemy*.
The musicality of Cagney's
performance, expressed
in his movement and
his distinctively New
York voice, showed the
potential of sound film.

working-class and immigrant communities. In the early sound gangster movies, even though the main criminal characters were officially meant to be seen as examples to avoid, they were still allowed to speak for themselves, and the richness of personality that spoke through their "street" accents and gangster argot made these characters both attractive and unforgettable.

In fact, it was James Cagney's Lower East Side of New York accent, his rapid-fire delivery, and the musicality of his speech that won him the role of Tom Powers. His speech pattern was so distinctive that he became one of the most imitated actors among comic impressionists. Tom Powers may lead a life of crime and violence, but we can't take our eyes off of him and, just as important, we love listening to what he says. Cagney's charismatic portrayal of Tom, his mix of humor, violence, and sexuality, led audiences both to sympathize with and fear him. He alternates in the movie between the attractive, as when he flirts with the rising screen idol Jean Harlow, and the frightening, as when he is stalking through the rain-soaked streets at night bent on vengeance against a rival gang for the murder of Matt. The most famous example of Tom's volatile character occurs at breakfast with his girlfriend Kitty (Mae Clark), when Tom, still seething over an argument with his older brother the night before and tired over "domestic" life in the hotel suite they share, viciously grinds a grapefruit half in Kitty's face.

The ending of *The Public Enemy* remains one of the starkest in American movie history. Kidnapped from a hospital by a rival gang, Tom is held hostage off screen. A phone call to his brother Mike raises hope that Tom may be released. While Tom's mother happily makes up Tom's room in anticipation of her child's return, Mike answers the doorbell. When he opens the door, we see the corpse of Tom Powers, wrapped like a mummy, his dead eyes staring at us. Tom's body falls to the floor inside the house, and the movie ends with an epilog reminding the viewers that crime doesn't pay.

Gangster movies like *The Public Enemy* became a particular target of those who feared for the negative influences of the movies on young people and those seen as "less educated," even though the vogue of the classic gangster movie lasted less than five years. More than simply the explicit representation of violence, heightened by the use of sound, gangster movies may have been seen as especially threatening because they presented a kind of dark side of the American dream. American movies in the gangster tradition, from *The Public Enemy* through *The Godfather* (Coppola 1972) to *American Gangster* (Scott 2007) and even cinematic television series such as *The Wire* or *Breaking Bad*, present us with characters intent on getting ahead and rising above the restrictive circumstances of their upbringing, characters who understand that money and power can equal status and respectability, no matter where that money and power come from.

A ten-year-old Martin Luther King, Jr., dressed as a plantation field hand, sings in a black Baptist choir at the Atlanta premiere of *Gone with the Wind*, December 14, 1939

Many of the invitees attending the lavish ball thrown by the Junior League of Atlanta as part of a three-day celebration of the premiere of *Gone with the Wind* had come in costume as members of the pre-Civil War slave-owning planter class that formed the focus of what was the greatest, most expensive Hollywood spectacle yet. The event was attended by hundreds of Atlanta's most prosperous citizens, and like virtually all events in the South in 1939, the ball was whites only. The only people of color present worked as employees, serving food and drinks and tending to the needs of the partygoers.

As part of the celebration of plantation culture, ball organizers had asked the Reverend Martin Luther King, Sr., pastor of the all-black Ebenezer Street Baptist Church, to provide a choir of young boys to sing slave songs and spirituals while also dressed in period costume as enslaved field workers. Little did those indulging in a romantic fantasy of the slave-owning past realize that one of the young singers in that choir, the ten-year-old pastor's son Martin Luther King, Jr., would be the key leader of the civil rights movement that would forever undermine their world of racial privilege.

The astonishing historical irony of one of the greatest figures of the twentieth century playing an enslaved field worker at the premiere of the most successful and iconic movie of the studio era underlines the enduring complexity of *Gone with the Wind* as an American screen experience. As with *The Birth of a Nation* a generation earlier, the movie served and still serves as a focal point for the contradictions and injustices centered on constructions of race and gender on the screen and in American society.

Fig 4.2
The ten-year-old Martin Luther King, Jr. is part of the choir dressed as field hands and performing at the Junior League ball the night before the premiere of *Gone with the Wind* in Atlanta. Source: George Karger/Getty Images.

Fig 4.3
Vivien Leigh as Scarlett
O'Hara and Clark Gable
as Rhett Butler in *Gone
with the Wind*, one of the
most successful movies of
all time, a classic example
of the studios era, and
another example of the
complicated and troubling
representation of race in
American cinema history.

When *Gone with the Wind* premiered in Atlanta two weeks before Christmas in 1939, it was the most expensive Hollywood movie ever made and one of the great gambles in movie history. *Gone with the Wind*, the only novel every published by the former Atlanta journalist Margaret Mitchell, was a surprise publishing sensation in 1936, winning the Pulitzer Prize for fiction and setting its own sales records. In bringing the official premiere to Atlanta, the legendary producer David O. Selznick banked on the popularity of the novel in the white South. Many of these readers saw Mitchell's novel as redemption for the defeat of the Confederacy, a fictional affirmation of the suffering and resilience of the white South.

Not all the stars of the movie were present at the premiere, however. Noticeably absent were the African American actors in the movie, most significantly Hattie McDaniels, who won an Academy Award (the first given to a black actor) for her portrayal of the main character Scarlett O'Hara's slave "Mammy," as well as Butterfly McQueen, who played another house slave "Prissy," and Oscar Polk, who played the slave "Polk." The Loew's Grand Theatre in Atlanta was strictly segregated, and while these actors would have been allowed to appear on stage as part of the acting company, they could not have entered the theater through the main entrance nor have sat in the audience. Neither could they have stayed in the same hotel with their white co-stars or attended the Junior League ball. Even when McDaniels won the first Oscar ever for a black actor in 1940, she still had to sit at a separate table apart from her co-stars at the awards ceremony in Los Angeles.

Gone with the Wind, like *The Birth of a Nation* before it, remains a lightning rod. Once again, the screen experience of the movies made visible and amplified questions of representation in relation to race, ethnicity, and gender. The diversity of reactions to *Gone with the Wind* since its 1939 premiere speaks to the diversity of screen experiences represented by those reactions. For some, issues of race and history dominate their experience of the movie. Other viewers identify strongly with the story of the main character, the prototypical Southern belle Scarlett O'Hara, admiring her as a rebellious, even radical character. These different screen experiences stem in complex ways from the different cultural and social experiences we all bring to the movies; one of the reasons to study and discuss the movies is to explore the screen experiences of others and how they cause us to reflect on how we understand our own experiences.

A Saturday afternoon matinee, 1943

For millions of Americans in the 1930s and 1940s, especially children and young people, Saturdays meant one thing: spending hours and hours in the dark of a movie theater, watching a matinee program. It's hard to imagine today what a dominant media presence the movies were in the early sound screen age, the era often called the "Golden Age" of Hollywood. Scholars estimate that in 1930 almost 70 percent of the population of the United States went to the movies at least once a week; by the late 1940s, that percentage was still well above 60 percent.

Nowadays, we tend to think of "going to the movies" more in terms of "going to the movie"; we go to see a single movie, and we tend to be very deliberate about what we want to see. The Saturday afternoon screen experience of the 1940s, however, was closer to channel or web surfing, turning on the television at random or flipping through our smart phone apps to see if we can find anything interesting. To be sure, matinee attenders had their favorites, and a popular star or movie series could definitely boost attendance, but the habit of going to the Saturday afternoon matinee was also a social experience. Those Saturday afternoons in the dark were a chance to spend time with friends and family, an inexpensive way to be entertained and catch up on the news of the day while munching on hot dogs, popcorn, and candy, and even a way to escape the heat of summer or the cold of winter.

What was the screen experience of the Saturday afternoon matinee like? If you were a child, you might show up at noon at one of dozens of downtown theaters in a big city or the local small town movie house with your ten-cent admission price. For that dime, you might spend the next four or five hours at the movies, watching a variety of films. The afternoon might start by looking ahead to next week with a series of Coming Attraction trailers, followed by a newsreel, followed by any number of short subjects. Filmed musical performances, a staple of the transition to sound in the movies, were early examples of what became music videos forty years later (there was even the invention of the "Panoram," a jukebox that played 16-millimeter musical shorts). Just as in the silent era, short comedies were a crucial part of the matinee program, featuring more well-known movie comedians such as Laurel and Hardy or Abbott and Costello or less well-known names (to us, not to the 1940s audience) like George O'Hanlon.

Cartoons were another staple of the matinees. As we will see below, the sound era created a boom in the development of movie animation, led by Walt Disney, the Fleischer brothers, and Leon Schlesinger, whose animation company became the basis of the famed Looney Tunes/Merrie Melodies cartoon unit at Warner Brothers. Matinee goers would look forward to the mix of slapstick, social satire, and surrealism that defined cartoons featuring Bugs Bunny, Daffy Duck, and other Warner characters (as well as modern television animated series such as *The Simpsons*, *South Park*, and *Family Guy*).

Fig 4.4
Clarence "Buster" Crabbe starring as Flash Gordon, space adventurer and one of the most popular serial comic strip adaptations. Crabbe was an Olympian champion swimmer who made the transition to the movies. He was well-known for appearing as Gordon, another comic strip space adventurer named Buck Rodgers, as well as Tarzan.

No matinee would be complete without showing the latest installment of a popular serial. Serials – a long-running adventure story told in weekly twenty-minute episodes – date back to the late nickelodeon age as exemplified by *The Perils of Pauline*, a 1914 serial starring Pearl White as the title character who found herself threatened by a variety of evildoers, with most episodes ending in a "cliffhanger" involving the hero facing certain death (such as hanging off of a cliff), requiring viewers to come back next week to find out what happened. If this format also sounds familiar, it is because it has endured as a key feature of narrative screen experiences, even more so in the current age of television dramas, where the term "spoiler alert" tells us that we still enjoy the suspense and continuity of the serials. The serials in a 1940s matinee would represent a wide variety of genres, and they were often made by smaller independent studios. Westerns, crime stories, science fiction – all were popular serial subjects, as were the then new medium of comic books. Perhaps no aspect of 1940s screen experiences would be more familiar to the contemporary multiplex-goer than posters advertising the adventures of Superman, Batman, the Green Hornet, Captain America, and others.

Although rarely featured prominently in overviews of American movie history, movie serials created immense affection and loyalty in their audiences, and their influence is everywhere in the screen ages of America cinema, from the homage/parody of both the *Star Wars* and various Indiana Jones movies to the aforementioned renaissance of superhero and comic book movies over the last twenty years. With the advent of television in the late 1940s, much of the Saturday afternoon matinee experience moved from the public to the private, as people gathered around their television sets and Saturday morning cartoons became a staple of young television viewers. As a result, the tradition of the Saturday matinee disappeared.

Screen ages

The movies in Depression-era America

The collapse of the stock market in 1929 brought economic devastation and record unemployment to the United States, creating the greatest social crisis since the Civil War. With almost one-quarter of the nation out of work, millions turned to the screen experiences of the movies for both escape and a way of making sense of the catastrophe that had occurred. The Depression arrived with the advent of sound, just when theaters needed to invest in installing the equipment they would need to show sound movies. The expense involved was too much for many independent theaters, but the larger studios were able to more readily finance the conversion of their own theater chains. The Depression would not spare the motion picture industry – almost every major studio with the exception of MGM would face economic difficulties and even bankruptcy – but it also had the effect of strengthening the position of the major studios, leading to what many call the "Golden Age" of the studio system over the next 15 years.

The studio system represented the latest effort of major movie producers to impose financial order and predictability on the expensive and inherently unpredictable business of making movies. Why have so many seen this particular screen era as a "Golden Age"? There are many reasons. For one, the movies, understood as the experience of buying a ticket at a local theater to watch a movie on a large screen, enjoyed their greatest period of media dominance from 1930 to just after World War II. While radio rapidly became a fixture in American homes during this time as well, other forms of visual entertainment such as vaudeville were in rapid decline. Television was still in its experimental stages, and while the movies were also the dominant media during the 1920s, the coming of sound and the development and increasing use of Technicolor film signaled what seemed like the final maturation of the movies as an art form.

The 1930s and 1940s also saw the widespread dominance of what the film scholars David Bordwell, Janet Staiger, and Kristin Thompson call the "classical" style of American filmmaking, featuring linear narratives focusing on the story of a main protagonist, continuity editing, and an emphasis on clarity and transparency in storytelling. In many ways, the classical style of screen narratives remains the dominant method of storytelling to this day, even as we have seen the recent development of less linear and focused forms of storytelling such as the multiple narrative story.

The idea of a "Golden Age" was also heavily promoted by the movie industry itself, as the star system achieved even greater prominence and studio publicity increasingly pushed the idea that the movies had transcended mere entertainment to become a defining feature of American culture. Around the world, the concepts of "America" and "Hollywood" became synonymous, as American movies circulated around the world and helped create their own mythology about the United States. Movie advertising would refer to "motion picture history" and the idea of movies as historical events, a form of rhetoric in keeping with the creation of the Academy Awards in the late 1920s. Studios focused on producing "prestige" pictures, often based on historical events, Broadway plays, and, as in the case with *Gone with the Wind*, literary works.

At the same time, the movies remained a popular and populist medium, always eager to provide a wide range of screen experiences to meet the demands of ticket buyers. While a prestige picture such as *Gone with the Wind* may have been the biggest box office success in the period (and in the history of American movies), some of the most popular stars of the era were young actors such as Shirley Temple, one of the top draws of the 1930s after becoming a star at age six with her appearance in *Bright Eyes* (David Butler 1934), Mickey Rooney (17 when he began to star in the popular series of *Andy Hardy* movies about the life of a "typical" American teenager), and Judy Garland, just 16 when she starred in *The Wizard of Oz* (Victor Fleming 1939). Throughout the 1930s and 1940s, comedians such as Will Rogers, the Marx Brothers, Bob Hope, and Abbott and Costello defined the mainstream American screen experience as much as those movies nominated for Academy Awards.

The studio system

The studio system brought the logic of factory production and monopoly capitalism to the making of movies. By controlling the production, distribution, and exhibition of movies, the studio system allowed a small group of companies – famously, the "Big Five" of Metro Goldwyn Mayer, 20th Century Fox, Paramount, Warner Brothers, and RKO, and the "Little Three" of Columbia, Universal, and United Artists – to dominate the American movie business in the 1930s and 1940s. Still, the studio system itself represents only about 30 years out of the over 100-year-long history of commercial American cinema.

Studio system The dominant organization of the American movie industry from the early 1920s until the Paramount decision of 1946 based on vertical integration and a factory-based model of production. Under the studio system, each of the major production companies tried to control all aspects of the movie business, from the development of movie projects through writing, planning, shooting, and post production to distribution and exhibition. Workers of all kinds, including actors, technicians, writers, directors, and designers, would be signed to long-term contracts, allowing studio executives to assign them to various projects.

Ironically, as we will see in later chapters, it was the model used by United Artists, the smallest of the "Little Three," a studio with virtually no production facilities and few theaters, which operated by providing funding and distribution deals for independent producers, that has proved more in keeping with the way Hollywood has made movies since the end of the studio system. Still, even if the studio system itself is long gone, the tremendous output of movies created during the period ensures our continuing interest in and significance of the period. And the names of the great studios of the period live on as well, representing some of the most enduring brand names in American commercial history, even if those brands are component parts of the massive entertainment conglomerates we will study in Chapters 7 and 8.

Studio factories and house styles

Who is responsible for creating the screen experiences we call the movies? As we saw in Chapters 1 and 2, as the making of movies became more and more specialized, attention began to focus on the director as the key figure in shaping the movie. The rise of star directors such as D. W. Griffith gave further support to this idea, and the role of the director still holds prominent place in most critical discussion of the movies, as reflected in the academic convention of identifying films by director and year.

At the same time, the rise of the star system led to the identification of movies as a "Mary Pickford" or "Rudolph Valentino" picture. After all, the actors are the most visible members of the creative team behind every movie, and we still see movie performers rated on the basis of their box office drawing power, regardless of the director of their films. Studios from the beginning of the commercial movie industry also marketed their films on the basis of the studio identity, encouraging viewers to look for the Biograph or Famous Players-Lasky name as the surest guarantee of what to expect on screen.

The studios era traded on all three ways of identifying and marketing movies: as the work of unique directors; as star vehicles; and as studio brands. Given the effort of studios to control every aspect of the movie production process, movie fans, reviewers, and scholars began identifying particular "house styles" for each of the major studios. These house styles encompass almost every aspect of the screen experience, from the subject matter and genre to the overall "mise-en-scène" of a movie, the combination of setting, costuming, lighting, and acting that creates the overall "look" of a movie. Studios played off of these associations in marketing their movies in ways similar to how the equally burgeoning automobile companies would create their own brand identities, from the inexpensive everyday transportation associated with Ford to the luxury automobiles produced by Cadillac.

Overview of house styles: The Big Five

Metro Goldwyn Mayer: Glitz and glamor

Under the leadership of studio head Louis B. Mayer and production chief Irving Thalberg, MGM quickly established itself as the biggest and most glamorous of the Hollywood studios. It was the only major studio not to face an economic crisis in the early years of the Depression, and movie fans quickly learned to associate MGM with expensive production values and big name stars. At its height, MGM came close to releasing a new movie every week, suggesting the astounding productivity of

Big Five/Little Three
A reference to the eight major companies of the studios era. The Big Five – Metro Goldwyn Mayer (MGM), Paramount, 20th Century Fox, Warner Brothers, and RKO – all owned their own systems of production, distribution, and exhibition. By contrast, the Little Three – Universal, Columbia, and United Artists – did not own any theater chains, and United Artists did not even own a production facility. While their smaller holdings put them at a disadvantage during the studios era, the Little Three were much less affected by the results of the Paramount Decision than their Big Five counterparts.

Fig 4.5
Two of the most famous faces from 1930s American movies, Greta Garbo and John Barrymore in MGM's lavish *Grand Hotel*.

the major movie companies during the studios age. Although MGM's image as the dominant American studio diminished somewhat in the 1940s, it remained the most famous and profitable of the "Big Five."

A lavish production such as 1932's *Grand Hotel*, directed by Edmund Goulding, a big hit at the box office and the winner of the Academy Award for Best Picture, represents MGM at its showiest, taking full advantage of the studio's vast resources to create a screen experience meant to dazzle audiences with its production design and star power. The setting and the story were also in keeping with MGM's focus on "prestige" productions. The story is a melodrama about a motley collection of characters who all happen to gather at the Grand Hotel in Berlin, including a member of the aristocracy turned jewel thief (John Barrymore), a fatally ill accountant (Lionel Barrymore) looking to spend his final days in luxury, a world-weary and suicidal Russian ballerina (Greta Garbo), and a corrupt industrialist and former employer of the accountant (Wallace Beery) who hires an aspiring actor (Joan Crawford) to work as his secretary while he tries to land a big deal.

Over the course of the movie, the lives of these characters become increasingly interconnected: the aristocrat befriends the accountant and falls in love with the ballerina (after first stealing her jewelry); the accountant confronts his ex-boss; and the secretary takes pity on the dying accountant. The plot climaxes with a confrontation when the industrialist discovers the aristocrat trying to steal from him. After he kills the aristocrat, the industrialist is arrested, the secretary leaves with the accountant, and the ballerina plans to meet the aristocrat at the train station, a meeting we know tragically will never happen. In spite of the European setting, the narrative of *Grand Hotel* contains elements that would resonate with Depression audiences: a once-rich aristocrat reduced to poverty; a humble but honest accountant whose whole life had been controlled by a greedy businessman; and a young actress trying to get ahead, caught between the temptation of selling herself to a rich man or remaining true to her ideals.

Just as lavish and expensive as *The Grand Hotel* but with a story that managed to combine the deprivation of Depression-era America with the glamor of Hollywood, *The Wizard of Oz* (Victor Fleming 1939) became one of the most famous and influential American movies ever made. *The Wizard of Oz* also features elaborate sets, including Dorothy's poor Kansas farm, the land of the Munchkins, the city of Oz, and the Wicked Witch's castle. The movie includes state-of-the-art special effects such as the cyclone that whisks Dorothy and Toto to the land of Oz and skies full of flying monkeys. An early triumph for the Technicolor process, the movie famously switches from a two-color sepia-tone to spectacular full color when Dorothy steps from her transported farmhouse into Oz. *The Wizard of Oz* also confirmed MGM's reputation for musicals, as Harold Arlen's songs for the movie quickly became familiar standards, including the haunting *Over the Rainbow*, a song of longing for a better, brighter world far away from the cares of an America still recovering from economic disaster and worried over the outbreak of war in Europe.

Case study 4.1: *The Wizard of Oz* and the Great Depression

When many people think of their screen experiences of 1939's *The Wizard of Oz*, they recall its unforgettable songs, from "Over the Rainbow" to "Follow the Yellow Brick Road," or the comic performances of Ray Bolger, Jack Haley, and Bert Lahr as the Scarecrow, the Tin Man, and the Cowardly Lion, or Judy Garland's beautiful singing voice, or how terrified they were as children by the flying monkeys sent out by the Wicked Witch of the West. They are less likely to think of *The Wizard of Oz* as a Depression-era movie, one that appeared after almost ten years of severe economic hardship and social trauma. Yet *The Wizard of Oz* is just as much a product of the Depression as it is a classic movie musical, a magical fantasy, and a special effects spectacular.

As a way of exploring how the different ideas and perspectives we bring to screen experiences affect the ways we think and react to the movies, explore *The Wizard of Oz* with the Great Depression in mind. You might begin by working in groups to review what you already know and believe about the historical event of the Depression as well as what questions you still have about it. You can then do some further research to fill in the gaps or to determine how accurate your assumptions are. Then watch *The Wizard of Oz* and consider in what ways we can see the influence of the Depression on how the filmmakers adapted L. Frank Baum's classic children's novel, which had originally appeared in 1900 at the dawn of the movies.

Consider, for example, how 1939 audiences familiar with the Dust Bowl and the mass exodus of farmers and farmworkers from the Midwest in the Depression, the subject of another classic movie from the same period, *The Grapes of Wrath* (John Ford 1940), would view the situation on the Gale family farm. How might the most celebrated formal features of *The Wizard of Oz*, such as the change from sepia tone to Technicolor when Dorothy lands in Oz, likewise reflect Depression-era experiences? To what extent do we think viewers at the time experienced the movie as an escape from the difficult economic realities outside the theater, and to what extend does the movie reference those realities?

Fig 4.6
Contrasting screen experiences from *The Wizard of Oz*: Dorothy (Judy Garland) in Depression-era Kansas, and Dorothy heading off on the Yellow Brick Road.

Paramount Pictures: Polish and sophistication

After becoming one of the most important studios in the 1920s, Paramount Pictures was hit hard by the Depression and almost disappeared when it declared bankruptcy in 1935. Throughout its economic struggles, however, Paramount maintained its reputation for sophistication and artistic ambition built up during its founding as Famous Players in the silent era. Although all the studios hired filmmaking talent from Europe, especially as the rise of Nazism drove many artists from the continent, Paramount became particularly well-known for stars such as the great German actor Marlene Dietrich, the French musical comedy star Maurice Chevalier, and the directors Josef von Sternberg and Ernst Lubitsch.

No picture evoked Paramount's reputation for European sophistication more than Ernst Lubitsch's 1932 *Trouble in Paradise*. Like MGM's *Grand Hotel*, the movie is set among wealthy and glamorous Europeans, all living in Art Deco splendor and wearing expensive, stylish clothing. *Trouble in Paradise* likewise features a debonair jewel thief, a pair of them, in fact, played by Herbert Marshall and Miriam Hopkins. They fall in love and team up – outside the bounds of marriage – to steal a fortune from a wealthy perfume manufacturer played by Kay Francis. Unlike *Grand Hotel*, however, there is no final accounting of right and wrong, no tragic death of the handsome thief.

At the same time, *Trouble in Paradise*, like *Grand Hotel*, is very much a Depression-era movie. The carefree existence of the idle rich in the movie contrasts with the masquerade of the jewel thieves Gaston and Lily, whose lives are defined by the need to get money and the wide gap between those who have so much and everyone else. *Trouble in Paradise* is also seen as one of the first screwball comedies, a series of Depression-era romantic comedies usually set in the dream world of the ultra-rich and often involving a romance between a wealthy and not-so-wealthy character. Like *Trouble in Paradise*, these movies feature witty dialogue, an undertone of playful sexuality, and an incongruous mix of sophistication and crazy farce involving improbable plot developments, such as the search for a missing pet leopard in *Bringing Up Baby* (Howard Hawks 1938).

If Paramount sought to project a more tasteful elegance than its powerful rival MGM, the studio also built a reputation for comedy, producing the signature films by the anarchic vaudeville comedians the Marx Brothers, daring sex comedies by Mae West that furthered the calls for censorship that led to the adoption of the Production Code, and the absurd domestic satires of W. C. Fields. Paramount was also the home of Bob Hope, one of the biggest comic stars of the studios era and

Fig 4.7
Gaston and Lily, the glamorous jewel thieves played by Herbert Marshall and Miriam Hopkins in Ernst Lubitsch's sophisticated comedy *Trouble in Paradise*.

beyond. In the 1940s, Hope teamed with Bing Crosby, a major singing and acting star in his own right, in a series of World-War-II-era "road" pictures that featured the two stars along with recurring love interest Dorothy Lamour traveling the globe in a series of comic misadventures.

Warner Brothers: Gritty realism

The success of sound in the movies made Warner Brothers into a major studio, and the profits it made before the stock market crash allowed it to purchase theaters and smaller studios in order to compete with the likes of MGM and Universal. At first, Warner Brothers built on the musical formula established in *The Jazz Singer* to create one of the first and most enduring styles of movie musical: the backstage musical. Featuring the musical stars Dick Powell and Ruby Keeler, these musicals focused on the backstage life of the musical comedy theater, as groups of singers, dancers, directors, and producers overcame obstacles to put on the big show. Typically, the stories centered on an unknown performer who finally gets his or her big break and becomes a star. The premise of the backstage musical allowed filmmakers to exploit the new medium of sound with snappy theater slang backstage and elaborate production numbers on stage, many choreographed and directed by the legendary Busby Berkeley. The popularity of the backstage musical has waxed and waned over the years, but it remains an enduring genre, most recently resurfacing in the *High School Musical* television movies and the series *Glee*.

As the popularity of musicals began to fade in the early 1930s, Warner turned to urban crime pictures and gangster movies such as *The Public Enemy* that cemented its reputation for grit over glamor. Warner Brothers produced some of the most openly political movies of the 1930s as well, such as the pro-prison reform movie *I Am a Fugitive from a Chain Gang* (Mervyn LeRoy 1932). The film tells the story of a man, played by the Warner star Paul Muni, who is wrongly convicted of a crime and forced to endure the brutalities of forced labor prisons. After ten years he escapes, assumes a new identity, and rebuilds his life as a successful businessman, only to be exposed and re-imprisoned. Escaping again at the end, he finds no salvation, but is apparently doomed to a life on the run and in the shadows.

The reference to shadows also applies to the look, or mise-en-scène, of many Warner Brothers movies. As opposed to the glitz and gloss of MGM movies, many Warner Brothers movies offered screen experiences that featured a darker, more mysterious look. The movies associated with one of Warner's most distinctive stars, Humphrey Bogart, exemplify this trend. Bogart himself, with his trademark persona of the tough guy with the soul of a poet and features that deviated from the conventionally handsome, embodied an everyman anti-hero. In roles such as the

Fig 4.8
From left, Mary Astor, Humphrey Bogart, and Jerome Cowan in Warner Brother's gritty and stylish detective thriller *The Maltese Falcon*.

hard-boiled detective Sam Spade in the early film noir *The Maltese Falcon* (John Huston 1941), the cynical but sensitive saloon owner Rick in *Casablanca* (Michael Curtiz 1942), or the equally cynical but sensitive fishing boat owner Harry Morgan in Howard Hawks' 1944 adaptation of Ernest Hemingway's *To Have and Have Not*, Bogart projected complex heroes who were equal parts brave and brooding, world weary and idealistic.

Not all Warner Brothers movies fit the bill of a darker, grittier style. The studio also made a star out of the Australian actor Errol Flynn, who became the Douglas Fairbanks of the 1930s by appearing in swashbuckling romantic adventure movies such as the Technicolor *The Adventures of Robin Hood* (Michael Curtiz 1938). As we will explore further later in the chapter, Warner also developed one of the most famous and influential animation units in Hollywood, Looney Tunes/Merrie Melodies, whose cartoon shorts starring Bugs Bunny, Daffy Duck, and Porky Pig actually surpassed the popularity of Mickey Mouse in the early 1940s. Still, even these characters, especially the fast-talking Bugs Bunny with his accent straight from the streets of Brooklyn, offered a cheeky, more urban alternative to Disney.

20th Century Fox: All-American populism

The major studio known as 20th Century Fox emerged in 1935 as a merger between William Fox's Fox Film Corporation, a giant of the silent era, and Twentieth Century Pictures, an independent production company formed in 1933 by the star producer Darryl F. Zanuck after he left Warner Brothers. When Zanuck became production head of the newly merged studios, he moved aggressively to create a new house style for the studio that would build on the popularity of Fox's biggest stars at the time, the homespun comedian Will Rogers and the child star Shirley Temple. Zanuck himself labeled this style "hokum," meaning an appeal to old-fashioned, "middle American" values, movies that aimed at providing reassuring entertainment more than challenging art.

Will Rogers and Shirley Temple both exemplify different aspects of this approach. The Oklahoma-born Rogers had become a star on the vaudeville circuit, in silent movies, and as a newspaper and magazine columnist. His trademark western drawl and his carefully cultivated image of a simple yet insightful everyman, able to see through the cant and jargon of politics and business with a kind of genial, down home sarcasm that recalled Mark Twain, made him one of the most popular celebrities in the country and one of the biggest box office stars of the early 1930s for Fox Pictures before his tragic death in a plane crash in 1931. Temple, as we have seen, was part of a wave of child stars that emerged in the 1930s. She projected a cheerful pluck and precocious optimism that Depression-era audiences responded to. Her signature songs "On the Good Ship Lollipop" and "Animal Crackers" became huge hits, even as their overt cuteness quickly made them targets of parody.

The actors that Zanuck signed to the new studio, such as Don Ameche, Alice Faye, and Tyrone Power, were all likeable performers who fit in well with the studio's output of populist family fair. *In Old Chicago* (Henry King 1938), a historical melodrama centered on fictional events leading up to the Great Chicago Fire of 1871 and featuring all three performers, illustrates the Twentieth Century house style of the late 1930s, a style that made the studio one of the most successful of the studios era. Ameche plays Jack O'Leary, a lawyer and crusading reformer of the corrupt politics that govern Chicago. His brother Dion, played by Power, follows a different route, becoming a gambler and falling in with the corrupt political machine his

Fig 4.9
Tyrone Power and Alice
Faye face an uncertain
future after the Great
Chicago Fire with resolve
and determination in 20th
Century Fox's historical
melodrama *In Old Chicago*.

brother opposes. Faye plays Belle Fawcett, a saloon singer with a heart of gold who falls in love with Dion.

The conflict between the brothers reaches its climax during the fire, when Jack is killed trying to save the city and Dion and Belle emerge reformed and dedicated to rebuilding the great city. The movie was a huge hit and earned an Academy Award nomination for Best Picture. Telling the story of one of America's great cities through the lens of a love triangle and featuring a spectacular recreation of the fire, *In Old Chicago* fulfilled Zanuck's desire to provide screen experiences that reflected rather than challenged the beliefs and desires of its audiences. Nevertheless, the movie still deals with the themes of political corruption as well as the struggles of immigrant families to find their place in America.

Towards the end of the 1930s, 20th Century Fox embarked on a program of making more "serious," prestige pictures, including the work of one of the most celebrated of Hollywood directors, John Ford. In a career that spanned the silent era to the 1960s, Ford became most celebrated for his westerns, a genre he helped revive with his landmark 1939 movie *Stagecoach*, a film that also made a star of John Wayne, who went on to become the most iconic embodiment of "All-American" masculinity. *Stagecoach* was made through United Artists, but Ford also had a long career at Fox, where he was teamed up with an actor who projected a quieter, more subtle version of American masculinity than Wayne, Henry Fonda.

In films such as *Young Mr. Lincoln* (1939), *Drums Along the Mohawk* (1939), and perhaps most famously the screen adaptation of John Steinbeck's moving and radical novel about the plight of dispossessed Oklahoma farm workers during the Depression, *The Grapes of Wrath* (1940), Ford and Fonda teamed up to create screen experiences that raised the artistic reputation of Fox while still evoking the populist strain that defined the studio's style. For a studio that specialized in what Darryl F. Zanuck called "hokum," *The Grapes of Wrath* remains one of the most provocative movies of the studios era.

RKO: Variety and experimentation

The newest and smallest of the major studios in the studios era, RKO was a creation of the sound era. RKO, short for "Radio Keith Orpheum," was the result of a merger brought about by David Sarnoff, the head of the Radio Corporation of America, Joseph Kennedy, the owner of the Film Booking Offices of America studio and father of the future president John F. Kennedy, and the Keith-Albee-Orpheum chain of movie theaters. Although in almost constant financial trouble and turmoil, RKO became known for its innovation and experimentation, and the screen experiences created or distributed by RKO are among the most memorable and influential of the studios era.

Two examples from the 1930s illustrate this innovation and experimentation, the first having to do with the evolution of the movie musical. While working for RKO, David O. Selznick signed the Broadway dance star Fred Astaire to a contract. Working with the choreographer Hermes Pan, Astaire and his on-screen partner Ginger Rogers starred in ten movies together from 1933 to 1939, including classics such as *The Gay Divorcee* (Mark Sandrich 1934), *Top Hat* (Mark Sandrich 1935), *Swing Time* (George Stevens 1936), *Shall We Dance* (Mark Sandrich 1937), and their final RKO musical together *The Story of Vernon and Irene Castle* (H. C. Potter 1939). Unlike the swooping, multi-camera dance spectacles created by Busby Berkeley for Warner Brothers, Astaire insisted on an almost still camera, full body shots, and long takes that allowed viewers to focus on the dance and the intricate and subtle interplay between Astaire and Rogers on the dance floor. Rather than interruptions to the story, the dances in the Astaire/Rogers movies were incorporated into the plot as part of the romantic seduction between the two characters. For Depression-weary viewers, these musicals fashioned a screen fantasy of elegance, beauty, and an implied eroticism that made these movies irresistible and that avoided interference from censors.

While the Astaire/Rogers movies revolutionized dance in the movies – and were among the most popular movies of the decade – RKO was also the home of another equally revolutionary but quite different screen experience, *King Kong* (Merian C. Cooper 1933). A landmark in the history of horror and adventure movies, *King Kong* represented the most ambitious use to date of the animation technique of stop-motion photography. A gamble by RKO, *King Kong* became a box office hit and made the special-effects-driven monster movie into a Hollywood staple that continues into the twenty-first century, including Peter Jackson's 2005 remake.

At the same time RKO also had an active B movie production schedule. The term **"B" movie** derived from the common exhibition practice of the double feature, where a typical bill would feature a major production (or "A" movie) preceded by a smaller, less expensive, and usually less star-studded B movie. Perhaps the most celebrated "B" production unit at RKO was the horror unit run by the writer and producer Val Lewton in the 1940s. Although Universal Pictures was more well-known for horror, the movies produced by Lewton were revolutionary in their focus on mood and atmosphere over monsters and terror, a choice that proved both artistic and economical. *Cat People* from 1942, for example, featured a young immigrant Serbian woman who is cursed to turn into a deadly panther whenever

"B" movie The original use of the term "B" movie referred to the second, less heavily promoted part of a double feature, as opposed to the "A" movie, which was considered the main attraction. Over time, "B movie" came to indicate any lower budget movie, especially those associated with popular genres such as westerns, horror, crime movies, and teen pictures. Although the double feature disappeared as a regular part of mainstream movie exhibition in the late 1960s, the term "B movie" has persisted as a way of describing these movies.

Fig 4.10
Ginger Rogers and Fred Astaire in RKO's elegant *Top Hat*. The Astaire and Rogers musicals revolutionized the genre and expanded the possibilities for sound movies.

she is stirred by passionate love. Directed by the film noir master Jacques Tourneur, the movie builds more on the anxiety and fascination aroused in audiences by the combination of sexuality and the "exotic" appeal of the main character Irina, played by the French actor Simone Simon, than by scenes of a terrifying monster. In fact, the whole movie is told in shadows, and we only see glimpses of Irina in "Cat Person" form.

The "Little Three": Universal, Columbia, and United Artists

The so-called "Little Three" studios – Universal, Columbia, and United Artists – lacked the vertical integration that defined the Big Five. Neither Columbia nor Universal ever acquired extensive fleets of theaters, and United Artists even lacked an actual studio, having been created to give filmmakers and producers more independence in how they made movies. It is one of the ironies of the idea of the studios era as a "Golden Age," or model of how movies "should" be made, that the United Artist approach to making movies ultimately proved more enduring than the vertically integrated factory model.

Universal Pictures

During the 1930s and 1940s, Universal made mostly smaller, "B" type movies with a few, high profile exceptions, such as their production of the landmark Rogers and Hammerstein musical *Show Boat* (James Whale 1936). During the 1940s, Universal was also the home of the comedy team of Bud Abbott and Lou Costello, two of the most popular stars of the era. Universal did make its mark in the 1930s with a series of horror movies that helped define the genre as a staple of American cinema. Universal had begun to specialize in horror during the silent era with the films of Lon Chaney, known as the "man of a thousand faces" for his extreme uses of makeup and costuming in movies like *The Phantom of the Opera* (Rupert Julian 1925) and *The Hunchback of Notre Dame* (Wallace Worsley 1923). Chaney died at age 47 in 1930 just as the sound era was beginning, but the Laemmles continued the horror legacy at Universal with a series of "monster" movies that would both establish characters – such as Dracula, the Mummy, Frankenstein's monster, and the Wolf Man – that continue to this day as staples of American cinema, and many of the screen experiences that have become cliches of the genre, including the dark and spooky castle, fog-shrouded moonlit exteriors, creaking staircases, and an ominous use of light and shadow borrowed from German Expressionist filmmaking.

The directors Tod Browning (*Dracula* 1931 and *Freaks* 1932), James Whale (*Frankenstein* 1931, *The Old Dark House* 1932, *The Invisible Man* 1933, *Bride of Frankenstein* 1935), and Karl Freund (*The Mummy* 1932) brought artistic

Fig 4.11
Boris Karloff as the monster in James Whale's *Frankenstein*, one of Universal's landmark horror movies from the 1930s.

sensibilities to horror. The Frankenstein films of James Whale, in particular, one of the only openly gay filmmakers of the era, complicated the horror screen experience by creating sympathy for the creature created by the egomaniacal Dr. Frankenstein. In spite of the terrifying and by now iconic makeup worn by the British actor Boris Karloff, the actor and director evoked the creature's confusion, fear, and loneliness, a loneliness that became the central theme of *Bride of Frankenstein*. These movies helped support Universal financially during the studios era, and they remain among the most well-known Hollywood movies ever made.

Columbia Pictures

For all the stability that motion picture companies sought in the studios era through vertical integration and a contract-based, assembly line model of production, there was still a great deal of volatility when it came to the men (and it was always men) who ran the studios. Columbia Pictures was different. From 1918 when he started the company with his brother Jack to his death forty years later in 1958, Harry Cohn was in charge at Columbia Pictures, serving as both president and head of production from 1924. Notorious for his temper and his dictatorial managerial style, Cohn controlled Columbia more completely than any other studio executive.

Like Universal, Columbia lacked its own chain of theaters. Beginning in the silent era, Columbia focused on making modestly budgeted genre movies and serials, a practice that continued with the addition of sound in the studios era. Columbia took the lead in bringing popular comic strips and comic books such as Batman and Superman to movie screens in the form of popular serials. Columbia was also the home of the knockabout comedians the Three Stooges and distributed the early animated cartoons of Walt Disney.

The work of the director Frank Capra helped raise Columbia's prestige and profile in the studios era of the 1930s and 1940s. In 1934, Capra directed one of the first screwball comedies, *It Happened One Night*, starring Clark Gable and Claudette Colbert. The story of a rich young woman fleeing her father's plans to have her marry a man she doesn't love and the fast-talking newspaper reporter who tracks her down and then falls in love with her himself, *It Happened One Night* combined sexual and social class tension as Colbert's character of Ellie Andrews learns about men and women whose lives were turned upside down by the Depression, all the while offering a fantasy of romantic fulfillment to Depression-era audiences.

It Happened One Night was a runaway hit for Columbia and became the first movie to win all five of the major Academy Awards: Best Picture, Best Director, Best Actor, Best Actress, and Best Screenplay. Having a Columbia movie win Best Picture established the studio as one of the majors, and *It Happened One Night* likewise

Fig 4.12
The runaway heiress Ellie Andrews (Claudette Colbert) shows jaded newsman Peter Warne (Clark Gable) how to bum a ride in Frank Capra's popular and daring early screwball comedy *It Happened One Night*.

established the screwball comedy as a Columbia specialty. Movies such as *Twentieth Century* (Howard Hawks 1934), *The Awful Truth* (Leo McCarey 1937), *Holiday* (George Cukor 1938), and *His Girl Friday* (Hawks 1940) rank as prime examples of the genre and helped make stars out of actors such as Cary Grant, Carole Lombard, and Rosalind Russell.

It Happened One Night was also the beginning of a run of popular and critically acclaimed movies for Capra at Columbia, especially his work with the screenwriter Robert Riskin. While Capra would continue to make screwball comedies, his later movies with Riskin created Capra's enduring reputation as the maker of screen experiences that defined a powerful vision of American democratic values and ideals. His movies combined an enduring sense of optimism and hope with a darker sense of the fragility of the American dream, a powerful mix that spoke powerfully to a wide range of viewers in the Depression era and that led to the adjective "Capraesque" to describe movies with a similar outlook.

In movies like *Mr. Smith Goes to Washington* (1939), *Meet John Doe* (1941), and *Mr. Deeds Goes to Town* (1936), and even his later, non-Columbia and non-Riskin classic *It's a Wonderful Life* (1946), Capra continued to mix light and dark, cynicism and optimism in ways that has led generations of moviegoers to remember his movies as positive and life-affirming, even when his screen experiences feature moments of despair, desperation, and, in the case of *It's a Wonderful Life*, suicide.

United Artists

It's ironic that United Artists, the company started in the silent era by Mary Pickford, Douglas Fairbanks, D. W. Griffith, and Charlie Chaplin to give actors and directors greater control and independence in the movie industry, has often been overlooked in many histories of the studios era. Not only did United Artists produce successful and influential movies during the 1930s and 1940s, but the model of independent production that the company championed, a model in direct contrast to the factory-style vertical integration of the major studios of the period, has proved to be far more enduring. Lacking any production facilities or theater chains of their own, United Artists managed to hold its own in the studios era and continue on into the next decades, remaining a significant force in the evolution of American cinema until the early 1980s. Even today, the United Artists brand name continues, now as a subsidiary of MGM.

Working with independent producers such as David O. Selznick and Samuel Goldwyn, and acting as the American distributor for the British producer Alexander Korda, United Artists compiled an impressive record of prestigious movies. In 1940, in fact, four of the ten movies nominated for Outstanding Production, or Best Picture, were associated with United Artists. The list included the first two American productions by the man who would become perhaps the most famous director in movie history, Alfred Hitchcock: *Rebecca*, the winner of the Oscar that year, and *Foreign Correspondent*.

True to its origins, United Artists also released Charlie Chaplin's studios-era masterpieces, *City Lights* (1931), *Modern Times* (1936), a satire on the alienation of modern industrial capitalism in the Depression that represented Chaplin's first use of spoken sound in a movie, and *The Great Dictator* (1940, his first real talkie in which Chaplin ridiculed Adolf Hitler and the Nazi Party, one of the first American movies to attack Hitler so directly). The "house style" of United Artists during the studios era, in effect, was not based on a particular style or set of featured genres dictated by

Fig 4.13
The housekeeper Mrs. Danvers (Judith Anderson, left) menaces the character played by Joan Fontaine (known only as "Mrs. de Winter"), the young second wife of a wealthy man who still seems to yearn for his dead first wife Rebecca in *Rebecca*, the movie that helped establish Alfred Hitchcock's Hollywood career.

the top-down control of production that was the rule at the major studios. Instead, United Artists was a place where a variety of producers and directors could work on projects of individual meaning and significance, a tradition that we will see carried on into the 1950s, 1960s, and especially the 1970s.

Poverty Row and independent filmmaking

Even though most film histories and retrospectives of the studios era focus on the most prestigious, expensive, or award-winning studio productions, the fact is that the economic viability of Hollywood in the 1930s and early 1940s rested not on the success of the most famous movies of the time, not even the megahit *Gone with the Wind*. Instead, the movie industry depended on the steady and rapid production of hundreds of smaller, lower budget movies, ranging from the "B" movie production units at all the major studios to the output created by the dozens of smaller studios that defined American cinema in the studios era as much if not more so than the majors. These smaller studios are sometimes grouped together under the name "Poverty Row," a reference to the many studios and production facilities that existed and still exist along Gower Street in Hollywood. The name "Poverty Row" reflects the condescending attitudes of the major studios and obscures the diversity of filmmaking and film viewing experiences created by these smaller operations.

The term "poverty" in Poverty Row referred to the generally lower budgets that characterized the movies made by these smaller studios, but in fact many of these studios did very well financially, in part by sticking to reliably popular genres and storylines, working quickly and efficiently, and avoiding the gamble of making large investments in the big budget "A" pictures that defined the major studios. Actually, when it came to the largest of the "Poverty Row" studios such as Monogram Pictures or Republic Pictures, there was often not much difference in budget between their movies and the "B" pictures coming out of the major studios, and many actors and directors worked for both the majors and the smaller studios. Columbia Pictures began the studios era as one of these smaller studios, rising to the status of a major with the success of Frank Capra's movies. Occasionally, a star would emerge from one of these smaller studios to become a major Hollywood figure, as with John Wayne, who leveraged his work in dozens of Monogram and Republic westerns in the 1930s to achieve his big breakthrough in John Ford's 1939 *Stagecoach*.

Studios like Monogram and Republic represent the "high end" of the Poverty Row studios, but there were also many production companies that really did operate on shoestring budgets, sometimes existing for only a year or two before going under.

Poverty Row A reference to the dozens of smaller studios that flourished in Hollywood during the studios era, including long-standing companies such as Monogram and Republic Pictures but also many smaller "studios" that were constantly appearing and disappearing. Many of these studios were located on Gower Street in Hollywood, and they were responsible for the hundreds of lower budget "B" movies – westerns, crime movies, melodramas, and action movies – that were a major part of the screen experiences of Americans in the studios era.

Fig 4.14
A young John Wayne as Stony Brooke in Republic Picture's *Overland Stage Raiders* in 1938, a year before his breakthrough performance in John Ford's *Stagecoach*.

Like all the smaller studios, these outfits focused on making action-oriented movies and were less interested in matters of character development and transformation than the major studios. In many ways, these studios and the popularity of the screen experiences they created point to the enduring importance of the actuality and spectacle aspect of the movies, a quality that continues to this day in the contemporary action movie.

Smaller studios were also more capable of creating movies that spoke to the diversity of cultural, regional, and ethnic experiences in the United States. The economics of the major studios dictated that they strive for screen experiences that would attract the greatest range of viewers possible. This need to create a large audience is one reason that many of the major studio movies in the studios era self-consciously tried to define and speak to a central "all-American" experience, as in the series of Andy Hardy movies starring Mickey Rooney from MGM depicting what the studio presented as a "typical" American family, even though very few families at the time had fathers who were judges.

Smaller outfits, however, could cater material to smaller markets, such as movies with country settings and characters for rural viewers, or working-class urban characters. There were movie companies that created experiences for specific ethnic markets, such as Yiddish-language and Jewish-oriented movies and movies in Spanish. As we saw in the example of Oscar Micheaux, there was also a tradition of African American cinema in the studios era. While Micheaux represents an effort to create a black cinema run by African American artists, other small movie companies run by black and white filmmakers developed to create movies featuring black characters and stories set in an African American experience. Studios such as Million Dollar Productions produced a wide range of movies for a primarily black film market, providing an important counterpart to the white-dominated Hollywood system.

Hollywood and World War II

Throughout the late 1930s, as Adolf Hitler and the Nazis rose to power in Germany and war once again broke out in Europe, Hollywood was reluctant to reflect these frightening developments in the movies. There are several possible reasons for this reticence. Some scholars have suggested that the major studios did not want to jeopardize the German market for American movies, although that once lucrative market shrank drastically after the Nazis came to power. The fact is that many American corporations, not just the movie studios, were eager to maintain business relations with Germany even as the Nazi government began aggressively taking over neighboring countries and territories. Overt anti-Semitism among many corporate leaders, most notoriously exemplified by Henry Ford of the Ford Motor Company, even harbored sympathy for the racist aims of the Nazi regime. There was also a strong anti-war movement in the United States during the 1930s based on the horrors of World War I, and while many in these movements were motivated by a moral repugnance against the mass slaughter of modern warfare and the fact that the poor and working classes bore the brunt of the suffering, some also appealed to this same home-grown American anti-Semitic sentiment as well.

As a result of the volatile political climate surrounding possible American involvement in the war, many Hollywood executives were wary of how best to address the situation. Still, a few Hollywood movies did eventually begin to address the rise of fascism and anti-Semitism in Europe. In 1939 Warner Brothers released *Confessions of a Nazi Spy*, directed by Anatole Litvak, another refugee from Nazi Europe, and starring the major Jewish American movie star Edward G. Robinson. The movie touched on many controversial issues, including the efforts by the Nazi government to encourage support for the German government among the large communities of German Americans in the United States. The movie was a major worldwide hit and was banned in Germany and Italy. Chaplin's *The Great Dictator*, a comedy openly mocking Adolf Hitler and starring Chaplin in a dual role as the dictator Adenoid Hynkle and a Jewish barber who winds up trading places with Hynkel, was released the next year.

The bombing of Pearl Harbor and the US declaration of war against both the governments of Germany and Japan in December 1941 dramatically changed the situation, and for the rest of the war Hollywood played an active role in representing and justifying the allied war effort. The US government set up the Office of War Information to create official propaganda for both domestic and international

Fig 4.15
Using documentary footage, montage sequences, and animation, the *Why We Fight* series sought to justify the US involvement in World War II to the American public.

audiences, and Hollywood played a major role in this effort. Hollywood stars became actively involved in morale efforts such as the United Service Organization (USO), which put on traveling shows to entertain the troops, both in the United States and in Asia and Europe.

Perhaps the most famous example of cooperation between Hollywood and the Office of War Information was the *Why We Fight* series of documentaries directed by Frank Capra. These movies were originally directed at members of the military, providing the rationale for American involvement in World War II, but they were later released for exhibition to the general public. Capra was inspired to counter the efforts of the German propaganda filmmaker Leni Riefenstahl, whose *Triumph of the Will* (1935) presented Hitler as a heroic and even mythic figure. Capra made innovative use of this movie and other German propaganda documentaries to present the war as a contest between free and enslaved countries, erasing the significant cultural and historical differences between Nazi Germany and imperial Japan to present them as part of a common threat to democracy and freedom. The *Why We Fight* series also highlighted the heroic efforts of allies such as Great Britain and, most controversially, the Soviet Union in battling the Nazis.

The major studios also began turning out war movie after war movie, each contributing to the construction of popular narratives about what the war meant and the importance of American unity. In an era before television and the Internet, millions of Americans flocked to movie houses for information about the war effort. The war features created by the studios and featuring familiar stars blended with newsreel footage and documentaries such as *Why We Fight* to create powerful screen experiences and equally powerful propaganda messages. As we have seen, war has always played an important role in the development of American cinema, and World War II's arrival at the height of the studios era dramatically affected how the war entered popular consciousness. To this day, World War II remains a kind of template for how we understand armed conflict in both the real world and the reel world of the screen.

The trauma of war

None of the major studios were interested in releasing any movie that could be seen as anti-war (and thus anti-American), a contrast with a series of anti-war movies throughout the 1920s and 1930s such as *All Quiet on the Western Front* (Lewis Milestone 1930) or *The Big Parade* (King Vidor 1925) that dramatized the senseless slaughter of World War I. Nevertheless, in striving to provide powerful, emotional screen experiences dealing with World War II, the major studios inevitably created complex experiences that evoked the trauma and tragedy of war, in spite of their desire to raise morale and promote optimism about the war effort. This duality is most obvious in movies set on the battlefield, where the violent death of characters we have come to sympathize with can produce feelings of admiration and sorrow, inspiration and despair.

It is in movies set on the home front, however, that we find screen experiences that express the trauma of wartime America in unexpected ways. For many Americans and especially for many American GIs, the contrast between the brutality and utter devastation occurring in Europe and Asia and the relative peace and security of the American mainland could be confusing and disconcerting. The 1944 20th Century Fox movie *The Fighting Sullivans* (Lloyd Bacon) played off of this disconnection – and expressed the duality between promoting morale and acknowledging horrific loss – by dramatizing the true story of the five Sullivan brothers of Iowa, who all enlisted in the Navy in 1942 and insisted on serving together. When their cruiser the *USS Juneau* was sunk later that year, all five brothers were killed. The movie asks audiences to both admire the heroism of the Sullivans and to sympathize with the devastating loss visited on their parents and other family members.

Even in movies that seemed to have nothing explicitly to do with the war, strains of the conflict colored audiences' experience of the films. The glossy, gorgeous MGM musical *Meet Me in St. Louis* (1944) starring Judy Garland, for example, seems an obvious attempt to escape from the anxieties of wartime America by transporting viewers to a mythical version of turn-of-the-century St. Louis, where we watch a year in the life of the white middle-class Smiths, an idealized version of the American family. No major tragedy or conflict visits the Smith family; the major plot development turns on whether Mr. Smith will accept a lucrative transfer to New York or keep his family in St. Louis.

Even in this legendary example of the MGM movie musical, directed by the equally legendary Vincente Minnelli, overtones of the war seep through. For one, the depiction of such an idealized version of America fits in with the propaganda aims of the Office of War Information to emphasize, as the Capra documentaries state, "Why We Fight." Beyond that, there are darker moments in this bright Technicolor story that would connect with the fears and anxieties of the wartime audience. The youngest Smith family member, the precocious little girl Tootie (Margaret O'Brien), has a taste for the macabre, reveling in stories of murder and conducting funerals for her dolls who "die." The Halloween sequence, which involves Tootie taking part in a prank that she believes results in murder, is filmed almost in the style of a horror movie. And Tootie's Christmas-Eve despair at her family's impending move results in her destroying the family of snowmen (surrogates for the Smith family) they have in the yard. The fact that these incidents all involve the cute and comical Tootie indicates we are not to take them too seriously, but add a disturbing awareness of death and mortality to a story about American optimism and idealism.

In *The Best Years of Our Lives*, released just after the war in 1946, director and war veteran William Wyler dealt openly with the trauma of the war on American society. The movie depicts the experiences of three returning servicemen, each representing a different social class and different form of war trauma, from the middle-class banker Al Stephenson (Fredric March) to the working-class soda jerk Fred (Dana Andrews). Real-life war veteran Harold Russell, who lost both hands during the war and had never acted before, played Homer, who dramatizes the

Fig 4.16
Al Stephenson (Fredric March) embraces his wife Milly (Myrna Loy) after finally returning from war while their children – and by extension the audience – watch in William Wyler's *The Best Years of Our Lives*.

difficult transition of severely wounded veterans. Remarkably for a Hollywood movie, the film does not shy away from dealing with both the physical and psychological injuries of war, including what we would now call post-traumatic stress syndrome. The movie won the Academy Award for Best Picture, and Russell received an Oscar for Best Supporting Actor.

If *The Best Years of Our Lives* suggested an openness to screen experiences involving the difficulties of the post-war experience, the fate of John Huston's documentary *Let There Be Light* demonstrates that there were still limits to what the government was willing to let audiences see. An important feature film director of such movies as *The Maltese Falcon* (1941), Huston made *Let There Be Light* while serving in Army Signal Corps and for similar reasons as Frank Capra's *Why We Fight* series. The movie depicts the experiences of veterans receiving psychological treatment in American psychiatric hospitals, and while the film emphasizes how successful the treatments are, the visual experience of ex-GIs struggling with chronic psychological trauma was too much for the Army, which banned its release until the 1980s.

Censorship and the Production Code

The creation of the Motion Picture Producers and Distributors of America in the 1920s under the leadership of Will Hays represented the first industry-wide attempt at self-censorship. Hays' office at first issued a list of "Don'ts and Be Carefuls" created by a committee of studio executives to guide film production by the major studios. The list of eleven "Don'ts" forbade movies from dealing with a wide variety of situations, from nudity to drug trafficking to "miscegenation," or any hint of an interracial romantic or sexual relationship. The twenty-five "Be Carefuls" cautioned moviemakers to avoid "vulgarity and suggestiveness" and to use "good taste" in regard to an even more diverse collection of subjects, including the "technique of committing murder," "sedition," and "excessive or lustful kissing."

The Hays office tried to enforce this list using persuasion and suggestion, but the lack of adequate staffing and any real enforcement mechanism made strict implementation of these guidelines impossible. With the advent of sound, calls for censorship began to grow, led in particular by various Catholic organizations. Arguments about the need for movie censorship once again echoed very different assumptions about what constituted "American" values, the proper social role of the arts, and just who was buying tickets for the movie theaters.

For most movie producers, movies were entertainment mainly enjoyed by adults who were capable of making their own decisions about what movies to see or not see. For others, such as the prominent Catholic activist Father Daniel A. Lord, the proper moral education of moviegoers was paramount, especially children, meaning that every screen experience should be geared to viewers of any age. This dichotomy between the idea of different screen experiences for different audiences and the idea that all screen experiences should be appropriate for all audiences has remained a central issue in American culture to this day, whether those screens are in movie theaters, living rooms, or on our computers and smart phones.

Negotiations between the MPPDA, Father Lord, and the influential Catholic journalist Martin Quigley resulted in the Production Code of 1930, a set of rules and guidelines that would define mainstream American moviemaking for the next 30 years. The MPPDA dramatically ramped up the enforcement mechanism of the Code in 1934 when Hays appointed Joseph Breen to head the **Production Code**

The Production Code
The Production Code was created in 1930 by the Motion Picture Producers and Distributors of America (MPPDA) as a form of self-censorship in order to forestall efforts at local and national government censorship. The Code was a list of what could and couldn't be included in movies, focusing in particular on issues related to sexuality, crime, religion, race, and ethnicity.

The Production Code Administration (PCA)
The Production Code Administration was instituted in 1934 under the leadership of Joseph Breen to more forcefully apply the Production Code. From 1934 until 1968, almost every Hollywood movie had to be approved by the PCA.

Fig 4.17
Joseph Breen (center), the head of the Production Code Authority, the movies' chief censor. Source: Rex Hardy Jr./ Getty Images.

Administration (PCA), an office specifically charged with enforcing the Code. The MPPDA used the power of vertical integration to insist that all movies receive official approval from Breen's office in order to achieve wide distribution in the United States. Producers and directors had to submit scripts and finished movies to Breen's office for official approval. The change was significant enough that the sound age before 1934 is called the "pre-Code" era, even though the original version of the Code had been around since 1930.

The need to get PCA approval for new movie projects led to frequent negotiations between filmmakers and Breen's office, and often with Breen himself. References to sex and sexuality were especially problematic. The Code insisted that the "sanctity of the institution of marriage and the home shall be upheld. Pictures shall not infer that low forms of sex relationship are the accepted or common thing" and that "[a]dultery, sometimes necessary plot material, must not be explicitly treated, or justified, or presented attractively." Moviemakers would substitute ambiguous language and double entendres to hint at sexual relationships between characters.

Sharp cut-aways from characters beginning to kiss to what seems to be some unspecified amount of time later, characters retreating behind closed doors, waves crashing on a beach; all of these became visual clues to signify sexual activity. Each relied on the fact that whatever the explicit content of a movie, the real screen experience was occurring in the minds of the audience.

Many movie fans and even filmmakers have even expressed nostalgia for the age of the Production Code, enjoying the ingenuity and subtlety required to get around the censors and appreciating how many of these successful subterfuges actually created greater erotic curiosity in the audience than if activities had been represented more explicitly. But the Code also served to legislate prejudice and discrimination into the screen experiences of the studios era. As we noted above, prohibitions against "miscegenation" made racism an established part of the Code. The injunction against "sex perversion or any inference to it" was a deliberate effort to prevent the very portrayal of homosexuality on screen, let alone sympathetic treatment of the lives of gay men and lesbian women. Again, filmmakers still found ways to suggest a range of sexual orientations among characters in the studios era, but these strategies often relied on stereotype and prejudice themselves.

The Paramount Decision and the end of the studios era

The administration of President Franklin Roosevelt sued the movie industry in 1938 over the issue of vertical integration, focusing specifically on studio domination of the exhibition industry. From the point of view of the government, and the point of view of independent producers and independent theater owners as well, vertical integration amounted to monopoly control of the movie business by the major studios. Even though the majors worked out a temporary understanding with the government in 1940 as the case moved through the courts, most of them knew that it was only a matter of time before they would be forced to sell off their theater holdings and suffer a major blow to their bottom lines.

The end finally came in 1948, when the Supreme Court ruled against the studios in what is commonly known as the "**Paramount Decision**" (the official name of the lawsuit was *United States v. Paramount Pictures, Inc. et al.*). Over the next decade, the major studios had to divest themselves of their theater holdings. Theater owners and exhibitors could now negotiate on a movie-by-movie basis with distributors. In order to try to make up for lost revenues, the major studios began raising their rental fees to the theaters, making the theater owners even choosier in picking which movies to exhibit.

While the Paramount Decision was a major contributor to the end of the studios era in American cinema, it was only part of a collection of dramatic changes in American society and culture that followed the end of World War II in 1945. The return of thousands of men who had fought in the war created pressure on the economy and tension with the similarly large numbers of women who had experienced independence and a new sense of freedom when they had responded to the call to assume the jobs and social roles men had left when they entered the military, leading to the beginnings of the modern women's rights movement. Similarly, African American communities, particularly in the Jim Crow South, frustrated by the continuation of racism at home after helping defeat a racist regime in Europe, began the process of activism and organization that led to the civil rights movement.

At the same time, the GI Bill provided working-class veterans with access to higher education, transforming American culture. With Europe and much of Asia in ruins, America enjoyed an economic dominance that manifested itself in an exploding consumer culture, and millions of mostly white Americans began leaving the cities for home ownership in the suburbs. Most worryingly for the movie industry, television quickly moved from a novelty to a staple of the American home, creating new screen experiences and intense competition for movie theaters, as many families opted to stay at home at night rather than venture out to the movies.

Movie attendance began to drop dramatically after the war and after the Paramount Decision, fueling the latest round of concern that the movies were doomed. As we will see in the next chapter, the next screen age in America did not result in the end but the next transformation of the movies and of the diversity of screen experiences that defined what "the movies" would mean to the next generation of Americans. As the myth of the "Golden Age" of movies suggests, the

Paramount Decision
The 1949 US Supreme Court Decision that held the major studios in violation of antitrust law for their practice of trying to control the production, distribution, and exhibition of movies. As the result of the decision, officially known as *United States v. Paramount Pictures, Inc. et al.,* the studios had to begin the process of divesting themselves of the movie theaters they owned. The Paramount Decision was one key factor in the end of what was known as the studio system.

trauma of the end of the vertically integrated studio system resonated far beyond the end of the studios era. In reality, future screen ages would continue to reflect and shape the changing contours of American culture, and many more powerful, moving, and influential screen experiences were still to come.

In development

Genres of gender: Film noir, the hardboiled detective, and the femme fatale

In the last chapter, we explored popular genres of female identity in the movies such as the sexually exciting and dangerous vamp, the innocent but tough girl next door, and the ultra-modern, convention-defying flapper, and how they reflected conflicting and ambiguous ideas about the meaning of masculinity and femininity, what it means to be a man or a woman, in the volatile culture of the late 1910s and 1920s. As we move into the studios era after the Depression, we see the rise of tough guy characters like Tom Powers in *The Public Enemy* as well as a soft-spoken but morally dependable midwestern archetype embodied by actors such as Jimmy Stewart and Henry Fonda. In terms of genres of female identity, the girl next door continued in many of the roles Judy Garland played, while the flapper morphed into glamorous modern women such as the screwball comedy heroines played by Claudette Colbert and Katharine Hepburn.

By the end of World War II in the mid-1940s, however, a new genre of American crime film emerged dubbed **film noir** or "black film" that featured complex genres of both masculine and feminine gender identity, genres that combined aspects of many of these previous gender genres. Film noir had its roots in literature; specifically, the growing popularity in the 1920s and 1930s of what has come to be called "hardboiled" detective fiction by writers such as Raymond Chandler and Dashiell Hammett. These stories featured lone wolf detectives – most famously, Chandler's Phillip Marlowe and Hammett's Sam Spade – who looked at the world with a jaundiced eye. They saw through traditional pieties about truth, justice, and the American way; for them, American society was defined by economic exploitation, government corruption, human greed, and selfishness. While they investigated crimes and tried to solve murders, they seemed motivated less by a sense of achieving justice than in following their own personal codes of ethics and conduct.

Film noir provided screen experiences, both bleak and exciting, that operated as a "dark" undercurrent of the bright Hollywood ideal of always giving the audience a clear hero to root for and a happy ending. Most important for our understanding of the screen experience and construction of gender identity during the studios era, film noir created two genres of gender – the hardboiled male hero and the dangerous woman, or "**femme fatale**" – that embodied and expressed a range of larger social anxieties and experiences of World-War-II-era America. These include the changing roles of women during the war (as both individual experience and official government policy encouraged women to enter the paid workforce in large numbers, particularly in jobs that had been traditionally reserved for men such as factory work), the internalized trauma of World War II, and the continuing economic dislocation/reorganization that followed the end of the war.

In this context, the femme fatale emerged out of a combination of the vamp and the flapper as an expression of gender anxiety in a male-dominated culture. A figure of both attraction and condemnation, of excitement and danger, the femme fatale drew on very old binary views of women as either good or evil, "madonnas

Film noir Film noir, or "black film," refers to a series of American crime movies released primarily from the late 1940s through the early 1950s. Featuring gender genres such as the hardboiled male hero and the dangerous femme fatale, films noir were defined by a sense of pessimism, doom, and existential anxiety, telling stories of cynical, world-weary characters whose futile pursuit of sex, money, and power ends in defeat and tragedy. Film noir is equally known for its distinctive visual style and tone, featuring the dramatic use of shadows and fast-talking characters.

Femme fatale A genre of female performance most associated with film noir, the femme fatale refers to a beautiful and dangerous woman who uses her intelligence and sexual attraction to manipulate men in the pursuit of money and power. The femme fatale was both a negative stereotype and an intriguing figure in film noir. While femmes fatale were represented as heartless villains and usually met violent ends, they were also powerful and fascinating characters, symbols of both masculine anxiety and female assertiveness.

Fig 4.18
Barbara Stanwyck as
the classic femme fatale
Phyllis Dietrichson with
Fred MacMurray as
the doomed insurance
salesman Walter Neff in
Double Indemnity.

or whores," maternal figures of self-sacrifice and devotion or diabolical figures of sexual temptation and selfishness. Likewise, the hardboiled male anti-heroes of film noir also featured contradictions. They were both tough and vulnerable, cynical and romantic, men who wouldn't "play the sap" for anyone, as Sam Spade (played by Humphrey Bogart) puts it in *The Maltese Falcon* (John Huston 1941), yet who seem unable to resist the attractions of the femme fatale.

Classic film noirs such as *Double Indemnity* (Billy Wilder 1944), *Out of the Past* (Jacques Tourneur 1947), *The Postman Always Rings Twice* (Tay Garnett 1946), and *Murder, My Sweet* (Edward Dmytryk 1944) tell the same basic story over and over: a hardboiled, world-weary man, sometimes a detective, sometimes a criminal, sometimes, as in *Double Indemnity*, a bored insurance salesman looking for a big score, who meets and falls for a beautiful, sexually powerful woman who tries to use and betray him as part of a scheme involving murder and money. Whatever the particular circumstances, these movies end in failure and death, a conclusion mandated by the logic of film noir and the needs of the Production Code Authority, who would only authorize such stories of crime and sexual desire if all the characters were suitably punished in the end.

The femme fatale is at the same time a sexist figure used to condemn women's ambition and sexual independence but also a strong, powerful, intelligent character, one the audience is supposed to hate but whose very outrageousness also makes her a figure of fascination and even envy. When we consider the importance of women to the Hollywood movie audience and studio box office receipts, we can see the complicated ways the femme fatale would draw on the most conventional and also the most potentially subversive reactions from mainstream audiences. The success of movies like *Double Indemnity* suggest that a war-weary audience stripped of illusions about a quick or easy end to the conflicts overseas was ready for a story that suggested the futility of any human endeavor, especially if that story was told with glamorous movie stars and more than a hint of dark humor. Film noir and the femme fatale emerged at the end of the studios era following World War II, but both genres have remained with us and continue to influence our screen experiences, on both small screens and large.

Case study 4.2: The Production Code in action: The case of *Double Indemnity*

A *New York Times* story written by reporter Fred Stanley in 1944 proclaimed:

> Hollywood, according to present indications, will depend on so-called "red meat" stories of illicit romance and crime for a major share of its immediate non-war dramatic productions: The apparent trend toward such material, previously shunned for fear of censorship, is traced by observers to Paramount's successful treatment of the James M. Cain novel, "Double Indemnity," which was described by some producers as "an emancipation for Hollywood writing."[2]

Hollywood had been interested in making a movie version of James M. Cain's story about adultery, murder, sex, and betrayal since it had first appeared in 1938, but Joseph Breen himself, the head of the Production Code Administration, had warned the studios that his office would never approve such a sordid and immoral story.

Six years later, Paramount Studios and the director Billy Wilder were finally able to bring *Double Indemnity* to the screen, and the result was one of the most famous and influential film noirs in American movie history. How were Paramount and Wilder able to overcome Breen's objections and produce a movie that featured two main characters – a bored insurance salesman named Walter Neff (Fred MacMurray) and a dangerous woman named Phyllis Dietrichson (Barbara Stanwyck) – who conspire to murder her husband for the insurance money? How does the example of *Double Indemnity* help us understand how the Production Code worked in the studios era of American cinema?

You might begin by reviewing the Production Code and watching *Double Indemnity* for yourself, taking note of how well you think the movie follows or doesn't follow the Code. Choose particular scenes from the movie, such as the famous "speed limit" interchange between Phyllis and Walter early in the film, and write about how you think the scene shows the influence of the Production Code and the creativity of the filmmakers in working within the Code. Then take a look at contemporary newspaper and magazine reviews of *Double Indemnity* from 1944. How did critics at the time react to how Paramount and Wilder worked within – or against – the Code? Finally, you can do further research by reading what film scholars such as Sheri Chinen Biesen have written about *Double Indemnity* and the Production Code.

Animation in the studios era

The studios era has not only been known as the Golden Age of Hollywood; for animation fans, the studios era is also the Golden Age of cartoons. The introduction of sound and the vertical integration system of the studios era provided a fertile environment for the development of the cartoon short subject, and no figure was more central to animation in the studios era than Walt Disney. When Walt Disney Cartoons released *Steamboat Willie* in 1928, the seven-and-a-half-minute movie was significant as both one of the first successful examples of a synchronized sound cartoon but also as the debut of one of the most recognizable movie stars ever to come out of Hollywood: Mickey Mouse. We will look at the career of Walt Disney in more depth below, but *Steamboat Willie* and subsequent cartoon shorts in the 1930s featuring Mickey, Minnie Mouse, Goofy, Pluto, and Donald Duck established Disney's company as the leader in movie animation, a source of both widespread

Fig 4.19

Anarchic, irreverent, and wildly imaginative, the Looney Tunes/ Merrie Melodies cartoons from Warner Brothers challenged the idea of animation as an exclusively children's medium. Here, a cross-dressing Bugs Bunny along with the hapless anti-hero Daffy Duck frustrate the hunter Elmer Fudd in the classic *Rabbit Fire*.

influence and intense competition. The Disney studios were also a breeding ground for an entire generation of movie animators who went to work for other studios and production companies, including the studio that would come to rival Disney's as the most popular producer of cartoon shorts and as an equally important influence on American cinema, the Looney Tunes/Merrie Melodies cartoons created by Leon Schlesinger Studios under contract for Warner Brothers.

A comparison of Disney and Warner Brothers cartoons illustrates the range of animation in the studios era as well as how cartoon short subjects pushed the boundaries between the sophisticated and the naive, the adult and the childlike. The Disney cartoons self-consciously embraced an all-American ideal, an appeal to the mainstream that also sought to raise the cultural esteem of animation. Warner Brothers, on the other hand, especially due to the early influence of the animator Tex Avery, created its own set of anthropomorphic animal stars, starting with Porky Pig and including Sylvester the Cat, Daffy Duck, and the true rival to Mickey Mouse, the fast-talking rabbit Bugs Bunny, that embraced the comic anarchy of the Marx Brothers to create screen experiences that featured social satire and a wild visual style that pushed the edges of what was acceptable to include in a cartoon.

For all their differences, both Mickey and Bugs still share much in common. With his gloved hands, wide-eyed appearance, dark fur/skin, and debut as a musical figure, Mickey drew on the same minstrel and vaudeville traditions as movies like *The Jazz Singer*. Bugs wore gloves as well, and his fast-talking comic style similarly reflected popular vaudeville comedy styles. As Mickey's fame grew in the 1930s and 1940s, however, his character became more of a Harold Lloyd figure, a middle-class striver and home owner who was often the sensible center of the storm surrounded by the slapstick antics of other Disney characters, especially the irascible and hot-tempered Donald Duck, who was a first cousin to Warner's perpetual schemer and equally hot-tempered Daffy Duck.

Bugs, however, beginning with his debut at the start of World War II, remained a multi-ethnic hybrid, a cross between the trickster figure from West African folklore that had become a part of African American folklore and the smart street hustler associated with immigrant inner-city neighborhoods. While Mickey spoke in an androgynous high-pitched voice aimed at children, Bugs spoke with a definite working-class Brooklyn accent. Like Groucho Marx, Bugs was always creating trouble for the sake of creating trouble, and his frequent targets would be "respectable" members of society, as in his long-running battle with the middle-class hunter Elmer Fudd. Warner Brothers' cartoons were always more risqué and indulged in more sexual humor than Disney Studios', and to this day many fans of movie animation still see Looney Tunes/Merrie Melodies as primarily cartoons for grown-ups.

Disney and Warner were not the only important animation companies during the studios era. Max and Dave Fleischer's series of Popeye the Sailor Man and Betty Boop cartoons were as equally popular as Mickey Mouse throughout the 1930s, although Boop's sexy flapper character had to be tamed after the creation of the PCA in 1934. At MGM, pioneering animators Joseph Barbera and William Hanna created the Tom and Jerry series in 1940. Tex Avery was hired by MGM in 1942, bringing the style he had developed with him from Looney Tunes/Merrie Melodies, and evident in his series of surreal Droopy Dawg cartoons.

The names above and below the title

Orson Welles

When *Citizen Kane* premiered on May 1, 1941, just days before the twenty-sixth birthday of its co-writer, director, and star, Orson Welles, the movie had been hotly anticipated, but few would guess the critical fame the film would garner, including the reputation of "greatest American movie ever made." Audiences were drawn to the movie because of Welles' reputation as a "boy genius" in the New York theater world. His radio production of H. G. Wells' Martian invasion fantasy *The War of the Worlds* on the day before Halloween in 1938 had become a media sensation after it was reported that many listeners had been fooled by the format of Welles' adaptation, which took the form of a mock radio news broadcast. However true this

Fig 4.20
Orson Welles. Source: Donald Keyes/The Kobal Collection.

reaction was, the broadcast further cemented Welles' reputation as a showman and innovator.

But audiences might also have been drawn to *Citizen Kane* by the campaign of newspaper tycoon and media mogul William Randolph Hearst to sabotage Welles' film out of anger that Welles had based the title character of Charles Foster Kane – a charismatic, self-absorbed newspaper tycoon and media mogul whose desire for power and attention destroys those around him and ultimately his own empire – on Hearst himself. A furious Hearst tried to have the movie shut down, forbidding his impressive chain of newspapers from accepting any advertising for the movie and pressuring RKO as well as the other major studios to cancel the project. Hearst was even behind an effort, led by MGM studio head Louis B. Mayer, to acquire and destroy the negative of the movie.

This combination of talent and controversy, big studio ambitions and the contrarian spirit of an experimental artist, marked Welles' brilliant but frustrating Hollywood career. Welles is simultaneously a symbol of both the studio system and of rebellion against that system; *Citizen Kane* a testament to the artistic achievements of the studios era but also an anomaly that showed the limits of the big studios. Welles was part of a generation of directors who had themselves grown up with the movies. He was born the same year that *The Birth of a Nation* premiered, and the possibilities represented by the screen experience of the movies formed a part of his artistic imagination from the earliest age.

In *Kane*, Welles set out to push the edges of what had become the "normal" way to make movies, to create a screen experience that would cause audiences to reflect on just what it meant to watch a movie, on what a movie meant. Like his contemporary, the avant-garde filmmaker Maya Deren, Welles was not satisfied with what had emerged as the "classic" style of Hollywood filmmaking. With *Citizen Kane*, he found himself in a unique position to challenge the studio system status quo from within, using the resources and talent of RKO to create one of the most influential screen experiences in world cinema history.

It is the way that Welles tells the story of Charles Foster Kane that marks the movie as a remarkable kind of screen experience. Welles begins the story with Kane's death, shown in gothic horror style in his empty mansion, and the mystery surrounding his last word "Rosebud." We then see a newsreel obituary about Kane's life, essentially telling us about everything we are about to see in the movie, before we find ourselves in the screening room with the reporters who are putting the story together. From there we follow one of the reporters, a man named Jerry Thompson (whose face we never clearly see), as he visits different associates of Kane, each telling their version of Kane's life, offering multiple points of view and interpretations of Kane, none of them able to answer Thompson's main question, "What is the meaning of Rosebud?"

These multiple points of view are reinforced by the use of different moviemaking techniques that play with the audience's expectations of the screen experience of a mainstream Hollywood movie, including a soundtrack that features characters speaking over one another's lines and the use of dramatic and startling sound bridges, as when a screaming cockatoo marks the transition from Thompson's interview with Kane's butler into a flashback from the last days of Kane's marriage to Susan.

Most famous of all these strategies is the use of deep focus, a photographic technique using widescreen lenses that keep objects both near and far away from

Fig 4.21
Orson Welles as the
newspaper tycoon turned
gubernatorial candidate
Charles Foster Kane in
Citizen Kane, a screen
experience based on the
intersection of money,
power, and the media,
including the movies.

the camera in focus, creating an illusion of depth but also preventing us from having a single aspect of the scenes to concentrate on, encouraging us to look at the relationships among all the people within the frame. Neither Welles nor his gifted cinematographer Gregg Toland invented deep focus for *Citizen Kane*, but few movies have used it so persistently or creatively. From beginning to end (which of course is the beginning again, as we watch workmen throwing Kane's massive accumulation of possessions into an incinerator and finally discovering what "Rosebud" is, a discovery that still doesn't explain its ultimate meaning), *Citizen Kane* plays with our expectations about what a movie experience should be. If *Citizen Kane* is one of the most elaborate and expensive "experimental" movies ever made, it is also immensely entertaining, a product of Welles the showman, an expert amateur magician as well as a gifted director.

The remainder of Welles' career as a director is a story of perpetual struggles with studio control (often exacerbated by Welles' own stubbornness), but struggles that produced some of the most innovative screen experiences in American cinema. His follow-up movie for RKO, *The Magnificent Ambersons*, an adaptation of a novel about turn-of-the-century America by Booth Tarkington, was equally remarkable and equally fraught. From spy thrillers like *The Stranger* (1946) to adaptations of Shakespeare such as his *Macbeth* (1948) to influential film noirs like *The Lady from Shanghai* (1947), and his last movie made for a major Hollywood studio, the masterpiece noir *Touch of Evil* (1958), Welles did not have a large output as a movie director, but just about every movie he did manage to finish has become a critical touchstone.

Several of Welles' signature visual experiences have been imitated by many later directors, including the famous house of mirrors shoot-out sequence from *The Lady from Shanghai* and the long continuous tracking shot of over three minutes that begins *Touch of Evil*, as the camera swoops through a town on the US–Mexico border following both a car with a bomb in its trunk and the two lead characters. Welles also maintained a successful career as an actor in movies like *Jane Eyre* (Robert Stevenson 1943) and *The Third Man* (Carol Reed 1949), and in the last decades of his life he became a kind of television celebrity, making frequent appearances on talk shows until his death in 1985. A product of the studios era, Welles would also become a role model for the later generation of American filmmakers who created the "New Hollywood" of the 1970s as well as the contemporary generation of independent directors.

Walt Disney

Walt Disney had reason to be nervous in December 1937, as he waited for the Los Angeles premiere of *Snow White and the Seven Dwarfs*, the first ever feature-length animated movie in color. His Walt Disney Studio, the cartoon production company he had founded with his brother Roy, had been working on *Snow White* for three years. Many in Hollywood predicted the project would be a costly disaster. Although Mickey Mouse had become one of the most recognizable cultural figures in the world by that point, and Disney animated shorts were a runaway success, many doubted that a feature-length cartoon would ever generate the box office revenues to offset the production costs and lengthy, painstaking animation process. After all, would anyone other than children be interested in an elaborate presentation of a fairy tale?

Disney – and Hollywood – had their answer after the premiere. The invited audience gave the movie a standing ovation, and *Snow White and the Seven Dwarfs* became the most popular movie in American cinema history until *Gone with the Wind* two years later. *Snow White* showed that animation could be used to develop characters as complex and compelling as "live action" movies, and the songs from the movie would also become American standards. After *Snow White and the Seven Dwarfs*, the dominance of the Walt Disney Studio in the field of American animation was permanently established.

But the name of Disney, of course, goes beyond the world of cartoons. "Disney" today represents a global media empire encompassing movies, television, theme parks, and consumer products. Disney is arguably the most famous brand name in American cinema and represents the most powerful and influential production company to emerge from the studios era. Ironically, the Walt Disney Studio of the 1930s and 1940s is never counted among the "Big Five" or "Little Three" of the studios era, and in many ways Disney and the company he created was the model of things to come in the American movie and media industries. A product of the "Golden Age" of the studios era, Disney the man and the company more clearly

Fig 4.22
Walt Disney in 1936 posing with cels from his landmark animated feature *Snow White and the Seven Dwarfs*. Source: Walt Disney/The Kobal Collection.

Fig 4.23
Disney's *Snow White and the Seven Dwarfs* both raised expectations for the screen experience of animation and created an enduringly popular genre of American movies.

foreshadow our contemporary screen age of giant media conglomerates designing consumer-driven entertainment experiences that cross a wide variety of media than the vertical integration model of MGM or Paramount.

Walter Elias Disney was part of a generation of American illustrators and animators who arrived in Hollywood in the 1920s just as sound and Technicolor were about to revolutionize the screen experiences of the movies in ways that were especially conducive to cartooning. After moving to Los Angeles in the early 1920s. Disney found success with a number of popular series, including a series of shorts combining live action and animation and starring a little girl named Alice and Disney's first "star" cartoon character, Oswald the Lucky Rabbit. After losing ownership of the Oswald character to his distributor, Disney worked with fellow animation pioneer Ub Iwerks to create Mickey Mouse, the character that would bring fame to the Walt Disney Studio and eventually become Disney's main trademark.

Disney managed not only to found a successful animation company, he made himself into a brand, the name "Disney" becoming a powerful signifier over the last half century of a wide collection of entertainment experiences and consumer products. In the 1950s, the Walt Disney Studio began making live action features as well as animation, and Disney moved aggressively into television as well, beginning in 1954 with a program called *Disneyland* (before the creation of the theme park of the same name) and continuing in some form until the present. The premiere of *The Mickey Mouse Club* the next year, a live action program aimed at children, further cemented the Disney brand.

Over the rest of the century, Disney expanded into the theme park business with the opening of Disneyland in 1955 and Walt Disney World in 1971, each built around the images and screen experiences of Disney movies. In the 1980s, this comprehensive form of media capitalism became known as "synergy," combining movies, television, consumer products, and theme parks, and extending the screen experience into a larger total consumer experience and identity. This became widely imitated from the 1980s to the present, with Disney becoming one of the six major media empires that dominate the contemporary entertainment industry (and which we will learn more about in Chapter 7).

Walt Disney himself hosted his television show until his death in 1966, and the identity of the Disney company brand became intertwined with Disney himself. His signature became the logo for his company, and he projected an avuncular identity as the friendly "Uncle Walt," a symbol of middle-American wholesomeness, suggesting that Disney and the Disney company were solely motivated by the desire to spread happiness and wonder. But Disney was also a shrewd and even ruthless businessman. He strongly resisted efforts by the Screen Cartoonists Guild to organize animators at the Walt Disney Company. In the post-World War II Red Scare, Disney became involved in the anti-Communist Motion Picture Alliance for the Preservation of American Ideal, and he was one of the first witnesses to testify before the House Un-American Activities Committee in 1947, where he accused several of the strike organizers of being Communists.

It is a testimony to the strength of the corporate brand Disney created that almost half a century after his death from lung cancer in 1966, his name remains one of the most famous to emerge from the studios era and indeed from the entire history of American movies. Although animation continues to be regarded as an interesting offshoot of film history, the empire that Disney built from Mickey Mouse and *Snow White* suggests that the screen experience of animation may be more central to understanding the cultural and artistic importance of American movies than many imagine. To this day, animated features continue to be a major source of profit for Hollywood, and the advent of computer-generated imagery (CGI) has only further blurred the lines between live action and animation, between "reality" and "cartoons."

Dorothy Arzner

The careers of Alice Guy-Blaché, Lois Webber, Frances Marion, Mary Pickford, and others show how integral the work of women filmmakers was in the first four decades of American cinema, both behind and in front of the camera. With the rise of the vertically integrated studio system came a more rigid subdivision and hierarchy of labor in the making of movies. The result was a major step backward for women directors and producers. Women remained central to the screen experience of the movies as actors and performers, but in other areas they found themselves limited to jobs that came to be stereotyped as "feminine" such as costume design. Where a director like Lois Webber was once as well-known and influential a director as Cecil B. DeMille or D. W. Griffith, by the studios era and the supposed Golden Age of Hollywood, women were no longer in charge on the set in the major studios.

Dorothy Arzner remains the singular exception to this rule in the studios era, a women who directed some twenty movies between 1927 and 1943 for major studios like Paramount and RKO. As a result, and because there wouldn't be another

Fig 4.24
Dorothy Arzner. Source:
The Kobal Collection.

woman directing mainstream Hollywood movies until Ida Lupino in the 1950s, Arzner has become a touchstone for movie critics and historians interested in the relationship between gender and the shaping of our screen experiences. Since Arzner was the only woman directing major studio releases in the studios era, we can't really draw broad conclusions about how her work represents the perspective and attitudes of all women; but as a gay woman making movies in an industry dominated by men and in a culture still dominated by rigid gender roles, Arzner's work reminds us that questions of gender and sexuality form a part of all our screen experiences, particularly in relation to mainstream Hollywood filmmaking, where so many of the narratives focused on stories of romance, sex, marriage, and betrayal.

A native Californian born just before the turn of the century, Arzner grew up in Los Angeles as the movie industry moved west and the institution of Hollywood was born. She was initially interested in becoming a doctor, but in the late 1910s she decided on a career making movies and landed a job at Paramount. Following her work on one of the movies that made Rudolph Valentino an international superstar, the bullfighting melodrama *Blood and Sand* (Fred Niblo 1922), she became one of Paramount's most successful and in-demand editors, leverage she was able to draw on when she threatened to leave the studio unless they allowed her to direct.

Arzner herself always had to negotiate a balancing act in her career as a director in regards to gender. While in interviews she was always insistent that she considered herself a director rather than a woman director, this insistence also reflected her awareness that a woman director would always face greater skepticism than male directors would, and studios were never hesitant to publicize her gender as a way of gaining more press attention for the films she made. Indeed, Arzner's characteristically "masculine" style of dress can be read both as a statement of her lack of difference from her similarly dressed male counterparts and as an assertion of her difference as a lesbian artist who remained officially in the closet.

On the basis of her early success as a director, Paramount entrusted her with the studio's entry into the sound era with *The Wild Party* in 1929. The movie was doubly important for Paramount, because it was also the sound debut for one of their biggest stars and sex symbols, Clara Bow. *The Wild Party* proved a great success, and as in many of the melodramas from the studios era that would come to be designated as "women's pictures," *The Wild Party* contrasts the main character's heterosexual romantic relationship with the close bonds – both friendships and rivalries – that she forms with other women in the movie. As Arzner moved confidently into the sound era, her films would continue to feature this tension between romance and independence. Watching these movies, we find ourselves torn between the conflicted desires of the main characters, trying to imagine ways strong, independent women can negotiate between the demands of the conventional romance narrative and their ambitions to defy gender conventions and lead a new kind of life.

In *Christopher Strong* (1933), for example, Katharine Hepburn, in only her second movie role, plays the aristocratic Lady Cynthia Darrington, a free-thinking modern woman who has forsaken romance to pursue, like Amelia Earhart, a career as a daring aviator. Her downfall appears in the form of the title character, Christopher Strong (Colin Clive), a married Member of Parliament with whom she has her first love affair, and a man whose own daughter has an affair with a married man. At the end of the movie, Darrington finds out she is pregnant, and to save the reputation of her lover she deliberately crashes her plane, concealing her suicide as a tragic accident, thus defining her as a character who is both self-assertive

Fig 4.25
Judy (Maureen O'Hara) gets ready to question a burlesque theater audience, as well as those of us watching the movie, about the ethics of being a spectator in Dorothy Arzner's *Dance, Girl, Dance*.

and self-sacrificing, someone who boldly defies gender prejudices yet in the end is destroyed by those same prejudices.

Arzner's most famous film for modern scholars and students is *Dance, Girl, Dance* from 1940, starring Maureen O'Hara and Lucille Ball. While the movie was a commercial failure in its day (in part because RKO failed to promote it properly), it remains a fascinating document not only about the struggles of ambitious women in the 1940s but also about the role of women and gender in mass entertainment. Unlike *Christopher Strong, Dance, Girl, Dance* is a kind of screwball romantic comedy. O'Hara plays Judy, an aspiring ballerina, who becomes friends with Ball's Bubbles, a world-weary chorus dancer. A complicated romantic plot line ensues involving Judy, Bubbles, a troubled rich boy, and a famous ballet impresario named Steve played by Ralph Bellamy. All the while, Judy struggles to start a career as a "serious" dancer while Bubbles finds fame – and money – as a burlesque dancer, eventually offering Judy a role in her act to help her make money.

In the end, Judy gets the man (Steve) and her career, but not before a falling out with Bubbles over the troubled rich boy and an amazing scene where Judy finds herself heckled by the burlesque crowd for her balletic dancing and unwillingness to strip. About to flee the stage, Judy instead confronts the audience, especially the men, scornfully expressing her disgust over their spending 50 cents to stare at naked women. In criticizing the on-screen audience, Judy also speaks of course to the movie audience as well, and her proto-feminist speech strikes a serious note in what is supposedly a screwball comedy.

Arzner left studio filmmaking after 1943 for reasons that are still unclear. She continued as a filmmaker, producing movies for the army and later television commercials, and she joined the faculty of the film school at the University of California, Los Angeles, where she taught until her death in 1979. Because of the effort of feminist scholarship in the 1970s to recover the stories of important women artists from writers to painters to musicians to filmmakers, Arzner's career was rescued from obscurity. Her experiences as a director in the studios era define the possibilities and limited opportunities for women in the "Golden Age" of Hollywood, limitations that only underscore Arzner's dedication and achievement.

Notes

1   Andre Sennwald, "The Public Enemy," *The New York Times*, April 24, 1931.

2   Quoted in Sheri Chinen Biesen, "Censorship, Film Noir, and *Double Indemnity*," *Film and History: An Interdisciplinary Journal of Film and Television Studies*, Volume 25, Numbers 1–2, 1995, pp. 40–52.

Explore further

Affron, Charles and Mirella Jona Affron, *Best Years: Going to the Movies, 1945–1946*. New Brunswick, NJ: Rutgers University Press, 2009.

Balcerzak, Scott, *Buffoon Men: Classic Hollywood Comedians and Queered Masculinity*. Detroit: Wayne State University Press, 2013.

Black, Gregory D., *Hollywood Censored: Morality Codes, Catholics, and the Movies*. Cambridge/New York: Cambridge University Press, 1994.

Bordwell, David, Janet Staiger, and Kristin Thompson, *The Classical Hollywood Cinema: Film Style and Mode of Production to 1960*. New York: Columbia University Press, 1985.

Christensen, Jerome, *America's Corporate Art: The Studio Authorship of Hollywood Motion Pictures*. Stanford, CA: Stanford University Press, 2012.

Couvares, Francis G. (ed.), *Movie Censorship and American Culture*. Amherst: University of Massachusetts Press, 2006.

Crafton, Donald, *The Talkies: American Cinema's Transition to Sound, 1926–1931*. Berkeley: University of California Press, 1999.

Decherney, Peter, *Hollywood and the Culture Elite: How the Movies Became American*. New York: Columbia University Press, 2005.

Dixon, Wheeler Winston (ed.), *American Cinema of the 1940s: Themes and Variations*. New Brunswick, NJ: Rutgers University Press, 2006.

Doane, Mary Ann, *The Desire to Desire: The Woman's Film of the 1940s*. Bloomington: Indiana University Press, 1987.

Doherty, Thomas, *Pre-Code Hollywood: Sex, Immorality, and Insurrection in American Cinema, 1930–1934*. New York: Columbia University Press, 1999.

—— *Projections of War: Hollywood, American Culture, and World War II*. New York: Columbia University Press, 1993.

Gehring, Wes D., *Forties Film Funnymen: The Decade's Great Comedians at Work in the Shadow of War*. Jefferson, NC: McFarland & Co., 2010.

Gomery, Douglas, *The Hollywood Studio System*. New York: St. Martin's Press, 1986.

Hanson, Philip, *This Side of Despair: How the Movies and American Life Intersected During the Great Depression*. Madison, NJ: Fairleigh Dickinson University Press, 2008.

Horne, Gerald, *Class Struggle in Hollywood, 1930–1950: Moguls, Mobsters, Stars, Reds, and Trade Unionists*. Austin: University of Texas Press, 2001.

Jewell, Richard B., *The Golden Age of Cinema: Hollywood, 1929–1945*. Malden, MA: Blackwell Publishing, 2007.

Leff, Leonard J. and Jerold L. Simmons, *The Dame in the Kimono: Hollywood, Censorship, and the Production Code*. Lexington: University Press of Kentucky, 2001.

Mayne, Judith, *Directed by Dorothy Arzner*. Bloomington: Indiana University Press, 1994.

Polan, Dana, *Power and Paranoia: History, Narrative, and the American Cinema, 1940–1950*. New York: Columbia University Press, 1986.

Schatz, Thomas, *The Genius of the System: Hollywood Filmmaking in the Studio Era*. New York: Henry Holt, 1996.

Shindler, Colin, *Hollywood in Crisis: Cinema and American Society, 1929–1939*. London/New York: Routledge, 1996.

Siomopoulos, Anna, *Hollywood Melodrama and the New Deal: Public Daydreams*. London/New York: Routledge, 2012.

Staiger, Janet (ed.), *The Studio System*. New Brunswick: Rutgers University Press, 1995.

Walsh, Frank, *Sin and Censorship: The Catholic Church and the Motion Picture Industry*. New Haven: Yale University Press, 1996.

CHAPTER 5

Theaters, drive-ins, and living rooms: Changing screens, changing movies, 1949–1966

Now playing

The premiere of *The Ten Commandments* at the Criterion Theatre, New York City, November 8, 1956

When Cecil B. DeMille's epic movie *The Ten Commandments* opened in the 1,700-seat Criterion Theatre in New York City, a luxurious art deco movie palace built twenty years earlier at the height of the studios era, movie fans had been anticipating the film for almost four years. At $13 million, it was the most expensive Hollywood movie yet, and it featured a huge cast of stars, including Charlton Heston as Moses, Yul Brynner as the Pharaoh Rameses, and Anne Baxter as Nefertiti, as well as thousand of extras. Shot partly on location in Egypt, huge sets were built for the film and intensive research went into the art and costume design. The special effects created for the movie became legendary, particularly the parting of the Red Sea. *The Ten Commandments* became a massive hit, playing at the Criterion alone for a year and a half and becoming one of the most profitable Hollywood movies ever made.

The movie also exemplifies both the challenges and successes that mainstream Hollywood filmmaking faced in the 1950s and early 1960s. Its director and producer, Cecil B. DeMille, was one of Hollywood's pioneers who had become

Fig 5.1
Combining spectacular visual effects such as Moses parting the Red Sea with an overlay of religious piety, Cecil B. DeMille's *The Ten Commandments* defined the Hollywood blockbuster in the 1950s.

a master of the big screen epic, crafting screen experiences made to overwhelm audiences with the intensity of their visual spectacle, beginning with his first version of *The Ten Commandments* as a silent movie in 1923. The 1956 film was meant to remind viewers that when it came to lavish, dazzling screen experiences, no one could compete with Hollywood, the visual majesty of imperial Egypt depicted in *The Ten Commandments* affirming the power and majesty of Hollywood as well.

That audiences might need reminding of Hollywood's unmatched ability to create screen spectacles speaks to the insecurity the American movie industry was feeling in the 1950s. The Paramount Decision, forcing the major studios to divest themselves of their theater chains, likewise was forcing Hollywood to remake how it made movies. Television had in a short period of time become a fixture in the American home, offering "free" screen experiences right in one's living room. As more and more middle- and working-class families began leaving the cities for the houses in the suburbs, television seemed designed exactly for a more private, domestic way of living, especially when most movie theaters remained in urban downtown areas.

Faced with these new competitive pressures, especially the proliferation of the new screen experiences represented by television, Hollywood looked to diversify the kinds of screen experiences associated with the movies, particularly those experiences that emphasized the limitations of TV. Not only did *The Ten Commandments* feature a huge story on an epic scale, it was also filmed in VistaVision, one of several versions of widescreen filmmaking developed in the 1950s. Along with such innovations as CinemaScope, Todd A-O, and Cinerama, VistaVision was designed to expand the width of the motion picture image, creating a large rectangular "vista" like nothing

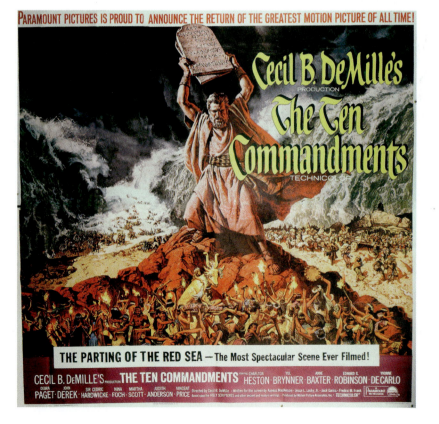

Fig 5.2
The lobby poster for this early re-release of *The Ten Commandments* emphasizes the movie's special effects, helping to draw a contrast with the small screen of television. Source: Paramount/The Kobal Collection.

that could be experienced on a television screen (or on most movie screens). Such innovation came at a cost; movie theaters wishing to show these new wide screen movies had to invest in bigger screens, new lenses, and, in the case of Cinerama, totally new projection equipment, an expense many theaters were unwilling to make.

The Ten Commandments was marketed as an "event" and exhibited as what came to be called a "road show" picture. Rather than playing on hundreds of screens across the country, a road show picture like *The Ten Commandments* only appeared in select movie theaters. Audiences attended these movies as they would a play, buying reserved seats in advance (at prices considerably higher than for regular movie admission) for one of the two daily showings. Not that there was time for more than two screenings: *The Ten Commandments* was 220 minutes long and included a ten-minute intermission. **Road show** movies like *The Ten Commandments*, *The Robe* (Henry Koster 1953), *Ben-Hur* (William Wyler 1959), *Around the World in 80 Days* (Michael Anderson 1956), or *Lawrence of Arabia* (David Lean 1962) continued until the early 1970s, when saturation booking – or flooding hundreds of theaters with the latest Hollywood blockbuster – became the norm for big budget movies. The idea of event movies emphasizing screen experiences unavailable at home has revived again in the digital era, with the screening of movies in 3D and IMAX at higher prices a regular feature of contemporary moviegoing.

With its biblical source material – filtered of course through the genres of romantic melodrama and action adventure movie – *The Ten Commandments* also played a role in Hollywood's ongoing project to stress the cultural importance and seriousness of the movies. In the case of the mid-1950s, the social and political pressures created by the anti-Communist government crackdown and the subsequent blacklist of suspected "subversives" in the movie industry (which we will learn more about below) led DeMille and Paramount Studios to describe the story of the exodus of Jewish slaves from bondage in ancient Egypt in terms of modern Cold War geopolitics. Since the end of World War II, international relations became increasingly described in terms of a confrontation between capitalism and communism centered on the struggle for global dominance and influence between the United States and the Union of Soviet Socialist Republics (USSR). After the lights dimmed on that autumn day in 1956, the audience at the Criterion Theatre saw another set of theater curtains projected on screen, from behind which Cecil B. DeMille himself emerged to explain that while the events in the movie had taken place thousands of years before, the real subtext was the conflict between the United States and the Soviet Union:

> The theme of this picture is whether men ought to be ruled by God's law or whether they are to be ruled by the whims of a dictator like Rameses. Are men the property of the state, or are they free souls under God? The same battle continues throughout the world today.

A showing of *Beach Party* at a drive-in theater, 1963

A line of cars idles on the side of a suburban road at twilight waiting for admission to a **drive-in theater**. Some of the cars carry entire families, both children and adults, including babies too young for a regular movie theater. Some of the younger children are wearing their pajamas, just in case they can't make it through the evening's entertainment. Other cars are filled with teenagers, excited by the chance to

Road show Refers to a form of exhibition that involves premiering a movie through a series of exclusive theatrical engagements featuring advance sale tickets at major cities across the country before opening the film in wider release. While the practice is as old as American cinema, the road show became a distinctive feature of the 1950s screen age, when Hollywood was seeking to maintain a competitive edge with television. Road show pictures such as *The Ten Commandments*, *Around the World in Eighty Days*, and *Ben-Hur* were usually lavish productions of over two hours in length, and during their road show tours they would often feature a musical overture and a ten-minute intermission.

Drive-in theater An outdoor movie theater where patrons would watch movies from their cars. Drive-ins became especially popular in America after World War II as more people moved to the suburbs and away from the city centers where most traditional movie theaters were located. Drive-ins became especially associated with youth culture, as teenagers and young adults were attracted to the convenience, economy, and privacy of the drive-in theater.

Fig 5.3
A drive-in movie theater in the 1950s. Source: Car Culture/Getty Images.

spend an evening out with their friends away from the prying eyes and ears of their parents; the single per car charge for admission is an added incentive as well, making the drive-in the cheapest ticket in town. Some vehicles have only two passengers, however; young people out on a date attracted by the cheap prices and the relative privacy of watching a movie from your car.

Once in the theater, the cars drive slowly over the raised berms and in between the rows of speaker stands, finally parking with the nose of the car raised toward the screen while the driver hangs the bulky speaker box on the car window. As the patrons wait for the sky to darken, they walk over to the concession stand for food, eat at picnic tables, or watch children play on swing sets and slides located underneath the looming outdoor screen. Finally it's showtime, and after jockeying for the best viewing position, everyone settles in to watch the movie, accompanied by the tinny sound from the speaker. If the weather is humid enough, someone in the front seat takes the responsibility to periodically wipe the condensation from the windshield.

Although the first drive-in movie theaters opened in the 1930s, the screen experience of the drive-in really came into its own in the 1950s and early 1960s. The popularity of the drive-in stemmed from several post-war developments: the movement of more and more families to suburban areas, where theaters were scarce but real estate plentiful; the growth of American car culture as part of the general consumer boom of the 1950s; the need to counter the competition of television with low-cost movie alternatives; and the rise in importance of the youth market and youth culture, especially as the first members of the post-war **baby boom** population began to reach driving age in the late 1950s.

The drive-in movie spoke to these issues by combining screen experiences. Like the interior of the car, the drive-in was both public and private, the car a kind of portable living room that provided the comfort of television viewing with the excitement of going out to the movies. For families with young children, drive-ins made it easy for everyone to go to the movies. For teenagers, the drive-in emphasized mobility and independence, as well the ability to be all alone in public. For that reason, drive-ins revived the old nickelodeon era concerns about the effect of dark theaters on young people, earning the nickname of "passion pits" for those patrons more interested in each other than what was playing on the screen. For all these reasons, drive-ins fit the era, and at their height they accounted for about one-quarter of all the movie screens in the USA.

The main feature on the screens this particular evening – *Beach Party* featuring the former star of the Mickey Mouse Club television show Annette Funicello and the teen pop music idol Frankie Avalon – also reflects the growing importance of the youth market to movies in the 1950s and 1960s as well as the move to independent production that marked this screen age. *Beach Party* was produced by American International Pictures, a small production company started in 1954 by James H. Nicholson and Samuel Z. Arkoff dedicated to making low budget movies aimed primarily at the teen market. These movies capitalized on the media fascination with and alarm over youth culture, from concerns about "juvenile delinquency" to changing sexual attitudes among young people, from the growing popularity of rock 'n' roll to the burgeoning civil rights movement. American International (AIP for short) also joined the wave of science fiction and monster movies that reflected Cold War anxieties over nuclear war and technology.

Sometimes, AIP would begin with a great title – such as *The Beast with 1,000,000 Eyes* (David Kramarsky 1954) – and would then build a movie to fit (sometimes very loosely) the title. With movies like *It Conquered the World* (Roger Corman 1956), *Shake, Rattle, and Rock!* (Edward L. Cahn 1956), *I Was a Teenage Werewolf* (Gene Fowler, Jr. 1957), and *The Amazing Colossal Man* (Bert I. Gordon 1957), AIP created a cult reputation for movies that might have been low on production values but were high on energy, imagination, and outrageousness. The legendary producer and director Roger Corman also helped turn AIP into a breeding ground for a generation of filmmakers who would go on to dominate serious American movies in the 1970s, including Martin Scorsese, Francis Ford Coppola, and Jonathan Demme.

Baby boom Refers to the generation of people born in the 18 or so years after World War II, from 1946 to 1964. This period marked a dramatic uptick in population growth in the 1950s as soldiers returned from the war and the US entered a period of relative economic prosperity.

Fig 5.4
The former Disney Mouseketeer Annette Funicello and the teen pop idol Frankie Avalon in *Beach Party*, a screen experience meant to appeal to as well as define youth culture in the early 1960s.

Fig 5.5
This poster advertising a double bill of *I Was a Teenage Werewolf* and *Dragstrip Girl* captures the low-budget excitement that American International Pictures targeted towards a mobile teenage audience. Source: AIP/The Kobal Collection.

Beach Party began the first of a series of surfing movies for AIP, films that featured teenage characters (even if the actors playing them were in their twenties) and fed into the early 1960s idea of California as a land of eternal sunshine and youthful optimism. The movies, including *Beach Blanket Bingo* (William Asher 1965) and *How to Stuff a Wild Bikini* (William Asher 1965) made a teen star of Funicello and walked a fine line between innocence and sexuality, between the promise of sexual pleasure and the ultimate reminder that Funicello, in the end, was always a "good girl." That both teens and families might be attracted to *Beach Party* also speaks to the last days of the Production Code and the idea that a movie should provide screen experiences appropriate for audiences of all ages. As we will see in the next chapter, by the end of the 1960s movies like *Beach Party* would come to seem quaint throwbacks to a more conformist era, even though that era was only a few years in the past.

With the rise of real estate values, uncertainty of weather conditions, and the emergence of cable television and VHS cassettes in the 1980s, the drive-in disappeared as an important form of screen experience, even though a few theaters remain in operation. Recently, however, the development of digital technology has created the "guerilla drive-in" movement, where just about anyone with a DVD player, digital projector, and low power FM transmitter can stage quick drive-in experiences anywhere there is an empty parking lot and a building with a large blank wall.

A television episode of *Alfred Hitchcock Presents*, January 3, 1960

When viewers at home turned on their television sets on the first Sunday night in January 1960, it took a little bit for the black and white cathode ray tube to warm up (and while color television had been officially introduced in the mid-1950s, the vast majority of television programming remained in black and white until the mid-1960s). They then saw a familiar, simple line drawing profile of arguably the most famous movie director in the world. To the eerie carnival-like strains of Charles

Fig 5.6
The iconic silhouette of Alfred Hitchcock opened each episode of his *Alfred Hitchcock Presents* television series, cementing his image as the most famous movie director in the world.

Fig 5.7
A future superstar of American movies, Steve McQueen (left) with a legendary star from Hollywood's studios era, Peter Lorre (ominously holding a meat cleaver) in a scene from "The Man from the South," an adaptation of a Roald Dahl short story on *Alfred Hitchcock Presents*.

Gounod's *Funeral March of a Marionette*, the director himself walked into the frame, matching his profile to the drawing (itself a creation of the director). This is how every half-hour episode of *Alfred Hitchcock Presents* (later expanded to *The Alfred Hitchcock Hour*) began. Hitchcock would provide an introduction and coda to each episode, on this night standing in front of a horse betting window to introduce a story about a strange wager called "Man from the South," starring Peter Lorre, a classic actor from the Golden Age of Hollywood, and the young Steve McQueen, a rising star who would become one of the most famous movie stars in the world just a few years later.

Why discuss a television show in a book about American movies? Wasn't television the major competition for movies after World War II? The answer to both questions is that television was equally a competitor and a collaborator with the movie industry in the 1950s and early 1960s, just as it is today. After all, the screen experience of early television was modeled in many ways on the movies. Most television screens of the time deliberately shared the same aspect ratio (the relation of length to width) most commonly used by the movies in the studios era, the screen experiences Americans were most familiar with. In the early twenty-first century, we find the lines between "television" and "movies" blurring even more as our screen options continue to expand, but from the beginning television represented as much an opportunity as a threat to the movies.

For one thing, the explosive growth in television sales and broadcasting in the 1950s and 1960s led to a huge demand for programming. As traditional movie attendance decreased in this screen age, both independent production companies and the major studios turned to creating material – including *Alfred Hitchcock*

Fig 5.8
TV as a member of
the family. This image
from 1957 promotes a
suburban American ideal
of a self-contained nuclear
family gathered around
the television set. Source:
Lambert/Getty Images.

Presents – for television. Overall movie production may have decreased after World
War II, but movie production facilities and personnel were turned toward providing
the programs, from westerns to situation comedies to police procedurals, that were
coming to define the television screen experience. Writers, actors, set designers,
costumers, all were happy for the steady work that television provided.

As television stations looked for more ways to fill their airtime, Hollywood
possessed a wealth of material in their vast storehouses of movies. Movies from the
first two decades of sound film, deemed too "old" for theatrical re-release, found
new life on television, as studios beginning with the failing RKO in 1955 began
contracting with television broadcasters for the rights to exhibit these older films. In
this way, you could say the movies provided competition with themselves, as viewers
could choose between a new movie at the local theater or watching an older film at
home.

To be sure, 1950s television provided a very different screen experience for these
movies than when they were originally shown in theaters. The small screen sizes
and poor visual resolution of early television lowered the level of detail visible and
shrank images from larger than life to smaller than life. Still, the flood of older
movies on television beginning in the mid-1950s provided unprecedented access to
movie history for millions of people and undoubtedly saved scores of films from
being discarded or lost. For generations of movie lovers (including the writer of this
book), television became a kind of do-it-yourself film school, allowing landmark
movies such as *Citizen Kane* to acquire a long-term critical acclaim after years away
from the big screen, and giving a second chance to neglected gems like Frank Capra's
dark yet inspiring Christmas movie *It's A Wonderful Life* (1946), which quickly
became a holiday tradition on the small screen.

Fig 5.9
The talented comedian and savvy businessperson Lucille Ball, along with her husband Desi Arnaz, made *I Love Lucy* into one of the first hit television sitcoms and a national sensation. Source: CBS-TV/ The Kobal Collection.

For a filmmaker like Alfred Hitchcock, television provided the opportunity to follow the leads of other movie veterans like Walt Disney and Lucille Ball and make himself into a household name. As Hollywood transitioned from the factory-style vertical integration of the studios era into a business based on putting together movie "packages," the fame and name recognition of creative personnel, both actors and directors, became more important than a studio brand. Ball, for example, had been a midlevel character actor during the studios era, but she demonstrated her keen business acumen when she and her then husband, Cuban-American bandleader Desi Arnaz, created Desilu Productions in 1950 to market a comedy series for the new medium of television. The show – *I Love Lucy* – not only became a runaway hit and a comedic touchstone for the first decade of American television, but Ball and Arnaz used this success to build Desilu Productions into one of the major producers of television programming. Along the way, Ball's brilliant comic portrayal on the show made her one of the most famous people in America, transforming her into one of the giants of the media industry.

With *Alfred Hitchcock Presents*, Hitchcock was able to bank his reputation as a director with a fondness for suspense and mystery into his own personal brand, becoming the most famous director in the world in the process. In "Names above and below the title" we will explore Hitchcock's significant contribution to American and world movie history, particularly his films from this screen age including *Rear Window*, *Vertigo*, and *Psycho*. Hitchcock's ability to make these challenging and sometimes controversial movies was enhanced by the name and face recognition created by *Alfred Hitchcock Presents* (a recognition reinforced by Hitchcock's trademark of always including himself in a brief cameo in his movies).

Screen ages

1949–1966: Conformity and contention

In the public imagination, the 1950s and early 1960s in America were a time of conservatism and conformity, an era where gender and racial roles were strictly defined, and the model of the middle-class suburban family – working dad, stay-at-home mom, and 2.3 kids – was the official ideal of the American dream. It was the world as depicted in television shows like *Ozzie and Harriet*, *Father Knows Best*, *Leave It to Beaver*, and, more recently and with a critical edge, in the cable series *Mad Men*. From this perspective, Hollywood is seen as being dominated by big screen, moralistic spectaculars like *The Ten Commandments* or teasing sex comedies like *Pillow Talk* (Michael Gordon 1959), where the characters played by stars Doris Day and Rock Hudson flirt with the promise of sexual freedom and new social roles for women before ultimately reinforcing the importance of traditional heterosexual marriage, even for a "career" woman.

As we will see, there is some justification for this stereotype, especially in the wake of the anti-Communist crusades in the late 1940s and early 1950s that sent shock waves through Hollywood and led to a shying away from "controversial" or overly political subjects among some filmmakers. But the era was also one of social challenge and tumult, as the growing **Cold War** confrontation between the United States and the Soviet Union stoked fears of global nuclear annihilation. The period saw the rise of the modern civil rights movement with the Birmingham bus boycott in 1955 led by the same Reverend Martin Luther King, Jr. who had sung in the "slave" choir at the premiere of *Gone with the Wind* less than twenty years earlier. At the same time, what would come to be called the Second Wave women's movement was in its early stages. Perhaps most spectacularly in terms of popular culture, the era also saw the rise of youth culture, signaled by the emergence of rock 'n' roll, as well as a growing counter-culture of avant garde and non-conformist artists across a wide variety of media, from Abstract Expressionism in painting to bebop jazz to the Beat movement in literature.

In terms of American cinema, the screen age of the 1950s and early 1960s also witnessed some of the most artistically ambitious and challenging movies Hollywood has ever produced. As mentioned above, Alfred Hitchcock created some of his most important screen experiences in the period, as did the legendary director John Ford and the brilliant stylist Nicholas Ray (both profiled below). Movies like the wartime melodrama *From Here to Eternity* (Fred Zinnemann 1953), the movie version of Tennessee Williams' landmark play *A Streetcar Named Desire* (Elia Kazan 1951) starring Marlon Brando, which brought Method acting to the movies, the dark

Cold War Refers to the historical period of tension, conflict, and competition after World War II between the capitalist countries of the USA and western Europe and the Communist countries led by the USSR and its satellite countries in eastern Europe as well as by the People's Republic of China. While the USA never went to war directly with either the USSR or China, the period was marked by a series of proxy wars fought in smaller countries such as the Korean War in the 1950s and the Vietnam War in the 1960s. The Cold War largely came to an end with the break-up of the Soviet Union in 1991.

Fig 5.10
In Alexander Mackendrick's darkly cynical *The Sweet Smell of Success*, Burt Lancaster portrays bullying newspaper columnist J. J. Hunsecker, who uses his media power to control the careers of entertainers and politicians alike, while Tony Curtis's character of Sidney Falco is an ambitious publicity agent willing to do anything to get ahead.

Fig 5.11
MGM's joyous musical comedy *Singin' in the Rain* casts a nostalgic and affectionate look back at the beginnings of sound movies only 25 years earlier. Here, Gene Kelly as silent movie star Don Lockwood and his director Roscoe Dexter (Douglas Fowley) struggle to convince vain screen idol Lina Lamont, played by Jean Hagen, to speak her lines into a microphone hidden in a potted plant.

and cynical *The Sweet Smell of Success* about the toxic relationship between show business and journalism (Alexander Mackendrick 1957), and the apocalyptic story of the world after nuclear war *On the Beach* (Stanley Kramer 1959) challenged the model of a tranquil and serene America. The actor, dancer, and director Gene Kelly helped expand the form of the musical with *An American in Paris* (Vincente Minelli 1951) and *Singin' in the Rain* (Gene Kelly and Stanley Donen 1952), and comedies like Billy Wilder's dark and sophisticated *Some Like It Hot* (1959) and *The Apartment* (1960) provided a counterpart to the conformist sexual morality of the Day/Hudson sex comedies. In fact, even those movies like *Pillow Talk* or the teen monster movies profiled in "Now playing" most associated with the conformist 1950s express social anxieties and social changes within the confines of familiar narrative genres.

Hollywood after the Paramount Decision: Divestment and diversification

As we have already seen from "Now playing," the aftermath of the Paramount Decision, requiring the Big Five studios to divest themselves of their theater chains (a process that in the case of MGM took almost the entire decade of the 1950s), along with the rise of television and the move towards privatized screen experiences centered on the suburban living room, once again led to a major reorganization of the movie industry. As the movies experimented with creating new screen experiences unavailable on the small cathode ray tubes of the television set, from widescreen exhibition to 3D movies, producers and other movie executives searched for new ways to minimize risk and create a new version of the media cartels that defined the studios era.

As average movie attendance declined from almost 90 million people per week at the end of World War II to less than half that number by 1960, and with studios now having to compete with each other to book movies into theaters, production shifted from the vertical integration of the studios era to a **package/project system**. Instead of an in-house assembly-line model, where studio executives assign producers, directors, writers, actors, and other professionals under contract to work on a particular movie, movies were now being developed as individual projects outside the studios, where a would-be producer would assemble a "package," often including a script, actors, and a director, and then contract with a studio to provide financing, production facilities, and distribution. These new producers included actors, such as Burt Lancaster, who with his partner Harold Hecht became one of the most successful producers as well as actors in the 1950s.

Package/project system
Refers to a system of movie production that involves a producer or agent assembling a "package" of talent – writers, a director, actors, etc. – to work on a given movie "project," which may then be brought to a movie studio for financing. The package/project system largely replaced the studio system after World War II.

The rise of the agents: MCA, Universal, and diversification

Often the people putting these packages together were talent agents, whose power and influence increased as the contract system of the studios era waned. Rather than simply negotiating studio contracts on behalf of the actors, directors, and others that they represented, agents now were uniquely situated to put movie packages together out of this diversity of talent. The case of Lew Wasserman and the Music Corporation of America (or MCA) is representative of both this screen age and the future of the movie business. MCA began as a talent agency in the 1920s representing musicians, but by the early 1950s it had become one of the most powerful agencies in Hollywood, and their star agent was Lew Wasserman.

Under Wasserman's leadership, MCA led the way in the creation of packages/projects built from the vast array of talent represented by the agency. MCA also moved aggressively into television production through its company, Revue Productions, including such well-known series as *Leave It to Beaver*. All along the way, MCA was the target of anti-trust investigations by the government, concerned that the company was becoming a new kind of entertainment monopoly. These fears were not unfounded. By the beginning of the 1960s, MCA had acquired Universal Studios (both the company and the production facilities), and although government pressure forced the company to get out of the talent agency business in order to take over Universal, their model of diversification, of building a media conglomerate involved in a wide variety of entertainment businesses, each of them reinforcing the other, was becoming the new dominant business model. Like Disney, MCA/Universal would combine movies, television, theme parks (beginning with Universal Studios), music, and other forms of entertainment. Through the dizzying number of acquisitions and mergers over the last 20 years, "MCA" has disappeared as a company name, but the latest version of the diversified conglomerate originally created by MCA (as of 2014 called NBCUniversal) remains one of the most powerful media empires in the world.

McCarthyism, the Cold War, and the blacklist

On November 24, 1947, ten Hollywood professionals – screenwriters Alvah Bessie, Herbert Biberman, Lester Cole, Ring Lardner Jr., John Howard Lawson, Albert Maltz, Samuel Ornitz, Adrian Scott, Dalton Trumbo and director Edward Dmytryk – were ordered to appear before the US House Un-American Activities Committee (or HUAC) to answer charges that they were members of the Communist Party intent on inserting Communist propaganda into mainstream Hollywood movies. It was not illegal – then or now – to be a member of the Communist Party in the USA, and many of these men had been members or had some involvement with the American Communist Party in the past, particularly in regard to labor organizing and the creation of the Screen Writers Guild in the 1930s. Radical and progressive politics were common in America, especially during the Great Depression, and the Soviet Union had actually been an ally of the United States during World War II before being recast as America's greatest enemy.

In the aftermath of World War II, prominent and influential conservative organizations and politicians in the United States began to warn of a Communist menace that was planning to overthrow the American way of life. The threat of Communism was linked to labor organizing and the growing anti-racist civil rights movements, and across the country any politically liberal attitudes or organizations ran the threat of being labeled as "subversive." This suspicion and even paranoia

Fig 5.12
Seven members of the Hollywood Ten arrive in Washington to testify before the House Un-American Activities Committee. From left, the screenwriters Samuel Ornitz, Ring Lardner, Jr., Albert Maltz, Alvah Bessie, Lester Cole, Herbert Biberman, and director Edward Dmytryk. Source: The Kobal Collection.

McCarthyism/Red Scare Refers to the period of investigations following World War II into what some claimed was widespread Communist influence and infiltration into American society. McCarthyism derives from the career of Republican US senator Joseph McCarthy, who rose to prominence with unfounded accusations that the government was riddled with Communist spies. The Red Scare led to a period of political fear and repression, particularly in the entertainment industries, where a series of "blacklists" ended the careers of many movie professionals suspected of subversive political beliefs.

about the supposedly widespread presence of Communist conspiracies is also know as "**McCarthyism**," after the Republican senator from Wisconsin Joseph McCarthy, who charged that the US government was riddled with spies from the Soviet Union. The American entertainment industry was a particular target of the "Red hunters," and the ten artists listed above, who came to be known as the "Hollywood Ten," became the focal point for a system – both formal and informal – of blacklisting that destroyed careers and sent a wave of fear throughout the movie and television industries.

The Hollywood Ten refused to answer the committee's questions – most notoriously, "Are you now or have you ever been a member of the Communist Party?" – and as a result they were cited for contempt of Congress and each sentenced to a year in prison. One, the director Edward Dmytryk, avoided prison by agreeing to testify and name others he knew who had been involved in "suspect" political activities. Thus began a pattern that would continue over the first part of the 1950s. Following the appearance of the Hollywood Ten, various blacklists were instituted, naming dozens of actors, writers, musicians, directors, and others suspected of Communist ties. Appearing on a blacklist meant an end to one's professional career. Some on the blacklist, like the director Jules Dassin, went into exile, continuing his film career in Europe. Others, like Dmytryk and the influential director Elia Kazan, agreed to testify and name names, leading to a rift in the Hollywood community that was still very much alive in 1999, when a 90-year-old Kazan was given an honorary Oscar in recognition of a film career that included landmarks such as *A Streetcar Named Desire* (1951), *On the Waterfront* (1954), and *East of Eden* (1955). While most in the audience applauded the award, a sizeable number of the Hollywood community in attendance sat on their hands, still angry over Kazan's actions almost half a century earlier.

The anti-Communist crusade swept up some of the biggest names in Hollywood, from Humphrey Bogart to early television superstar Lucille Ball. Anti-Semitism and racism also fueled the investigators, including the notorious Mississippi congressman John Rankin, who did nothing to conceal his bigotry. When asked in 1947 by the liberal Californian congresswoman Helen Gahagan Douglas to actually name movies that Rankin thought were pro-Communist, he answered by pointing out the ethnicity – and by implication, the loyalty – of Hollywood stars who had protested the Hollywood Ten hearings:

> One is Danny Kaye. We found his real name was David Daniel Kaminsky. Then there was Eddie Cantor. His real name was Edward Iskowitz. Edward G. Robinson, his name is Emmanuel Goldenberg. There's another one here who calls himself Melvyn Douglas, whose real name is Melvyn Hesselberg.[1]

Douglas happened also to be the congresswoman's husband.

Ironically, although the goal of the blacklists was to eliminate "Communist" influence in Hollywood, the episode did reveal the powerful connections between Hollywood and conservative politics. The Hollywood Ten hearings featured "friendly" testimony by the actor Ronald Reagan, president of the Screen Actors Guild, who endorsed the committee's work. A former New Deal Democrat, Reagan became increasingly active in Republican politics over the ensuing years, leading to his election as governor of California and later president of the United States.

The blacklist began losing its power in the late 1950s and early 1960s, particularly when the producer/director Otto Preminger openly hired the blacklisted writer Dalton Trumbo to write *Exodus* in 1960 and the actor Kirk Douglas insisted that Trumbo also be openly credited as the writer of Stanley Kubrick's *Spartacus* later that same year. Nevertheless, the blacklist destroyed and damaged many careers, even leading to a number of suicides and early deaths. The blacklist also fueled a reluctance to openly address social issues such as poverty, workers' rights, or racism in major films.

Still, the blacklist can be seen as informing several movies in the screen age. Fred Zinnemann's 1952 western *High Noon*, for example, about a small town sheriff abandoned by his fellow citizens and left to face a gang of criminals on his own, and written by the blacklisted writer Carl Foreman, was seen by many as an allegory of what were coming to be called "witch hunts" (the basis for Arthur Miller's 1953 stage allegory about anti-Communist hysteria, *The Crucible*). In 1956, *Storm Center*, directed by Daniel Taradash and starring Bette Davis, directly addressed the Red Scare with a story about a small town librarian fired for refusing to remove a book about Communism from the library shelves. The overall cautiousness about tackling controversial issues on screen during this period would result in an explosion of new filmmaking and the counter-culture in the mid-1960s, where mainstream American cinema began to openly engage with the social revolutions that began sweeping through the country during that decade.

Hollywood and the world

Before World War II, the movie business was truly international. For American moviemakers, the global box office was as important a source of revenue as the domestic market, and while American movies enjoyed popularity around the world, European movies also formed a significant part of American screen experiences. The

Fig 5.13
Gary Cooper as Marshal
Will Kane in *High Noon*
finds himself abandoned
by his friends and
community members when
they learn that a notorious
criminal has gotten out
of prison and is intent
on revenge against Kane.
Many viewers have seen
the movie as an allegory
of the anti-Communist
witch hunts of the late
1940s and early 1950s.

French Pathé company had studios in the United States during the silent era, and the French silent comedian Max Linder was one of the most famous and popular stars all around the world, including the United States.

World War I dramatically disrupted the international movie market, but World War II had an even more disastrous impact on the vibrant movie cultures of Europe, especially those of Germany, France, Italy, and the United Kingdom. Most of the European mainland was cut off from American movies during the war, and in the war's immediate aftermath American movies and media were able to dominate world markets, especially in war-devastated Europe. This dominance would prove to be shortlived, however, as European movie industries began to recover, often with help from European governments. Many countries set up laws favorable to local production of movies, including quotas on the number of foreign movies that could be shown, subsidies to encourage movie production, and financial restrictions on the profits that could be exported out of the country.

At the same time, as we have seen, the American movie business faced declining domestic sales as the result of competition from television and the impact of the Paramount Decision. As ticket sales declined at home, studios and producers in the United States became even more dependent on robust global sales to make their business profitable, a situation that continues to this day, as contemporary American studios depend on the international market for movies in order to turn a profit. The opening and rebuilding of Europe represented a great opportunity for American studios to expand audiences for their movies, even with the imposition of quotas and other financial restrictions.

Since American movie production was no longer connected to any particular studio in the package/project model of filmmaking, American and European producers found they could create useful partnerships with each other, and American filmmakers were attracted to the lower production and labor costs they found in other countries. When Cecil B. DeMille made his silent version of *The Ten Commandments* in 1923, for example, he shot all the exterior scenes in southern California; for his epic 1956 blockbuster, he went to Egypt and the Sinai Peninsula for filming. International production allowed American movies to feature far-flung locations that were exotic to domestic audiences (a reprise of the international travelogues that were popular actualities in the early silent era), visual screen experiences unavailable to television audiences at the time. The use of international locales and actors also made American movies more attractive to global audiences.

Runaway production
Refers to the practice
of American movie
production filming
overseas to take
advantage of lower labor
costs in other countries,
in effect "running away"
from higher costs in the
United States.

Throughout the 1950s and early 1960s, dozens and dozens of movies were shot in other countries, from epics like *The Ten Commandments* and *Ben-Hur* to musicals like *Funny Face* (Stanley Donen 1957) and *The Sound of Music* (1965). In Hollywood, these movies were called "runaway productions," recognizing that in filming overseas producers were "running away" from more expensive domestic costs in Hollywood. The practice of **runaway production** also continues to this day, as do concerns about the consequences of this practice for American movie professionals. Turn on a contemporary television program or movie supposedly set in a city in the United States, and you may just as easily be watching Vancouver or Toronto standing in for Chicago or New York.

The renewed globalization of the movie industry after World War II also raises interesting questions about just what we mean by "American" movies. For example, the Academy Award winner for Best Picture in 1958, *The Bridge On the River Kwai*, was produced by the Austrian-American Sam Spiegel, based on a novel by the French writer Pierre Boulle (who also wrote the novel *Planet of the Apes*) about a group of mainly British prisoners-of-war in Asia during World War II. The screenplay was written (anonymously at the time) by the blacklisted American writers Carl Foreman and Michael Wilson, and the movie was directed by the British director David Lean, featuring a mixed American/British cast including Alec Guinness, William Holden, and Sessue Hayakawa. Finally, the entire movie was shot entirely in Sri Lanka. Is this an "American" movie? A "British" movie? However we describe it, the movie provided a screen experience popular with audiences in both the United States, the United Kingdom, and around the world. Again, the movie business remains international to this day; the *Harry Potter* movies are a good example of films made entirely in Great Britain for an "American" movie studio, Warner Brothers.

International influences

This internationalizing of film production also led to the influence of world filmmaking, particularly from Europe, on American movies. Italian neo-realism as exemplified by such movies as *Bicycle Thieves* (Vittorio De Sica 1946) and *Open City* (Roberto Rossellini 1945), a stripped-down, almost documentary style of filmmaking that created screen experiences focused on the day-to-day struggles of poor and working-class people in post-war Italy, shot on location and often with non-professional casts, led American filmmakers to import versions of this approach into Hollywood movies. Films like Elia Kazan's *On the Waterfront*, about efforts to clean up a corrupt labor union (and seen by some as an effort to justify those who named names as part of the anti-Communist crusade) and Delbert Mann's *Marty* (1955), based on a television play about a shy thirty-something butcher looking for

Fig 5.14
The American movie star
William Holden (left) and
the British movie star Jack
Hawkins in the British
director David Lean's
*The Bridge on the River
Kwai*, an international
production that defies
national labels like
"American" or "British."

Fig 5.15
Movies like Elia Kazan's *On the Waterfront*, starring Marlon Brando, whose "Method" acting style revolutionized American cinema, show the influence of Italian neo-realism in its use of location shooting and focus on working-class characters.

love, both reflect the influence of neo-realism with their decidedly non-glamorous locations and stories of working people. Even a movie like the Elvis Presley vehicle *Jailhouse Rock* (Richard Thorpe 1957), meant to capitalize on Presley's rock 'n' roll stardom, features a gritty, neo-realist approach.

Likewise, the French *Nouvelle Vague* or "New Wave" movement, which also stressed realistic location shooting and deeply personal and sometimes experimental approaches to moviemaking, had a major impact on the beginnings of a new kind of independent, artistically ambitious American moviemaking. The actor turned filmmaker John Cassavetes' 1957/1959 movie *Shadows*, for example, used improvisation and handheld camera work to tell a story about the bohemian artist culture of 1950s New York. A kind of American New Wave movie, *Shadows* anticipates the growth of both avant garde moviemaking in the United States during the 1960s and the revolutions that would shake Hollywood soon thereafter.

Finally, international movies themselves found a growing market in major American cities with the growth in popularity of "art" cinema houses. "Foreign film" became a powerful signifier that referred to both critically acclaimed new movies from major new filmmakers around the world, including Ingmar Bergman in Sweden, Akira Kurosawa and Yasujiro Ozu in Japan, Federico Fellini in Italy, and François Truffaut and Jean-Luc Godard in France, as well as to the greater freedom to show nudity and sexual expression found in many international movies. Indeed, the influx of international movies into art house theaters outside the enforcement of the Production Code Authority became a significant factor in the erosion of power of the PCA throughout the 1950s and early 1960s.

The end of the Production Code and the beginnings of the ratings system

With the Paramount Decision mandating that the major studios give up their theater chain holdings, the Production Code Administration lost a major means of enforcement when it came to censoring movies. Remember that the Production Code Administration had been set up by the Motion Picture Producers and Distributors of America (renamed the Motion Picture Association of America, or MPAA, at the end of World War II), a trade organization of the movie industry, not the US government, so enforcement of the Production Code depended on theaters not showing movies that did not have PCA approval. As theatrical exhibition became separated from motion picture production, studios could threaten the newly independent theaters that they would not allow them to show their product if they ever exhibited movies that didn't have the PCA seal of approval. At the same time, however, theaters were becoming more selective in the movies that they would rent for exhibition, meaning the studios still had to remain on friendly terms with the theater owners.

With the increased competition from television and the switch to the package/project system of production, opportunities opened for independent producers to challenge the Production Code system. As we have seen, American cinema needed to find ways of creating screen experiences that would dramatically distinguish the movie screens from TV screens. Technological innovations were one way of doing this; another was to offer more challenging, explicit, and daring screen experiences than could be shown on television. Rather than follow the model of the Production Code, where all films had to be appropriate for all audiences, some filmmakers specifically targeted more mature, adult audiences. We see a similar strategy followed by subscription television channels such as Showtime and HBO today, which feature more explicit language, violence, and sexuality than traditional network television.

As the previous section pointed out, the influx of significant foreign films into boutique American theaters exposed audiences to compelling screen experiences produced outside the authority of the PCA. Nudity, the ability to explore the complexity of human sexuality both within and outside of traditional marriage, a greater freedom of personal expression – these qualities of many European movies both inspired American filmmakers and provided even more competition for the moviegoing public.

In 1952, the showing of one such foreign film – the Italian anthology movie *L'Amore*, or *Ways of Love* when it was shown in the USA – led to a Supreme Court decision that would pave the way for greater freedom of expression in American cinema. The movie had been both acclaimed by movie critics and condemned by conservative religious leaders, and the controversy led the state of New York to revoke the film's distribution license. When the argument reached the Supreme Court, the court's decision reversed its earlier ruling in 1915 that denied freedom of expression rights to the movies and instead ruled that movies were indeed examples of free speech covered by the First Amendment to the Constitution, making legal censorship very difficult.

One of the first movies to seriously challenge the PCA was *The Moon is Blue*, a 1953 romantic comedy produced and directed by Otto Preminger. To contemporary viewers, it might seem difficult to understand why the movie was controversial. The plot centers on a young woman played by Maggie McNamara who moves to New York to become an actress. Most of the movie centers on a dinner party she attends at the home of an architect played by William Holden. At the party, both

Fig 5.16
Although it probably strikes modern viewers as anything but scandalous, Otto Preminger's *The Moon is Blue*, starring (from left) David Niven, Maggie McNamara, and William Holden, challenged the Production Code by discussing sex in a lighthearted and comic way.

the architect and an older man played by David Niven attempt unsuccessfully to seduce her. Instead, they all engage in a spirited and playful discussion about sexual morality. The next day, she accepts the architect's marriage proposal.

No nudity, no sex, and the movie ends with an endorsement of marriage. Why did the PCA object to the script for *The Moon is Blue*? Simply because the characters discussed issues of sexual behavior in a flippant and comical way. When negotiations with the PCA broke down, Preminger and United Artists decided to make the movie anyway and distribute it without PCA approval. When it opened, some theaters restricted attendance to "Adults Only." Three states actually banned the movie. In spite of or, more likely, because of the controversy, *The Moon is Blue* became a major hit. Just as important, it showed that not only could producers and theaters survive defying the Production Code, such defiance could even be a major selling point.

Throughout the rest of the 1950s and early 1960s, the Production Code saw its authority erode further and further. The MPAA revised the Code to give filmmakers more freedom, and the PCA became more and more reluctant to withhold its approval, fearing that movies would be released without it anyway, further undermining the authority of the Production Code. By the end of this screen age, although the Production Code was still technically in force, it no longer played any significant role in movie censorship. With filmmakers around the world increasingly challenging and expanding the range of subjects and types of screen experiences in the 1960s, the MPAA would look to a new means of forestalling government regulation with the ratings system, which we will examine more closely in the next chapter.

In development

The western

If the post-World War II crime movies of film noir openly questioned traditional American values, the western in the 1950s and early 1960s provided a more covert if no less pointed critique of social values and American history. The western, which had been experiencing something of a decline as a genre, experienced a renaissance of both popularity and artistry in this screen age. Themes and issues that had driven many early westerns in the silent era, such as the meaning of the frontier to American history, the situation of Native Americans, and questions of masculine identity, returned in the post-war western. We will examine the most important filmmaker associated with this western renaissance, John Ford, in more depth below, including his disturbing, fascinating, and beautiful movie *The Searchers*, but many other directors, writers, producers, and actors created screen experiences with the western that connected with the anxieties and concerns of post-war moviegoers.

In an era of overt repression brought about by the anti-Communist crusades, the conventional view of the western as exemplifying a traditional, patriotic representation of the United States featuring the pioneer values of rugged independence, self-reliance, and entrepreneurship provided cover for this most American of genres to question these very ideals, even as they appeared to reinforce them. The relation of the individual to the community, the purpose of government, even racism and the colonial exploitation of Native peoples – we can find all of these potentially explosive issues informing the screen experiences of the post-war western, even if in ambiguous or contradictory ways. By questioning the values of the past, these movies began to question the values of the world built on that past.

As we have seen, Fred Zinnemann and the blacklisted writer Carl Foreman were able to mount an allegorical critique of blacklisting in *High Noon*, relying on the iconic narrative of the gunfight and the all-American star power of Gary Cooper (himself an outspoken anti-Communist) to show what happens when fear and suspicion tear a community apart. Or viewers could simply watch the movie as an exciting western. At the same time, the director Anthony Mann worked with another famous example of big-screen all-American decency, Jimmy Stewart, to create a series of westerns, including *Winchester '73* (1950), *Bend of the River* (1952), *The Naked Spur* (1953), *The Far Country* (1955), and *The Man From Laramie* (1955), that relied on the definitive qualities of Stewart's screen persona – his soft-spokenness, his emotional understatement, and his core of inner strength and resolve – to create what would come to be called "anti-heroes," characters in the traditional role of the western hero who nonetheless raise questions about their motives and beliefs in ways that can make us doubt the overall moral logic of the stories we experience.

In *The Far Country*, for example, Stewart portrays a rootless cattle driver named Jeff Webster who claims to live by the rule of only looking out for himself, in spite of his close friendship with his partner, the grizzled oldtimer Ben Tatum (Walter Brennan). Early on the movie plants the suspicion that Jeff may also be a killer, before entering into the main conflict involving Jeff and the ruthless political boss (dictator, really) Judge Gannon (John McIntire) of the Alaskan frontier outpost of Skagway during the Yukon Gold Rush at the end of the nineteenth century, and a femme fatale saloon owner Ronda Castle (Ruth Roman). In featuring glorious Technicolor panoramas of the Canadian Rockies, *The Far Country* presents a visual

Fig 5.17
In *The Far Country*, James Stewart's Jeff Webster is a troubling anti-hero who claims to care only about his own well-being until the brutal shoot-out at the movie's conclusion.

Fig 5.18
Delmer Dave's *3:10 to Yuma* starring Glenn Ford (right) as the wanted outlaw Ben Wade and Van Heflin as Dan Evans, the struggling rancher who agrees to transport him to jail for money, another 1950s Western that questioned the mythology of the American frontier.

spectacle meant to contrast with the tiny television screen (where westerns were equally growing in popularity), but in its narrative *The Far Country* is more like a claustrophobic film noir, with many scenes taking place in the cramped interiors of gold camps and frontier saloons. In the end, Jeff finally abandons his "selfish" personal code to embrace the idea of building community, but only after a violent blood bath that results in the death of both Ben and Ronda.

The Far Country was a big budget production, but smaller westerns continued this critical examination of the classic American loner hero. In Delmer Dave's 1957 *3:10 to Yuma*, based on a short story by the legendary American crime writer Elmore Leonard, Van Heflin portrays Dan Evans, a family man in the mold of Gary Cooper's Will Kane from *High Noon*, who undertakes the dangerous, almost suicidal, mission of delivering the murderous outlaw Ben Wade, played by Glenn Ford (an actor who usually portrayed all-American heroes) to a nearby town in order to catch the train of the movie's title. Evans is motivated as much by economic desperation as a desire to see justice done, as his commission will be paid by a wealthy stage coach owner. As in *High Noon*, Evans is eventually abandoned by almost everyone except for his wife and the town drunk who agrees to serve as his deputy.

Right when Evans is about to be overpowered by Wade's gang, Wade, seemingly impressed by Evan's dogged heroism, helps him avoid the gang and make the train. This supposedly successful ending to Evans' mission is undercut at the end by Wade's confidence that he'll still be able to escape from the Yuma jail after Evans delivers him, raising questions about the whole point of Evans' courage and commitment to seeing the job through. Both *The Far Country* and *3:10 to Yuma* conclude with endings that conform to the Production Code mandates, but neither can be taken as wholehearted affirmations of the American past. At the end, both raise more questions than they answer about what the mythology of the western tells us about American culture and history.

Science fiction

"A horror horde of crawl-and-crush giants clawing out of the Earth's steaming depths!" This promotional line from the poster for *Them!* (Gordon Douglas 1954), a low-budget movie about giant atomic mutant ants that threaten Los Angeles, captures for many the spirit of one of the most popular genres of the 1950s and early 1960s – popular both at the time and with legions of fans since – science fiction. Science fiction is as old as cinema itself and films like George Méliès's *A Trip to the Moon* in 1902, but the genre really came into its own in this post-World War II screen age in America.

There are several reasons for the development of science fiction after World War II, beginning with the growing fascination with and anxiety over science and technology. On the one hand, the booming consumer culture of the 1950s sold the idea of technology as the key to prosperity and happiness, from household appliances to the increasingly ubiquitous television set. It's no accident that when Disneyland first opened in 1956, Tomorrowland, featuring attractions sponsored by corporations such as Monsanto showing off their latest technological innovations, offered a futuristic counterpoint to the nostalgia of Main Street, USA. Science in the form of the atomic bomb was also credited with victory over Japan in World War II.

But atomic weaponry also fueled fears of nuclear annihilation as the Cold War between the USA and the USSR intensified. Science and technology represented power, power that could promise future benefits but power that might also lead

Fig 5.19
A poster for the 1950s atomic monster movie *Them!* about a colony of giant mutant ants threatening the city of Los Angeles. Source: Warner Bros/The Kobal Collection.

to destruction and loss of control. Such ambivalence gave rise to the anti-nuclear weapons movements of the late 1950s and early 1960s and the beginnings of the environmental movement following the publication of Rachel Carson's *Silent Spring* in 1962. The science fiction movies of this screen age express this ambivalence over science and technology, even if in the end it is often scientists who save the day from the problems caused by science. Science fiction movies were made by both big studios and smaller independent companies. The market for these movies was also fueled by the same growth of the teen market discussed in "Now playing," and atomic monster movies were a regular part of drive-in programs.

Themes of invasion and contamination – threats from the outside and threats from within – inform many of the most influential kinds of science fiction movies in the period. A combination of anti-Communist hysteria and a fascination with the beginnings of what would become the space program led to a series of "invaders from space" movies. In some movies, such as *The Day the Earth Stood Still* (Robert Wise 1951), the alien visitor Klaatu has a human form and brings a cautionary message to the planet: turn away from the path of nuclear war or face destruction. In others, such as *The Thing From Another World* (Howard Hawks 1951) and *The Blob* (Irvin Yeaworth 1957), the alien invaders are monsters who threaten to destroy all human life, fears linked to humanity's development of weapons capable of doing the same thing.

Part of Cold War propaganda stressed the USSR as just such an alien invader, but the anti-Communist blacklists also promoted the fear of an invasion from within, when Communist ideas would insinuate themselves into the hearts and minds of otherwise all-American citizens. Coupled with the growing understanding of the effects of atomic radiation and fallout, a number of science fiction movies provided screen experiences focused on this invader from within, usually as the result of atomic testing gone awry. In monster movies such as *Them!* and *The Beast from 20,000 Fathoms* (Eugène Lourié 1953), ordinary animals such as ants mutate into giant killers, or, as in *The Beast* (as well as the influential Japanese anti-atomic monster movie *Godzilla* [Ishiro Honda 1954]), atomic testing awakens dormant dinosaurs.

Even more psychologically intriguing are the movies where the transformation occurs within humans. In *The Incredible Shrinking Man* (Jack Arnold 1957) and *The Fly* (Kurt Neumann 1958), exposure to radiation leads to the main character of Scott Carey (Grant Williams) in the first movie shrinking in size until he is on the verge of disappearing altogether, providing the opportunity for the use of outsize props and other special effects to change our perspective to that of a small animal and even an insect. One of the most unforgettable scenes involves Carey fleeing for his life from his house cat, the one-time pet turned relentless predator. In *The Fly*, a scientist named Andre Delambre (David Hedison) becomes a victim of his own hubris when his attempts to invent a matter transporter result in the creation of two mutants: one featuring the body of Delambre and the head of a house fly, and the other Delambre's head on the body of fly trapped in a spider's web. Delambre's high-pitched cries of "Help me!" as the spider approaches have become iconic in movie history.

Don Siegel's *Invasion of the Body Snatchers* (1956) – one of the most influential screen experiences of 1950s science fiction – combines both the outside/inside threats of invasion to create a movie that has inspired viewers and critics to see the film as a Cold War allegory, but one with contradictory readings. The alien invaders in this movie take the form of seed pods that grow exact reproductions of the citizens of a small central Californian town, reproductions that kill the originals as part of a process of taking over the Earth. These replicants are identical in every way except that they seem somehow lifeless, devoid of free will and emotion. It's up to the hero of the movie, Dr. Miles Bennell (Kevin McCarthy), to figure out what is going on and try to alert the world before it's too late. In the original ending, we see him rushing down a highway, shouting at the passing cars with little effect. The studio deemed

Fig 5.20
"They're here already! You're next!" Residents of a small Californian town played by (from left to right) Dana Wynter, King Donovan, Carolyn Jones, and Kevin McCarthy react in horror after discovering pod people duplicates of themselves growing in a backyard greenhouse.

this ending too dark, and insisted on a prologue and epilog showing Bennell being treated for psychological delusions until he finally convinces the FBI to take action.

The idea of people turning into mindless followers with no free will of their own inhabits many science-fiction plots in movie history, including a fascination with robots and the enduring popularity of zombies (and in fact the plot of *Invasion of the Body Snatchers* resembles that of 1953's *It Came From Outer Space* directed by Jack Arnold). Since *Invasion of the Body Snatchers* first appeared in 1956, people have seen it as both an anti-Communist allegory, with the "pod people" (a phrase that has entered the popular vernacular) representing the supposedly mindless conformity of life under Soviet Communism. Others, however, make equally committed arguments that the mindless conformism being criticized here is that of those taking part in the anti-Communist witch-hunt. Both interpretations speak to a sense of paranoia and loss of control beneath the official gloss of post-war economic boom. The screen experience of *Invasion of the Body Snatchers* has proved so haunting and suggestive that there have been at least three major remakes of the movies, the latest in 2007.

Genres of gender in the 1950s and early 1960s: Marilyn Monroe and James Dean/Rock Hudson and Doris Day

Contemporary visual narratives such as the television series *Mad Men* or the movie *Revolutionary Road* (Sam Mendes 2008 and based on Richard Yates' 1961 novel) express our current sense of the transition from the 1950s into the 1960s, especially the tensions and contradictions bubbling below the surface of images of suburban affluence and contentment, tensions and contradictions that would fuel the social revolutions of the 1960s and 1970s. One particularly fraught source of these tensions and contradictions centers on the performance and meaning of gender in the 1950s and early 1960s. Of course, at the time neither filmmakers nor audiences knew about the dramatic changes that would soon sweep American society, but neither were they unaware nor uninterested in the changes that were already occurring.

Screen experiences in this screen age reflected two opposing forces: a greater cultural interest and openness in questions of sexuality and gender, an interest that fed moviemakers' desire to challenge both television and the Production Code by pushing the boundaries of what could be represented on film. On the other hand, conservative forces, including official government policies, sought what was seen as a return to more traditional gender roles after the disruptions of World War II, disruptions that included the greater entry of women into the workplace. Many women, however, were not interested in going back. The beginnings of the Second Wave of the women's rights movement along with a growing counter-culture challenged the idea and ideal of a traditional status quo with clearly differentiated roles for men and women, although these challenges had yet to overtly penetrate most mass media entertainment. Teen culture, however, especially the rise of rock 'n' roll music, did enjoy higher visibility and became a symbolic focus of concern over issues of gender, sexuality, and morality that extended throughout the larger society.

In this section, we will look at four actors – Marilyn Monroe, Rock Hudson, Doris Day, and James Dean – and the genres of gender they performed as an introduction to some of these tensions and contradictions regarding gender, tensions and contradictions you can then explore through other actors and screen experiences of this screen age. In their performances of gender, these actors reflect both a cultural desire to stabilize and more clearly define the differences between men and women

Fig 5.21
Marilyn Monroe in *Some Like It Hot*.

Fig 5.22
Doris Day and Rock Hudson in *Pillow Talk*.

and a growing interest, fluctuating between anxiety and attraction, in the disruptive force of sexuality to undermine this very stability.

There is no more legendary American screen figure than Marilyn Monroe (her birth name was Norma Jeane Mortenson), and her gender genre as the ultimate 1950s blonde bombshell can be taken as an extreme form of crafting an exaggerated version of female sexuality. Along with actors like Jayne Mansfield, Monroe's gender performance combined sweetness and naiveté with amplified symbols of female sexuality, especially focused on breast size, as a way of reinforcing gender difference. Roles in movies like *Gentlemen Prefer Blondes* (Howard Hawks 1953), *The Seven Year Itch* (Billy Wilder 1955, resulting in the iconic image of Monroe standing over a subway grate with the wind blowing up her dress), and *Some Like It Hot* (Billy Wilder 1958) seemed to reinforce this bombshell image, although Monroe herself resisted the narrowness of this identity, consciously working on her craft as an actor, seeking out a wider variety of roles, and moving into the producer's role. Her early death at age 36 from a drug overdose in 1962 has symbolized for many the tragic dimensions of a gender performance Monroe could never completely escape.

Tall, clean-cut, physically fit, Rock Hudson embodied an exaggerated version of American masculinity, which his none-too-subtle stage name of "Rock" is meant to emphasize (his real name was Roy Scherer). His gender genre is a clear inspiration for the image of Don Draper in *Mad Man*. In his continuing need to hide his identity as a gay man, Hudson also inspired the idea of how a carefully crafted and polished image can be used to hide a more complicated reality. Still, in sex comedies with Doris Day such as *Pillow Talk* (Michael Gordon 1959) and *Lover Come Back* (Delbert Mann 1961) and in the lush melodramas directed by Douglas Sirk, *Magnificent Obsession* (1954), *All That Heaven Allows* (1955), and *Written on the Wind* (1956), Hudson was meant to represent an ideal of unquestioned straight masculine identity.

The gender genres created for both Monroe and Hudson were meant to stabilize the idea of rigid differences between men and women, especially in relation to sex and sexuality. But sex remained an explosive arena, resistant to containment within traditional marriage, a source of anxiety and uncertainty, and the more exaggerated the efforts to stabilize those identities the more those identities risked becoming parodies and cartoons. Doris Day, Hudson's opposite in *Pillow Talk* and *Lover Come Back* and the star of a string of extremely popular sex comedies into the early 1960s, showed in her performances of gender the fault lines in these efforts to both exploit and contain gender and sexuality on screen. In these sex comedies Day portrayed at the same time characters identified as "eternal virgins" but who were also independent career women in charge of their own lives, a pairing of qualities that strained believability. As the 1960s progressed, this strain proved increasingly unsustainable, and by 1968 her film career was more or less over.

But even in the screen age in which she enjoyed her greatest success, Day's performances of gender ranged across an array of genres, from a sexy nightclub singer in *Love Me or Leave Me* (Charles Vidor 1955) to the title character of *Calamity Jane* (David Butler 1953) who spends most of the film dressed in men's clothing to portray the gender-defying nineteenth-century frontierswoman of the movie's title. A gifted singer and an underrated actor, Day negotiated genres of gender that both looked back to supposedly more stable, domestic genres of female performance before World War II (although as we have seen, screen experiences of gender have always been in flux) and also suggested possibilities for greater freedom in terms of expressing female sexual desire.

In the 1956 epic *Giant* (George Stevens), Hudson co-starred with both Elizabeth Taylor and a young actor making his final screen appearance, James Dean. Dean had only three major roles in movies before dying in a car crash in 1955 at age 24, but like Monroe he has become a tragic cult symbol of the costs of defying the conformism of 1950s American culture. More to the point, his performance of gender in these three movies – in addition to *Giant*, *East of Eden* (Elia Kazan 1955) and most famously *Rebel Without a Cause* (Nicholas Ray 1955) – had an eccentric, stylized, and androgynous quality that challenged conventional ideas about masculinity and femininity.

In *Giant*, it seems at times as if Hudson and Dean are in two different movies. Hudson follows a traditional Hollywood performance style, a presentational mode focused on maintaining a consistent image and way of movement. Dean, on the other hand, was part of the burgeoning Method acting movement that was revolutionizing American theater and movies, a movement associated with the acting teacher Lee Strasberg, the director Elia Kazan, and stars like Marlon Brando. Method actors

Fig 5.23
James Dean (foreground) and Rock Hudson in *Giant*, with Mercedes McCambridge and Elizabeth Taylor.

spent preparation time trying to understand the inner emotional and psychological lives of characters they were portraying in an effort to produce what they saw as more natural, realistic performances. The result, performances that featured intense emotional outbursts and dramatic expressions of physicality, appear now as stylized as the more conventional approaches of a Rock Hudson, but at the time the Method, which has gone on to become the dominant style of American screen acting, caused excitement and controversy, as fans both embraced and criticized this seemingly "wilder" form of performance.

Case study 5.1: A new kind of acting: Movies and the Method

When movie viewers in 1951 went to see the film version of *A Streetcar Named Desire*, Tennessee Williams' play about an emotionally fragile southern woman who goes to live with her sister and her volatile husband in working-class New Orleans, they not only saw a break-out performance by Marlon Brando, who had starred in the play on Broadway and would become one of the biggest movie stars of his generation, they were also seeing a new kind of acting style. Called "Method Acting," this approach was based on the "the Method" taught by the influential acting teacher Lee Strasberg at the Actors' Studio, an acting school started in 1947 that has influenced generations of American actors. Strasberg based his "Method" on the theories and techniques of the turn-of-the-century Russian teacher Constantin Stanislavski.

The idea of the Method was rooted in a desire for psychological realism, for dramatic performances based on the authentic expression of emotion rather than conventional techniques and mannerisms. Explore the Method revolution in post-World War II movie acting by watching films that feature Method and non-Method actors working together. In *A Streetcar Named Desire*, for example, the Method-trained Marlon Brando, working with the Method-proponent director Elia Kazan, co-stars opposite the classically trained Vivien Leigh. In *Giant*, the Method actor James Dean stars opposite the more traditional Hollywood acting styles of Elizabeth Taylor and Rock Hudson. As you experience these movies, how would you describe the difference in acting styles and the effect they have on you among the different actors in the movie? Expand your exploration by reading reviews and essays of the time that discussed the use of Method acting in these films.

Finally, consider different examples of the Method and the legacy of the Method in later movies and in current-day American cinema. What contemporary actors seem to be or identify as Method actors? How has Method acting and its ideal of a more "realistic" portrayal of emotion influenced what we think of as good or effective acting?

Dean's performances, especially as the misunderstood teenager Jim Stark in *Rebel*, along with his early death, led to him becoming a teen idol and sex symbol, but his gender performance also confused clear lines of differentiation between male and female. Like Elvis Presley, Dean's long (for the time) hair, his contorted body movements, and his extravagant emotionalism contrasted sharply with the more contained masculine personas of Hudson, Jimmy Stewart, Gregory Peck, and other major stars of the era. Both pretty and handsome, both sensitive and violent, the gender genre performances of Dean and Presley, and in particular their popularity, showed the complexity of gender identity in 1950s American culture and cinema.

The names above and below the title

John Ford

The career of the director John Ford spans a half-century of American cinema, from the silent era to the 1960s, and he remains one of the most influential and revered of American filmmakers. During the 1930s, 1940s, and 1950s, there was no more important director in Hollywood, and shortly after the beginning of the screen age featured in this chapter, he won his still unequaled fourth Best Director Oscar. Although his work spanned several genres, as evidenced by films such as *Young Mr. Lincoln* (1939) and *The Grapes of Wrath* (1940), he is most associated with the western, a genre he helped revive with his 1939 classic *Stagecoach*, a movie that also made a star out of John Wayne, an actor who became closely associated with Ford.

Although the western is often thought of in terms of simple morality plays – as in the "Black Hat/White Hat" cliché – Ford's westerns showed an awareness of the moral complexity of the western experience in America, based as it was on the violent dispossession of Native peoples from their lands and culture. Rather than relying on one-dimensional models of virtue and bravery, Ford's westerns featured conflicted, even psychologically damaged heroes whose ultimate motives remain ambiguous to viewers. The flawed, complicated heroes of Ford's westerns serve as recognition of the traumatic psychological impact of frontier violence and the conquest of Native peoples. Placed in the context of the late 1940s and 1950s, when Ford made some of his most important westerns – movies like *My Darling*

Fig 5.24
John Ford on the set of his revisionist western *The Man Who Shot Liberty Valance* (1962), flanked by co-stars James Stewart and John Wayne. Source: Paramount/The Kobal Collection.

Fig 5.25
John Wayne as the menacing ex-Confederate office Ethan Edwards, obsessed with avenging the murder of his brother's family and retrieving – and possibly executing – his niece in *The Searchers*.

Clementine (1946), *Fort Apache* (1948), *She Wore A Yellow Ribbon* (1949), *Rio Grande* (1950), *The Searchers* (1955), and *The Man Who Shot Liberty Valance* (1962) – we can see these traumatized heroes as implicit expressions of the violence of World War II, in which Ford served and was wounded as a filmmaker.

Ford's 1955 movie *The Searchers*, starring the epitome of all-American masculine heroism John Wayne in a dark and unsympathetic role, is a prime example of the western renaissance in the 1950s described above, and it remains a beautiful, compelling, and disturbing screen experience. The plot centers on the obsessive, years-long quest by Wayne's character, the former Confederate officer Ethan Edwards, to avenge the murder of his brother's family by Comanche warriors and to rescue his kidnapped niece Debbie (as an example of the extensive influence of Ford's movie, the death of Luke Skywalker's family in the original *Star Wars* is based on the harrowing massacre sequence in *The Searchers*).

The ostensible hero of the movie, Ethan is a frightening figure, quick to violence and with a murky past (he suddenly shows up with no explanation at his brother's Texas homestead several years after the end of the Civil War). He is openly racist in his view towards Indians, including Martin Pawley (Jeffrey Hunter), his half-Indian adopted nephew and fellow searcher. Over the years of their searching, Ethan's goal moves from rescuing Debbie to murdering her after she becomes a wife to his main Comanche adversary Scar, a character who we find is much like Ethan in his obsession with vengeance against the white settlers who have murdered his own people. Ethan and Martin eventually do find the now-teenaged Debbie (played by Natalie Wood), slaughter Comanche warriors and families, and brutally scalp Scar. In the end, Ethan decides to spare Debbie's life and return her to the white settlement before he heads off alone into an uncertain future.

Over the years, viewers have experienced *The Searchers* as both reinforcing racist views of Native peoples as savage killers and as presenting a searing indictment of that racism through the humanity of Martin and his opposition to the bloodthirsty Ethan. Given Ethan's unapologetically Confederate loyalties and the movie's appearance the same year as the Montgomery bus boycott, Ford's emphasis on Ethan's racism and violence can't help but evoke comparisons to the growing African American civil rights movement as well. Visually, *The Searchers* features Ford's trademark long shots of beautiful and lonely western vistas, dwarfing the human characters moving across them. A sense of isolation and dread pervades the movie; in its moral complexity and disturbing representations of frontier violence, *The Searchers* serves as an example of the turbulence roiling under the surface of 1950s American culture.

Nicholas Ray

No director's reputation from this screen age has grown over the years more than Nicholas Ray's. In part, his interest for later generations comes from how his movies from the 1950s seem to anticipate the social and cultural revolutions of the later 1960s and 1970s, both in subject matter and in his distinctively flamboyant style. In an era defined by a growing consumer culture and a repressive political climate, Ray made movies featuring non-conformist characters out of synch with a world dominated by the values of money, status, and power. His movies provide dramatic and emotional screen experiences driven by the volatile passions of his conflicted, unpredictable characters. In his landmark *Rebel Without a Cause*, Ray helped define the cultural idea of the misunderstood teenager, of young people frustrated by what they see as the hypocrisy and false values of the adult world, an attitude that would come to define the social protests of the next decade.

Raised in Wisconsin and Chicago, Ray moved to New York when he was twenty-three and become involved in the politically engaged theater of the Depression. His sympathy for underdogs and his critical view of American capitalism managed to remain a defining feature of his work throughout his film career, even during the height of the Hollywood blacklist, and the idea of the rebel informs Ray's movies. Films like *They Live By Night* (1949), *In A Lonely Place* (1950), and especially his astonishing western *Johnny Guitar* (1954), feature characters who are all rebelling in different ways, unwilling or unable to go along with social expectations or play conventional social roles, whether because of social class and the unfairness of the criminal justice system (*They Live By Night*), the commercial demands of Hollywood filmmaking (*In A Lonely Place*), or, in *Johnny Guitar*, a western that concludes with a shoot-out between the two main female characters, because of restrictive constructions of gender.

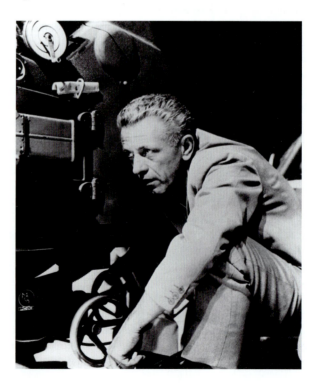

Fig 5.26
Nicholas Ray. Source: The Kobal Collection.

Fig 5.27
Misfit teens Plato (Sal
Mineo), Jim (James Dean),
and Judy (Natalie Wood)
find temporary refuge in
an abandoned mansion in
Rebel Without a Cause.

Case study 5.2: Constructing the teenager: Images of youth in 1950s screen experiences

The screen age after World War II is marked by Hollywood's efforts to create screen experiences designed specifically to appeal to teenagers. But as the title to Jon Lewis' study of youth movies, *The Road to Romance and Ruin*,[2] suggests, Hollywood movies have also been influential in shaping our ideas of what it means to be a teenager, and many of these ideas took shape in the screen age of the 1950s and early 1960s.

Depending on which movies you have watched, you might have seen teenagers portrayed as either silly overgrown children or menacing young adults, as either a source of humor or of fear and anxiety. Explore the ways that movies in the 20 years after World War II portrayed teenagers by comparing and contrasting an example of a movie about troubled youth and what were called "juvenile delinquents" such as *The Blackboard Jungle* (Richard Brooks 1955) or *Rebel Without a Cause* (Nicholas Ray 1955), with an example of a movie about fun-loving teens such as *Gidget* (Paul Wendkos 1959) or one of the "Beach Blanket" movies. As you watch the movies, consider:

- What kind of emotional response in relation to teenagers does the movie seem to be trying to create?
- What different audiences is the movie appealing to?
- How might these different audiences have divergent reactions to the movie?
- What do these screen experiences suggest about the larger concerns and anxieties in the time period?

Expand your exploration by reading movie reviews from the period. What aspects of the screen experiences do these writers respond to? In what ways do their reactions echo or differ from your own? Finally, you might read scholars like Lewis to gain more perspective about why teenagers were such a focal point for filmmaking in the 1950s and 1960s.

In *Rebel Without a Cause*, James Dean gives the performance that would define him as a star and a cult figure. The movie tells the story of three lonely teenagers – Jim Stark, the son of wealthy parents more interested in status and keeping up appearances than with the emotional needs of their son; Judy (Natalie Wood), a young woman whose father can't deal with her sexual maturity; and "Plato" (Sal Mineo), a small, emotionally troubled young man largely abandoned by his own wealthy, divorced parents – who come together to form a kind of substitute family. In Ray's movie, what was already becoming the Hollywood cliche of the "juvenile delinquent" is given sympathetic treatment as most of the teenagers in the movie, including the supposed tough-guy bully/gang leader Buzz Gunderson (Corey Allen), prove in the end to be vulnerable, sensitive, and emotionally honest, eager for understanding, love, and guidance from adults which they have never received.

The characters in *Rebel* resist the rigid expectations they feel imposed on them by the larger world, especially the idea that appearances matter more than feelings. In the tragic story of Plato, who idolizes Jim as a combination of older brother, best friend, and love interest, Ray also introduces issues of sexuality into his story. The subject of youth rebellion, Dean's intense, Method-driven performance, along with Ray's innovative and stylish use of framing (as in the film's opening, where we are down in the ground in close-up on the drunken Jim playing with a toy monkey, or later when we get an upside-down shot reflecting Jim's point of view as he lays sprawled across a sofa) seem to anticipate the changes that would sweep through Hollywood in the late 1960s and the 1970s. As a result, many viewers and filmmakers have seen Ray as a director ahead of his time, and he has influenced a wide range of artists from the French New Wave directors to Martin Scorsese. Both because of his increasing reluctance to conform to expectations for Hollywood filmmaking and the effects of a substance abuse problem on his health, Ray's Hollywood directorial career ended when he collapsed during production of *55 Days at Peking* in 1963. Ray died in 1979, but in the years since his reputation has only grown as an innovative and daring stylist.

Alfred Hitchcock

- A famous photographer laid up with a broken leg thinks he sees evidence of a murder while playing peeping Tom with his neighbors. Was there really a murder, or was it all a projection of his guilty imagination?

Fig 5.28
Alfred Hitchcock on the set of *Psycho*, a movie that would redefine the Hollywood thriller. Source: Paramount / The Kobal Collection.

- A police detective on medical leave watches as his fear of heights prevents him from saving the life of the woman he is following for a friend, and with whom he has fallen in love. When he sees a woman on the street who looks like the dead woman, he works his way into her life and makes her over into a duplicate of the first woman, before she meets a similar fate.
- A young woman on the run after stealing money from her employer stops at a remote motel run by a strange young man who lives alone with his mother, where she is brutally murdered in the shower by a mysterious figure. First a private detective and then the woman's sister come to investigate, and we soon learn that the young man has a horrifying secret.

These three brief plot synopses, each featuring ambiguous protagonists harboring deep secrets and suggesting a world where chaos and violence lurk just beneath the surface of even the most innocent or innocuous situations, belong to three of the most famous movies of this screen age and of American cinema history: *Rear Window* (1954), *Vertigo* (1958), and *Psycho* (1960). All were the product of perhaps the most famous filmmaker of all time, Alfred Hitchcock, from what many see as his greatest period of filmmaking, an especially bold claim given that Hitchcock, like John Ford, had been a major figure in the movies since the silent era. Hitchcock's career also spanned two continents; he is one of the greatest directors in both British and American movie history, having established himself at the top of his profession in his native England before emigrating to the United States just before World War II and becoming one of the most popular and acclaimed directors in Hollywood.

In the fourteen movies he made during this era, Hitchcock crafted a wide variety of screen experiences, from tense character studies (*Strangers on a Train* 1951) to glamorous and romantic thrillers (*To Catch A Thief* 1954) to thrilling big screen spectacles (*North by Northwest* 1959) to, at the beginning of the 1960s, a pair of horror classics (*Psycho* and *The Birds*) that defied the Production Code and opened Hollywood to the power and box office popularity of more explicit representations of violence. Known as a master of suspense and mystery, Hitchcock had been producing work considered master works of American cinema since his spectacular Hollywood debut with *Rebecca* (1940), but in many ways his approach seems especially well-suited to America in the 1950s.

If the characters in Nicholas Ray's movies wear their hearts – and their emotional and psychological traumas – on their sleeves, Hitchcock famously focused on characters who try to stay cool and collected but who slowly start to come apart, sometimes, as in *Rear Window*, to finally triumph in the end (although with a second broken leg); sometimes, as in *Vertigo* and *Psycho*, to find the world irretrievably

Fig 5.29
In *Rear Window*, James Stewart plays a photojournalist turned peeping Tom whose curiosity reveals a possible murder.

broken. Hitchcock specialized in playing movie stars against their types or placing them in situations where their screen personas would be tested and even undermined. His interest in secrets lurking beneath the surface of even the most seemingly "normal" and conventional situations and people created a dramatic counterpoint to advertising images of a sunny, optimistic, prosperous American paradise of consumer goods and stable nuclear families, and the current of paranoia running through his movies echoes the political tensions and repressions of the early Cold War.

In Hitchcock's movies, these secrets include hidden desires, fears, and obsessions, troubled family histories featuring unresolved Oedipal relationships between sons and mothers, and a discomfort and anxiety over the power of sexuality to introduce chaos and disorder into the world. Like film noir, his movies often include a kind of femme fatale in the characters of young, beautiful, and blonde-haired women who function as objects of obsession and desire, from Grace Kelly, who is targeted for murder and then falsely accused of murder herself when she kills her attacker in *Dial M for Murder* (1954) to Kim Novak in *Vertigo* to Janet Leigh in *Psycho*, the ostensible star of the movie who is violently murdered not long after the movie begins. Unlike the classic femme fatale, many of these women are more victim than perpetrator. Throughout these movies, Hitchcock emphasizes the disturbing role of chance and arbitrary accidents in determining our fates.

In *Psycho*, Alfred Hitchcock crafted a screen experience that dramatically broke with the Hollywood studio tradition of glossy movie escapism in ways that helped usher in the next screen age. Even though Hitchcock was the most famous director in the world at the beginning of the 1960s, studio executives at Paramount were not happy with his choice of *Psycho*, a lurid story of a serial killer based on a novel by Robert Bloch (itself based on the story of real-life serial killer Ed Gein), preferring a more glamorous, star-studded project like his very successful *North by Northwest* instead. Recognizing how movie production had changed since the end of the studios age, Hitchcock offered to finance the movie on his own as a low-budget project using the production crew and facilities from his television show, with Paramount only distributing the movie.

Shot in a stark black and white with a tense, staccato score from his regular composer Bernard Herrman, *Psycho* became a huge hit and showed the power of low-budget, independent filmmaking. The murder of Marion Crane in the shower of her room at the Bates Motel at the hands of Norman Bates has become one of the most famous scenes in movie history. Known simply as "the shower scene," the sequence uses rapid editing between images of Janet Leigh screaming, parts of her naked body, a flashing knife, and blood circling down the drain to produce shock and excitement in the audience and cause us to think we see more than we really

Fig 5.30
Janet Leigh as the doomed Marion Crane caught mid-scream in the shower scene from *Psycho*, one of the most famous screen experiences in American cinema history.

do. That the movie was finally approved by the Production Code Administration shows how weakened the PCA had become by the beginning of the 1960s. The box office success of *Psycho*, Hitchcock's biggest hit, showed that audiences were ready for more daring and provocative screen experiences. A product of the studios age, Hitchcock with *Psycho* pointed the way to the dramatic changes that would transform American filmmaking over the next twenty years.

Notes

1   Friedrich, Otto, *City of Nets: A Portrait of Hollywood in the 1940s*. Berkeley: University of California Press, 1986, p. 321.
2   Jon Lewis, *The Road to Romance and Ruin: Teen Films and Youth Culture*. New York: Routledge, 1992.

Explore further

Baty, S. Paige, *American Monroe: The Making of a Body Politic*. Berkeley: University of California Press, 1995.

Buhle, Paul and Dave Wagner, *Blacklisted: The Film Lover's Guide to the Hollywood Blacklist*. New York: Palgrave Macmillan, 2003.

Byars, Jackie, *All That Hollywood Allows: Re-Reading Gender in 1950s Melodrama*. Chapel Hill: University of North Carolina Press, 1991.

Ceplair, Larry and Steven Englund, *The Inquisition in Hollywood: Politics in the Film Community, 1930–60*. Urbana: University of Illinois Press, 2003.

Davis, Blair, *The Battle for the Bs: 1950s Hollywood and the Rebirth of Low-Budget Cinema*. New Brunswick, NJ: Rutgers University Press, 2012.

Doherty, Thomas, *Teenagers and Teenpics: The Juvenilization of American Movies in the 1950s*. Philadelphia: Temple University Press, 2002.

Friedrich, Otto, *City of Nets: A Portrait of Hollywood in the 1940s*. Berkeley: University of California Press, 1986.

Hall, Sheldon, and Steve Neale, *Epics, Spectacles, and Blockbusters: A Hollywood History*. Detroit: Wayne State University Press, 2010.

Hoberman, J., *An Army of Phantoms: American Movies and the Making of the Cold War*. New York: The New Press, 2011.

Humphries, Reynold, *Hollywood's Blacklists: A Political and Cultural History*. Edinburgh: Edinburgh University Press, 2008.

Jones, Darryl, Elizabeth McCarthy, and Bernice M. Murphy (ed.), *It Came from the 1950s!: Popular Culture, Popular Anxieties*. New York: Palgrave Macmillan, 2011.

Kaplan, E. Ann (ed.), *Women in Film Noir*. London: BFI, 1998.

Krutnik, Frank, Steve Neale, Brian Neave, and Peter Stanfield (eds.), *"Un-American" Hollywood: Politics and Film in the Blacklist Era*. New Brunswick, NJ: Rutgers University Press, 2007.

Lev, Peter, *Transforming the Screen*, *1950–1959*. Berkeley: University of California Press, 2006.

Lewis, Jon, *Hollywood v. Hard Core: How the Struggle over Censorship Saved the Modern Film Industry*. New York: New York University, 2000.

Naremore, James, *More Than Night: Film Noir in its Contexts*. Berkeley: University of California Press, 2008.

Pomerance, Murray (ed.), *American Cinema of the 1950s: Themes and Variations*. New Brunswick, NJ: Rutgers University Press, 2005.

Wager, Jans B., *Dames in the Driver's Seat: Rereading Film Noir*. Austin: University of Texas Press, 2005.

CHAPTER 6

Movies big and small: Art movies, blockbusters, and the new Hollywood, 1967–1980

Watching *Nashville* at a suburban multiplex, summer 1975

The patrons who drove up to the suburban movie theater on a lazy summer night in late June 1975 had a choice of four movies playing on four different screens. The innovation of a single movie theater featuring multiple screens – called a **multiplex** – had taken off in the late 1960s and throughout the 1970s. While the first multiplexes featured only two or three screens, by 1975 a theater that had only four screens was starting to seem old-fashioned. Often located in or near the equally new 1970s consumer phenomenon of the shopping mall and featuring ample free parking, multiplexes appealed to the car-based culture of suburbanites.

The four movies playing this evening offer a microcosm of the 1970s screen age in American cinema, ranging from mass-market blockbusters to more personal, idiosyncratic, even experimental films. The largest of the four screens was devoted to that summer's runaway hit, a horror action movie about a New England beach town terrorized by a giant shark and directed by a young man named Steven Spielberg making only his second Hollywood feature, *Jaws*. The movie was a box office sensation, providing a thrilling screen experience that would dramatically influence how Hollywood would make movies and the first big hit for Spielberg, who would go on to become the most successful director in American movie history.

Theater two was also showing an exciting, violent action movie, *Rollerball*, a dystopian science fiction story set in what seemed like the distant future (2018!), where America is controlled by a giant corporation and the public is kept entertained by the brutal sport of Rollerball, a variation of roller derby involving heavily armored teams of roller skaters and often resulting in death. While the movie featured fast-moving action sequences in the Rollerball arena, the film, directed by Norman Jewison, a filmmaker with a reputation for politically engaged movies, also worked as a dark satire on the intersections among government, big business, and the entertainment media.

The third screen featured a sequel, an increasingly popular type of movie in the 1970s, *French Connection 2* (John Frankenheimer), a continuation of the 1971

Multiplex A movie theater that features a number of smaller theaters all showing different movies. The multiplex arose as part of suburban mall culture in the late 1960s and has become the dominant kind of movie theater in the contemporary screen age. The first multiplexes had only two or three screens, although now multiplexes of twenty or more screens are common.

crime thriller *French Connection* directed by William Friedkin that had won the Academy Award for Best Picture. Both *French Connection* movies married the traditional police procedural movie with a gritty, realistic atmosphere and a sense of world-weary cynicism about the criminal justice system. The main character of the New York police detective Popeye Doyle, played by Gene Hackman, was a classic anti-hero, driven to complete his assignment but prone to outbursts of violence and racism.

Moviegoers who chose the fourth theater would have perhaps the most innovative screen experience of all these choices: Robert Altman's ensemble comedy/drama, *Nashville*. A sprawling story about the world of country music and the state of America in the mid-1970s, *Nashville* featured almost two dozen characters and interwove several story lines, including a presidential campaign, the comeback attempt of a sensitive country singer, a legend of the music business being courted by the presidential candidate, aspiring musicians hoping to make it big, and a mysteriously troubled young man.

Altman had established himself as one of the most distinctive and adventurous filmmakers of the 1970s and a central figure in what has come to be called the **New American Cinema**, the Seventies Renaissance, or the New Golden Age of American film. *Nashville* displayed his signature cinematic style. No one figure emerges as the central character of the story, and most scenes contain multiple plot lines occurring all at the same time. Characters speak over each other, and viewers have to put the narrative together out of various interconnected fragments. The movie is at the same time comic and tragic, cynical and sentimental, and the ending remains ultimately unresolved. That a screen experience as challenging and unconventional as *Nashville* was also a popular success (although nowhere near the success of *Jaws*) speaks to why so many critics point to the 1970s as a high point in American cinematic creativity.

A college film society screening of *The Godfather*, October 1976

A crowd begins to gather in a school auditorium for the latest Friday evening screening by the college film society, a group of students from various majors all interested in studying the movies with the same attention and seriousness as courses in literature, music, and theater. Every week they show a different movie they consider of artistic, social, or historic significance, from both America and around the world, from silent classics to tonight's presentation, *The Godfather* from 1972. Unlike commercial movie theaters, the film society rents 16-millimeter versions of

Fig 6.2
Screen legend Marlon
Brando as the Godfather
Don Vito Corleone, head
of the Corleone crime
family, in Francis Ford
Coppola's epic reinvention
of the gangster movie, *The
Godfather*.

their films from distribution companies aimed at the most professional theaters. The
sound for the movie comes solely from the speaker in the projector.

All in all, then, the screen experience for tonight's showing of *The Godfather* will
be noticeably different than when the movie first premiered in 1972. The images and
sounds will be smaller and quieter, but still not as different from the bigger screen
version than when the movie was first televised in 1974, on both color and black-
and-white screens, ranging from living room consoles to small portable sets. Still,
across all of these screen experiences (a range that will only become more diverse
over the coming decades), the movie remains popular and powerful.

The Godfather has developed a reputation not just as one of the most critically
acclaimed of all American movies, but as the film whose box office success helped
save Paramount Pictures and heralded an era in Hollywood filmmaking focused on
the star director. The **auteur** (literally "author") **theory** of filmmaking, developed
in France during the 1950s and imported to the US soon after, elevated the role of
director to that of the visionary artist, the "author" of a movie the way a writer is
author of a book. With *The Godfather*, Paramount reluctantly took a chance on
the 32-year-old director Francis Ford Coppola to make the movie adaptation of
Mario Puzo's bestselling novel about the mafia. Instead of simply making a formula
gangster movie, Coppola structured *The Godfather* like grand opera as he told the
story of the Corleone crime family's violent efforts to maintain their position at the
top of the organized crime hierarchy.

The great set piece of the movie involves a series of executions ordered by the
rising young godfather Michael Corleone (Al Pacino) in retribution for an almost
fatal attack on his father, Don Corleone (Marlon Brando). While we watch the
baptism of Michael's nephew in an ornate church, the camera cuts back and forth
to the various killings, all while we listen to the priest's invocations and Michael's
pledge to renounce evil. The overwhelming success of *The Godfather* suggested
that audiences were becoming receptive to more mature, sophisticated, and violent
filmmaking, and the movie opened the doors for a generation of innovative young
directors.

The very existence of college film societies also speaks to the changing audience
for movies. As the great population shift away from cities and towards the suburbs
continued throughout the 1960s, fewer and fewer families and older Americans made
moviegoing a regular part of their leisure time. Young people under thirty, however,
were going to the movies, and they brought with them both a desire for films that

**Auteur theory and
auteurism** An influential
theory of criticism and
interpretation that views
movies as the unique
stylistic and thematic
expression of their
directors, the relationship
of director to movie
similar to that of author
to book. Auteur theory
developed among a
group of rebellious young
French film writers and
directors in the 1950s
and was popularized in
the US by the movie critic
Andrew Sarris in the early
1960s. Auteur theory has
had a profound effect on
how movies are studied
and discussed and was
influential in the rise
of the New American
Cinema.

spoke more to their own historical perspectives growing up in the turbulence of the 1960s while also providing more thrilling and daring screen experiences. Many older studio executives had a hard time coming to grips with these changes. Box office hits like *My Fair Lady* (George Cukor 1964) and *The Sound of Music* (Robert Wise 1965) looked back to the Hollywood of the 1940s and 1950s, but in many ways these represented the last gasp for this more traditional model of screen experience.

At the same time these musicals premiered, the first film school directors began to enter the movie business. The first efforts at making the study of movies a formal part of academic study date back to the silent era, but it was really in the 1950s and 1960s that colleges and universities began to embrace film as a serious discipline of training and study. These new young filmmakers brought with them an awareness of film history and an international perspective that made them eager to experiment with and challenge long-standing conventions of filmmaking, to create screen experiences they felt more accurately expressed the changing society around them. Francis Ford Coppola, who did his graduate study at the UCLA film school, is a prime example of this new generation of American filmmakers, as were Martin Scorsese (New York film school), George Lucas (USC), and Steven Spielberg (Cal State Long Beach).

Still, even with the expansion of film schools and academic departments, the formal study of cinema was only a fragmented part of many college curriculums, with a few classes offered here and there in theater, English, and communications departments. The proliferation of college film societies, along with the growth of urban art house movie theaters devoted to showing smaller and foreign films, signaled the growing interest in seeing movies as a major art form among many young people. While all of these endeavors at pursuing the study of movies outside the main exhibition structure of Hollywood would be both undermined and transformed by the home video revolution, the structure of the independent "art" movie versus the Hollywood blockbuster endures as a cultural category.

Star Wars premieres at Mann's Chinese Theatre, Hollywood, May 1977

The mainly young crowd who had waited outside for hours to file into the aging theater on Hollywood Boulevard in Los Angeles were able to get a taste of the screen experiences of their parents' and grandparents' generations. The theater called "Mann's Chinese Theatre" in 1977 was still more famously known as "Grauman's Chinese Theatre," a classic downtown movie palace that first opened half a century earlier at the height of the silent age. The extravagant exterior resembled a giant pagoda with an equally flamboyant interior done up in red and gold.

The most famous part of this most famous theater was the large outdoor forecourt, where for decades movie stars and celebrities had planted their footprints and handprints in concrete, one tradition that was still in operation in 1977, even after the theater had been acquired by the multiplex chain of Mann theaters in 1970. Still, the palace was showing signs of its age. As the customers took their seats, they could look up to see netting spread out under the ornately decorated ceiling, there to catch pieces of falling plaster in case of earthquake. Downtown big city theaters, even landmark palaces like the Chinese Theatre, were no longer regular parts of most screen experiences in the 1970s, as the multiplex suburban theater chains dominated the movie exhibition business.

Instead, a trip to a theater like the Chinese was more of a special event, and there was no more special movie event experience in spring 1977 than the opening of

Fig 6.3
Faded but still lavish, the courtyard to what was called Mann's Chinese Theatre at the time this picture was taken in 1982; a survivor from the screen age of downtown movie palaces, when it was called Grauman's Chinese Theatre after its legendary original owner Sid Grauman. Source: Stephanie Colasanti/The Kobal Collection.

George Lucas' space fantasy, *Star Wars*. Seen as a big gamble by 20th Century Fox, *Star Wars* was an amalgam of genres – including science fiction and the western – that seemed out of fashion, and industry insiders were unsure whether the movie's combination of special effects action sequences and tongue-in-cheek campy humor would work with audiences. The thousands of moviegoers who have seen *Star Wars* multiple times over the years since the movie opened have proved that Fox's gamble was right. At the same time, a whole mini-industry arose devoted to selling *Star-Wars*-related products, from action figures to clothing to board games and even records and television specials, producing profits that surpassed box office receipts and creating what came to be known as a franchise movie, a money-generating entertainment vehicle that grew out of the screen experiences of viewers like those waiting for the show to begin at the Chinese Theatre.

Both *Star Wars* and *Jaws*, box office blockbusters that reset the standard for the money that could be produced by a hit movie, are credited and blamed for the significant changes in the movie industry during the screen age of the 1970s. In the negative version of the story, both movies are described as superficial action stories focused more on providing sensational screen experiences than on challenging the expectations and ideas of their audiences. The idea of a franchise movie such as *Star Wars* creating a whole fan culture that would provide the basis for endless consumer products and subsequent can't-miss sequels would come to dominate how studios – and more important, the megacorporations who now owned those studios – would approach the business of making movies. Instead of the openness towards experimentation and creativity that defined other significant Hollywood movies in the 1970s, so this argument goes, Hollywood would retreat into producing thrill rides for young people, chasing the next new box office sensation. Increasingly, Hollywood began focusing on the big summer blockbuster to serves as a "**tentpole**" picture, a hugely popular megahit that would financially support the rest of the studio's business.

There is a great deal of truth to this argument, as we will see in the following chapters, but the actual screen experience of that audience in 1977 also suggests a more complicated reality. Both Spielberg and George Lucas, for example, were products of the film school movement, and both had started their careers with small, personal movies very much in keeping with the new, more adventurous filmmaking of the early 1970s: Spielberg's *The Sugarland Express* (1974), a quirky chase movie based on a true story featuring two charismatic and likeable anti-heroes, and Lucas's *American Graffiti* (1973), a warm and nostalgic look back at small town California in 1962 (based on Lucas's own teenage experiences), right on the cusp of the dramatic changes that would sweep the country over the next ten years.

Star Wars itself is rooted in both Hollywood and world cinema history, including the Japanese master Akira Kurosawa's *The Hidden Fortress* (1958) and John Ford's *The Searchers*. The witty, fast-talking banter between the assertive, far-from-passive Princess Leia (Carrie Fisher) and the charismatic outlaw Han Solo (Harrison Ford) recalls screwball comedies like *His Girl Friday* (Howard Hawks 1940) and *The Awful Truth* (Leo McCarey 1937), right down to the inclusion of slang terms from that earlier screen age as in Leia's description of Han Solo as a "flyboy." The movie even opens like a 1940s Saturday matinee serial, with a screen crawl describing what we are about to see as "Episode Four," as if these are characters we had been following every weekend for months.

If the opening screen crawl invited viewers to think of an earlier screen age, the next shot provided a thrilling visual and sonic spectacle that represented the state of the art in 1970s special effects: a vast starry vista of outer space is suddenly filled with a giant space ship looming over our heads, chasing a smaller craft into the distance, the sound of the ship's engines rumbling the theater (the fact that there would really be no sound in outer space has not bothered the movie's legions of fans). For the fans in the once glamorous movie palace, experiencing *Star Wars* on a

Tentpole movie The "tentpole" movie refers to a huge summer blockbuster whose profits will support a movie studio's overall operations for the year. Steven Spielberg's massive hit *Jaws* is usually credited – or blamed – as the first tentpole movie.

Fig 6.4
The wise-cracking banter between the characters of Luke Skywalker (Mark Hamill), Princess Leia (Carrie Fisher), and Han Solo (Harrison Ford) links *Star Wars* to the fast-talking screwball comedies of the 1930s and 1940s.

huge screen provided both an up-to-date visual thrill and a sense of reliving the past, of what it must have been like to watch a movie in what was already being called the "Golden Age" of Hollywood. In this way, the screen experience of *Star Wars* looks both forward and backward, recalling (and redefining) the magic of the past of Hollywood while also creating new models for the future of screen experiences in America.

Case study 6.1: *Star Wars* and its sources

Although the original *Star Wars* movie is often seen as part of a decisive change from older styles of moviemaking towards the contemporary focus on blockbuster franchise movies heavy on special effects and light on character development, we can also look at former film student George Lucas's movie as a complex homage to the history of American and world cinema. We have already suggested that *Star Wars* pays tribute to the Saturday matinee adventure serials of the 1940s; the popularity of the *Star Wars* franchise has led to an explosion of research and scholarship, both formal and informal, into other sources for Lucas's original movie, some specifically pointed out by Lucas, such as the Japanese director Akira Kurosawa's 1957 samurai movie *The Hidden Fortress*, and others derived from interpretive arguments made by fans and critics.

You can learn more about *Star Wars* and about how screen experiences evolve and influence one another over time by exploring some of the sources for *Star Wars*. Begin with published interviews with Lucas about his influences for the movie and supplement this with the work of academic scholars and serious movie critics. Then, seek out some of these cinematic sources and watch them for yourself, looking for specific evidence of both thematic (i.e. what the story is about) and stylistic (i.e. how the story is told) influences on *Star Wars*. Then, write about how you think these influences informed the choices and creative decisions made by Lucas in creating *Star Wars* as well as how your research into these sources has affected your own experience of the movie.

Screen ages

The turning point

The 1960s and 1970s were among the most turbulent decades in American history. The civil rights movement led by Dr. Martin Luther King, Jr. ended legal segregation in the South and dramatically transformed race and politics in the country. King's subsequent murder was part of a wave of political violence beginning with the assassination of President John F. Kennedy and later his brother, the presidential candidate Senator Robert Kennedy, demonstrations at the 1968 Democratic National Convention in Chicago, and the shooting of college students during anti-Vietnam war protests at Kent State University and Jackson State University in 1970. The war, America's longest before the war in Afghanistan in the twenty-first century, killed almost 60,000 US soldiers and over a million Vietnamese and fractured the national community in ways that resonate to the present.

In terms of American cinema, this atmosphere of conflict and protest, of challenges to social constructions of racial, gender, and sexual identity, also decisively changed the course of the movies. There have been many dividing lines in American

Fig 6.5
The March on Washington for Jobs and Freedom on August 28, 1963, one of the largest human rights protests in American history, was a landmark in the civil rights movement, culminating in the Reverend Martin Luther King, Jr.'s stirring "I have a dream" speech. Source: Magnum Photos. © Leonard Freed/Magnum Photos.

cinema history – from silent to sound, from the studios era to the television era – but the late 1960s and the 1970s mark an irreversible change in terms of presentations of violence and sexuality, in the style and form of movie narratives, and in the screen expectations of viewers. While movies like *The Godfather*, *Star Wars*, and *Apocalypse Now* show some signs of their late 1960s and 1970s context, they still seem more contemporary to us, more in line with our expectations for representations of violence, sexuality, and attitudes towards government and society, than films made just a few years earlier such as *The Sound of Music*, *Pillow Talk*, or *The Ten Commandments*.

The late 1960s and the 1970s connect to contemporary cinema in another important way. It is one of the ironies of this screen age that what many critics have described as a Second Golden Age of American movies in terms of artistry, innovation, and the willingness to create screen experiences that challenged audiences, was also the era in which the main movie companies were absorbed into multinational corporations. Rather than existing as companies devoted solely to the making and distribution of movies, the major studios would increasingly function as component parts of massive conglomerates that started as automobile parts manufacturers (Gulf+Western, which acquired Paramount Studios), finance and insurance companies (Transamerica, which acquired United Artists), and hotel owners (Kirk Kerkorian, who acquired MGM). Since then, the ownership of the major movie studios (or at least the brand names of major studios) has changed hands many times as these conglomerates merged, took over one another, and transformed into the massive international entertainment industry of today. That this move towards greater incorporation of the movies into globalized capitalism occurred at the same time as a flourishing of artistic creativity defines one of the tensions that defined this screen age.

Screen experiences big and small

As the 1960s turned into the 1970s, the screen experiences available to fans of visual narrative continued to expand and diversify. Television technology continued to produce screens that were ever bigger and featured increasingly sharp images. Color television grew from being a novelty to the norm, and as a result, the movies also adopted color as the default medium for film production, in part to match the expectation of audiences accustomed to color TV, and in part to ensure that television would remain interested in broadcasting Hollywood movies. In fact, television viewing continued to develop as a major part of movie experience, further blurring the distinctions between movies and TV. Networks competed for the rights to be the first to show hit movies on television during prime time. For millions of Americans, the small screen of television was the main way they experienced some of the most significant and groundbreaking movies of the screen age, as when NBC aired *The Godfather* in 1974. At the same time, the television networks themselves began creating "television movies." One of Steven Spielberg's most important early movies, *Duel* (1971), was made for television.

Movie exhibition became at the same time bigger – with the proliferation of multiplexes – and smaller – from those same multiplexes squeezing ever tinier screening rooms into their theaters, and "art house" theaters opening focused on boutique screenings of "art" films and historically significant movies. The idea of "boutique" screenings went along with the idea of going to the movies as more of a special event than a regular routine. Where a fan in the 1940s might go to the movies two or three times a week, seeing whatever happened to be playing, Hollywood marketing in the 1970s increasingly focused on the idea that the individual movie itself was the draw. Seeing *The Godfather* or *The Exorcist* wasn't sold as just another entertainment experience; advertising promoted them as significant cultural events, urging viewers to join in an important collective cultural experience.

The idea of movies as "special events" – as opposed to the mundane quality of television – was part of Hollywood's continuing efforts to differentiate the movie experience, efforts that resulted in the final breakdown of the Production Code. Studio executives, producers, distributors, and exhibitors were convinced that movies needed to become ever more daring, explicit, and sensational, providing experiences and exploring subject matter unavailable to viewers on the smaller screen, from language to nudity to violence. A single, uniform Production Code had become increasingly anachronistic, especially as movie audiences grew younger. The idea of a single production code instead defined the broadcast television experience, where the Federal Communication Commission defined standards of obscenity and decency, as referred to in the late comedian George Carlin's 1972 satirical routine, "Seven Words You Can Never Say on Television." Carlin's ridicule took on added relevance given that those same seven words were now regularly heard in the multiplex as the ratings system took hold.

The ratings system

The movie ratings system – the same system in use today – was created in 1967 by the MPAA as the result of negotiations between studios and exhibitors. Rather than demanding that all movies meet the standards of a single code, the rating system followed the British practice of creating categories of movies that could only be shown to certain audiences. The initial rating system ranged from the still-existing "G" for general audiences to "M" for Mature, "R" for Restricted to those over sixteen or minors with an adult, and "X" for adults over 18 only. In theory, moviemakers could now make their films any way they wanted, and the MPAA would then sort them in terms of which rating is appropriate. In practice, studios targeted specific ratings for their productions based on box office projections, and just as in the Code era producers and directors began to negotiate with the MPAA over these rating designations. Still, the immediate impact of the ratings system was dramatic, as filmmakers embraced this greater freedom of expression.

Vietnam and the end of the American empire

The period immediately following World War II saw the United States emerge as a massive world power, politically, economically, and culturally. With much of Europe in ruins, the US was able to dominate the world economy in the 1950s and 1960s. The Cold War defined the US and the Soviet Union as the two major "superpowers" vying for global influence and power. As one European colony after another began achieving independence, both the US and the USSR sought to extend their influence over these newly liberated countries, often using and fomenting conflicts in these fledgling countries as a means of challenging each other. Korea, Guatemala, Iran, the Dominican Republic, Cuba – each became a battleground used by both countries as part of this political struggle.

The war in Vietnam began after France abandoned its former colony in the 1950s in the face of a revolution led by Marxist guerillas. Concerned that the new government in Vietnam would become a satellite of the Soviet Union, the United States picked up where France left off, first with military advisors and CIA operatives, but then with an open military conflict. It's almost impossible to overestimate the impact of the war in Vietnam on the culture of the 1960s and 1970s. With the final defeat and expulsion of US forces in 1975, the war shattered illusions about American supremacy and moral superiority, especially among the large population of "baby boomers" who came of age during the period and who supplied the soldiers who fought in the war.

The civil rights movement further demanded that Americans confront the legacy of racial oppression and brutality by insisting on the justice of full economic, social, and political equality for African Americans, a struggle that continues to this day. The Watergate scandal, involving the cover-up of activities by White House officials

Fig 6.6
American helicopters create their own movie soundtrack by blaring Richard Wagner's "Ride of the Valkyries" from loudspeakers as they attack a Vietnamese fishing village in Francis Ford Coppola's *Apocalypse Now* (1979), a movie that reflects the profound divide in the United States created by the war in Vietnam.

in the Nixon administration to sabotage the Democratic Party candidate George McGovern in the 1972 presidential election, led to the unprecedented resignation of President Richard Nixon. For millions of Americans, especially young Americans, this history of violence and scandal made them skeptical of conventional Hollywood narratives that now seemed formulaic or naive, and this dissatisfaction was increasingly reflected in declining box office revenues.

Always wary of taking risks, the established Hollywood studios were initially slow to register this impact. Many of the studio executives were older men raised in earlier screen ages of the movies, and they felt as disconnected from the rapidly changing American society around them as these younger viewers felt by the usual movie fare. At the same time, the takeover of major studios by giant corporations that had started with MCA's acquisition of Universal Studios in 1962 brought increasing pressure on the bottom line. It was evident that Hollywood needed yet another new business model.

Getting bigger by getting smaller

As we have said, a central paradox of this period of massive change in Hollywood revolves around the fact that movies in this screen age became at the same time more corporate and more adventurous, both bigger and smaller. One way of exploring this seeming contradiction between art and business is in terms of the economic crisis faced by Hollywood in the mid-1960s. We can understand what has come to be called the New American Cinema less in terms of whether the studios suddenly became more artistically sensitive and more as a case of a greater willingness to bankroll various experiments as part of chasing a younger, more critical audience.

These experiments involved movies that displayed a more critical social awareness and used new modes of storytelling as well as films that promised more exciting and sensational screen experiences, often in the same movie. While it is possible to see movies like Robert Altman's *Nashville* and George Lucas' *Star Wars* as representing two completely different strands in 1970s Hollywood, it can be just as useful to see them as equally products of the New American Cinema. Some of the key films of the late 1960s that signaled this new openness to experimentation, including the groundbreaking *Bonnie and Clyde* (Arthur Penn 1967), *The Graduate* (Mike Nichols 1968), *2001: A Space Odyssey* (Stanley Kubrick 1968), *M*A*S*H* (Robert Altman 1970), and especially *Easy Rider* (Dennis Hopper 1969), underlined the box office power of the youth audience.

Fig 6.7
"We rob banks." Profoundly influenced by the intimacy and experimentation of French New Wave filmmakers, Arthur Penn's *Bonnie and Clyde*, starring Faye Dunaway and Warren Beatty as the Depression-era bank robbers/folk heroes Bonnie Parker and Clyde Barrow, was a surprise box office hit and helped inaugurate a new era in American filmmaking.

All of these movies challenged narrative conventions and were much more critical of the cultural status quo than older Hollywood films, including the American dream in *The Graduate*, the war in Vietnam in *M*A*S*H*, and ideas of right and wrong in American history in *Bonnie and Clyde*. At the same time, these films were also more shocking and explicit in their representations of sexuality, nudity, and violence compared to the Production Code era. The relationship between social criticism and visual sensation was and remains complex and intertwined. A movie such as Sam Peckinpah's revisionist western *The Wild Bunch* (1969) was both widely praised and criticized for its graphic depictions of violence involving slow motion sequences and exploding blood packs. At the same time, viewers both then and now made connections between this story of a group of aging outlaws who became entangled as hired guns in the Mexican revolution of the 1910s and the war in Vietnam.

None of these early successes came easily. There was great reluctance to make *Bonnie and Clyde* and much skepticism over its prospects. *Easy Rider*, an ultra low budget road movie about two hippie bikers looking to make a drug deal before being murdered by right-wing thugs, all to a modern rock soundtrack, took Hollywood completely by surprise when it became the third highest grossing movie of 1969. The critical and commercial success of *The Godfather* in 1972 opened the space for investing in more personal, director-centered movies by filmmakers such as Hal Ashby (the cult black comedy *Harold and Maude* in 1971; the political and social satire *Shampoo* in 1975; the anti-war *Coming Home* in 1978), Alan Pakula (the neo-film noir *Klute* in 1971; the conspiracy thriller *The Parallax View* in 1974; the Watergate scandal in *All the President's Men* in 1976), and Martin Scorsese (*Mean Streets* in 1972; the ultra-violent *Taxi Driver* in 1976; the boxing epic *Raging Bull* in 1980).

Fig 6.8
Made for less than $400,000 and earning more than $40 million at the box office, the success of the road movie *Easy Rider*, featuring co-producer and writer Peter Fonda (in the stars and stripes helmet) and co-producer, writer, and director Dennis Hopper (on the other motorcycle) as two hippies crossing the country on their way to Mardi Gras, shocked the Hollywood establishment and demonstrated the growing influence of the 1960s counterculture. The movie also featured a young Jack Nicholson (wearing the football helmet), who would go on to become one of Hollywood's biggest stars.

Case study 6.2: Youth culture and Hollywood: The case of *Easy Rider*

The astonishing box office success of *Easy Rider* in 1969, an ultra low-budget, largely improvised road trip story about hippies traveling across the country on motorcycles with a soundtrack featuring rock artists of the day such as Jimi Hendrix and The Byrds, took mainstream Hollywood by surprise. Made by Dennis Hopper, a longtime Hollywood actor, and Peter Fonda, the son of Hollywood legend Henry Fonda and brother of Jane Fonda, *Easy Rider* sparked an intense debate among movie industry professionals, film critics, and movie fans about what the movie meant for the future of American cinema. To this day, critical opinion remains divided about why exactly *Easy Rider* was such a landmark movie, what influence it has had, and even whether it is a very good film.

Explore this landmark movie in 1960s and 1970s American cinema by reading what people at the time were saying about *Easy Rider*. Begin with your own screen experience of the film. What is your overall reaction? What about the movie strikes you as most "typical" of the time in which it was made? Can you see traces of *Easy Rider* in later movies you have seen? Write some initial speculations and guesses about why you think the movie was so popular and controversial. Next, read through reviews and articles from 1969 about *Easy Rider*. What kind of a critical conversation emerged about the movie? What did the filmmakers say? What do you find most surprising about these comments? Which seemed to have been the most farsighted? Finally, read more recent scholarship and discussions of *Easy Rider* that attempt to place the movie in historical context. Complete your exploration by writing about how you now think about the significance of *Easy Rider* in American movie history.

Fig 6.9
Often featuring casts of fading Hollywood legends and television character actors, movies like *The Poseidon Adventure* showed that screen experiences promising spectacular visual effects and stories of daring escapes remained a popular way to differentiate the big screen of the movie theater from the small screen of television in the 1970s. Source: 20th Century Fox / The Kobal Collection.

The 1970s saw other new trends and genres that also built on creating screen experiences that took advantage of the greater freedoms offered by the ratings system, experiences that further underlined the differences between what could be seen at the movies and what could be shown on TV. Many of these new genres have continued to this day, further underlining the connections between this screen age and now. **Disaster movies**, for example, built on the success of *Airport* (George Seaton 1970), a story of a crippled airliner attempting to land after a bomb explodes mid-flight. These movies usually featured large casts combining older movie stars and television actors, and followed a basic plot line of disaster victims struggling to survive. *The Poseidon Adventure* (Ronald Neame and Irwin Allen 1972) featured an ocean liner overturned by a tidal wave; *The Towering Inferno* (John Guillerman 1974) a skyscraper on fire; and *Earthquake* (Mark Robson 1974) a killer earthquake striking Los Angeles (selected theaters showing *Earthquake* also boasted of offering the movie in Sensurround, a bass-heavy sound system that produced vibrations meant to simulate the on-screen earthquake). The disaster movie genre would later be hilariously parodied in the 1980 cult classic *Airplane!* (Jim Abrahams, David Zucker, and Jerry Zucker).

Don Siegel, the great action movie director responsible for *Invasion of the Body Snatchers*, helped start a cycle of vigilante movies in the 1970s with *Dirty Harry* (1971) starring Clint Eastwood, the first in a series of five films centered on the character of Harry Callahan, a rogue San Francisco cop who takes the law into his own hands. Subsequent movies such as *Walking Tall* (Phil Karlson 1974) and *Death Wish* (Michael Winner 1974) likewise featured characters (in the first a small-town sheriff, in the second a "regular guy" whose wife is raped and killed) disgusted by government corruption and what they see as the inability of the authorities to protect the community from crime and lawlessness, who similarly act as their own judge and jury.

The idea of the righteous vigilante takes the archetype of the "Lone Ranger" from the tradition of the western and creates another enduring figure in American cinema, from *Bullitt* (Peter Yates 1968) to *The French Connection* to *The Seven Ups* (Philip D'Antoni 1973) in this screen age, to later incarnations such as the *Die Hard* and *Lethal Weapon* series and the angrier version of Batman seen in Christopher Nolan's *Dark Knight* series in the 2000s. These movies often embody a conservative and even reactionary response to the tumult and counter-culture of the 1960s and 1970s (the serial killer in *Dirty Harry* is loosely associated with hippie culture), although a low-budget cult film such as *Billy Jack* (Tom Laughlin 1971) can be

Disaster movies A popular subgenre of movies in the 1970s, typically centered on an ensemble cast of characters each trying to survive a particular kind of disaster, from the man-made (a ship capsizing in *The Poseidon Adventure*, a skyscraper on fire in *The Towering Inferno*) to the natural (such as *Earthquake*).

Fig 6.10
"Do you feel lucky?" The character of the vigilante cop "Dirty" Harry Callahan, played by Clint Eastwood, who specialized in action anti-heroes, expressed reactionary anxieties over the social revolutions of the 1960s and 1970s, with a hero who both defended and rebelled against the status quo.

seen as a left-wing vigilante movie, as the title character uses martial arts skills to defend a counter-cultural multiracial school. *Bullitt* reintroduced the exciting car chase, a staple of early silent cinema, to the movies with a new degree of realism, a screen experience that continues in the *Fast and Furious* series. Martin Scorsese's groundbreaking *Taxi Driver* is itself a kind of commentary on vigilante movies, as the psychotic title character becomes an unlikely media star after he murders a pimp.

Horror also benefitted from the openness to a greater intensity of screen experiences, with results that obscured the distinction between artistically ambitious "auteur" movies and genre favorites. Both *Rosemary's Baby* (Roman Polanski 1968) and *The Exorcist* (William Friedkin 1973) were directed by critically acclaimed "auteur" directors but also became box office hits, a pattern that culminated in Stanley Kubrick's adaptation of Stephen King's *The Shining* (1980). Towards the end of the decade, John Carpenter's low-budget box office hit *Halloween* (1978) was part of an emergence of a new kind of horror movie, the slasher film, that built on the example of *Psycho* to initiate a long-standing subgenre that combined psychotic killers and fears about teenage – specifically female – sexuality with almost comically graphic violence to create a popular and influential subgenre that continues today with movies like the *Hostel* and *Saw* series.

Sequels and franchises

To the multinational corporations that were acquiring movie studios in the 1960s and 1970s, movies were seen less as works of art or even exciting cultural experiences than as potential profit generators. As part of the perpetual search for a business model that provided stability and predictability, Hollywood increasingly turned to the sequel as a means of building on audience affection and familiarity in order to create a lucrative movie franchise. George Lucas' *Star Wars* movies, Sylvester Stallone's *Rocky* and *Rambo* movies, and Steven Spielberg's *Indiana Jones* series are prime examples, but throughout the 1970s any successful movie was guaranteed to produce sequels that slapped a number on after the original title. While sequels developed a poor reputation as unoriginal knock-offs or repetitions of the original, the practice extended to more critically praised movies as well. *The Godfather Part II* (Francis Ford Coppola 1974) was as well received as the first, and both movies won Best Picture Oscars. Of all the trends to emerge from this screen age, perhaps none is as enduring or significant in terms of the movie business than the reliance on sequels and the **franchise movie**.

By the end of the 1970s, the franchise model seemed to promise a new stable business model for the conglomerates. At the same time, a backlash developed

Franchise movie A movie popular enough to spawn sequels as well as a wide range of cross-marketing opportunities, from soundtrack albums to toys to sponsor tie-ins. The most successful franchise movies, such as *Star Wars* or the *Indiana Jones* movies, have become cultural icons, almost a part of American folklore. Beginning in the 1970s, the major Hollywood studios have focused on creating franchise movies in order to ensure large and predictable sources of income.

Fig 6.11
The *Rocky* franchise, one of the most lucrative of the 1980s, started with a personal, low-budget, character-driven movie written by and starring Sylvester Stallone, who would go on to become an international action superstar.

against the "auteur" approach, the idea of giving certain star directors free reign to come up with bold new screen experiences as a way of exciting audiences. The franchise model and the intensely loyal fan base created by movies such as *Star Wars* seemed a safer, more profitable way of engaging and keeping young people coming to the movies. Two controversial productions from the end of this screen age – Francis Ford Coppola's Vietnam war epic *Apocalypse Now* (1979) and particularly Michael Cimino's equally epic western *Heaven's Gate* (1980) – became notorious for running far over budget and taking far longer to finish than originally planned, and for many Hollywood executives they signaled the need to control costs and exert much greater control over the production process. Ironically, while *Heaven's Gate* was a box office dud, *Apocalypse Now* did turn a respectable profit and is now seen as a classic of the era (even *Heaven's Gate* found a more favorable critical reception in later years). Still, Coppola's movie was not the surprising hit his *The Godfather* had been ten years earlier. Although it was number four at the box office that year, the movies at number three and number five – *Rocky II* (Sylvester Stallone) and the first movie adaptation of the cult TV show *Star Trek* (Robert Wise) – both seemed less risky choices in the multinational conglomerate film business at the end of the 1970s.

In development

Comedy in the 1970s: Woody Allen and Mel Brooks

Through the first seventy-five years of American movie history, most film comedians had come from vaudeville, burlesque, and music hall traditions, essentially pre-cinema traditions that filmmakers such as Charlie Chaplin and the Marx Brothers adapted to the still relatively new medium of the movies. In the late 1960s and into the 1970s, however, new generations of comic artists raised on movies began to make movies. Rather than adapting older styles of comedy to the movies, these filmmakers were steeped in traditions of movie comedy, and this cinematic awareness informed and transformed the comic screen experiences they created. No two filmmakers were more influential and important in this regard than Mel Brooks and Woody Allen.

Both Brooks (born Melvin James Kaminsky) and Allen (born Allen Stewart Konigsberg) grew up in New York City and began their comic careers as stand-up comedians and writers for the television in the 1950s. Just as important, both were also steeped in the rich traditions of Jewish-American humor. This tradition forms one of the key components of American humor and has deeply influenced the development of movie comedy, from the Marx Brothers to Jerry Lewis. Like many earlier Jewish movie comedians and entertainers, both Brooks and Allen adopted less "ethnic"-sounding stage names at the beginnings of their careers, but when they turned to filmmaking, neither hid their religious heritage. Indeed, their Jewish identities worked as defining parts of their film personas and a key source of humor as they used their outsider status to satirize American society.

Brooks is most well-known for his parodies of cinema history, screen experiences that build and rely on his audience's familiarity with that history, beginning with his work on the 1960s television show *Get Smart*, an absurdist parody of James Bond spy movies. His first movie, *The Producers* (1968), established Brooks as a comic filmmaker unafraid of challenging viewers' expectations. An outrageous parody of show-business greed and a bold satire of anti-Semitism, the movie follows

Fig 6.12
Mel Brooks. Source: 20th
Century Fox/The Kobal
Collection.

Fig 6.13
As Sheriff Bart (Cleavon
Little) rides across the
American west, the
moving camera reveals
jazz legend Count Basie's
orchestra playing the
soundtrack we hear
in the background in
Mel Brooks's surreal,
provocative, and earthy
western parody *Blazing
Saddles*.

the efforts of a lovably corrupt theater producer and his naive partner to create a
sure-fire Broadway flop in order to fleece investors. The play they fund, *Springtime
for Hitler*, a musical tribute to the founder of the Nazi Party, becomes a surprising
camp hit. Brooks's willingness to ridicule racism with chorus lines of high-kicking
stormtroopers made *The Producers* into a cult hit and helped establish a tradition of
outrageous movie comedy.

   In his most popular movies of the 1970s, Brooks parodied westerns (*Blazing
Saddles* 1974); classic Universal horror movies (*Young Frankenstein* 1974); and
Alfred Hitchcock (*High Anxiety* 1977). He even made a tribute to silent filmmaking,
appropriately titled *Silent Movie* (1976). As much parodies of the moviemaking

process as of specific movie genres, these are screen experiences made by a movie fan for other movie fans, constantly breaking the illusion of movie reality for comic effect, as when in *Blazing Saddles* an exterior panning shot set to a lush musical soundtrack suddenly reveals a full orchestra in formal attire playing in the middle of the desert. As in *The Producers*, Brooks consistently tackled and satirized issues of race and ethnicity in ways traditional Hollywood movies had been too timid to address.

Woody Allen also shared the same traditions of Jewish humor and love for American film as Mel Brooks, but he combined his talent for physical and verbal comedy with a deep appreciation for global art cinema, moving from gag-filled early movies to reinventing the romantic comedy in *Annie Hall* (1977). His first major movie, *Take the Money and Run* (1969), the supposedly true story of an inept career criminal named Virgil Starkwell, is a forerunner of the mockumentary tradition seen in later movies such as *This is Spinal Tap* (Rob Reiner 1984) and television programs like *The Office*. The movie is more a collection of comic set pieces than a real narrative, a model Allen would follow in his early comedies.

His early successes with *Bananas* (1971), a joke-based satire of revolutionary politics, and especially *Sleeper* (1973), a comedy set 200 years in the future that makes fun of the pop culture, politics, and gender relations of the early 1970s, established Allen along with Brooks as a major American comic filmmaker. Allen also used these early movies to establish his trademark screen persona of the nebbish, a perpetual failure who is socially awkward, physically inept, bookish, intellectual, and sarcastic. As deliberately crafted and almost as well-known as Chaplin's Little Tramp, this screen persona continued to inform those movies of his in which he also stars, even as his narratives became more realistic and less gag-driven.

Love and Death (1975), a parody of both Russian literature and Russian film history, showed Allen's increasing ambitions as a filmmaker, with sequences that reference images from silent classics such as Sergei Eisenstein's *The Battleship Potemkin* (1925). With *Annie Hall*, Allen's critical reputation decisively changed. One of the most influential romantic comedies in American cinema history, *Annie Hall* rewrites the basic rules of the genre, one that had been in serious decline since the early 1960s. Social challenges to restrictive conventions of sexual behavior and gender identity suddenly made the traditional courtship story seem not just old-fashioned, but even repressive and reactionary.

Fig 6.14
Diane Keaton as the title character and Woody Allen as the neurotic comic Alvy Singer in Allen's *Annie Hall*, a romantic comedy that reflected the rapidly changing gender roles for men and women in the 1970s.

Rather than a story of a successful courtship and marriage, *Annie Hall* tells the story of an ultimately failed but still meaningful and worthwhile relationship. *Annie Hall* is told in retrospect with Allen's character of Alvy Singer as a voice-over narrator, and makes inventive use of split-screens, subtitles, and even animation. At the end of the movie, Alvy and the title character (played by Diane Keaton) are no longer romantically involved, but they part as friends, with Singer admitting how much their love affair meant to him. *Annie Hall* became one of the few comedies to win the Best Picture Oscar and has become one of the most influential films of the 1970s, echoed in movies from *When Harry Met Sally* (Rob Reiner 1989) to *500 Days of Summer* (Marc Webb 2009).

Allen ended the decade with *Manhattan* (1970), a multi-character ensemble romantic comedy shot in gorgeous black and white by cinematographer Gordon Willis that also serves as a love letter to his native New York City. From his first movies in the late 1960s to the present, Allen has remained one of the most prolific and inventive filmmakers in American cinema history, having directed over 45 movies so far, including comedies, dramas, and various combinations of both.

Blaxploitation movies

Blaxploitation cinema refers to a popular and controversial series of movies focused on African American inner-city life that became popular with multiracial audiences across the country in the 1970s. Usually focused on the struggles of poor and working-class young black men and women, most Blaxploitation films were versions of crime action movies. The protagonists ranged from black detectives – either private eyes or cops – fighting both urban crime and white racism, as in *Shaft* (Gordon Parks 1971) and *Cotton Comes to Harlem* (Ossie Davis 1970) to the vigilante-style characters portrayed by Pam Grier in *Coffy* (Jack Hill 1973) and *Foxy Brown* (Jack Hill 1974), up-and-coming gangsters in the drug trade like Ron O'Neal's Priest in *Superfly* (Gordon Parks, Jr. 1974), and even versions of classic horror characters like the title character of *Blacula* (William Cain 1972).

As we have seen throughout the early screen ages of American cinema history, mainstream Hollywood had been reluctant to make movies by and about African Americans. In fact, many of the most influential screen experiences produced by Hollywood, from *The Birth of a Nation* to *Gone with the Wind* reinforced an American racial and ethnic mythology that racial harmony depended on every group knowing and accepting their place in the social hierarchy. Filmmakers like Oscar Micheaux had to work in a separate but unequal tradition of black film in order to present more complex and even subversive experiences of the variety and pressures of African American life.

The civil rights movement of the 1960s and 1970s presented a decisive challenge to these racial hierarchies and mythologies. At the same time, African American audiences were proving to be among the most loyal moviegoers as attendance began declining in the 1960s. As white audiences moved to the suburbs, downtown movie theaters began serving greater numbers of black and Latino fans. Hollywood gradually became more open to movies that highlighted race and racial discrimination as themes. Movies like *In the Heat of the Night* (Norman Jewison 1967), about a black police detective from Philadelphia who investigates a murder with a white southern sheriff, and *Guess Who's Coming to Dinner* (Stanley Kramer 1967), a social comedy about interracial romance, became box office hits. Both films starred Sidney Poitier, who became the most popular black movie star in American

Blaxploitation A series of movies popular in the 1970s focused on the lives and experiences of working-class, urban, African American characters. Most movies labeled as Blaxploitation are lower-budget films, often though not exclusively crime movies focused on the drug trade. Blaxploitation movies arose in response to the surprising (to Hollywood executives) success of Melvin Van Peebles's independent *Sweet Sweetback's Baadasssss Song* and MGM's *Shaft* (Gordon Parks), both from 1971. Proponents of Blaxploitation cinema credit the movement with providing greater visibility and filmmaking opportunities for black actors and directors as well as creating innovative and exciting new approaches to action moviemaking; critics point out that many of these movies reinforce stereotypes about inner-city black life, especially the prevalence of crime and violence.

Fig 6.15
Richard Roundtree (left)
as the hardboiled private
eye John Shaft in the most
successful and influential
of the Blaxploitation
movies, *Shaft*.

film history to that point. Soon thereafter, the economic success of films like *Cotton Comes to Harlem*, *Shaft*, and the low-budget, independent feature *Sweet Sweetback's Baadasssss Song* (Melvin Van Peebles 1971) started the Blaxploitation trend.

Why were these movies seen as controversial? On the one hand, Blaxploitation films featured African Americans as the center of action and drama, and they provided entry points for a new generation of black film directors including Van Peebles, Ossie Davis, Gordon Parks, and even Sidney Poitier himself. Black actors such as Richard Roundtree, Pam Grier, and the former football stars Fred Williamson and Jim Brown all became movie stars and household names across the US. Almost all of these films used soundtracks featuring contemporary soul and rhythm and blues music. Both Isaac Hayes' score for *Shaft* and Curtis Mayfield's for *Superfly* became bestsellers and soul classics. For the first time in American cinema history, movies about African American life were a major part of the movie landscape and a major genre of Hollywood filmmaking.

On the other hand, these movies could also be seen as reinforcing racist stereotypes of the urban black male as hustler, pimp, or drug dealer. Worse, as with the gangster films of the early 1930s, some feared that these movies glorified criminal activity, making these drug dealers and pimps into glamorous, exciting, and charismatic figures. Did Blaxploitation really represent a breakthrough for black culture and filmmaking, or were these films simply modern versions of the stereotypes that had long defined the worst of Hollywood's depictions of black life and identity? Whatever the answer, these screen experiences were clearly enormously attractive to millions of mostly younger Americans of many races, both urban and suburban.

1970s Blaxploitation cinema profoundly influenced the development of hip-hop and rap culture, including much of its visual culture and mythology, from the late 1970s to today. In film, the resurgence of black action movies in the early 1990s can be seen as a homage to and updating of the Blaxploitation film. For many contemporary directors, most famously Quentin Tarantino in movies like *Jackie Brown* (1997) and *Django Unchained* (2012), the energy, creativity, and stylized violence of 1970s Blaxploitation cinema remains a powerful influence.

Genres of gender: Nontraditional leading men: Dustin Hoffman, Al Pacino, Richard Dreyfuss

What is a leading man? A cinematic gender genre that embodies ideas and ideals of sexual attractiveness, charismatic heroism, and cultural values? Over the course of American cinema history, we can trace how the model of the leading man changes and evolves, from the debonair sophistication of John Gilbert in the silent era to larger-than-life, action-oriented figures like John Wayne, to brooding, intense, passionate characters such as James Dean. The gender genre of the leading man means more than just a central character in a cinematic narrative; the leading man also reflects larger ideas and participates in conflicts about ethnicity, social class, race, gender, power, and authority.

In the 1960s and 1970s, the stars of *Butch Cassidy and the Sundance Kid* (George Roy Hill 1969) and *The Sting* (George Roy Hill 1973) – Paul Newman and Robert Redford – exemplified an older ideal of the leading man: tall, thin, with blue eyes. Coded as white, their ethnic identity was supposed to be invisible and generic, registering simply as "American." Both were among the biggest stars of this and subsequent screen ages. But as the history of America and American cinema has shown, there is no such thing as "simply American," and in the late 1960s a group of actors achieved stardom whose appearance and behavior signaled a new openness to the idea and ideal of the "leading man." These new versions of the gender genre of the leading man suggest the dissatisfaction with older narrative conventions in the wake of the business downturn of the late 1960s and an effort to find screen actors who embodied different conceptions of masculinity.

Dustin Hoffman

When he rose to stardom after his role in *The Graduate* (Mike Nichols 1967) as Benjamin Braddock, the disaffected college graduate who drifts into an affair with an older woman before running away with her daughter, Dustin Hoffman definitely broke with the classical Hollywood model of the leading man. Shorter than most

Fig 6.16
Paul Newman (left) as Butch Cassidy and Robert Redford as the Sundance Kid, two of Hollywood's biggest stars and the definition of mainstream gender genres of masculine beauty in the 1960s and 1970s.

Fig 6.17
As the alienated recent college graduate Benjamin Braddock in *The Graduate*, Dustin Hoffman defined a less glamorized, more conflicted gender genre of the masculine romantic hero.

of his co-stars, with a prominent nose and nervous, even neurotic persona, his performance spoke to the disillusionment and anxiety of college-age moviegoers in an era of cultural and social upheaval. Hoffman seemed more obviously "ethnic" – another way of saying that his presence foregrounded the idea of ethnicity as a fundamental part of all versions of the American identity. Over the course of the 1970s and beyond, he played a wide variety of roles, from the street hustler Ratso Rizzo in *Midnight Cowboy* (John Schlesinger 1969) to the title character of the anti-Vietnam war western *Little Big Man* (Arthur Penn 1970) to the investigative journalist Carl Bernstein in *All the President's Men* (Alan J. Pakula 1976), a movie in which he co-starred next to the more traditional leading man, Redford.

Al Pacino

Also small in stature but known for the fierce intensity of his performing style, Al Pacino was chosen by director Francis Ford Coppola, Jr. for the central role of Michael Corleone in *The Godfather* over more traditional leading men like Warren Beatty and Redford. Coppola wanted an Italian American actor for the part. Rather than building audience identification and sympathy by conforming to previous Hollywood models of masculine beauty, Pacino used this intensity and emotionality to rivet the viewer's attention. With his appearances in *The Godfather Part II*, the police department exposé *Serpico* (Sidney Lumet 1973), and as the anti-hero bank robber in *Dog Day Afternoon* (Sidney Lumet 1975), Pacino rivaled Hoffman as one of the top male stars of the decade.

Richard Dreyfuss

Dreyfuss crafted a screen persona that very much resembled Woody Allen's: verbal, intelligent, vibrating with nervous energy. Unlike Allen, however, Dreyfuss became yet another convention-defying leading man in the 1970s, from his role as a bookish,

Fig 6.18
Al Pacino became one of the most influential actors of the 1970s with roles in movies such as *The Godfather* and *The Godfather Part II*, *Serpico*, and here in *Dog Day Afternoon*, Sidney Lumet's gritty, neo-realist movie based on a true story about a hapless bank robber hoping to steal enough money for his lover's sex-change operation.

Fig 6.19
Cerebral and intense, Richard Dreyfuss's character of Matt Hooper makes for an unconventional action hero in one of the biggest blockbuster movies of the seventies, *Jaws*.

ambitious high school senior wondering about his future in the nostalgic *American Graffiti* to playing the nonconformist proto-hippie romantic lead in *The Goodbye Girl* (Herbert Ross 1977), for which he won the Academy Award for Best Actor. He also starred in two of the biggest Steven Spielberg blockbusters of the 1970s, movies that changed the business model of the movie industry: *Jaws* and *Close Encounters of the Third Kind* (1977). As the blockbuster model took hold over the next several decades, Hollywood would both return to older conventions of leading men and also embrace exaggerated versions of ultra-masculinity in the figures of Sylvester Stallone's Rocky character and the movies of Arnold Schwarzenegger. That an actor with an identity as distinctive and unconventional (in Hollywood terms) as Dreyfuss would be cast to star in two major action pictures illustrates the changes and experiments that marked Hollywood in the 1970s.

The names above and below the title

Jane Fonda

In the career of Jane Fonda, daughter of Henry Fonda, one of the most important actors from the studios age of American cinema, we can see the changes and upheavals that define the screen age of the late 1960s and the 1970s. Beginning her movie career as a rising young ingénue, a career arc reflecting the managed creation of movie stars from the older era, Fonda sought out more challenging and unconventional roles, first in France and then as part of the new experiments in Hollywood filmmaking. Just as she was establishing herself as one of the most important and serious screen actors, her political activism, especially in the anti-Vietnam War movement, took her away from acting and made her a controversial political lightning rod. Then, in the second half of the 1970s, she resurrected her movie career to again become one of the most popular actors in America over the next fifteen years.

After a privileged but troubled upbringing – her mother Frances Ford Seymour struggled with mental illness and committed suicide when Fonda was thirteen – she decided to follow in her father's footsteps and trained in Method acting as part of the Actors' Studio in the 1950s. After working on the stage she entered the movies at age 22 with a starring role in the romantic comedy *Tall Story* (Joshua Logan 1960) opposite Anthony Perkins, just months before his legendary appearance as the serial killer in Alfred Hitchcock's *Psycho*. Fonda was a gifted and popular actor, regularly appearing in movies throughout the early 1960s.

But just as Hollywood began to change in the mid-1960s, so did Fonda. She began spending time in France, where she married the movie director Roger Vadim

Fig 6.20
Jane Fonda as a conservative army wife whose experience with the impact of the Vietnam War leads to personal and political transformation in Hal Ashby's *Coming Home*.

and became more interested in politics, especially the civil rights and anti-war movements, events she felt she had been sheltered from before. She became far more selective about her screen roles, waiting for screen experiences that promised to be more serious and socially relevant, such as the part of Gloria in *They Shoot Horses, Don't They?* (Sidney Pollack 1969), a grim and sober story based on Horace McCoy's Depression-era novel about the desperate participants in a 1930s dance marathon, a story that ends with Gloria successfully begging her partner to kill her and release her from a life of poverty and hopelessness. She won an Oscar for her portrayal of an expensive prostitute who becomes part of a murder investigation in the sophisticated mystery *Klute* (Alan J. Pakula 1971).

As the 1960s turned into the 1970s, Fonda became more and more active in the anti-war movement, moving away from filmmaking to devote more time to the cause. A 1972 tour she made of North Vietnam, the country the United States was fighting in the war, became a media firestorm, and supporters of the war began calling her "Hanoi Jane" and questioning her loyalty and patriotism. For some, she became a symbol of the "Hollywood radical" and tapped into Cold War fears over movies as culturally subversive. In contrast to these accusations that the movie industry was becoming politically radicalized, the multinational conglomerates that were acquiring Hollywood movie companies in the era were more interested in profitability and economic stability than promoting revolution, and Fonda seemed an increasingly polarizing and alienating figure.

Despite this controversy, Fonda did successfully return to filmmaking with a role in the satirical romantic comedy *Fun with Dick and Jane* (Ted Kotcheff 1977). Her interest in politics undimmed, she publically announced that she was only interested in making movies that were socially relevant. Rather than damaging her marketability, her popularity only grew with her role as an investigative reporter in *The China Syndrome* (James Bridges 1979), a movie about an impending meltdown at a nuclear power reactor, eerily released just two weeks before the actual partial meltdown at the Three Mile Island reactor in Pennsylvania. She received her second Oscar for *Coming Home* (Hal Ashby 1978), an anti-war movie about the traumas afflicting returning Vietnam veterans. She entered the 1980s as one of the top box office stars in the country, her popularity burnished by her series of exercise videos that took advantage of the burgeoning home video industry, which would dramatically transform the movie industry as well.

Steven Spielberg

Steven Spielberg is arguably the most successful director in American movie history, based on both box office returns and cultural influence. Several of his movies – *Jaws* (1975), *Close Encounters of the Third Kind* (1977), *Raiders of the Lost Ark* (1981), *E.T. the Extra-Terrestrial* (1982), and *Jurassic Park* (1993) – are among the most popular American movies of all time. His 1975 hit *Jaws* (along with George Lucas' *Star Wars*) is either credited or blamed as the movie that changed Hollywood forever, establishing the creation of the megahit blockbuster franchise as the primary business goal of the movie industry.

As screen experiences, his movies provoke similarly divided opinions. His champions praise his talent for creating visual excitement and sweeping narratives that engulf the viewer in a completely imagined alternative reality. His critics fault Spielberg for substituting simple emotional reactions in place of more complex or challenging approaches. The opening of *Jaws*, featuring a shark attack we only see

Fig 6.21
Steven Spielberg. Source:
LucasFilm Ltd/Paramount/
Eva Sereny/The Kobal
Collection.

from above the water, as a young woman swimming in the ocean at night shouts with fear as she fights with an unseen force beneath the surface before she disappears completely, leaving the viewers to imagine what has taken place below the waves, is a prime example. The scene provides an ominous opening, all the more terrifying for its restraint and subtlety; at the same time, the format of beginning a movie with an exciting and even shocking action episode quickly turned into a standard and often stale cliche in the Hollywood movies of Spielberg's many imitators.

In truth, there is no simple approach to Spielberg's career. It includes the "tentpole" blockbusters described above but also historical epics dealing with slavery (*Amistad* 1997), the Holocaust (*Schindler's List* 1993), World War I (*War Horse* 2011), and World War II (*Saving Private Ryan* 1998); literary adaptations, including *The Color Purple* (1985) and *Empire of the Sun* (1987); and even a fascinating science fiction "collaboration" with Stanley Kubrick (a director whose cerebral, analytical approach to movies seems the opposite of Spielberg's) on a project that Kubrick had initiated but handed off to Spielberg before Kubrick's death in 1999, *A.I. Artificial Intelligence*, a film about a lonely robot that spans 2,000 years.

Spielberg's screen experiences, in fact, express the idea of Hollywood both big and small. Even at their showiest and most special effects-driven, Spielberg's movies are equally defined by their attention to character and close social observation.

E.T. the Extra-Terrestrial, for example, tells a fantastic story about a friendly space alien trying to return to his home planet as part of a poignant and sweetly comic exploration of a working single mother and the rhythms of modern American suburban life. In effect, Spielberg can be seen as offering audiences small movies within big movies. A child of divorce, Spielberg's movies regularly feature stories about families in transition and parent–child relationships, themes that echoed with the changing family dynamics of the 1960s and 1970s.

In American cinema history, only Alfred Hitchcock and Walt Disney rival Spielberg in terms of fame and name recognition. Spielberg's influence can be clearly seen throughout the contemporary generation of American filmmakers, especially in J. J. Abrams, whose *Super 8* (2011) was both produced by and is a homage to Spielberg. Remarkably, forty years after his directing debut, Spielberg remains one of the most important and prolific American filmmakers.

Martin Scorsese

There is no more acclaimed contemporary American filmmaker than Martin Scorsese, and no filmmaker better exemplifies the film school generation of young directors who came of age in the late 1960s and early 1970s. He grew up in a working-class Italian American family on New York City's Lower East Side. Chronic asthma prevented him from much physical activity as a child, but the screen experiences of movies provided both sanctuary and a rich fantasy life. After college, he earned a graduate degree in film at New York University in 1966, and throughout his career Scorsese has been famous for his encyclopedic knowledge of world movie history.

Over the course of his by now over 20-year movie career, Scorsese has worked in a wide variety of genres and dealt with an equally diverse range of subjects, from musicals (*New York, New York* 1977) and musical documentaries (such as *The Last Waltz* 1978) to horror thrillers (*Shutter Island* 2010) and comedies (*After Hours* 1985), period dramas (*The Age of Innocence* 1993) and even a biography of the Dalai Lama (*Kundun* 1997). One of his first movies, *Alice Doesn't Live Here Anymore* (1974), is one of the earliest mainstream Hollywood movies to show the influence of the growing feminist movement in the 1970s, telling the story of a recently widowed single mother who takes her young son on a cross-country trip in search of a singing career.

However, Scorsese is most closely identified with screen experiences rooted in his Lower East Side Italian American upbringing, especially movies dealing with the culture of the criminal underworld. His movies are associated both with a sensitive artistry and graphic depictions of violence. These two seemingly contradictory

Fig 6.23
Martin Scorsese on the set of *Alice Doesn't Live Here Anymore* in 1974. Source: Warner Bros/The Kobal Collection.

aspects of Scorsese's work express the changes in Hollywood filmmaking in the late 1960s and 1970s as American movies sought to appeal to a younger, more movie-savvy audience, an audience that Scorsese was very much a part of.

On the one hand, Scorsese's passionate commitment to the movies as a serious art very much fits in with Hollywood's grudging willingness to support producers, writers, and directors interested in creating new and innovative screen experiences that challenge audience expectations and appeal to younger viewers. On the other hand, his early experiences working with the great low-budget producer Roger Corman and American International Pictures, for whom he made *Boxcar Bertha*, a Bonnie-and-Clyde-style story of two outlaws during the Depression, showed that his fondness for movies included both action pictures and art movies. In fact, like many of his contemporaries, Scorsese exemplified that part of 1970s moviemaking that challenged old distinctions between "A" and "B" movies, between big-budget prestige pictures that aspired to the status of high art and more sensational, low-budget movies that provided thrilling visual spectacles.

The new ratings system allowed filmmakers like Scorsese to create intense, graphic, and provocative screen experiences, blurring the lines between whether viewers were attracted more by his bold new ideas and approaches to movie storytelling or by shocking new images and sensations. Bringing an art film sensibility to genres associated with sex and violence like the gangster movie and the crime thriller, Scorsese created movies that had wide appeal across a range of audiences.

His first major success, for example, was *Mean Streets* (1972), a highly personal film set in the Lower East Side about a thoughtful young gangster named Charlie (played by Scorsese regular Harvey Keitel) who tries to look out for his more impulsive and self-destructive friend Johnny Boy, played by Robert De Niro, an actor who more than any other has become identified with Scorsese's work. Although a low-budget movie, *Mean Streets* is full of formal and artistic innovations, including a home-movie-style title sequence and the use of pop and rock music on the soundtrack. The movie presents a gritty, seemingly realistic view of life on the streets, but Scorsese's use of colored lighting and unusual camera perspectives always remind us that we are watching a movie.

At the same time, *Mean Streets* also represents a more graphic take on the classic gangster movie. The characters revel in their use of obscenity, and the violence is sudden and graphic. As with many of the movies associated with "New Hollywood" in the 1970s, critics were divided in their reception. Most praised *Mean Streets* as a bold and original screen experience, one that rejects the squeamishness or sentimentality of older movie traditions to more directly confront issues of loyalty, faith, honor, and duty. To some critics, the artistry of *Mean Streets* was not enough to overcome their discomfort with the more graphic representations of violence and sexuality. Like those who supported the early efforts at movie censorship in the first screen age of American cinema, they linked these new movies to what they saw as a coarsening of the culture (what conservative politicians denounced as a new "permissiveness").

The movie Scorsese made just three years later, *Taxi Driver* (1976), only heightened these tensions, becoming one of the most critically acclaimed and controversial movies of the 1970s. Again starring De Niro and featuring Keitel, *Taxi Driver* follows the actions of Travis Bickle, a lonely, disaffected, and deeply troubled young man living on his own in 1970s Manhattan, earning a meager living as a taxi driver and himself becoming more and more disgusted by what he sees as the cultural decadence around him, represented most powerfully in the person of the 12-year-old prostitute Iris, played by the then 13-year-old Jodie Foster. We watch as Bickle descends into madness, finally breaking with reality and going on a bloody killing spree to "rescue" Iris after his initial plan to assassinate a political candidate fails. Ironically, Bickle winds up becoming a media hero, still driving the streets in his taxi at the end of the movie.

Both the subject matter and the graphics in *Taxi Driver* are intense and brutal, especially in the sadistic gun and knife battle in the rundown brothel. Again, Scorsese presents striking images and visual experiences, such as the overhead tracking shot as we follow the blood-soaked aftermath of Bickle's killing spree from room to room, all the while listening to the highly stylized, jazzy soundtrack by the legendary Bernard Herrmann, who had composed music for Hitchcock's greatest films, including *Psycho*. Still, Scorsese had to negotiate with the MPAA in order to avoid an X rating for the movie because of the violence, and many critics were disturbed by Foster's role as a child actor playing a prostitute.

It might seem strange to say so, but in some ways both *Taxi Driver* and *Star Wars*, released the next year, can be seen as representing the same kind of generational and cultural divide that marked the upheavals of this important screen age in American cinema. While *Taxi Driver* was an intense, R-rated crime drama that challenged boundaries of what could acceptably be shown in a "mainstream" Hollywood movie and *Star Wars* was a big-budget science fiction fantasy associated with children and adolescents, both were screen experiences that did not fit neatly into the studios era notions of "A" and "B" movies, of "respectable" movies and

Fig 6.24
A dramatic overhead shot of the bloody aftermath of the title character Travis Bickle's (played by Robert De Niro) vigilante-style killing spree in *Taxi Driver*.

exploitation pictures. Some critics, in fact, see these two movies, and the two men who directed them, Martin Scorsese and George Lucas, as themselves standing for two opposing trends in 1970s American movies, one towards more personal, artistically ambitious movies, the other towards simplistic popcorn movies that aim to provide spectacle over intellect.

Yet many contemporary movie viewers of all kinds, from everyday fans to scholars and critics, particularly those who came of age in the 1970s and after, enjoy both dark, gritty Scorsese films like the boxing epic *Raging Bull* (1980) and the densely imagined and exciting mythology of the *Star Wars* series. As the movie industry decisively changed in the late 1960s and 1970s in ways that we will continue to explore in the next two chapters, we have in many ways returned to the diversity of the earliest screen ages of American movies, including the debates about just what the movies are. Just as early critics and writers debated whether film was more like a form of sideshow carnival entertainment or potentially one of the fine arts, critics in this screen age returned to basic questions about art, meaning, and social purpose in the movies, questions that resonate into our current screen age.

Explore further

Bapis, Elaine M, *Camera and Action: American Film as Agent of Social Change, 1965–1975*. Jefferson, NC: McFarland, 2008.

Biskind, Peter, *Easy Riders, Raging Bulls: How the Sex-Drugs-and-Rock 'n' Roll Generation Saved Hollywood*. New York: Simon & Schuster, 1998.

Casper, Drew, *Hollywood Film 1963–1976: Years of Revolution and Reaction*. Malden, MA: Wiley-Blackwell, 2011.

Cook, David A., *Lost Illusions: American Cinema in the Shadow of Watergate and Vietnam, 1970–1979*. Berkeley: University of California Press, 2002.

Corrigan, Timothy, *A Cinema Without Walls: Movies and Culture after Vietnam*. New Brunswick, NJ: Rutgers University Press, 1991.

Friedman, Lester D. (ed.), *American Cinema of the 1970s: Themes and Variations*. New Brunswick, NJ: Rutgers University Press, 2007.

Gilbey, Ryan, *It Don't Worry Me: The Revolutionary American Films of the Seventies*. New York: Faber and Faber, 2003.

Grant, Barry Keith (ed.), *American Cinema of the 1960s: Themes and Variations*. New Brunswick, NJ: Rutgers University Press, 2008.

Guerrero, Ed, *Framing Blackness: The African American Image in Film*. Philadelphia: Temple University Press, 1993.

Harris, Mark, *Pictures at a Revolution: Five Movies and the Birth of the New Hollywood*. New York: Penguin Press, 2008.

Jacobs, Diane, *Hollywood Renaissance*. New York: Dell, 1980.

Kirshner, Jonathan, *Hollywood's Last Golden Age: Politics, Society, and the Seventies Film in America*. Ithaca, NY: Cornell University Press, 2012.

Lawrence, Novotny, *Blaxploitation Films of the 1970s: Blackness and Genre*. London/New York: Routledge, 2008.

Lewis, Jon (ed.), *The New American Cinema*. Durham: Duke University Press, 1998.

Palmer, William J., *The Films of the Seventies: A Social History*. Metuchen, NJ: Scarecrow Press, 1987.

Sims, Yvonne D., *Women of Blaxploitation: How the Black Action Film Heroine Changed American Popular Culture*. Jefferson, NC: McFarland, 2006.

CHAPTER 7

Shopping malls, video stores, and cable TV: Movies in the franchise era, 1981–1997

Now playing

***Sex, Lies, and Videotape* screens at the Utah/US Film Festival, January 1989**

1989 would prove to be another year of big-budget blockbusters for Hollywood, with movies like Tim Burton's *Batman*, Steven Spielberg's *Indiana Jones and the Last Crusade*, as well as sequels to previous hits including the buddy cop movie *Lethal Weapon 2* (Richard Donner), and the time-travel teen comedy *Back to the Future Part II* (Robert Zemeckis). The fans attending the United States Film Festival in Park City, Utah, that year, however, were looking for something different, something smaller and more personal. The festival had started twelve years earlier in Salt Lake City based on the idea of celebrating independent American movies made outside of the major studio funding and distribution structure. The festival had moved to the skiing resort of Park City in the early 1980s, and since 1985 had been run by the actor Robert Redford's Sundance Institute, an organization likewise devoted to nurturing new and diverse filmmakers outside of the main commercial movie industry.

Fig 7.1
Graham (James Spader), a young man who can connect with others only through the viewfinder of his camcorder, prepares to interview Cynthia (Laura San Giacomo) about her sex life in Steven Soderbergh's *Sex, Lies, and Videotape*.

Videotape/VHS A
method of recording
sound and images using
magnetic tape. VHS, or
"Video Home System,"
refers to a particular kind
of video recording and
playback using cassette
tapes. While industry use
of videotape goes back
to the 1950s, the sale
of consumer videotape
cameras and recorders
took off in the 1980s,
allowing anyone to create
their own sound movies,
record programming from
their television sets, and
play prerecorded tapes
at home.

The fans taking their seats at the Egyptian Theatre, an art deco classic from the silent era of American cinema, were there to see just such an example of what would quickly be called "indie" filmmaking, the debut theatrical feature by a 26-year-old director named Steven Soderbergh titled *Sex, Lies, and Videotape*. Made for just over $1 million, a fraction of the almost $50 million budget of *Indiana Jones and the Last Crusade*, *Sex, Lies, and Videotape* had no elaborate special effects, chase scenes, or battle scenes. Instead, the movie told the story of four young adults: Ann (Andie McDowell) and her yuppie lawyer husband John (Peter Gallagher), her free-spirited artist sister Cynthia (Laura San Giacomo), who is having an affair with John, and the person whose arrival would precipitate Ann's reassessment of her life and the end of her marriage, John's old college friend Graham (James Spader). The title of the movie refers both to the deceptions that the characters practice with one another and to Graham's use of a home video camera – part of a **video tape** revolution that was transforming the movie industry – to record women talking about their sexual histories.

The film became the surprise hit of the festival. To Soderbergh's shock it led to a distribution deal with Miramax Film – a company that would specialize in finding interesting new independent filmmakers like Soderbergh (and, just three years later, Quentin Tarantino), winning the Palme D'Or at the Cannes film festival (maybe the most prestigious film award in the world), and becoming a box office hit, not on the scale of a *Batman*, but enough to inspire articles about the rebirth of independent cinema and making the United States Film Festival – renamed the Sundance Film Festival in 1991 – a focus for discovering new movie talent. *Sex, Lies, and Videotape* would become a part of a narrative about American cinema that divided movies between "studio" films and indies, between mass-market blockbusters and smaller, more personal movies.

As we have seen, such neat distinctions are never that neat, and the major media conglomerates that have dominated mainstream movie production since the 1970s would seek to make "indie" movies just another part of their product lines. Soderbergh's own career has moved between both worlds, from big-budget franchise movies like *Ocean's Eleven* (2001) and its two sequels, and smaller, experimental movies like *Bubble* (2005) and *The Girlfriend Experience* (2009). Both Soderbergh's career and his first movie recognize that there were audiences for a wide diversity of screen experiences, just as his movie's focus on videotaping, on the ability of just about anyone to create their own screen experiences, equally recognized the technological and cultural developments that would create a revolution in what we mean by movies, cinema, and media.

A family watches *Raiders of the Lost Ark* on HBO in their home, 1984

Cable television A
method of transmitting
television programming
that relies on cables
connected to television
sets rather than
broadcasting through
the air. Unlike broadcast
television, which
generates revenues
by selling commercial
advertising, cable
television directly
charges each viewer for
subscribing. While cable
television has been
around since the 1950s,
it became a major means
of television transmission
in the 1980s.

The family settling into the living room couch to watch a movie on television didn't think of themselves as part of a revolution. They had recently subscribed to a **cable television** service, Home Box Office, or HBO, and they were excited about all the new movies they would be able to watch as a result. Like millions of people around the world, they had been fans of Steven Spielberg's action-packed homage to 1940s Saturday matinee movie serials, *Raiders of the Lost Ark*, since they had first seen it at the local multiplex three years earlier. They also knew that the movie would eventually show up on network television, but not as it turned out until 1986. The movie had already been released on laserdisc and videotape, but the family liked the convenience of having a range of movies available on HBO.

The 1980s would mark the greatest proliferation of movie viewing options and screen experiences since the earliest days of American cinema, the days of peep shows and nickelodeons. The development of various pay cable television networks and pay-per-view systems, along with the home video explosion in the form of video cassette players and camcorders, dramatically changed the landscape for the movie-viewing experience. If the abandonment of the Production Code for the ratings system and the growing corporatization of the movie business in the late 1960s and 1970s defined one beginning of our contemporary relationship to the movies, the cable and video revolution of the 1980s along with the growth of global media conglomerates defined the other.

Movies had been a staple of broadcast television programming since the 1950s and an important part of the screen experience, both in providing access to movies and movie history to millions of viewers and in helping finance the movie industry. The rise of cable television, for-pay subscription services carried over overhead and underground cables, not only greatly expanded this market through new networks like HBO and the American Movie Channel (AMC) but also destabilized the movie business, as the studios and producers looked to contracts with cable companies as part of financing the movies and pay-per-view and cable television premieres became a regular part of how movies were released. As we will see in the final chapter, the rise of cable and later satellite television would further blur the lines between movies and television. Where the screen experiences we still refer to as "the movies" first became available for viewing would become increasingly diverse, with the bricks-and-mortar movie theater no longer the only place to see a first-run "movie."

As the family begins watching *Raiders of the Lost Ark*, we can see how these new viewing opportunities created very different screen experiences of the supposedly "same" movie. The opening temple raiding sequence of the movie, for example, culminating in the main character of Indiana Jones (Harrison Ford) running for his life towards the camera and away from a huge rolling stone ball, had been designed to overwhelm audiences in movie theaters, the giant ball almost 30 feet tall, the sound booming out of multiple speakers, all in a large dark room full of excited fellow moviegoers. Our family this evening, by contrast, is sitting in a well-lit living room, their television screen only 26 inches across diagonally. To accommodate the widescreen size of the movie, the image runs with a black band at the top and the bottom. The opening sequence is still exciting but not visually overwhelming, and the ability to watch the movie multiple times changes the emotional reaction of the viewers from awe to affection, as Indiana Jones became a well-loved character as much as a dynamic action hero. Free from the constraints of the movie theater, family members are even able to easily discuss the movie while they watch.

Fig 7.2
Harrison Ford, as the archeologist/adventurer Indiana Jones, narrowly escapes with his life from a Mayan temple in *Raiders of the Lost Ark*, initiating one of the most lucrative franchise series of the 1980s and 1990s.

Synergy A business theory widely adopted by entertainment conglomerates in the 1980s that focused on creating cross-marketing opportunities connecting movies to the sale of related consumer products such as toys, video games, action figures, and clothing, and the promotion of other consumer goods such as fast food, soda, and automobiles.

These new screen experiences would become part of an effort by media conglomerates to reestablish the business model of vertical integration – under the banner of "synergy" – in the latest effort to stabilize and control the movie business. The individual movie would more and more function as a catalyst for a variety of viewing experiences and marketing opportunities, and the economic logic of the blockbuster – the massive profits that could be reaped from a single giant hit franchise – would become even more firmly entrenched.

College students watch a VHS copy of *Pulp Fiction* in their college dorm room, 1997

Since the 1960s, college students had become an increasingly important part of the movie audience in terms of marketing and ticket sales. Intellectually and artistically curious, with flexible life schedules and disposable income (at least, enough to pay the price of a movie ticket), college students in particular and young people in general could also be enthusiastically devoted to screen experiences they loved, returning over and over again to their favorite movies. In the early 1990s, no movie had a stronger campus following than Quentin Tarantino's *Pulp Fiction* (1994). The follow-up to his stylish, hyperviolent, low-budget crime movie *Reservoir Dogs* (1992), *Pulp Fiction* was both an exciting crime movie but also a dizzying compilation of movie and popular culture history.

Drawing its title and spirit from the legacy of cheap crime novels, featuring exciting stories written in equally exciting and deliberately anti-literary prose, *Pulp Fiction* interwove three stories involving a pair of philosophical hit men (played by John Travolta and Samuel L. Jackson), two hapless Bonnie-and-Clyde-wannabes (Tim Roth and Amanda Plummer), and an aging boxer looking for one last big score (Bruce Willis), moving backwards and forwards in time, finally tying all the story lines together in a screen experience that draws on film noir, horror, martial arts movies, and even westerns and musical comedies. Made outside of major studio financing and distributed by the same Miramax Company that had discovered *Sex, Lies, and Videotape*, which specialized in finding indie gems, *Pulp Fiction* became a worldwide hit, especially among young people.

The students gathered around the tiny television set hooked up to a cheap VCR in the dorm room had already watched Tarantino's career-making movie many times already. In fact, the screen experience of *Pulp Fiction* seemed designed to take advantage of the home video age. The complexity and density of the narrative structure, filled with all sorts of allusions to other movies and intricate plot connections, made multiple viewings almost a necessity. And this very density of *Pulp Fiction*'s references to other movies equally spoke to the impact of the video rental industry. Seemingly overnight in the 1980s, thousands of video rental stores and companies had sprung up across the country (and around the world), from ultra-small businesses similar to the grungy "RST Video" featured in Kevin Smith's microbudget cult movie *Clerks* that came out in the same year as *Pulp Fiction*, to Blockbuster Video, which would become a multibillion-dollar company in the 1990s before almost disappearing in the digital screen age of the twenty-first century.

Video rental stores, along with public libraries, which had also begun making tapes available for checkout, made it easier for young movie fans to educate themselves about movie history, especially the history of low-budget action movies and other "exploitation" genres. Part of Tarantino's growing legend, which we will return to below in "Names above and below the title," was his own self-education

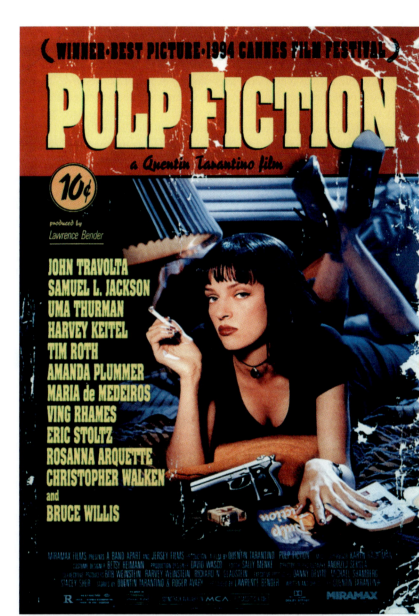

Fig 7.3
This poster for Quentin Tarantino's *Pulp Fiction* featuring Uma Thurman as gangster's wife Mia Wallace, in the style of a cheap 1950s paperback cover, was a staple of dorm rooms in the early 1990s. Source: Miramax/Buena Vista/The Kobal Collection.

Fig 7.4
John Travolta (left) as Vincent Vega and Samuel L. Jackson as Jules Winnfield, the hyper-talkative hit men from *Pulp Fiction*.

working as a video store clerk, an alternative to formal film school training. *Pulp Fiction* challenged and inspired many of its fans to search out the dozens and dozens of movie references in the film, from noir classics like *Kiss Me Deadly* (Robert Aldrich 1955) to the French New Wave experiments of Jean-Luc Godard.

Home videotape technology represented the greatest challenge and greatest opportunity to the movie industry since the invention of the cinema. After first fighting the proliferation of video cassette recorders, which allowed home viewers to record their favorite movies off of the television, movie companies saw the sale of video cassettes (and later DVDs in the late 1990s) turn into a vital part of movie marketing, surpassing the importance of movie ticket buyers to the corporate bottom line in the 1980s. For the first time, movie fans could create their own personal libraries of favorite movies to go along with their collections of books and music.

While these home collections strengthened the emotional attachments of movie fans to their favorite screen experiences, video cassettes also began raising questions about intellectual property – about just what we are buying when we buy a theater ticket or a video copy of a movie, indeed about just what we mean by "copy" and "original" – that would come to define the coming digital age. After the 1980s, movie fans would come to experience the movies as increasingly interactive, as the lines between creating movies and watching movies became more and more fuzzy.

Screen ages

Opposing forces in the franchise era

When Ronald Reagan took the oath of office as president of the United States in January 1981, many people saw his election, as well as that of other conservative leaders around the world such as Margaret Thatcher in the United Kingdom, as a sign of a right-leaning political reaction against the turbulent social, political, and economic changes of the 1960s and 1970s. There is certainly some truth in this interpretation, as in his campaign Reagan himself emphasized a return to so-called traditional American values and a mythic vision of what American was like before the 1960s, often with not very subtle appeals to race-based fears on the part of white voters. Over the course of his eight years in office and the subsequent four-year term of his successor and former vice president George H. W. Bush, Reagan advocated for sweeping deregulations of big business and a weakening of organized labor, policies that would have a major impact on the movie industry.

But if leaders like Reagan and Thatcher represented a conservative turn in politics, they did not usher in a period of political and cultural consensus. Throughout their terms in office, they were polarizing figures, inspiring both devotion and fierce opposition in equal measure, forces that would lead in the US to the election of the Democratic baby boomer Bill Clinton in 1992, someone who was very much a product of the 1960s. The political and social culture of the 1980s were marked by what came to be called the "**Culture Wars**," a continuation of the revolutionary social changes introduced in the 1960s that included the civil rights movement and, perhaps most significantly, the Second Wave feminist movement. In the 1980s, arguments about women's rights, especially reproductive rights and the politics of abortion, the multicultural nature of American society, and an acceleration of demands for the civil rights of gays and lesbians, fueled by the AIDS pandemic, came to dominate media discussion of culture and the arts. The disintegration of the Soviet

Culture wars Refers to a broad collection of controversies and debates around social issues and values that was part of defining various political divisions in the United States during the 1980s. These issues included reproductive and abortion rights, the growing multicultural identity of American society, the role of religion in politics, civil rights for gay and lesbian people, and the proper response to the AIDS epidemic. In terms of the movies, the culture wars represented an extension of long-standing arguments about the impact of cinema on American values and beliefs.

Union and Eastern European Communism at the end of this screen age, and the first Gulf War, would mark a decisive political turn at the beginning of the 1990s, one fueled by the changing demographics of the country and the rise of digital culture.

The movie business in the 1980s

Hollywood in the 1980s and early 1990s found itself searching for new ways to contend with powerful forces moving in opposite directions. As we saw in "Now playing," the 1980s witnessed an explosion in the variety of screen experiences available to movie fans. The move to the home as a center of family media entertainment, a process that began with radio and accelerated with the television age, now included the idea of the "home theater" and the beginning of our contemporary screen age, where the majority of our cinema screen experiences occur outside formal movie theaters. The expansion of home videotape technology and videocassette recorders along with cable television would forever change the viewing practices of movie fans. The introduction of the personal computer – the IBM PC in 1981 and the Apple Macintosh in 1984 – had little initial impact on the movie business, but they would soon become the most transformative media of them all by the turn of the century. For the major movie studios and the corporate conglomerates that owned most of them, many of these centrifugal forces affecting the movie business were seen as both threats and opportunities.

At first, some companies fought these changes, including the unsuccessful lawsuit brought by Universal Studios against Sony challenging the sale of machines that would allow people to make videotape recordings of television programming. However, with the election of a president in favor of removing regulations that had been designed to limit the power and influence of big business, the movie businesses

Fig 7.5
One of the most iconic images from 1980s screen experiences, Elliott (Henry Thomas) goes for a midnight bike ride courtesy of his new friend, the title character of Steven Spielberg's *E.T. the Extra-Terrestrial*, a movie that combined sentimentality and nostalgia with darker tones of menace and loneliness.

Fig 7.6
Elliott in *E.T. the Extra-Terrestrial* with one of the favorite Earth foods of the little lost alien, a handful of Reese's Pieces candy. The Hershey Company paid for this example of product placement after the makers of M&Ms passed on the opportunity.

looked to take advantage of this changing environment of less government oversight through a return to vertical integration, or the practice of trying to acquire control over all aspects of media production, distribution, and marketing, under the name of "synergy" and the idea of the franchise. These centripetal forces meant a greater and greater concentration of money and power in the formation of giant media conglomerates. Since the 1960s, the businesses we still call "studios" had really become movie-financing companies. A "Paramount" movie no longer meant that the movie was made at a production facility owned by Paramount; instead, it meant that Paramount functioned as the main financial organizer and center of distribution for the movie, wherever and by whomever it was actually made. The business of movies was actually the business of deal and package making.

Throughout the 1980s and into the 1990s, a wave of mergers and acquisition began a process of creating global media empires, collections of companies that developed "properties" involving theatrical exhibition, cable TV companies, videocassette sales, the sale of movie-related merchandise and clothing, music, and cross-promotional advertising, including what came to be called "**product placement**," as when the title character of *E.T. the Extra-Terrestrial* (Steven Spielberg 1982) turns out to have a fondness for Reese's Pieces, or when Marty McFly in *Back to the Future* (Robert Zemeckis 1985) is mistakenly identified as "Calvin Klein" on the basis of his designer underwear.

These mergers, including the creation of Time Warner, Sony's acquisition of Columbia Pictures, Rupert Murdoch's purchase of 20th Century Fox, and Viacom's absorption of Paramount, began a process that continues to this day. The Disney Company, one of the pioneers of media "synergy," reinvented itself in the 1980s, creating a movie division aimed at more grown-up movies and reviving its animation division to spectacular success with *The Little Mermaid* (Ron Clements and John Musker 1989). In the early 1990s, their purchase of ABC Television led to Disney becoming one of the giants of contemporary media.

Movies in the 1980s and 1990s: Bigger, louder, costlier

As the economic structure of the movie business shifted more and more to the franchise model, with the individual "movie" operating as the center of a massive marketing strategy involving multiple screens and entertainment venues, the focus centered more and more obsessively on the drive to create the next blockbuster. Both *Star Wars* and *Raiders of the Lost Ark* became models for Hollywood. The terms

Product placement A form of synergy and cross-marketing that involves companies paying moviemakers to include their products in the movies. While the practice actually spans the entire history of American cinema, product placement became especially widespread beginning in the 1980s. Prominent examples of product placement include references to Reese's Pieces in *E.T. the Extra-Terrestrial* (1982), and Calvin Klein underwear and Pepsi Cola in *Back to the Future* (1985).

Fig 7.7
After a decade-long decline, both Disney and movie animation in general made a successful comeback, beginning with *The Little Mermaid*.

"Star Wars" or "Indiana Jones" (the main character of *Raiders of the Lost Ark*) took on cultural meanings greater than any particular movie, becoming what we would now call cultural memes. Toys, collectible souvenirs, video games, amusement park rides, these movie franchises formed a new relationship towards the movies that has only intensified in the digital age through online communities, fan fiction, and digital mash-ups.

Just as the ideas of the 1930s and 1940s as a Golden Age and the 1970s as the renaissance of New American Cinema have become part of the dominant mythology of Hollywood history, the 1980s is often thought of as the age of the blockbuster franchise. *E.T. the Extra-Terrestrial* (Steven Spielberg 1982); *Ghostbusters* (Ivan Reitman 1984) and *Ghostbusters II* (Ivan Reitman 1989); *Beverly Hills Cop* (Martin Brest 1984), *Beverly Hills Cop II* (Tony Scott 1987) and *Beverly Hills Cop III* (John Landis 1994); *Die Hard* (John McTiernan 1988), *Die Hard 2* (Renny Harlin 1990), and three more sequels; *Lethal Weapon* (Richard Donner 1987), *Lethal Weapon 2* (Donner 1989), and two more sequels; *The Terminator* (James Cameron 1984, the movie that made Arnold Schwarzenegger an international superstar), *Terminator 2: Judgment Day* (Cameron 1991), and two more sequels; *Top Gun* (Tony Scott 1986); these movies were marketed as cultural events, screen experiences that existed in multiple formats. By mid-decade and for the first time in the history of cinema, more movie watching occurred inside the home – via videocassette and cable television – than in movie theaters.

Studios increasingly planned movies in terms of multiple marketing opportunities and multiple ways for consumers to have a franchise experience. Actually watching the movie was just one of these experiences. As a result, producers searched for ideas and stories that would produce the greatest variety of marketing opportunities. Tim Burton's *Batman* (1989), for example, represented one of the first examples of a trend that would define mainstream movies from that time to the present – the movie based on a classic comic book. A comic series like Batman came with a pre-existing fan base and cultural familiarity. The stylized heroes of *DC* and *Marvel* comics, with their elaborate and character-defining costumes, their equally colorful cast of evildoers, and the various paraphernalia associated with superheroes – in the case of Batman, his car, helicopter, and motorcycle, his bat cave, the dozens of clever weapons at his disposal – were tailor-made to follow the example of *Star Wars* in terms of toys, games, costumes, and a whole subculture of role playing and other opportunities for fan involvement.

Fig 7.8
Television star Bruce Willis became a movie star with his role as detective John McClane in *Die Hard* and its various sequels. An updating of the classic cowboy hero, the character of McClane was part of a move towards a more aggressive, less conflicted image of dominant American masculinity in 1980s cinema.

Many critics described the franchise movie trend, for both good and bad, in terms of cinema as amusement park thrill ride, a way of experiencing the movies that actually hearkens back to the earliest days of cinema and what the scholar Tom Gunning has called the "cinema of attractions," screen experiences based more on the production of wonder and spectacle than the development of narrative or character.[1] The logic of the franchise and the desire for marketing synergy eventually led to the metaphor of movie as thrill ride becoming literally true, as theme parks that were also owned by the emerging media megacorporations began creating rides based on their blockbuster movies, culminating with the premiere of *Pirates of the Caribbean: The Curse of the Black Pearl* (Gore Verbinski 2003), a franchise movie based on a popular Disneyland and Disney World thrill ride.

The example of *Rambo*

Of all the movie franchises that came to define the 1980s in the minds of many, there was no more symbolic – and notorious – example than the *Rambo* series. The series featured Sylvester Stallone, a struggling actor in the 1970s who rose to prominence in 1976 by writing and starring in the surprise hit *Rocky* (John Avildsen), a small, old-fashioned underdog story about a struggling boxer that won the Best Picture Oscar. From its low-budget beginnings, *Rocky* went on to become one of the biggest franchises of the 1980s and spawn five sequels. As the *Rocky* movies became bigger and bigger, so too did Stallone, both in terms of fame and physical size. Along with the former body building champion Arnold Schwarzenegger, Stallone's highly sculpted, exaggerated physical appearance defined a cartoonish new gender genre of masculinity in the 1980s (see "In development" below) that fit the larger-than-life, black-and-white conflicts between good and evil that defined many 1980s blockbusters, including the *Rambo* series.

Although Rambo came to be identified as a symbol of a simplistic American patriotism and associated with Reagan-era conservatism, the first movie in the series, *First Blood* (Ted Kotcheff 1982), from a novel by David Morrell and co-written by Stallone, can actually be seen as a kind of anti-war movie in the tradition of Vietnam films like *Apocalypse Now* (Francis Ford Coppola 1979). The main character of John Rambo is a traumatized Vietnam vet upset by the deadly effects of the defoliant chemical Agent Orange on his former platoon members. Psychologically fragile and suffering from flashbacks, Rambo is provoked to acts of violence by a cruel small-town sheriff, resulting in an extended battle between Rambo and the police that ends with his arrest.

Fig 7.9
Sylvester Stallone as the embittered Vietnam war veteran John Rambo in *First Blood*, the first movie in the *Rambo* movie franchise. The name "Rambo" became synonymous with the more conservative and militaristic foreign policy of the Reagan era in American politics.

From a troubled but sympathetic figure in *First Blood*, one of the biggest hits of the early 1980s, Rambo went on in the subsequent movies *Rambo: First Blood Part II* (George Cosmatos 1985) and *Rambo III* (Peter MacDonald 1988) to become a less complex and more politicized figure, symbolically refighting the war in Vietnam not just as part of a personal mission but as a sort of cultural catharsis meant to restore the idea of America as a powerful and morally unambiguous superpower. The character actually goes on a mission in Vietnam in *First Blood Part II*, where his comment "Do we get to win this time?" became a way of rewriting the disaster of Vietnam as stemming from a lack of national toughness and will, making Rambo into a metaphor for conservative, aggressive foreign policy. The *Rambo* series became a political flashpoint, a way of dividing political beliefs and loyalties and reinforcing the idea that America in general and the movies in particular were becoming more and more conservative in the 1980s.

But saying that either America as a whole or American movies became more conservative in the 1980s is too simplistic. While there were blockbuster movies that were seen as pro-military such as *Top Gun* (Tony Scott 1986), a movie about hot-shot navy fighter pilots that the US Navy actually used as part of their recruitment campaign, other movies such as Oliver Stone's *Platoon* (1986), based on Stone's own experiences in Vietnam, and *Born on the Fourth of July* (1989), a movie about the real-life anti-war disabled Vietnam veteran Ron Kovic, were both popular successes and deeply critical of the Vietnam war. An example of the complexity of 1980s American cinema, *Born on the Fourth of July* starred Tom Cruise, who also played the lead in the more pro-military *Top Gun*. A star of both comedies and action movies who emerged as a megastar in the 1980s, Tom Cruise (along with other stars such as the former television actors Tom Hanks and Michael J. Fox) evoked a genre of masculine performance, both boyish and sensitive, heroic yet vulnerable, that worked as a counterpart to the more muscle-bound retro version of machismo represented by Stallone and Schwarzenegger that we will explore further in "In development."

Fig 7.10
Some saw movies like Tony Scott's *Top Gun*, starring the emerging superstar Tom Cruise (left) as hotshot navy pilot Pete "Maverick" Mitchell, as part of Hollywood's embrace of an unambiguous celebration of the American military in the 1980s. The Navy even credited the popularity of *Top Gun* with helping their recruiting efforts.

Fig 7.11
Tom Cruise's portrayal of Vietnam war veteran turned anti-war activist Ron Kovic in Oliver Stone's *Born on the Fourth of July* just three years after the success of *Top Gun*, showed that mainstream screen experiences centered around America's military history remained complex in Reagan-era America.

Indie movie Refers to
movies made more
or less independently
of mainstream studio
production. Independent
movies are as old as
the movie industry.
The term "indie movie"
became popular in the
1980s as the result of
a wave of smaller, more
personal filmmaking that
developed in contrast
to Hollywood's growing
reliance on big-budget
blockbuster movies. The
indie movie movement
is especially associated
with the rise of various
film festivals across the
country, including the
Sundance Festival in Park
City, Utah and the South
by Southwest Festival in
Austin, Texas. Examples
of early indie movies
include Spike Lee's *She's
Gotta Have It* (1986),
Steven Soderbergh's
Sex, Lies, and Videotape
(1989), Quentin
Tarantino's *Reservoir
Dogs* (1992), and Kevin
Smith's *Clerks* (1994).

Alternatives to the blockbuster: The rise of indie movies

As the logic of the movie franchise increasingly thought of movies as commodities
to own as much as events to attend, movie companies began to rely more and more
heavily on the massive profits produced by the blockbuster. The growth in home
video sales also increased global sales potential, as copies of the latest Hollywood
hit could be shipped around the world. While these hits and new sources of revenue
did produce tens of millions of dollars in revenue, the need to produce ever more
impressive and exciting screen experiences also tremendously increased movie
production costs.

And the truth was that most movies weren't blockbusters. The search for the
next megahit franchise was fed by the age-old desire to control the notoriously
volatile movie business, as was the formation of global media corporations linking
together movies, television, cable, video, music, and merchandising. Ironically,
this desire to stabilize profits only increased risk-taking in terms of the enormous
amounts of money being funneled into the production and marketing of what
companies hoped was the next can't-miss hit. The original *Star Wars* in 1977, for
example, cost approximately $11 million; by contrast, *Batman* cost $48 million
to make in 1989, the majority of that money devoted to marketing, publicity, and
advertising to try to ensure its success.

But while the idea of the 1980s as the era of the blockbuster does have some
truth to it, it doesn't tell the whole story. The same developments in multiple screen
experiences and multiple ways of seeing movies, especially the development of home
video, also helped produce the counter-movement to the blockbuster in American
cinema described in the "Now playing" feature on Steven Soderbergh's *Sex, Lies, and
Videotape*: the indie movie movement. Just as the rapid expansion of movie theaters
and the implementation of the double-bill created a huge demand for new films to
fill screens in the 1930s and 1940s, the videocassette industry led to a similar new
demand in the 1980s. Part of this demand was met by the issuing of older movies on
video, but the growing demand for videocassettes also created opportunities for new
screen experiences.

Fig 7.12
Michael Keaton as the title
character in Tim Burton's
wildly imaginative
blockbuster *Batman*, one
of the biggest hits of
the franchise era which
helped establish the comic
book movie as one of the
dominant genres of our
contemporary screen age.

Case study 7.1: What makes an indie movie an indie movie?

The simplest definition of "indie movie" refers to any movie made outside of mainstream production. But "indie movie" came to have an artistic meaning as well, suggesting not just how a movie was financed but also a certain formal and aesthetic style and sensibility. "Indie movie" has become its own genre, a category on streaming services like Netflix, and a term of both praise and criticism. Explore what we mean by an indie movie sensibility by watching several key 1980s and early 1990s independent movies. As you review your screen experiences of these movies, what qualities would you say these movies have in common? These qualities can include subject matter, narrative structures, formal aspects such as the use of handheld cameras, location and sets, pacing, the use (or non-use) of music, even particular actors who seem to be indie movie regulars. Your goal is to formulate an answer to the question, "What makes an indie an indie?"

Further expand your research by comparing these early indie movies to more recent examples. Since the 1980s, a critical discussion has also grown around the question of what makes an indie an indie, including concerns about to what extent a kind of conventional indie movie structure has developed that seems at odds with the idea of indie movies as experimental or more willing to take risks than mainstream movies. Finally, supplement your analysis by exploring scholarly discussions of indie movies since the 1980s, including the issue of how entertainment conglomerates have absorbed supposedly "indie" movie production into their mainstream production practices.

Not surprisingly, the adult sex movie industry took quick advantage of the privacy that the home video market offered viewers (a development that anticipated the similar privacy of viewing experience that would define the Internet), and the production of sex movies rapidly increased over the decade. A whole new category of movie distribution – the "straight to video" market – grew just as rapidly, operating under the radar of most official media reporting about Hollywood, which still mainly focused on movies that premiered in traditional theaters. Genres like horror and action movies were especially popular in the direct-to-video market. A whole new sub-genre, the "erotic thriller," crime mysteries that featured both explicit violence and sexuality, took advantage of the same privacy that benefitted the sex film industry. The erotic thriller also carried over into the mainstream movie industry with movies like the controversial *Basic Instinct* (Paul Verhoeven 1992).

If the expanding venues for screen experiences benefitted the "exploitation" movie industry, it also opened up opportunities for a new generation of filmmakers interested in making smaller, more personal movies that did not fit the mass audience blockbuster formula. These were screen experiences directed at more particular audiences, including viewers who may have enjoyed many of the franchise hits but were also interested in a greater diversity of stories, characters, and approaches to visual storytelling. As the major media corporations worked to focus their energies on creating massive box office sensations, a whole new alternative film culture developed: the independent movie.

In addition to Steven Soderbergh, filmmakers like John Sayles, Jim Jarmusch, and Jonathan Demme all began their careers in the independent film movement of the 1980s. The directing brothers Joel and Ethan Coen gained international attention with their low-budget but high-attitude film noir *Blood Simple* in 1984.

Like their contemporary Quentin Tarantino, the Coens were stylistic magpies in their moviemaking, combining elements from all eras of movie history in their reworking of classic genres like the screwball comedy (*Raising Arizona* 1987) and the gangster movie (*Miller's Crossing* 1990).

The indie movement also slowly began to open doors for a greater variety and diversity of filmmakers. Spike Lee, profiled below in "Names above and below the title," was able to use his low-budget romantic comedy *She's Gotta Have It*, featuring an African American cast, to unexpectedly enter the Hollywood mainstream. Julie Dash's *Daughters of the Dust* (1992) became the first movie directed by an African American woman to receive general distribution. Robert Townsend's *Hollywood Shuffle* (1987) satirized Hollywood's long history of racial stereotyping. John Singleton's critically acclaimed *Boyz n the Hood* (1991) began a series of dramas and action movies focused on inner-city black life and informed by hip-hop culture, an updating of the Blaxploitation cycle of the 1970s.

Similarly, women directors such as Susan Seidelman began achieving mainstream success and visibility after decades of being marginalized in Hollywood. Seidelman's feminist comedy *Desperately Seeking Susan* (1985) starred the pop superstar Madonna and became a major hit. Amy Heckerling's high school comedy *Fast Times at Ridgemont High* (1982) was another box office success, and the actors Barbra Streisand and Penny Marshall began directing careers. The director Kathryn Bigelow, who would go on to become the first – and to date only – woman to win a Best Director Oscar in 2009 with *The Hurt Locker* also began her career in the 1980s with the vampire western *Near Dark* (1987).

Latino directors, almost completely non-existent in mainstream American cinema history, began to gain attention as well. Gregory Nava's *El Norte* (1983), the harrowing and moving story of a brother and sister fleeing political violence in Guatemala and trying to create a life in the United States as undocumented workers, brought Hollywood's attention to the importance of Latino culture in the United States. Hollywood had long valued the Latin American market for American films, and many countries in Latin America had their own extensive and popular film industries, especially Mexico, but until the 1980s there had been little interest in movies starring Latino characters or in stories told by Latino filmmakers. The playwright Luis Valdez also turned to movies in the 1980s with *Zoot Suit* (1981) and *La Bamba* (1987), signaling the beginnings of a new understanding of the importance and diversity of the growing Latino American audience.

Fig 7.13
The brother team of Joel and Ethan Coen emerged as one of the most influential filmmakers of contemporary American cinema with their low-budget, independent film noir *Blood Simple* in 1984. Here, the doomed bartender Ray (John Getz) peers into the Texas night trying to find out who is following him and his lover, the wife of his bar-owner boss.

Fig 7.14
The rise of independent filmmaking in the 1980s held out the promise to reflect a more diverse representation of multicultural America than most mainstream Hollywood screen experiences. While much of that promise still remains more possibility than reality, movies such as Gregory Nava's *El Norte*, telling the story of two political refugees from Guatemala, Enrique (David Villalpando) and his sister Rosa (Zaide Silvia Gutiérrez), and their perilous struggle to find a better life in the United States, expanded the range of American screen experiences.

This relative increase in the diversity of filmmakers in the 1980s and early 1990s did not represent a complete restructuring of who got to make movies in America. The ranks of directors remained overwhelmingly dominated by white men, and the supposed advent of a "new wave" of filmmakers, whether women, African American, Latino, gay and lesbian, or any other under-represented group, has become a recurring media story, reappearing every few years whenever there happens to be an apparent bump in the number of minority filmmakers. Still, this development in the 1980s registered the continuing demographic changes in America as well as the opening of new screens and screening experiences, and while the diversification of American filmmakers remains wildly uneven and progresses in fits and starts, it does represent the future of American cinema.

In development

Slasher movies

An insane killer wearing an ominous papier-mâché mask terrorizes a young babysitter, killing her friends and chasing her through a suburban home before she turns the tables on him, stabbing him with his own knife. The appearance of John Carpenter's *Halloween* in 1978 was both a major hit and marked a new sub-genre of horror movie, one that for many people became synonymous with the genre in general: the slasher movie. Throughout the 1980s, the slasher movie became a staple of American movies, both in theaters and in the direct-to-video market, and in so doing became a flashpoint for recurring arguments about the possible negative influence of movies on American life.

The slasher movie typically featured a remorseless, maniacal killer, sometimes supernatural, sometimes not. The names of these characters – Michael Myers in *Halloween*, Jason Vorhees in *Friday the 13th* (Sean Cunningham 1980), Freddie Kruger in *A Nightmare on Elm Street* (Wes Craven 1984) – became widely known, even among those who had never seen the movies. The main targets of the killer's wrath were typically teenagers – also the target audience for these movies – and usually sexually active teenagers. The slasher movie shows the clear influence of Alfred Hitchcock's *Psycho* in the mix of a "psychotic" serial killer working out some kind of psychological trauma and the use of shocking, often sexualized violence.

Fig 7.15
The masked killer Michael Myers (Will Sandin) emerges from the shadows to terrorize Laurie Strode (Jamie Lee Curtis) in John Carpenter's *Halloween,* one of the key franchises in the slasher movie genre of horror.

In keeping with the marketing trends of the 1980s, franchise movies spawning a series of sequels dominated the sub-genre (*Halloween* led to seven sequels, *Friday the 13th* to twelve, and *Nightmare on Elm Street* to nine), but dozens of imitators followed. The slasher movie initiated a widespread contemporary association between horror and extreme violence, an association that continues in the more recent sub-sub-genre of "torture porn," including the *Saw* (James Wan 2004) and *Hostel* (Eli Roth 2005) series. While the larger horror genre included a wide variety of 1980s and early 1990s movies, from Stanley Kubrick's *The Shining* (1980) to Ridley Scott's science-fiction horror movie *Alien* (1979) and even comedies such as *Ghostbusters* and *Beetlejuice* (Tim Burton 1988), the connection between horror and bloodletting remains persistent.

Horror, both in literature and on film, has long focused on anxieties over the body and sexuality, and many see the common slasher film fixation on the sexuality of young women as both a defining quality of the sub-genre and the source of much of the controversy over slasher movies. Slasher movies can be seen as similar to the revenge and vigilante movies of the 1970s, and even the *Rambo* series of the 1980s, as further reactions against the cultural redefinitions of traditional gender and sexual roles that began in the 1960s. From this point of view, killers like Michael Myers, Jason, and Freddie Krueger are punishing young people – and especially women – who violate traditional sexual morality. These movies provide screen experiences that condemn the sexual morality of these same young women while also offering sexualized images of young women being tortured and murdered, expressing the audiences' mixed desire for both titillation and punishment.

Others, however, argue that something even more complex may be going on. While these movies do traffic in traditionally objectifying and violent images of young women, the narratives also often feature a young woman as the main protagonist and ultimate victor over the killer. The film critic Carol J. Clover refers to such characters, beginning with Jamie Lee Curtis's portrayal of Laurie Strode in *Halloween,* as the "final girl."[2] She argues that both male and female viewers of slasher movies come to identify with the final girl. As a result, some viewers might enjoy the slasher movie as a kind of revenge against violence against women, or at least as a more complicated arena for working through conflicted and evolving social ideals about sex and gender.

Case study 7.2: Why do we like horror movies?

As we discussed in the "In development" section, a new kind of horror movie exemplified by *Halloween* (1978), *Friday the 13th* (1980), and *A Nightmare on Elm Street* (1984) was among the most popular franchises of 1980s American cinema. The graphic depictions of violence in these movies once again raised a long-standing question about the horror genre: Why do people like having screen experiences meant to frighten and terrify them? Explore this question for yourself by watching two or three examples of 1980s horror and carefully examining your own reactions. How would you define your own screen experiences? What would you describe as the most and least enjoyable aspects of watching these movies? Begin to place your own experience into context by comparing the reactions of different people in the class. How do the responses of self-described fans of horror differ from those who do not enjoy these kinds of movies?

Expand your discussion by reading reviews and articles about the movies you watched from the time they first appeared in theaters. What larger social developments or values do these writers reference? The work of film historians and theorists can then help you to understand these 1980s horror movies in relation to the history of movie horror and ideas about what social and psychological purposes horror serves.

Finally, the potentially comic elements of the slasher movie – especially in Wes Craven's *Nightmare on Elm Street* series, where the main killer Freddie Krueger fatally inhabits the dreams of his young victims and metes out his revenge with a dark sense of humor – adds another dimension to understanding the appeal of the screen experience of horror. A genre defined by its experiential effect on the viewer rather than by setting or plot element, horror has always produced mixed reactions in viewers, never more so than in slasher movies. Just listen to an audience watching a slasher movie – screams of fear are equally accompanied by anxious laughter, a reaction that makes the slasher film perhaps the ultimate "thrill ride" cinema.

John Hughes and new teen movies

One of the most enduring and beloved movies of the 1980s was not a special-effects-laden, big-budget blockbuster, but a story that takes place almost completely within a high school library on a Saturday morning, as a group of students that represents a range of high school stereotypes – a jock, a nerd, a popular girl, a delinquent, and a weirdo – serve detention together and gradually come to bond over their shared hopes, fears, and insecurities: *The Breakfast Club* (1984), one of a series of closely observed teen comedy dramas written and directed by John Hughes. Featuring a group of young actors, including Molly Ringwald, Anthony Michael Hall, Emilio Estevez, Judd Nelson, Andrew McCarthy, Rob Lowe, and Ally Sheedy, who were labeled the "Brat Pack" by the media because they appeared in combination together in a number of 1980s movies, the John Hughes teen movie tried to offer what Hughes hoped was a more realistic, less exploitive image of adolescence than previous Hollywood movies.

The idea of the teenager as representing a separate and unique stage of human development began in the early twentieth century but really took hold in the years after World War II. "Teenagers" came to be seen almost as their own specific tribal group, with a distinctive culture, set of rituals, and ways of talking. Economically, teens became a major consumer group from the 1950s to the present, especially for the entertainment industry. The teen high school movie has become a regular staple of American cinema over the last half century, creating screen experiences both aimed at and focused on young ticket buyers.

Of course, while the youth market was a primary target for movies about teenagers, teenagers were not involved in making these movies in ways other than acting. Unlike the music industry, where teenagers and young adults were writing and performing their own music, the movies were made by older adults and reflected their own understanding and concerns about teenagers. There was the troubled, psychologically disturbed teen as in the character of Jim Stark from *Rebel Without a Cause* (Nicholas Ray 1955), the goofy love-happy teens of American International Pictures "Beach Blanket" movies of the early 1960s, and in the late 1970s and into the 1980s, the sexually obsessed teens in comedies such as *Porky's* (Bob Clark 1982), a precursor to such later movies as *American Pie* (Paul Weitz 1999).

Hughes, a former writer for the comic magazine *National Lampoon*, first achieved movie success with the script for the film version of a story he had first published in the *Lampoon*. *National Lampoon's Vacation* (Harold Ramis 1983) is a broad comedy about a family road trip that goes all wrong. The movie was a big hit, and it enabled Hughes to both write and direct the teen movies for which he is most widely known: *16 Candles* (1984), *The Breakfast Club* (1984), *Pretty In Pink* (1986), and *Ferris Bueller's Day Off* (1986). In these movies, Hughes offered representations of young people as neither sex-obsessed, goofy, nor menacing, but as instead psychologically complex, intelligent characters who are struggling to find meaning and purpose for their lives on the cusp of adulthood.

With the exception of the more fantasy-driven *Ferris Bueller's Day Off*, these movies were realistic and gently comic character studies focused on the challenges of adolescence – peer pressure, parental expectations, the impact of social class – that many young adult viewers then and now could relate to. Even *Ferris Bueller's Day Off*, structured around a series of increasingly improbable adventures by a group of three friends playing hooky from school, such as Ferris (Matthew Broderick) taking control of a parade float and leading all of downtown Chicago in a dance video while he lip synchs the Beatles' version of "Twist and Shout," ultimately focuses on the same personal issues found in all of Hughes's teen movies and features the heart-to-heart confessional scenes that were another trademark of these films.

Fig 7.16
The Breakfast Club, John Hughes' movie focused on a group of teenagers stuck in Saturday detention who overcome stereotypes and high-school cliques to bond and provide emotional support to one another, recalled earlier movies about adolescent trauma like Nicholas Ray's *Rebel Without a Cause*. Here, from left, the school "princess" Claire (Molly Ringwald), "brain" Brian (Anthony Michael Hall), "athlete" Andy (Emilio Estevez), "basket case" Allison (Ally Sheedy), and "criminal" John (Judd Nelson) share stories about the pain of teenage life.

Hughes made several other successful 1980s comedies, some higher concept movies featuring teens (*Weird Science* 1985) and some adults (such as *Planes, Trains, and Automobiles* 1987). He stepped back from active directing in the 1990s, although he continued to write screenplays and produce movies, including *Home Alone* (Christopher Columbus 1990), the most successful live action comedy ever made, before his tragic early death from a heart attack at age 59 in 2009. But it is his revision of the teen movie for which he has been most remembered and which has had the most lasting influence; when people to this day refer to a "John Hughes"-style movie, they are thinking of movies like *Sweet 16* and *The Breakfast Club*.

Genres of gender: The bodybuilder hero

As we discussed in the section on Rambo, this character both simplified and exaggerated the idea of the masculine hero, especially in physical terms. Both Rambo and the superstar who portrayed him, Sylvester Stallone, grew in size from film to film, with ever more bulging biceps and ever more massive pectoral muscles. With this new form of 1980s blockbuster hero, a new genre of movie masculinity was born: the bodybuilder hero. In its pursuit of the comic-book action hero come to life, the bodybuilder hero can seem like either an insistence on or parody of an ideal of the male body.

Since the development of the bodybuilder hero in the 1980s, fans and critics have argued about what this genre of gender performance says about our culture. Seen as a regressive expression of unambiguous masculinity in reaction against feminism and the blurring of traditional gender roles, the bodybuilder hero fits in with the idea of a conservative backlash against a changing American society. Seen as a parody, however, the bodybuilder hero suggests the impossibility – and undesirability – of "turning back the clock," revealing the ridiculousness of uncontested male supremacy and macho posturing; bodybuilding as a sport, after all, is literally built on the idea of posturing. In fact, in its embrace of physical extremity and focus on personal appearance, the bodybuilder gender genre even begins to confuse conventional stereotypes about men and women.

The bodybuilder gender genre actually has a long history in American movies, starting with the Edison Company's short films of Sandow the Strongman in turn-of-the-century Kinetoscope parlors. Sandow's reputation as a "physical specimen" marked the bodybuilder genre as outside the most typical movie and stage

Fig 7.17
Former champion bodybuilder Arnold Schwarzenegger as the robot assassin title character in James Cameron's *The Terminator*. That the character is a cyborg is especially appropriate in that Schwarzenegger's appearance suggested a meticulously crafted and manufactured version of hypermasculine identity.

performances of masculinity. While many iconic male movie stars were portrayed as physically active and strong – especially the early cowboy heroes – none were bodybuilder types. The bodybuilder hero was reserved for specific kinds of film roles, the most famous being the various versions of Tarzan. Based on a series of pulp novels by Edgar Rice Burroughs, Tarzan was a decidedly exotic hero, an English aristocrat raised by apes in Africa. In finding a visual expression of Burroughs' character, Hollywood often turned to athletes such as the Olympic swimming champions Johnny Weissmuller and Buster Crabbe.

The prime example of the 1980s bodybuilder hero is, of course, Arnold Schwarzenegger, an actual professional bodybuilder from Austria who became one of the biggest action heroes of the 1980s and 1990s. Schwarzenegger's movie career actually began more like that of the actors who played Tarzan, in specialty roles that emphasized his carefully constructed physical appearance. His first major screen appearance was a documentary about bodybuilding, *Pumping Iron* (George Butler 1977), but he had earlier played the title role (under the name "Arnold Strong") in the low-budget *Hercules in New York* (Arthur Allan Seidelman 1969).

From there, he built a career playing other novelty characters that exploited his bodybuilder figure and heavily accented English, most significantly in *Conan the Barbarian* (John Milius 1982). His fame grew exponentially playing a character that was literally meant to be seen as a built body, an assassin robot from the future in *The Terminator* (1984), the movie that also launched the career of blockbuster director James Cameron, who would go on to direct some of the most successful movies of the last 20 years, including *Titanic* (1997) and *Avatar* (2009). Following the lead of the Rambo character, Schwarzenegger moved into action hero roles portraying supposedly "real" characters, such as the military Special Forces hero in both *Commando* (Mark Lester 1985) and *Predator* (John McTiernan 1987).

As a star, Schwarzenegger was always primarily identified by his gigantic physique, and he played off of the potentially comic aspects of his bodybuilder physique in order to become increasingly mainstreamed as a masculine character. Comedies like *Twins* (Ivan Reitman 1988), where he plays the fraternal twin of the five-foot-tall Danny DeVito, and *Kindergarten Cop* (Ivan Reitman 1990), where he plays many scenes with a group of five-year-olds, acknowledged Schwarzenegger's outsized physique for comic purposes, but they also tried to convince audiences to see him as a more well-rounded human character.

The most extreme example of the mainstreaming of Schwarzenegger may be Cameron's *True Lies* (1994), where he plays an undercover CIA agent masquerading as a suburban computer salesman, in spite of an outsized physical presence that would make him seem an unlikely candidate for any "undercover" assignment. For the most part, the other characters in the movie take his bodybuilder physique for granted, as if there were nothing unusual about it. Still, the movie banks on the audience's recognition of Schwarzenegger as bodybuilder hero, and his physical appearance remains his most distinguishing feature as a star.

The bodybuilder hero marks an ongoing trend in Hollywood genres of gender focused on a sculpted, weight-trained, and possibly chemically reinforced ideal for both men and women. As *True Lies* demonstrates, this mainstreaming of the bodybuilder hero has also created moments of dissonance as characters who are otherwise supposed to be economically struggling or harried by life's problems seem to be spending hours in the gym. The change in Hollywood gender genres over the decades, for example, was an issue in the casting of Curtis Hanson's tribute to film noir, *L.A. Confidential* (1997), based on James Ellroy's crime novel set in the 1950s. As Hanson put it, action stars from the 1950s "all had that kind of beefy, masculine look that was in the pre-aerobic nautilus era … these guys never worked out in any way, apart from maybe some push-ups or something."[3] Casting such a movie in the early 1990s, it was hard to find male actors who didn't spend a lot of time in the gym. In fact, one of the stars of the film, Guy Pearce, had himself been a bodybuilder.

Parody or ideal? From the 1980s movies of Stallone and Schwarzenegger to more contemporary movies like the CGI-laden *300* (Zack Snyder 2006) to the prevalence of superhero movies, the bodybuilder hero remains both a significant contemporary genre of masculine performance in the movies and a target of criticism and ridicule. The extremity of the bodybuilder physique – especially the focus on large pectoral muscles – makes the bodybuilder hero align with a similar focus on exaggeration in genres of female identity. As some scholars have argued, the bodybuilder hero has become a kind of drag character, a gender genre that so exaggerates stereotypes of masculine physical identity that it reveals masculinity as a kind of costume. In this way, the bodybuilder hero may allow audiences to both idealize and laugh at this performance of masculine power at the same time.

The names above and below the title

Spike Lee

The Best Picture Oscar for 1989 was *Driving Miss Daisy*, a heartwarming adaptation of a play about the twenty-five-year relationship between an affluent white Southern woman and her African American driver during the turbulence of the

Fig 7.18
Spike Lee. Source: Columbia Tristar / The Kobal Collection.

civil rights movement in the 1950s and 1960s. Although the movie does reference these events, the core of the film focuses on how Miss Daisy and her driver Hoke, played by the great American actors Jessica Tandy and Morgan Freeman, develop a moving friendship over the years, finding commonality across barriers of race, gender, and class. In spite of the violence and conflict that defined the fight against racial segregation, *Driving Miss Daisy* ends on a hopeful and sentimental note, implying that the friendship of these two charming characters can undo centuries of institutionalized oppression. Although the movie was a box office success and an award winner, the movie divided critical opinion over whether its depiction of race relations didn't actually reinforce older stereotypes about race, an argument that resurfaced twenty years later in relation to *The Help* (Tate Taylor 2011).

There was another screen experience in 1989, however, that offered a more challenging, less reassuring view of American race relations, one not set in the past but in the immediate present: Spike Lee's *Do the Right Thing*. A graduate, like Martin Scorsese, of the New York University film school, Lee had gained attention with his independent low-budget comedy *She's Gotta Have It* (1986) and the politically-conscious college comedy *School Daze* (1988). *Do the Right Thing* tells another story about relationships across racial lines, this time involving Sal (Danny Aiello), the Italian American owner of a pizzeria in a predominantly black, multiethnic Brooklyn neighborhood, and Mookie (played by Lee himself), his African American delivery man. Simmering tensions in the neighborhood erupt when police kill a young black man, Radio Raheem (Bill Nunn), who had been playing his music too loud in Sal's pizzeria. A riot ensues, one begun when Mookie picks up a trash can and throws it through the window of his long-time employer. At the end of the movie, Mookie and Sal meet again in front of Sal's destroyed business, Sal angry at what he sees as Mookie's betrayal and Mookie demanding back pay. Sal pays Mookie, and the two part after an ambiguous reconciliation.

Do the Right Thing became one of the most critically acclaimed and discussed movies of the year, boldly addressing race and racism in ways that mainstream American cinema had never really done before, so boldly that the Academy of Motion Picture Arts and Sciences did not nominate the movie for Best Picture. While Lee's film directly confronts American racism, it does not do so in a black and white way. Both Sal and Mookie are complicated characters. Sal is a dedicated business and family man who takes pride in serving a diverse community, but he

Fig 7.19
Spike Lee as Mookie prepares to hurl a trash can through the window of his employer Sal's pizzeria at the climax of *Do the Right Thing*.

also harbors racist ideas and attitudes, as do his sons. Mookie is both charismatic and self-centered, using his wits to survive economically while being criticized by his Latina girlfriend for lack of initiative and attention to their son. The relationship between the two men is equally complicated, one of mutual respect and wariness, intimacy and distance.

Rather than providing the consolation of *Driving Miss Daisy*, Lee wants the screen experience of *Do the Right Thing* to consistently challenge his viewers, examining their own attitudes and reactions, as in the famous montage sequence featuring neighborhood characters of every ethnicity and race spewing stereotypes about each other directly at the camera, and therefore at the audience. Just when some viewers might expect Sal and Mookie to defuse the growing neighborhood anger over the death of Radio Raheem, Mookie instead throws the trash can that sets off the uprising (in interviews, Lee has insisted that audience reactions to Mookie's action divided along lines of race, with many white viewers shocked and disappointed, but many black viewers understanding why Mookie does what he does). The title sequence of the movie begins with Mookie's girlfriend Tina (Rosie Perez) dancing to Public Enemy's rap anthem, "Fight the Power"; the movie ends with two seemingly contrasting quotations, one from Malcolm X and one from Martin Luther King, Jr. about the use of violence for political ends. The movie does not explicitly endorse either point of view, and in fact the more one thinks about them, they begin to seem less opposed than they had seemed.

With *Do the Right Thing*, Lee emerged as one of the most important and influential contemporary American filmmakers of the 1980s and perhaps the most famous black filmmaker to date in mainstream American film. Part of the generation of directors who came of age in the independent films of the 1980s, Spike Lee has continued to create screen experiences that challenge audiences to confront the complex operations of American racism across a variety of genres, from the epic biography *Malcolm X* (1992), the sports story *He Got Game* (1998), the documentaries *4 Little Girls* (1997, about the bombing of the 16th Street Baptist Church in Birmingham by Ku Klux Klan terrorists in 1963), and *When the Levees Broke* (2006), about the aftermath of Hurricane Katrina, to comedy, as in *Bamboozled* (2000), a satire about racial stereotyping in media. He has also pushed back against being pigeonholed as a "black" director by showing his directorial range in the crime thrillers *Summer of Sam* (1999), *25th Hour* (2002), and *Inside Man* (2006). He remains a fascinating and important voice in American cinema.

Susan Seidelman, Amy Heckerling, Martha Coolidge

As visual narrative has grown into our dominant form of mass cultural expression over the last century, there has been no greater issue in American movie history than the persistent gender imbalance among the filmmakers who create our screen experiences. As late as 2013, women directed just 6 percent of the 250 top-earning movies in the United States.[4] The careers of three women directors who found box office success in the 1980s and early 1990s – Susan Seidelman, Amy Heckerling, and Martha Coolidge – exemplify both hope and frustration, both the possibility for change and the continuing obstacles faced by women who want to direct. These three directors each created major hits, yet their careers also show how even these successes did not provide the same benefit of the doubt that male filmmakers have enjoyed.

As we saw in Chapters 1 and 2, women such as Alice Guy-Blaché and Lois Weber played central and formative roles in the early decades of American movies in a wide range of roles, both behind and in front of the camera, but with the advent of the studio system, women found themselves increasingly restricted to a smaller group of gender-defined roles in movie production, from acting to costume design to film editing. While a director like Dorothy Arzner managed to forge a career in the studio system, and later the actor Ida Lupino was able to direct a series of movies in the late 1940s and early 1950s for her own production company, they were definitely the exceptions rather than the rule in Hollywood, even as the women's rights movement grew in the 1960s and 1970s.

As the 1970s turned into the 1980s, however, the social changes brought about by the women's movement, along with the growth of college film schools that fostered many of the important male directors of the 1970s, began providing new entry points for women into the director's chair, including the three profiled here. Susan Seidelman, Amy Heckerling, and Martha Coolidge were all products of the New York University film program. Between them, they were responsible for some of the most popular comedies of the 1980s and early 1990s, from *Fast Times at Ridgemont High* (Heckerling 1982) to *Desperately Seeking Susan* (Seidelman 1985), *Real Genius* (Coolidge 1985), and *Clueless* (Heckerling 1995). In spite of these successes, however, all three faced a greater reluctance to finance their movies among producers, studios, and investors than male counterparts with much less consistent track records.

Seidelman first attracted attention with *Smithereens* (1982), an indie movie about a wayward young woman eager to become part of the New York punk rock scene in the early 1980s. Featuring actual punk musicians like Richard Hell, *Smithereens*

Fig 7.20
The director Susan Seidelman (right) with Madonna on the set of *Desperately Seeking Susan*. Source: Orion/The Kobal Collection.

Fig 7.21
Madonna as Susan, a free-spirited member of the downtown New York arts scene, in *Desperately Seeking Susan*.

Fig 7.22
Director Amy Heckerling on the set. Source: Branti Film/Cockamamie/Mary E. Matthews/The Kobal Collection.

showed Seidelman's understanding of the alternative music scene, an awareness she brought to her breakthrough film, *Desperately Seeking Susan*. Pushing for younger actors than the producers originally wanted for this story of a bored New Jersey housewife who finds herself propelled on an exciting adventure in the Manhattan underground arts scene, Seidelman cast the twenty-five-year-old Rosanna Arquette as Roberta, the bored housewife. Most famously, she cast Madonna, at the time an up and coming pop singer who had never acted in a movie before, in the title role. By the time the movie premiered, Madonna had become a music superstar, and the energy and cheekiness of the story resonated with younger audiences.

Heckerling showed a similar ability for finding new talent in her first movie, *Fast Times at Ridgemont High*, a comic story about contemporary high school life based on the non-fiction book by the screenwriter Cameron Crowe. Two years before John Hughes' *Sixteen Candles*, Heckerling demonstrated how to be both funny and sensitive in dealing with the challenges of adolescence, mixing silliness with real poignancy, including the issues of date rape, pregnancy, and abortion. A surprise hit, *Fast Times* launched the careers of several important young actors, including Jennifer Jason Leigh, Phoebe Cates, Judge Reinhold, and most famously Sean Penn, who

Fig 7.23
Sean Penn in a break-out
performance as the genial
stoner surfer Jeff Spicoli
in Amy Heckerling's *Fast
Times at Ridgemont High.*

Fig 7.24
Martha Coolidge. Source:
Rysher Entertainment/
Bruce McBroom/The Kobal
Collection.

steals the movie with his hilarious yet also affectionate portrayal of the stoner surfer
Jeff Spicoli.

After more box office success with another unlikely hit, the gimmicky *Look
Who's Talking* (1989), that used special effects to feature talking babies, Heckerling
wrote and directed one of the trademark American movies of the 1990s, *Clueless.*
A surprisingly faithful adaptation of Jane Austen's classic novel *Emma* from 1815,
Clueless gently lampoons the materialistic culture and slang of a group of affluent
Beverly Hills high school students, showing her pitch perfect ear for teen speak.
Following Austen's example, Heckerling uses the apparent triviality of her characters'
striving for popularity and romance to explore more serious questions of ethics,
loyalty, and the importance of compassion, all the while maintaining the air of
glamor and fantasy associated with the greatest of screwball comedies.

Fig 7.25
A scene from Martha Coolidge's *Valley Girl*, a Romeo and Juliet story about the romance between Hollywood punk Randy (Nicolas Cage) and "valley girl" Julie (Deborah Foreman).

A pattern soon emerged of these filmmakers taking material seemingly aimed to exploit stereotypes about young people and turning them into more thoughtful, emotionally convincing screen experiences, and Martha Coolidge is no exception. After directing a semi-documentary independent movie about date rape, *Not a Pretty Picture* (1976), she was given the chance (for a token salary) to direct *Valley Girl* (1983), a movie the producers saw as an exploitation picture meant to capitalize on the silly and sexist stereotype of the southern California "valley girl." Instead, like Heckerling, Coolidge took her characters seriously as multidimensional human beings, and along with including the required valley-speak, creates a Romeo and Juliet story about a relationship between a rich suburban girl and a working-class punk boy. Coolidge would bring that same perspective to *Real Genius* (1984), another potentially gimmicky comedy about science nerds in college.

Since their emergence in the 1980s, all three have managed to maintain directing careers, in large part thanks to television. The careers of all three reveal a central challenge that still confronts women (and other "non-traditional" – i.e. non-white male) directors: a persistent skepticism among movie financers about their abilities that results in a low tolerance for perceived failure, and a reluctance to provide the artistic freedom that would allow these directors to display the very qualities that first brought them to attention. Throughout their careers, Seidelman, Heckerling, and Coolidge have been saddled with generic movies that ignore their strengths and interests, and all three have struggled to find support for their own ideas and projects.

In fact, grouping them together as "women directors" is part of the problem that women in film still face. While the emergence of directors like Seidelman, Heckerling, and Coolidge in the 1980s signaled the possible opening of mainstream Hollywood to the idea of women in charge of movie production, the history since then continues to be a series of stops and starts. The opening of the digital and online age has created new opportunities for a wide range of filmmakers, and in Chapter 8 we will examine the significance of directors like Kathryn Bigelow, who have worked to push the idea that women can direct all kinds of movies, not just supposedly "women's" genres like comedy and romance. Today, another new generation of women filmmakers, including Bigelow, Nicole Holofcener, Nancy Meyers, Sofia Coppola, and Lynn Shelton, continue to challenge the long exclusion of women from the director's chair. The future of their and other's careers is part of our own involvement in the contemporary screen experience of American cinema.

Quentin Tarantino

The rise of indie film culture in the late 1980s and early 1990s launched the careers of a generation of artistically adventurous directors who continue to be among the most influential and innovative in American cinema today, including Steven Soderbergh, Spike Lee, Richard Linklater, David O. Russell, Paul Thomas Anderson, Wes Anderson, and Kevin Smith, among others. Of this group, there is no filmmaker who has been more famous, controversial, and influential than Quentin Tarantino. From the initial sensation created by his incredibly stylish, ultra-violent, and low-budget crime film *Reservoir Dogs* at the Sundance Film Festival in 1992, Tarantino has produced a series of screen experiences defined by his encyclopedic knowledge of movie history, especially exploitation and genre movies, a playful sense of experimentation with narrative structure and movie form, a love of elaborately staged scenes of violence, and a refusal to follow safe or predictable formulas. Both action-oriented and extremely talky, fast-moving and sprawling, Tarantino's films inspire strong reactions in viewers, making him one of the most popular and criticized of contemporary filmmakers.

As was suggested in the "Now playing" section on *Pulp Fiction*, Tarantino's biography is almost as legendary as his films, his life story often described as another version of the "self-made" genius model of earlier directors like Erich Von Stroheim and Orson Welles. Born in 1963, Tarantino dropped out of high school in the late 1970s to attend acting school, which he also left. Rather than studying film in college, Tarantino is largely a self-taught filmmaker, his main "school" the video store he worked in, part of the impact of the videotape revolution of the 1980s (although in interviews Tarantino has expressed regret that he missed out on studying movies in college).

Fig 7.26
Quentin Tarantino. Source: Universal/The Kobal Collection.

As "Now playing" pointed out, part of the fun of watching a Tarantino movie involves being on the lookout for references from a wide range of cinema history, from French New Wave filmmaking to silent comedy, but Tarantino is most influenced by the Italian-made "spaghetti westerns" of the 1960s and early 1970s and the Hong Kong martial arts movie industry of the 1970s to the present. What both these action movie traditions have in common is that they are hybrids and hodgepodges, crossing lines of cultures and combining genres, challenging conventions between "serious" and "exploitation" movies, the trivial and the profound. All of these qualities define Tarantino's screen experiences as well. Like these movies, Tarantino's films focus on visual excitement and movement, including intricate choreographies of violence, as in the many battle set pieces throughout the two *Kill Bill* movies, themselves tributes to both the martial arts and western traditions.

As we saw in "Now playing," Tarantino's hugely successful follow-up to *Reservoir Dogs*, *Pulp Fiction*, became one of the defining movies of the 1990s, and made him one of the most talked-about directors in the world. Tarantino's next project was another crime movie, *Jackie Brown* (1997), but in Tarantino's characteristically unconventional style one that featured a middle-aged African American women played by the great Blaxploitation star Pam Grier as the hero. Tarantino's movies have always featured prominent African American characters, and his treatment of race and especially the use of the word "nigger" have provoked debates about whether his screen experiences challenge or merely exploit the brutal history of this epithet, particularly from his contemporary Spike Lee. The fact that Tarantino's movies resist maintaining a consistent tone, combining comedy, tragedy, violence, and irony, only intensifies the diversity of viewers' reactions to his work, part of Tarantino's goal as a director.

Never one to shy away from controversy, Tarantino has more recently tackled serious and contentious historical issues that mainstream American movies have been either reluctant to address or have only done so with an air of earnest seriousness. *Inglourious Basterds* (2009, with a title taken from a 1970s Italian World War II movie) tackled World War II and the Holocaust with a story of a select group of Jewish soldiers who go on vigilante commando raids against the Nazis, culminating in a fantasy of executing Hitler and the Nazi high command in a literal kind of fiery holocaust – in a movie theater, no less. In *Django Unchained* (2013), Tarantino takes on American slavery, combining realistic and comic-book violence in a movie that is both historical document and another superhero revenge fantasy, as the title

Fig 7.27
The title sequence from Quentin Tarantino's first movie, *Reservoir Dogs*, demonstrates his stylized approach to constructing his screen experiences, as the team of criminals (portrayed by, from left, Michael Madsen, Harvey Keitel, Tim Roth, Quentin Tarantino himself, and Steve Buscemi) walk down the street in slow motion, all dressed in matching suits and shades.

character, a former slave named Django (named after a similar avenging hero from a series of spaghetti westerns) teams up with a German bounty hunter to rescue his wife from slavery and exact his own retribution. As in *Inglourious Basterds*, Tarantino is unafraid of bending historical truth in the name of confronting the violence of racism and slavery. Audacious, provocative, talkative, and endlessly imaginative, no contemporary filmmaker's work continues to be more anticipated than that of Quentin Tarantino.

Notes

1   Tom Gunning, "The Cinema of Attraction: Early Film, Its Spectator and the Avant-Garde," *Wide Angle*, 8.3 & 4, Fall 1986: 63–70.
2   Carol J. Clover, *Men, Women, and Chain Saws: Gender in the Modern Horror Film*. Princeton, NJ: Princeton University Press, 1993.
3   Roddick, Nick, "Hanson, Curtis: LA Confidential," *Urban Cinefile*, March 13, 2014, http://www.urbancinefile.com.au/home/view.asp?a=531&s=Interviews_Archives
4   Martha M. Lauzen, "The Celluloid Ceiling: Behind-the-Scenes Employment of Women on the Top 250 Films of 2013," *Women Make Movies* website, March 13, 2014, http://womenintvfilm.sdsu.edu/files/2013_Celluloid_Ceiling_Report.pdf

Explore further

Bernstein, Jonathan, *Pretty In Pink: The Golden Age of Teenage Movies*. New York: St. Martin's Griffin, 1997.

Clover, Carol J., *Men, Women, and Chain Saws: Gender in the Modern Horror Film*. Princeton, NJ: Princeton University Press, 1993.

Grant, Barry Keith (ed.), *The Dread of Difference: Gender and the Horror Film*. Austin: University of Texas Press, 1996.

Herbert, Daniel, *Videoland: Movie Culture at the American Video Store*. Berkeley: University of California Press, 2014.

Holmlund, Chris (ed.), *American Cinema of the 1990s: Themes and Variations*. New Brunswick, NJ: Rutgers University Press, 2008.

Jordan, Chris, *Movies and the Reagan Presidency: Success and Ethics*. Westport, CT: Praeger, 2003.

Kord, Susanne and Elisabeth Krimmer (eds.), *Contemporary Hollywood Masculinities: Gender, Genre, and Politics*. New York: Palgrave Macmillan, 2011.

Lyons, Charles, *The New Censors: Movies and the Culture Wars*. Philadelphia: Temple University Press, 1997.

Nadel, Alan, *Flatlining on the Field of Dreams: Cultural Narratives in the Films of President Reagan's America*. New Brunswick, NJ: Rutgers University Press, 1997.

Nystrom, Derek, *Hard Hats, Rednecks, and Macho Men: Class in 1970s American Cinema*. Oxford/New York: Oxford University Press, 2009.

Palmer, William J., *The Films of the Eighties: A Social History*. Carbondale: Southern Illinois University Press, 1993.

Pierson, John, *Spike, Mike, Slackers and Dykes: A Guided Tour Across a Decade of American Independent Cinema*. New York: Miramax Books/Hyperion, 1997.

Prince, Stephen, *A New Pot of Gold: Hollywood Under the Electronic Rainbow, 1980–1989*. New York: C. Scribner's, 2000.

Redding, Judith M. and Victoria A. Brownworth, *Film Fatales: Independent Women Directors*. Seattle: Seal Press, 1997.

Rhines, Jesse Algernon, *Black Film, White Money*. New Brunswick, NJ: Rutgers University Press, 1996.

Stringer, Julian (ed.), *Movie Blockbusters*. London/New York: Routledge, 2003.

Tasker, Yvonne, *Spectacular Bodies: Gender, Genre, and the Action Cinema*. London/ New York: Routledge, 1993.

Wasko, Janet, *Hollywood in the Information Age: Beyond the Silver Screen*. Austin: University of Texas Press, 1995.

Willis, Sharon, *High Contrast: Race and Gender in Contemporary Hollywood Film*. Durham, NC: Duke University Press, 1997.

Wood, Robin, *Hollywood from Vietnam to Reagan – and Beyond*. New York: Columbia University Press, 2003.

Wyatt, Justin, *High Concept: Movies and Marketing in Hollywood*. Austin: University of Texas Press, 1994.

CHAPTER 8

The digital era: Back to the future, 1994–present

Now playing

***Titanic* plays on a small screen embedded in the back of an airplane seat, 1998**
The young woman on board the non-stop flight from New York to Los Angeles has settled into her seat and looks at the small screen embedded in the seat back in front of her. She is excited to see that the airline is showing a movie that happens to be the biggest hit of the past year, James Cameron's *Titanic* (1997), the latest movie retelling of one of the most famous transportation disasters of all time, the sinking of the luxury liner *RMS Titanic* in 1912 after a collision with an iceberg in the north Atlantic, killing more than 1,500 people. Cameron has developed a reputation as a master of **computer generated imagery (or CGI)** effects in his movies, and *Titanic* combines an intimate story about two doomed lovers from different social classes – the wealthy Rose (Kate Winslet) and working-class Jack (Leonardo DiCaprio) – with an epic recreation of the disaster itself.

The movie dominated box offices and the Academy Awards and provided theatergoers with a visually overwhelming screen experience in the classic style of the movie epic, as the giant ship breaks apart and hundreds plunge to their deaths. The young woman on our flight had loved the movie when it came out, and as she put her headphones on she was looking forward to watching it again. But is the movie she will be watching really the same screen experience that she enjoyed in the movie theater where she first saw *Titanic*? Rather than gazing at a 30-foot tall screen rising to the ceiling above her head, she peers at a tiny nine-inch video monitor. Rose and Jack are still there, and the *Titanic* still breaks in two before disappearing beneath the black waves, but the images are no longer overwhelming, the sound over the small headset no longer booming. Still, she finds the love story just as moving and the conclusion just as tragic, no matter the small size of the screen.

Computer-generated imagery (CGI) Refers to a broad range of digital special effects that involves creating screen images solely using computer technology. These images range from static backgrounds to action sequences that can involve hundreds of completely computer-generated characters, as in the battle sequences in the three *The Lord of the Rings* movies directed by Peter Jackson. Computer animation, especially as pioneered by Pixar studios, involves animated movies completely generated using computer software.

Fig 8.1
Leonardo DiCaprio and Kate Winslet as the ill-fated lovers Jack and Rose in James Cameron's *Titanic*, a canny mix of melodrama and CGI special effects that became one of the most popular American movies of the 1990s.

While airline companies began screening movies on airplanes as early as the 1920s, for the most part these exhibitions were stunts or gimmicks until the 1960s, when the advent of portable projectors and later videotape made movies a regular feature of longer plane flights. Where a single screen at the front of the cabin had been the norm in airplanes, in the late 1990s seatback screens became the latest innovation in inflight entertainment. Just three years later in 2001, Apple would introduce the iPod, allowing anyone to watch a movie on a screen that fits in one's hand. By the early 2010s, airline passengers found themselves surrounded by screens, as people watched movies, television shows, and videos on a wide variety of phones, tablets, and other devices. In fact, some predict that the built-in screen will soon be a thing of the past on planes, completely replaced by personal viewing devices.

While most passengers welcome the increasing array of screening options available to them, especially on long transcontinental or overseas flights, this dizzying variety of screen experiences made possible by the advent of the latest in digital technology is returning us to the question that we began with at the dawn of American cinema: Just what is a movie? Personal viewing devices give us an unprecedented ability to manipulate and customize our screen experiences, starting and stopping play, repeating scenes and skipping others, even cutting, pasting, and re-editing parts of the visual narratives we see. "Movies" exist in movie theaters, on cable television, on an iPad, on a smart phone. Just as filmmakers, viewers, and writers wrestled with the question of just how to define the new art form that emerged at the turn of the twentieth century, at the beginning of the twenty-first century we find ourselves facing many of the same questions.

Two high school students watch a VHS cassette of *The Phantom Edit* on a home entertainment center, 2001

The videocassette came from a friend of a friend of a friend. Soon after the tape is popped into the VCR player, a familiar phrase appears on the television screen in front of a black background: "A long time ago in a galaxy far, far away..." followed by the ringing opening chords of John Williams' famous score, the unmistakable block design letters of *Star Wars*, and the title "Episode 1: The Phantom Menace." But this isn't quite the long-anticipated "prequel" to the *Star Wars* series that writer and director George Lucas had released in 1999. Instead, these two teenagers are watching an unauthorized version of that movie known as *The Phantom Edit*.

As its name suggests, this movie is a re-editing of the original *Phantom Menace*. "The Phantom Editor," later identified as professional editor Mike J. Nichols, took his own video copy of *The Phantom Menace* and made hundreds of changes to the movie that he felt strengthened the storyline. The most famous of these changes, the one that attracted the most publicity for *The Phantom Edit*, involved dramatically lessening the impact of a new addition to the *Star Wars* universe, the character of Jar-Jar Binks.

Jar-Jar Binks had quickly emerged as a point of contention among die-hard fans soon after *The Phantom Menace* premiered. Enabled by the radical new opportunities for communication and interactivity created by the explosive growth of the Internet, many had immediately taken to chat rooms and discussion boards to critique the movie and especially to register their unhappiness with Jar-Jar. A tall, gangly alien created completely through CGI featuring bulbous eyes, a protruding snout, and long ears that hung like dreadlocks down his back, some viewers saw him not only as a ridiculously comic figure out of step with the increasing seriousness

Fig 8.2
The completely computer-generated character of Jar-Jar Binks, here with the "real-life" actors Liam Neeson as Qui-Gon Jinn, Hugh Quarshie as Captain Panaka, and Natalie Portman as Queen Amidala, emerged as a controversial figure in George Lucas' reboot of the *Star Wars* franchise, *The Phantom Menace*.

Fanediting A form of interactive digital culture that consists of individuals re-editing existing movies into different versions, sometimes in an effort to improve the movie, sometimes to transform the movie in terms of genre or to combine it with other movies, a process also known as remixing or "mash up." The first significant instance of fanediting was *The Phantom Edit*, a revision of *Star Wars Episode I: The Phantom Menace*.

Fan fiction A kind of creative writing that involves stories based on characters and incidents from favorite books and movies. Fan fiction, especially understood as the retelling of popular stories, is as old as literature, but the accessibility of the Internet has created an extensive global network of fan fiction sites. The growth of fan fiction, a form of what is also known as "user-generated content," has played an extensive role in the increasingly interactive nature of what it means to be a fan and consumer of popular culture.

with which fans regarded the *Star Wars* mythology, but even as a kind of racial stereotype, as Jar-Jar's wide-eyed gullibility, his exaggerated reactions, and especially a speech pattern based on Jamaican patois suggested the demeaning representations of black people that has been a disturbing staple of American cinema history. While in the past such objections and arguments would remain at the level of discussions and disagreements among fans, *The Phantom Menace* represented a new kind of response. Rather than merely argue about the movie, the Phantom Editor tried to fix it.

The appearance of the *The Phantom Edit* quickly became a focus of media coverage and debate at the beginning of the twenty-first century, in large part because it exemplifies two crucial developments resulting from the rise of digital technology and the Internet. The first is the radical interactivity made possible by digital technology. Rather than simply watching movies and other screen experiences, viewers can now remake, remix, and recombine any form of digital media. Although the Phantom Editor Mike Nichols actually made the original *The Phantom Edit* using pre-digital videotape, the technical move from film and tape to the ones and zeroes of digital information allows anyone with a laptop and some basic editing software to follow Nichols' example. Since *The Phantom Edit*, a whole subculture called "**fanediting**" has grown, allowing anyone with the time and interest to become a "redirector" and customize their own versions of their favorite movies.

The second development involves the growth and development of fan culture enabled by the Internet. The cross-marketing of franchise movies like *Star Wars* we examined in the previous screen age had already turned this discrete series of movies into an entire commercial subculture, including action figures, video games, clothing lines, a series of novels based on the movie mythology, and most of all a devoted fan base who attended conventions, wrote newsletters, and became intellectually and emotionally invested in the series. The widespread access to the Internet that began in the mid-1990s both increased and transformed these fan activities. **Fan fiction**, the creation of new stories based on the characters of popular novels, movies, and television shows, had been an underground activity since the 1970s, but Internet publication fostered an explosion of fan-based production and creativity.

Fans created their own elaborate websites devoted to *Star Wars*, and Hollywood slowly began to comprehend the power and influence of these online fan communities. Conventions like Comic-Con, which had started as small gatherings of comic book and popular culture enthusiasts, would become major marketing and publicity venues for moviemakers. Internet fan culture embraced the interactivity of the digital age, insisting on its own "ownership" of the franchises fans loved. Our screen experiences have now expanded to include the creative interactivity of fan culture, from fan fiction and fan edits to projects like *Star Wars Uncut*, in which people from around the world have fashioned their own recreation of fifteen-second clips from the original movie, all reassembled into a new "movie" of its own. For the movie industry, these new developments were seen as both opportunities and threats, both strengthening the emotional investment of consumers in the screen experiences they were producing but also challenging what it means to "own" a screen experience.

A college film student watches *The Birth of a Nation* on YouTube, 2010

A student sits in her dorm room and reviews her writing assignment for her History of American Film class: write an interactive blog essay analyzing two scenes involving representations of race and gender in D. W. Griffith's *The Birth of a Nation*. She has already settled on two she wants to write about: the first shows the character of "Mammy," the enslaved black housekeeper for the Cameron family, played in blackface by the white actor Jennie Lee, helping to rescue the head of the Cameron family at the end of the Civil War, placing her former owner's safety above her own freedom; the second involves the infamous pursuit of the virginal Sofie Cameron (Mae Marsh) by Gus (Walter Lang, again in blackface), leading to his brutal lynching by the supposedly heroic Ku Klux Klan. Griffith himself had defended his movie against charges of racism in this second scene by pointing to the depiction of "good" (in Griffith's estimation) characters like Mammy in the first. In addition to arguing that both scenes represent damaging racial stereotypes, the student has also decided to argue that both Mammy and Flora reinforce equally restrictive historical ideas about the proper roles for women at the time.

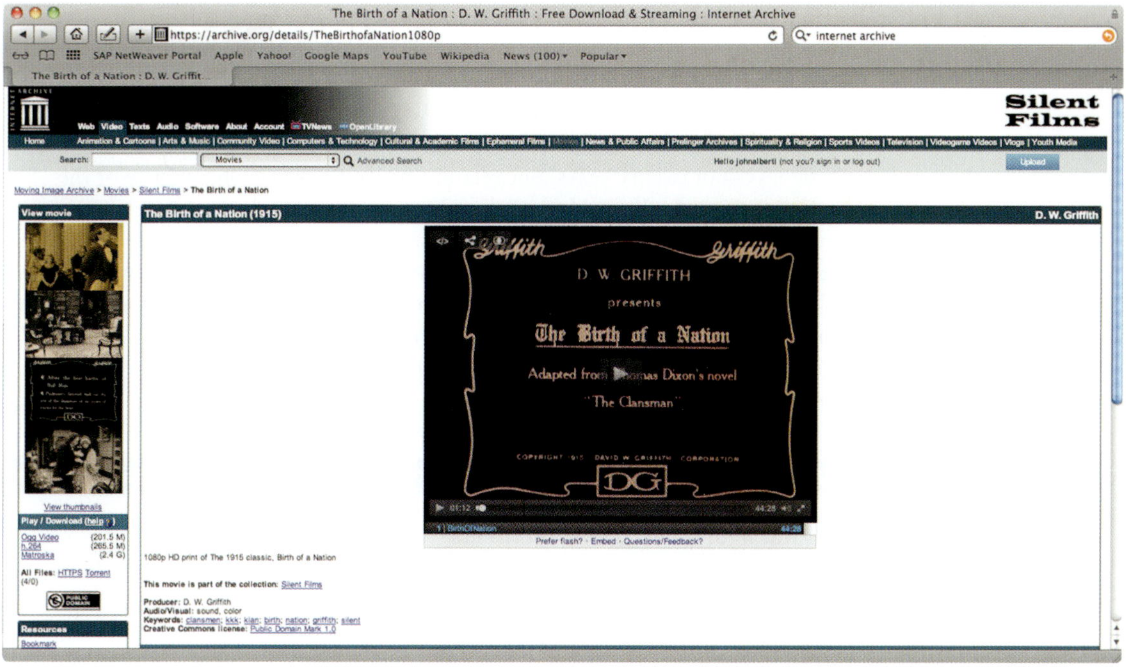

Fig 8.3
Online resources such as the *Internet Archive* digital library (https://archive.org/) have made hundreds of movies from even the earliest days of American cinema easily accessible to anyone with a computer, tablet, or smart phone. Source: https://archive.org/details/TheBirthofaNation1080p.

What are her next steps in composing her essay? If she were a student in 1980, her options would have been limited to relying on her notes and memory of seeing *The Birth of a Nation* for the first and only time when her professor had screened it in class. Books and journal articles would include verbal descriptions of the movie, all filtered through the particular interpretations of the writers, and these same texts might also contain some photographic reproductions of scenes and frames. If she wanted to see the actual movie again, however, she would have to wait for another public screening of the film.

Were she writing ten years later in 1990, she could now rent or borrow a videotape of the movie, allowing her to rewind and watch these two scenes multiple times and giving her a chance to explore her reactions to this screen experience in detail. The growing availability of videos from public and school libraries had dramatically opened up American film history to anyone interested in learning more about the evolution of American cinema, and her ability to rewatch the movie multiple times on her own would help enrich her research experience of reading those books and articles about *The Birth of a Nation*, creating a greater familiarity with the movie that would make the commentary and arguments from film scholars all the more meaningful.

In 2010, her options for exploring *The Birth of a Nation*, one of the screen experiences that established movies as a major artistic and cultural medium in America, have expanded in ways unimaginable even ten years earlier. Rather than physically going to a library, she can easily access the movie on YouTube, a video sharing site that came online in 2005 and quickly became the most popular "movie theater" in the history of the world. She can just as easily download the digital file of the movie from sites like the *Internet Archive*, allowing her to not only watch the movie but to grab clips to embed in her online blog essay, where she can provide her own recorded commentary to accompany her own viewer's/reader's screen experience of her analysis. She can place these clips from *The Birth of a Nation* in contrast with clips from dozens of other movies from the history of American cinema, creating exciting new opportunities for new insights and new lines of discussion and debate.

Because her blog essay is online, she can communicate her ideas to people around the world interested in race and gender in *The Birth of a Nation*, reducing and even erasing the line between "student" and "scholar," "amateur" and "professional." In a little less than twenty years, our relationship to the screen experience of the movies has been radically transformed, as we now have for the first time in movie history easy access to the means of creating screen experiences. From one of the most expensive of artistic mediums, moviemaking is now available to anyone with a smart phone and a personal computer. For those of us interacting with movies at the beginning of the twenty-first century, we are experiencing the beginnings of a new visual media age as exciting and transformative as the dawn of American cinema at the turn of the last century.

Screen ages

The digital age: A new dawn of cinema

Perhaps no movie better expresses the contradictions and anxieties surrounding media in the digital age than *The Matrix* (Andrew and Lawrence/Lana Wachowski 1999) a $63 million massive special effects extravaganza from Warner Brothers, part of the equally massive Time Warner company, a global media conglomerate

Fig 8.4
The rebel fighters Trinity (Carrie-Anne Moss) and Neo (Keanu Reeves) prepare to do battle against the intelligent machines that have enslaved the human race in *The Matrix*, the Wachowskis' dystopian allegory about the threat posed by digital technology, although the movie is itself an example of the power of computer-generated imagery in creating spectacular new screen experiences.

that controls television networks, magazines, comic books, and movie studios. *The Matrix* tells the story of a contemporary computer hacker named Neo (Keanu Reeves) who finds out that our ideas of individuality and personal freedom are all an illusion, a fantasy fed directly into our brains so that our bodies may lie dormant and serve as an energy source for machines that have grown intelligent and taken over the world. Neo then leads a revolution against the machines and the fantasy world they have created – known as the "Matrix" – leading a rag-tag group of freedom fighters against the technology that not only controls our actions but our very thoughts and feelings.

In evoking a dystopian world where the machines that humans have created to serve us have instead enslaved us, *The Matrix* draws on a long twentieth-century tradition of movies and novels that express our uneasiness over rapid technological and social change, from Fritz Lang's silent classic *Metropolis* (1927) to the *Terminator* series. The fact that a giant media conglomerate such as Time Warner, a company that critics of media consolidation consider its own kind of "matrix," dominating and controlling our access to information and our screen experiences, would bankroll a movie that champions the idea of the individual rising up against the faceless, impersonal entities that enslave our bodies and imaginations, seems either ironic or cynical, or maybe a little bit of both.

The contemporary screen age that begins with the opening of the Internet to millions of computer users around the world in the mid-1990s and continuing through the rapid evolution of digital technology to include smart phones, personal tablets, and ever more interactive and extensive means of communicating and connecting with one another and with the global information network defines a revolution in media technology that is reshaping our relationship to screen experiences on an almost daily basis. While the cultural activity we call "the movies" remains a significant art form, source of cultural influence, and economic activity in the digital age, these changes are also raising fundamental questions about just what we mean by calling something a "movie" that recall the earliest days of American cinema. For both moviemakers and movie fans (if we can even continue to differentiate between the two), these changes suggest both promise and fear, optimism and pessimism, over the future of American movie history.

Freedom and control: The push and pull of the digital age

The basic premise of *The Matrix* draws on two significant currents and cultural ideas about the impact of technology in the digital age: on the one hand, the concentration of power and information in the hands of a small group of global institutions beyond the control and even understanding of the individual; on the other, the

growing ability of the individual to access information and communicate with others
in unprecedented ways beyond the control of these large social institutions. Does
the Internet signal an unprecedented democratization of information and media,
empowering ordinary citizens in ways impossible to imagine only a few years before?
Or does the Internet represent the latest development of consumer capitalism,
allowing corporations and governments access to our most private information?

Such arguments continue to swirl in the contemporary screen age, and evidence
exists supporting both points of view. The Internet has in fact allowed literally tens
of millions of people to interact with each other and express their opinions and ideas
with a speed and global reach that was impossible in the analog world of printing
presses and paper. As we discussed above in "Now Playing," the rise of interactive
fan culture has exponentially increased the interactivity of our screen experiences,
and digital technology has also dramatically cut the costs involved in creating
visual narratives, increasing access to moviemaking in unprecedented ways. The
rise of "DIY" (Do It Yourself) moviemaking will become one of the most important
developments of our current screen ages, and websites like Flickr, YouTube, Vimeo,
and others allow for virtually cost-free worldwide distribution of anyone's creation
(even if they can't guarantee that anyone will want to watch).

At the same time, the concentration of media ownership has also accelerated,
enabled by these same technological and culture changes. By the second decade of
the twentieth century, we can point to a "**Big Six**" of global media companies –
Comcast, the News Corporation, Disney, Viacom, Time Warner, and CBS – that
control 90 percent of media in the United States and dominate mainstream movie
production. Confusingly, these giant megacorporations also produced "independent"
movies through companies like Fox Searchlight (the News Corporation) and
Focus Features (Comcast). "Independent" movies now can range from a movie
like Jonathan Caouette's award-winning autobiographical documentary *Tarnation*
(2003), made for a little over $200 using home movies and the iMovie program
on his Mac computer to any movie with an "indie" feel such as Wes Anderson's
Moonrise Kingdom (2012), financed by Focus Features for $16 million, modest
by blockbuster standards (the biggest hit of 2012, Joss Whedon's comic-book
adaptation *The Avengers*, cost over $200 million), but still beyond the reach of
most moviemakers. As the variety of screen experiences continues to proliferate in
the digital age, the competition between these various forces, both towards greater
concentration and control and greater access and diversity, becomes ever more
heated and complicated.

Big Six A reference to
the small number of
giant megacorporations
that control the vast
majority of media
production – including
movies – in the US
and around the world.
The actual number and
composition of these
megacorporations tends
to vary from year to year
as various mergers and
acquisitions change their
specific makeup, but
the trend of increasing
concentration of media
ownership in a small
group of powerful
conglomerates continues.
As of this book's writing,
the "Big Six" consists
of Comcast, the News
Corporation, Disney,
Viacom, Time Warner,
and CBS.

Globalization, 9/11, and the movies

The fall of the Berlin Wall in 1990 followed the next year by the dissolution of the Soviet Union seemed to signal the end of the Cold War, the confrontation pitting the United States and western Europe against the USSR and the People's Republic of China, with massive arsenals of nuclear weapons on each side aimed at one another. The Cold War had been the defining global narrative since the end of World War II, and hopes were built that a new spirit of international cooperation might follow. With the collapse of the Soviet Union, some political leaders in the United States envisioned a period of unchallenged American leadership (in spite of the fact that China remained a formidable economic and military power) and even dominance, an idea encapsulated in President George H. W. Bush's invocation of a "New World Order" led by the US.

The end of the Cold War and the growth of digital technology and the Internet did begin to rapidly and radically accelerate the globalization of the world economy, as money and digital information – including movies – could travel around the world instantly, 24 hours a day. As we have seen, the mainstream American movie industry has always depended on a global cinema culture and box office as a crucial source of funding and influence, and the importance of global distribution and sales has only increased in the digital age. The prospect of international sales is a primary consideration in what kinds of movies get funded today and has further accelerated the focus on spectacular franchise action adventure blockbusters. As we will see below in the "In development" section, global marketing has been a key driver in the rise of the comic-book superhero action movie ever since the success of Tim Burton's *Batman* in 1989, as stark battles between good and evil punctuated with visually impressive CGI action sequences create screen experiences that travel easily across borders of culture and language.

The end of the Cold War did not mean the end of global conflict, however, and the digital age has also come to be defined by the legacies of European and American colonialism and the battle for control of the world's natural resources, especially the oil that fuels the global economy. The first Gulf War between the United States and Iraq in 1990–1991 presaged that the historically complex politics of the oil-rich Middle East would replace the Cold War as the focus of US foreign policy, a development that would come to a head with the disastrous terrorist attacks on September 11, 2001, leading to the controversial wars in Afghanistan and Iraq that would become the longest in American history. The so-called "Global War on Terror" as defined by the second president Bush came to symbolize the dark side of globalization for many, splitting Americans between those believing that security needs required the US to forcefully assert its global military dominance and those

Globalization A catch-all term indicating a wide variety of economic, political, and cultural developments that stress the increasingly interconnected and interdependent nature of global activity, particularly in relation to the digital communications revolution. As money and capital is able to circulate around the world 24 hours a day, seven days a week, the lines between the global and local are becoming increasingly blurred. In terms of movies, the major production and distribution companies view the market for their screen experiences in terms of a broad global market, thus complicating our sense of what it means to describe a movie as "American."

Fig 8.6
George Clooney as Major Archie Gates, Ice Cube as Staff Sergeant "Chief" Elgin, and Mark Wahlberg as Sergeant First Class Troy Barlow scheme to locate stolen Kuwaiti gold before their consciences are stirred by the plight of Iraqi dissidents abandoned by the US military in David O. Russell's Gulf War satire *Three Kings*.

feeling that a continuing insistence on this global dominance would only lead to more conflict and violence.

As with the Vietnam War in the 1960s, American studios were at first reluctant and unsure about whether and how to create screen experiences dealing with these complex and controversial wars. Would American viewers flock to or avoid movies about such tragic and divisive events? Over the last twenty years, movies like David O. Russell's *Three Kings* (1999), a darkly satirical movie set in the First Gulf War, and Kathryn Bigelow's Best-Picture-winning *The Hurt Locker* (2008) about a bomb disposal squad in the Iraq War, have expressed skepticism over the political motivations behind the wars and focused instead on the heroism and trauma of the soldiers involved. Some critics have seen other action adventure movies, especially the comic-book superhero movies referred to above, as providing either escapist fantasies allowing audiences to forget the war by experiencing less morally ambiguous displays of American heroism or, particularly in terms of the conflicted versions of superheroes as in Christopher Nolan's *Dark Knight* Batman trilogy, a version of the audience's growing ambivalence about the very idea of a superhero, or a superpower.

Since the election of the Democrat Bill Clinton in 1992, followed by the contested election of the Republican George W. Bush in 2000, the American political climate has been divided and divisive, in many ways a reflection both of what seems to many a more confusing international arena following the simple binary oppositions of the Cold War and of the accelerating demographic and technological changes that are defining the twenty-first century in the United States. At the beginning of the twentieth century, the wave of immigration that was changing American culture led to a tension between those who wanted to resist these changes and those who embraced new visions of a more diverse American culture and identity, and these conflicts were reflected in the development of early cinema, especially as these newest Americans formed a major part of the early moviegoing public.

The first decades of the twenty-first century are witnessing similar arguments as the US adapts to the quickly arriving reality (already here in states like California) that by the middle of the century there will be no statistically dominant ethnic or racial group in the United States. The historic and even astonishing election and re-election of Barack Obama, the first African American president, is one powerful indicator of the changing nature of American society. In terms of the

Fig 8.7
An improvised explosive device is about to claim the life of bomb disposal expert Staff Sergeant Matthew Thompson (Guy Pearce) in Kathryn Bigelow's stark and visceral portrayal of the Iraq War, *The Hurt Locker*.

movies, Hollywood can be seen as reacting slowly to these changes, still creating screen experiences that overwhelmingly focus on the lives and adventures of white male characters. The growing globalization of the movie business reflects the same conflicting pressures between concentration and diversity that define the media culture of the digital age. While the dominance of global media conglomerates results in theaters around the world showing blockbuster franchises like *Iron Man* (Jon Favreau 2008), digital technology has also brought more diversity to American movie culture, as movies from around the world have become more readily available than ever before.

The continuing importance of DIY and indie cinema

In the first decades of the twenty-first century, the category of the "indie" film remains as important – and its meaning just as murky – as ever. As much an attitude as anything else, "indie" remains a useful way to describe screen experiences that moviegoers find particularly original, challenging, or just plain "different." In a globalized film economy based on the idea of synergy and the multi-platform of franchise movies, we need a category to talk about movies – whether we see them on the screens of movie theaters or our smart phones – that suggest a more personal, individually crafted approach to cinema storytelling. It's probably no coincidence that as Internet commerce continues to grow in size and importance, a similar space has opened up online for handmade and artisanal products on websites like Etsy.com.

The rise of global media conglomerates and the proliferation of screens and viewing platforms have caused many to question whether the entire cultural experience we call "the movies" is about to undergo a radical transformation. Both Steven Spielberg and George Lucas have speculated about a cinema future divided between blockbuster movies that charge twenty-five dollars or more for a ticket and smaller "movies" only shown online or on television.[1] At the same time, however, the digital screen age has also witnessed the remarkable careers of a diverse group of directors, which challenge the idea of the 1970s as the last "Golden Age" of personal, artistically ambitious movies.

Over the last twenty years, this group of directors has created a space between the ideas of "mainstream" and "indie" with screen experiences that combine the ambition of Hollywood studio movies with the intimacy of personal art movies. These filmmakers include Paul Thomas Anderson (*Boogie Nights* 1997; *Magnolia* 1999; *Punch Drunk Love* 2002; *There Will Be Blood* 2007; *The Master* 2012); Richard Linklater (*Dazed and Confused* 1993; *Before Sunrise* 1995; *Waking Life*

Do-it-yourself (DIY) A philosophy of artistic activity that emphasizes creative independence from corporate, academic, or other professional cultural institutions. A practice long associated with home improvement and arts and crafts, "DIY" was taken up by various radical and experimental artistic movements, especially punk rock, in the 1970s and 1980s as a counter to consumer marketing and corporate influence. The digital age has greatly expanded the opportunities for DIY activity, as digital technology has dramatically increased the means and lowered the costs of producing "homemade" music, videos, and movies.

Fig 8.8
The earnest but hapless police officer Jim Kurring (John C. Reilly, background) gives would-be burglar Donnie Smith (William H. Macy) a second chance in Paul Thomas Anderson's ambitious *Magnolia*. The movie, in the style of Robert Altman, weaves multiple characters and multiple story lines together in a tale about a group of lonely people in Los Angeles' San Fernando Valley who are each searching for redemption in their own ways.

2001; *School of Rock* 2003; *Before Sunset* 2004; *A Scanner Darkly* 2006; *Fast Food Nation* 2006; *Me and Orson Welles* 2008; *Bernie* 2011; *Before Midnight* 2013; *Boyhood* 2014); Wes Anderson (see below in "Names above and below the title"); David O. Russell (*Flirting with Disaster* 1996; *Three Kings* 1999; *I* ♥ *Huckabees* 2004; *The Fighter* 2010; *Silver Linings Playbook* 2012; *American Hustle* 2013); David Fincher (*Seven* 1995; *The Game* 1997; *Fight Club* 1999; *Panic Room* 2002; *Zodiac* 2007; *The Curious Case of Benjamin Button* 2008; *The Social Network* 2010; *The Girl with the Dragon Tattoo* 2011); Joel and Ethan Coen (*Fargo* 1996; *The Big Lebowski* 1998; *Oh Brother, Where Art Thou?* 2000; *The Man Who Wasn't There* 2001; *Intolerable Cruelty* 2003; *The Ladykillers* 2004; *No Country for Old Men* 2007; *Burn After Reading* 2008; *A Serious Man* 2009; *True Grit* 2010; *Inside Llewyn Davis* 2013); Spike Jonze (*Being John Malkovich* 1999; *Adaptation* 2002; *Where the Wild Things Are* 2009; *Her* 2013); Sofia Coppola (*The Virgin Suicides* 1999; *Lost in Translation* 2003; *Marie Antoinette* 2006; *Somewhere* 2010; *The Bling Ring* 2013); Darren Aronofsky (*Pi* 1998; *Requiem for a Dream* 2000; *The Fountain* 2006; *The Wrestler* 2008; *Black Swan* 2010; *Noah* 2014); and Todd Haynes (*Safe* 1995; *Velvet Goldmine* 1998; *Far From Heaven* 2002; *I'm Not There* 2007; *Carol* 2015).

Filmmakers who came of age in the 1970s experienced a creative renaissance as well in the digital screen age, from the late Robert Altman (*The Player* 1992; *Short Cuts* 1993; *Gosford Park* 2001) to Woody Allen and Martin Scorsese. In spite of his concerns about the unsustainable economics of the Hollywood blockbuster culture, Steven Spielberg, the director both credited and blamed for the blockbuster franchise movie, has made some of his most interesting and personal movies in the digital age, from the anti-slavery epic *Amistad* (1997) to his collaboration of sorts with Stanley Kubrick *A.I. Artificial Intelligence* (2001) to his thoughtful historical biography *Lincoln* (2012).

At the same time, digital technology has also empowered a truly indie movement of do-it-yourself filmmaking, from fanedits like *The Phantom Edit* to websites such as YouTube, Vimeo, and others that have democratized the process of creating screen experiences in unprecedented ways. The marketing of eight-millimeter "home movie" technology just after World War II had greatly expanded the chance for millions of amateurs to experience filmmaking on a small scale, and many of the indie filmmakers listed above – as well as major directors such as Spielberg – got their first taste of directing with their parents' home movie cameras, a trend that expanded even further with sales of video camcorders in the 1980s and 1990s. Today, the almost universal presence of smart phones with movie technology, along with inexpensive editing software and the ability to share digital screen experiences for free over the web, points to a future where moviemaking is as accessible as writing poetry, drawing a picture, or making up a song.

The relative cheapness of digital technology compared to film along with the proliferation of cable television channels and online streaming services has helped fuel the recent boom in documentary moviemaking over the last twenty years. The 2000s also saw the rise of other low-budget, DIY movements such as the group of highly individual filmmakers known collectively, and against the wishes of many of these filmmakers, as "**mumblecore**." Made by recent college graduates and based on the experiences of young adults trying to find their way in the fragmented economy of the twenty-first century, these movies have shown that in spite of the perennially dire predictions about the future of movies and the total control imposed by giant

Mumblecore Refers to a "DIY" group of American independent filmmakers in the early 2000s characterized by extremely low budgets, a focus on the everyday lives of college-educated 20-somethings, and a reliance on improvisation. Filmmakers associated with mumblecore include Andrew Bujalski, Mark and Jay Duplass, Joe Swanberg, Lynn Shelton, and Aaron Katz.

Fig 8.9
Julie Delpy and Ethan Hawke as Céline and Jesse in Richard Linklater's *Before Sunrise* (1995), a movie that focuses solely on the one evening two young people spend falling in love as they wander the streets of Vienna before Jesse must catch a flight the next morning. The creative trio of Delpy, Hawke, and Linklater have returned to these characters twice more in *Before Sunset* (2004) and *Before Midnight* (2013), movies that chart the effect that the passage of time has had on their evolving relationship.

Fig 8.10
After emerging as part of the indie film movement in the 1980s, the Coen Brothers' reputation has only grown on the basis of movies like *Fargo* (starring Frances McDormand as Minnesota police officer Marge Gunderson), a screen experience that combines deadpan comedy, brutal violence, and philosophical reflection.

Fig 8.11
Bill Murray as Bob Harris, a disaffected movie star in Tokyo to film a whiskey commercial, who meets a young woman uncertain about her own future in Sofia Coppola's character study *Lost in Translation*.

Fig 8.12
A lonely little boy who also happens to be a robot finds and loses a family and ultimately witnesses the extinction of humankind over the span of 2,000 years in Steven Spielberg's *A.I. Artificial Intelligence*, a project begun by the late screen legend Stanley Kubrick.

media companies, filmmakers are still finding new ways to create exciting screen experiences and gain the attention of a broader movie audience. Over the next decade, we may be talking about filmmakers such as Mark and Jay Duplass, Andrew Bujalski, Joe Swanberg, Aaron Katz, Kelly Reichardt, Lynn Shelton, Behn Zeitlin, and Ryan Coogler in the same way as the list of indie directors listed above.

From *The Matrix* to *Her*: Fear and hope for the future

If *The Matrix*, made as the Internet was becoming our dominant means of communication technology and just before the events of 9/11 would upend the post-Cold War status quo in America, expresses trepidation and anxiety about our changing relationship to technology (even as the movie itself was a product of advanced digital technology), a more recent movie by the current auteur Spike Jonze suggests a less apocalyptic, more poignant, and perhaps even more hopeful vision of the digital future. In *Her* (2013), set in the Los Angeles of the near future, a lonely, introverted writer of customized "personal" letters for other people, named Theodore Twombly and played by Joaquin Phoenix, finds himself falling in love with his new computer operating system. The system, named "Samantha" and voiced by Scarlett Johansson, represents the future of artificial intelligence technology as she is able to learn and evolve from her experiences (just as a flesh-and-blood person does), challenging our distinctions between the human and the machine in ways that echo cultural theorists on "cyborgs" and the post-human world, such as Donna Haraway and Raymond Kurzweil.

Rather than asking us to regard the growing relationship between Theodore and Samantha as either ridiculous or frightening, *Her* instead draws on our long familiarity with romantic comedy movies to suggest that rather than dehumanizing us, as *The Matrix* seems to be warning, digital age technology may just as easily represent the latest expression of our ancient human need for connection and community, love and intimacy. The bittersweet ending of *Her* does not provide easy answers one way or the other, but like the earliest screen experiences, from the kiss shared by May Irwin and John Rice in 1896 to the excitement of an early narrative like *The Great Train Robbery*, Jonze's movie uses the wonder and power of the screen experience to allow us to consider what it means to experience love and loss, joy and heartbreak; in short, what a screen experience can tell us about the human experience.

Fig 8.13
Joaquin Phoenix plays a lonely writer named Theodore Twombly who unexpectedly finds love and intimacy with the operating system of his computer (the voice of Scarlett Johansson) in Spike Jonze's wistful but optimistic romantic comedy *Her*.

In development

Television versus movies/television as movies

For many movie critics, the year 1999 was a watershed for American movies in the digital age, a year that could rival 1939, the golden year of the golden age of movies, in terms of quality and significance. The year 1999 brought a wealth of fascinating, powerful, and challenging screen experiences from an equally wide range of talented filmmakers. Sam Mendes' suburban satire *American Beauty*, Paul Thomas Anderson's epic study of celebrity, media, and the enduring need for human connection *Magnolia*, Kimberly Pierce's moving story of homophobia and prejudice *Boys Don't Cry*, Wes Anderson's breakthrough coming-of-age comedy *Rushmore*, Spike Lee's taut, provocative study of New York in the 1970s *Summer of Sam*, David O. Russell's Iraq War comedy *Three Kings*, David Fincher's disturbing movie about masculinity at the end of the century *Fight Club*; these were just a few of the notable films of 1999.

That same year, the cable television network HBO premiered a television series that would also come to be seen as a turning point, one that many critics and viewers felt was the equal of any of these movies in terms of its complex characters, smart writing, and sophisticated portrayal of the relationships among family, greed, loyalty, and violence in contemporary America: David Chase's *The Sopranos*, the story of an affluent suburban New Jersey family headed by a psychologically troubled mob boss, played by James Gandolfini, who regularly visits a therapist to deal with his panic attacks. Over its eight-year run, *The Sopranos* would rack up an impressive array of awards, draw flattering comparisons with movie classics like *The Godfather*, and help change the debate about how we understand the difference between movies and television.

Fig 8.14
Edward Norton (foreground) as a depressed but unnamed salesman who falls under the influence of Tyler Durden (Brad Pitt) in *Fight Club*, David Fincher's controversial adaptation of the novel by Chuck Palahniuk. Early reviewers were divided as to whether the movie was a celebration or satire of regressive male sexism. Not a major commercial success when it was first released in 1999, *Fight Club* went on to become a cult favorite.

Fig 8.15
Hilary Swank (left) as transsexual Brandon Teena, whose relationship with Lana (Chloë Sevigny) ends in tragedy when he is raped and murdered by homophobic acquaintances in Kimberly Pierce's *Boys Don't Cry*.

Fig 8.16
James Gandolfini as the troubled crime boss Tony Soprano, and Lorraine Bracco as his psychiatrist Dr. Jennifer Melfi, in David Chase's *The Sopranos*, a groundbreaking cable television show.

Fig 8.17
"I'm as mad as hell, and I'm not going to take this anymore!" When legendary news anchor Howard Beale (Peter Finch) is fired for low ratings, he delivers an on-air rant that galvanizes the viewing audience in Sidney Lumet's *Network* in 1976, a dark and bitter satire of the empty values dominating the television industry.

From the rise of television as a mass medium in the 1950s to the end of the twentieth century, the movie business has worked hard to emphasize the differences between the two kinds of screen experiences. Television may have been convenient and "free" (if you didn't mind commercials), the studios would argue, but even the most expensive cathode ray picture tubes could not match the beauty, detail, and subtlety of projected film images, never mind the sheer thrill provided by the big screen experience. Although movie attendance continued to decline into the 1960s and television continued to grow in popularity and influence, a pervasive cultural belief emerged that television could never match the movies, whether in terms of picture quality, production values, the complexity of the stories told, even the level of acting. Films like Sidney Lumet's 1976 satire *Network*, written by the legendary television writer Paddy Chayefsky, reinforced this distinction, picturing television as dominated by infantile programming and sensationalistic journalism.

The growth of cable television and videocassette and later DVD players in the 1980s and 1990s signaled a decisive shift in where audiences were watching movies; now, more people watched movies on their television sets at home than on a screen in a movie theater, thus undermining the advantage in picture quality enjoyed by the movies. In spite of this trend, the popular sense of movies and television as very different screen experiences endured, and for the most part the two mediums still featured a different set of stars and actors and were made by a separate group of writers and directors.

The digital age, however, has set in motion a series of developments that are increasingly blurring these lines between movie, television, and Internet screen experiences in ways that are changing what we mean by "movies" and "TV." Technologically, the increasing conversion of both movie and television production from film to much less expensive digital recording, along with the development of high definition video as the default viewing experience both on home televisions and on movie theater screens, has made the term "film" almost obsolete, especially as a way of differentiating between movies and TV (although it is important to emphasize that reports of the demise of film are still very premature). In terms of our viewing habits, the explosion of entertainment sources available to us, from literally hundreds of channels on cable and satellite television systems to thousands of websites, has divided the audiences for screen experiences into a dizzying variety of "niche" groups, each devoted to a particular subgroup of screen experiences, whether at the movies or on television.

Long form episodic "television" series such as *The Sopranos* and *Breaking Bad*, *Mad Men*, *Homeland*, *The Walking Dead*, *Orange is the New Black* and others began to incorporate what we thought of as "cinematic" production values and artistic ambition at the same time that many blockbuster franchise movies seemed to abandon the character-driven narratives that had dominated movies since the studios age. Streaming net-based services such as Netflix, Amazon, and Hulu combine "television" and "movie" content in their menus of available screen experiences. The popularity of "binge viewing" – watching multiple episodes of a "series" in a single viewing session – can produce multi-hour screen experiences that further complicate what it means to "watch" a movie or a television show. Many "movies" now premiere simultaneously in movie theaters (still a necessity to be considered for an Academy Award) and as video-on-demand. As a result, maximizing the accessibility and variety of screen experiences available to a potential viewer, rather than the merits of any particular form of screen experience, is growing in importance as a business model in ways that disturb some filmmakers and could change the basic economic structure of the "movie" business.

As a sign of the changing times in the digital screen age, even Steven Spielberg admits that financial pressures led him to consider bringing his critically acclaimed movie *Lincoln* to HBO rather than movie theaters, and the Sundance Film Festival pioneer Steven Soderbergh is claimed to have renounced moviemaking, focusing more on "television" productions like *Behind the Candelabra* (2013), complete with "movie" stars Michael Douglas and Matt Damon (to complicate matters even

Fig 8.18
Michael Douglas as showbusiness legend Liberace (right) and Matt Damon as his lover Scott Thorson in Steven Soderbergh's *Behind the Candelabra.*

further, *Behind the Candelabra* was shown in movie theaters across the United Kingdom and Europe). It's far too soon to say that the distinction between "movies" and "television" has disappeared, and cultural rituals such as the Academy Awards continue to reinforce the uniqueness of the movies. Still, it's interesting to speculate whether at some point in the future, the distinction between the "Best Made for TV Movie" and "Best Picture" may collapse into one another.

The comic-book movie

In 2012, the most popular movie in America was *The Avengers* (Joss Whedon), based on a *Marvel* comic-book series about a team of superheroes that had first appeared almost forty years earlier. In fact, just as each member of the comic book *Avengers* was the star of his or her own line of comics, so too four of the main characters of the Avengers – Iron Man, Captain America, Thor, and the Hulk – had already been featured in their own movies (Iron Man twice) in the four years leading up to *The Avengers*. Not only that, but three other movies in the box office top ten that year were also based on comic-book characters: *The Dark Knight Rises* (the third movie in Christopher Nolan's Batman series); *The Amazing Spider-Man* (Mark Webb), and *Men in Black 3* (Barry Sonnenfeld).

The case of *The Amazing Spider-Man* was as significant as that of *The Avengers*, given that the movie was not really a sequel but a "reboot," a way of starting over a successful franchise from the beginning as Christopher Nolan had done with *Batman Begins* (2005), a **reboot** of the 1989 *Batman*. Yet the franchise Columbia Pictures was starting over with *The Amazing Spider-Man* was the very successful trilogy of Spider-Man movies directed by Sam Raimi – *Spider-Man* (2002), *Spider-Man 2* (2004), and *Spider-Man 3* (2007) – that had ended just five years earlier. The character of the Incredible Hulk from *The Avengers* movie had also gone through two recent "reboots" – *Hulk* (Ang Lee 2003) and *The Incredible Hulk* (Louis Leterrier 2008). This sample from 2012 exemplifies a major genre of action movie in the digital age, one that has proved durably popular but also that causes concerns for many movie fans: the comic-book superhero movie.

As we have seen, Hollywood has often turned to the comics and comic books for screen material. The intensely visual energy and action of comics lend themselves well to movies, and, as with movies based on popular novels, comic-book movies attract an audience of fans already interested in following their favorite characters on screen. Throughout the screen ages of the twentieth century, comic-book superheroes have periodically reappeared in movies – Richard Donner's *Superman* (1978) was

Reboot The process of continuing a popular franchise series by starting over, introducing a new group of actors, new plotlines, and often a new style or approach to the series. Christopher Nolan's *Batman Begins* (2005) is considered a "reboot" of the Batman series begun by Tim Burton's *Batman* (1989). Other examples include *Spider-Man* (Sam Raimi 2002) and *The Amazing Spider-Man* (Marc Webb 2012), and *Superman* (Richard Donner 1978), *Superman Returns* (Bryan Singer 2006), and *Man of Steel* (Zack Snyder 2013).

Fig 8.19
Iron Man (Robert Downey, Jr.) and Captain America (Chris Evans) prepare to battle Norse gods and other extraterrestrials in Joss Whedon's *The Avengers*.

a major success – but the popularity of Tim Burton's stylish, even campy *Batman* (1989) marked the beginning of a torrent of superhero movies, one that has lasted into the second decade of the twenty-first century.

Why are these movies so popular with Hollywood? To begin with, there are some basic economic reasons. The idea of the "pre-sold" property that has always motivated movie producers has only intensified in the era of globalized media giants looking to create synergy – the latest term for this is "convergence" – among a variety of consumer goods and experiences all focused around a franchise. The connections between the contemporary superhero and ancient mythological stories, connections made explicit in comic-book versions of actual mythological characters such as Thor, allow these stories to resonate with indigenous mythic traditions around the world. More simply, action-oriented screen experiences built on clear distinctions between heroes and villains translate easily across borders of culture and language. These movies also appeal across a range of age groups, from children and teen viewers to adults who have been lifelong fans of comics, especially *Marvel* comics, which came of age with the baby boomer generation in the 1960s.

Yet the appeal of contemporary comic-book superhero movies is anything but simplistic. While these stories do seem to feature straightforward confrontations between good and evil, the storytelling strategies of many of these movies are often more complicated. Both Burton's 1989 *Batman* and Christopher Nolan's *Dark Knight* movies were directly influenced by Frank Miller's *Dark Knight* comic-book series in the 1980s. Miller was the first to portray Batman as a tormented middle-aged figure in a story influenced by the moral ambiguities of film noir, a view reflected in Miller's own film version of his noir-inflected graphic novel *Sin City* (2005). Burton's mixing of comedy and horror, fantastic sets, and dark lighting, suggests the evolution of darker, more sarcastic, and morally ambivalent superheroes for a complicated age.

The shock of the 9/11 attacks, which some commentators thought would result in a new desire among audiences for simpler, more clear-cut heroes, has instead not seemed to diminish this trend towards ambivalent superheroes. Christopher Nolan's Batman movies – *Batman Begins* (2005), *The Dark Knight* (2008), and *The Dark Knight Rises* (2012) – starring the intense Method actor Christian Bale, embraced Miller's Dark Knight concept to both economic and critical success. In *The Dark Knight* in particular, Batman's battle with the psychotic criminal Joker (a role that brought the equally intense actor Heath Ledger a posthumous Oscar) seems less a war between good and evil than an internal conflict within Batman himself. Both damaged sons who feel like outcasts in the world, Batman and the Joker are as much

Fig 8.20
Christian Bale as a brooding, tormented Batman in Christopher Nolan's *The Dark Knight*.

twins as opponents, and the destruction caused by their violent conflict leads to the deaths of hundreds (including Batman/Bruce Wayne's lover Rachel Dawes, played by Maggie Gyllenhaal) as well as massive property damage.

The Dark Knight seems as much to question whether we really need or want superheroes as to celebrate them (an ambivalence that also provides the central conflict in the 2008 action comedy movie *Hancock*, starring Will Smith and directed by Peter Berg). Part of the *Marvel* comics heritage is its reputation for creating modern, psychologically complicated characters, from the *X-Men* series, an allegory of multicultural America that plays off of the idea of superheroes as social outsiders, to Spider-Man, the classic insecure teen who unwittingly finds himself both gifted and burdened with superpowers, a theme also present in J. K. Rowling's astonishingly successful Harry Potter series. It is no accident that all of these stories about reluctant heroes have become successful digital-age movie franchises.

For some, the comic-book superhero genre represents a troubling development in the digital age of American movies, crowding out funding for smaller, more character-driven movies less reliant on CGI effects and fantastic storylines. Yet the argument can also be made that the increasing use of irony and satire in these movies points to the ways that the indie movie movement may also be influencing the franchise superhero movie, especially in the work of Joss Whedon, the writer and director of *The Avengers* who developed a reputation with television series like *Buffy the Vampire Slayer* and *Firefly* for developing fantasy and science-fiction stories that feature witty dialogue and strong women characters reflective of the screwball comedies of the studios age in American cinema. Whedon himself used some spare time during post-production work on *The Avengers* to make us his own ultra-low-budget digital indie movie, a critically acclaimed contemporary adaptation of Shakespeare's *Much Ado About Nothing* (2013). In any case, it's perhaps appropriate that the critical debate about comic-book superhero movies is marked by such ambivalence, given the role of these movies in creating heroes for a skeptical age.

Bromances and chick flicks

The leading man and the leading woman: throughout *Screen Ages* these stable-sounding gender genres, visual representations of what Hollywood has offered as the ideals of male and female beauty, have changed and evolved over the years, reflecting larger cultural changes regarding our definitions, attitudes, values, and even laws about gender and sexuality. One vivid way we can chart these changes in gender

Bromance A sub-genre of the romantic comedy popular in the early 2000s that features or focuses on the emotional relationship between two or more male characters as much if not more than the traditional heterosexual romance story. Examples include *The 40-Year-Old Virgin* (Judd Apatow 2005), *Wedding Crashers* (David Dobkin 2005), *Superbad* (Greg Mottola 2007), and *I Love You, Man* (John Hamburg 2009).

Fig 8.21
Fran Kranz as a very southern Californian Claudio in Joss Whedon's low-budget contemporary version of William Shakespeare's *Much Ado About Nothing*. Whedon, the director of the huge tentpole comic book movie *The Avengers*, has proved himself adept at creating screen experiences for screens of every size.

genres is through changes in the narrative genre of the romantic comedy. Beginning with the provocative marriage comedies of Cecil B. DeMille in the late 1910s and 1920s (such as *Male and Female* [1919] and *Why Change Your Wife?* [1920]) and continuing through the screwball comedies of the studios screen age and the Doris Day/Rock Hudson sex comedies of the 1950s and 1960s, the romantic comedy has been both an enduring genre and one sensitive to changes in gender roles, constructions of sexual identity, and how we understand the roles of love, sex, and romance in our lives.

In our digital screen age of American cinema, we have seen the romantic comedy seem to divide along lines of gender. On the one hand, many romantic comedies have come to be labeled "chick flicks," suggesting in a not-very-flattering way that the genre is mainly of interest to women. The appearance of a raucous comedy in 1998 by the writing and directing team of Peter and Bobby Farrelly called *There's Something About Mary* pointed towards the emergence of a new subgenre of romantic comedy, one involving insecure, emotionally underdeveloped, and sometimes unattractive young men and (apparently) confident, successful, and ambitious women: the bromance.

At first, *There's Something About Mary* seems like a broad parody – complete with jokes about embarrassing bodily functions – of the romantic comedy. But there is also a kind of sweetness to the main character of Ted, played by Ben Stiller, who has a lifelong crush on the unattainable title character, a beautiful and brilliant surgeon played by Cameron Diaz, that acts as a counterpoint to the aggressiveness of much of the movie's humor. The traditional gender role reversals involved in the plot – Ted is shy and socially awkward, Mary is wealthy, successful, and independent – along with the strange relationship that emerges involving Ted and two other suitors/ stalkers, points to a new mix of the heterosocial and homosocial, a focus as much on the emotional relationships between men as much if not more than the traditional heterosexual romance between men and women. The bromance may be the latest reflection of our changing ideas about what it means to be a "man" or a "woman" in an age of rapidly expanding options for gender and sexual identity and equality.

If the romantic comedy has traditionally served as a barometer of changing attitudes towards gender, sex, and marriage, the dramatic social revolutions of the 1960s almost spelled the end of the genre altogether in the 1970s. Demands for social, economic, and political equality for women along with loosening moral prohibitions against sex outside of marriage made the old formula of "boy meets girl, boy loses girl, boy gets girl," all leading to the marriage altar, seem obsolete and

Fig 8.22
Ted (Ben Stiller) reunites with his old high-school crush Mary (Cameron Diaz) in the Farrelly brothers' bawdy take on the romantic comedy, *There's Something About Mary*.

sexist. Woody Allen's landmark romantic comedy *Annie Hall* expressed this new reality, telling a story where the couple splits up at the end, each walking in opposite directions from each other in the film's concluding scene.

In the late 1980s and through the 1990s, however, the writer and director Nora Ephron led a revival of the form, creating fantasies of romance and marriage that were also rooted in the social realities of changing gender roles and a feminist insistence on gender equality. Her hit movies *Sleepless in Seattle* (1993) and *You've Got Mail* (1998), along with others such as *When Harry Met Sally* (Rob Reiner 1989) and a string of films starring Julia Roberts – including *My Best Friend's Wedding* (P. J. Hogan 1997), *Runaway Bride* (Garry Marshall 1999), and *Notting Hill* (Roger Michell 1999) – established a pattern for what some came to call the "chick flick" romantic comedy. Significantly, many of these new romantic comedies explicitly referenced how the history of romantic comedy movies has shaped our understanding of gender and romance. Both *Sleepless in Seattle* and *You've Got Mail*, for example, were remakes of earlier classics: *An Affair to Remember* (Leo McCarey 1957) and *The Little Shop Around the Corner* (Ernst Lubitsch 1940). The characters in *Sleepless* actually watch scenes from *An Affair to Remember* and talk about how these movies have shaped our expectations, for good and ill, of romantic love.

The accusation that these movies had little to say to male audiences actually speaks to the overwhelming and continuing gender imbalance of traditional Hollywood screen experiences. Unusually for any screen age but unfortunately especially so for our own, these movies focused primarily on the experiences, desires, and lives of the central woman character. Roberts' own screen and star persona, combining conventional standards of movie beauty with an athleticism and intelligence reminiscent of Katharine Hepburn, provided a psychologically complex fantasy figure for many women to identify with. Some men, accustomed to movies that only featured fantasy figures of masculine identity, were perplexed by stories so focused on issues related to women's identity. Most women viewers, however, have had no choice but to develop a lifelong familiarity with screen experiences about men's gender issues.

It is in this cultural context that the bromance has emerged. The word "bromance" refers to key aspect of these movies: the fact that the real "romantic" relationship seems as much about the men in the movie as the traditional heterosexual marriage plot. Movies like *Superbad* (Greg Mottola 2007), *Old School* (Todd Phillips 2003), *I Love You, Man* (John Hamburg 2009), the *Hangover* series

Fig 8.23
In John Hamburg's bromance *I Love You, Man*, the budding friendship between Sydney (Jason Segel, front) and Peter (Paul Rudd) is as much the center of romantic interest as the relationship between Paul and his fiancée Zooey (Rashida Jones).

(*The Hangover* Todd Phillips 2009; *Part II* Todd Phillips 2011; *Part III* Todd Phillips 2013), and *Wedding Crashers* (David Dobkin 2005) define the bromance as a successful marketing strategy for Hollywood – movies that combined the romantic comedy with gross-out humor that could appeal to both men and women – and have provoked a lively debate. Do these movies represent a backlash against the idea of gender equality – with immature men behaving badly and still winding up with a beautiful female partner at the end – or a grudging acceptance of changing ideas about gender genres of masculinity, as these emotionally immature men learn to acknowledge their own desire for intimacy with their male friends before they are ready to be an emotionally responsive romantic partner?

The former television writer and producer Judd Apatow has emerged as a kind of bromance auteur. His movies *The Forty-Year-Old Virgin* (2005), *Knocked Up* (2007), *Funny People* (2009), and *This Is 40* (2012), have earned a mix of praise and criticism for their portrayal of male sexual insecurity and immaturity. Apatow also produced *Bridesmaids* (Paul Feig 2011), a female "bromance" starring and co-written by the gifted comedian Kristen Wiig that shows how the tone of the bromance – one combining gross-out humor with a sensitivity about the complexities of contemporary gender relations – can work across genres of gender identity.

The names above and below the title

Kathryn Bigelow

When Kathryn Bigelow became the first woman to win the Best Director Academy Award in 2009 for *The Hurt Locker*, her intense portrait of three members of an army bomb disposal unit in the Iraq War, her breakthrough was both a hopeful sign of progress for women in the movie industry and an indication of how slow that

Fig 8.24
Director Kathryn Bigelow.
Source: Paramount/George Kraychyk/The Kobal Collection.

progress has been and remains. Bigelow is only one of four women ever nominated for that award: in addition to Bigelow, the German director Lina Wertmüller in 1976 for *Seven Beauties*, the New Zealand director Jane Campion in 1993 for *The Piano*, and Sofia Coppola for *Lost in Translation* in 2003. As of the writing of this textbook, no other woman has been nominated since.

One barrier faced by many filmmakers considered "nontraditional" (that is, other than straight white men) is having producers, studios, and financers pigeonhole them based on their identities. Spike Lee, for example, has spoken often about his frustration with being perceived as a director who can only make films about the African American experience. Over the course of Hollywood history, those few women able to make it into the ranks of movie direction, whether as a "mainstream" or even "indie" director, have struggled with the same prejudice that has relegated women directors into specific genres considered more "feminine," such as romances and comedies (the careers of the three women profiled in Chapter 7 – Susan Seidelman, Amy Heckerling, Martha Coolidge – are cases in point). Throughout her own career, however, Bigelow has pushed back against these boundaries, establishing herself as one of the premier directors of serious action-oriented movies about subjects such as war and terrorism, which had long been the sole domain of male directors.

Bigelow was born in California in 1951 and originally studied to be a painter before switching to filmmaking in the 1970s at Columbia University, where she studied with cutting-edge film theorists, evidence of the critical perspective she brings to crafting the tense, nerve-wracking action sequences that have become her signature as a filmmaker. From the very beginning of her career as an independent filmmaker in the 1980s, Bigelow was drawn to action-oriented genres that defied Hollywood expectations for women filmmakers. Her first movie, *The Loveless* (1981), is a movie about a biker gang that terrorizes a small town, a la the classic 1953 teen rebel movie *The Wild One* (László Benedek). *Near Dark* (1987) mixes the western with a vampire story (years ahead of the contemporary vogue of vampire stories like *Twilight* and *True Blood*) and is about a young man in a small town in the west who becomes a vampire after being bitten by a young woman who belongs to a roving gang of the undead.

With *Blue Steel* (1989) and *Point Break* (1991), Bigelow attracted wider attention and also critical disagreement. *Blue Steel* tells the story of a woman police officer (played by Jamie Lee Curtis) who is unjustly suspended after shooting an armed robber and subsequently finds herself both the romantic and violent target of an insane millionaire. *Point Break* is another genre mixer, a kind of surfer crime movie starring Keanu Reeves playing an FBI agent and Patrick Swayze as the leader of a group of surfer/bank robbers. Both movies feature recurring areas of interest for Bigelow: tortured, sometimes pathological male heroes and, in the case of *Point Break*, members of a team facing extreme pressure and tension in a morally ambiguous atmosphere. Many reviewers of *Point Break* had difficulty reconciling the movie's combination of surfer speak and undeniably exciting chase sequences.

These themes continue in her cult classic *Strange Days* from 1995, a science-fiction crime story set in the future about an illegal trade in selling people's memories. The idea of using technology to experience what others have seen and experienced has clear parallels to the fundamental appeal of the movies. For Bigelow, the action movie, and more specifically the composition and rhythm of specific cinematic action sequences, are never simple and uncomplicated but speak to what we find most powerful and fascinating about the movies as a form of human communication, of sharing our memories and experiences with one another.

Strange Days and a subsequent action movie *K-19: The Widowmaker* (2002), loosely based on an actual near-disaster aboard a Russian nuclear submarine in the early 1960s, were not box office successes, and for the next six years Bigelow, like many contemporary women directors, found what work she could directing television. With her next two movies, however, Bigelow has gained almost complete control over development and production, allowing her to more freely realize her vision for action movies about complex, controversial subjects.

Both *The Hurt Locker* and *Zero Dark Thirty* focus on the wars in Iraq and Afghanistan, making Bigelow one of the few American filmmakers to directly address these defining and divisive conflicts. Both combine taut, suspenseful action with complex examinations of the psychological toll on the men and women involved in dangerous, exciting, but also morally troubling missions. The bomb squad in *The Hurt Locker*, based on the war reporting of the movie's writer and co-producer Mark Boal – and particularly the central character of Sergeant James (Jeremy Renner), constantly find their lives in danger against a backdrop where, as in the Vietnam war forty years earlier, the lines between civilians and combatants, "friends" and "enemies" is murky and uncertain.

In *Zero Dark Thirty* – likewise written by Boal and based on the true story of the hunt for and assassination of Osama bin Laden, the leader of al-Qaeda, the group behind the attacks of 9/11 – a fanatically dedicated CIA operative named Maya Lambert (Jessica Chastain) works with a team of intelligence agents to track down the elusive Bin Laden. While Lambert never doubts the justice of her mission, a belief reinforced by the death of her colleague and friend, her own methods of investigation, including the use of torture, also confuse the moral landscape in which she operates. At the end, her theory about bin Laden's whereabouts is key to his execution, but after identifying the terrorist leader's body, the movie ends with Lambert sitting in a military aircraft flying out of Afghanistan. Unable to answer the pilot's questions of where she wants to go next, she sits quietly weeping.

Zero Dark Thirty's depiction of the torture of suspects and witnesses has divided viewers over whether the movie means to endorse or criticize the brutal methods used by the CIA and military intelligence, but in both movies we can argue that Bigelow uses the visceral excitement and our experience with action narratives to cause us to question our own investment in violence, revenge, and the glorification of war. In both movies, the characters of James and Lambert are horrified by the

Fig 8.25
CIA operative Maya Lambert (Jessica Chastain) flees from a hotel bombing in Kathryn Bigelow's tense and suspenseful screen experience about the killing of Osama bin Laden, *Zero Dark Thirty*.

destruction they see but are also drawn to and invigorated by it, as James finds that civilian life lacks the danger and excitement of the war zone, leading him at the end of the movie to once again leave his wife and young child to re-enlist. As viewers, the screen experiences that Bigelow provides us are equal parts emotionally involving and draining, thrilling and disturbing. At the conclusions of these two war movies, Bigelow refuses to provide us with neat resolutions or clear emotional cues about how we should feel about what we have just seen and experienced. In this way, her action movies operate as challenging reflections on the function of war and violence.

Wes Anderson

Of all the indie filmmakers who have entered American cinema since the Sundance Film Festival and the coming of the digital era and who have made the term "indie" synonymous with the creation of deliberately unconventional, stylized, and even eccentric screen experiences, no one has seemed more "indie" than Wes Anderson. Anderson's screen experiences have become so distinctive – the term "quirky" is often applied to him – that he rivals his contemporary Quentin Tarantino in terms of an immediately recognizable style. The eight feature films he has released since 1996 – *Bottle Rocket* (1996), *Rushmore* (1998), *The Royal Tenenbaums* (2001), *The Life Aquatic with Steve Zissou* (2004), *The Darjeeling Limited* (2007), *Fantastic Mr. Fox* (2009), *Moonrise Kingdom* (2012), and *The Grand Budapest Hotel* (2014) – speak to the complex meaning of "indie" moviemaking in the contemporary screen age: his highly personalized filmmaking, like the DIY movement, speaks to a "craft" response to the idea of the franchise.

Fig 8.26
Wes Anderson on the set of *The Darjeeling Limited*. Source: Fox Searchlight/ The Kobal Collection.

Part of what defines Anderson's career – and defines what makes him different from a more consumer-driven approach to the movies – is his unusual and unpredictable range of subject matter. He has made movies about a misfit at an exclusive prep school (*Rushmore*), a world famous documentarian of marine life (*The Life Aquatic*), three brothers on a comic voyage of self-discovery to India (*Darjeeling Limited*), and even a stop-action animated movie based on Roald Dahl's story about a charming and roguish fox (*Fantastic Mr. Fox*), none of them fitting any Hollywood model of sure-fire and familiar plot lines. In spite of this range, however, there are thematic links and interests that recur in Anderson's screen experiences, especially the familiar story of a sensitive, imaginative boy in search of a father figure.

For example, the main character of Max Fischer (Jason Schwartzman) in *Rushmore*, the movie that established Anderson's reputation as an important new filmmaker, is the son of a gentle, widowed barber. Inspired by the love and confidence of his late mother, Max has become a student at Rushmore, a private school mainly for the sons of the wealthy, where he tries to reinvent himself as a child of privilege, joining every club on campus (and starting many others, including beekeeping) and staging elaborate dramatic productions based on gritty 1970s movies. His search for role models leads him to become a kind of surrogate son to a rich but melancholy industrialist while also embarking on a doomed courtship of one of the faculty members.

In the end, Max's neglect of his schoolwork leads to his expulsion from Rushmore and enrollment at the local public school, and he finds himself in a ridiculous love triangle with the industrialist and the teacher (a triangle in his mind only). Max finally abandons the pretense of a privileged background and appreciates his real father's kindness and support, but he never abandons his imaginative ambition and individuality, and in the end all the characters come together to celebrate his astonishing school play version of the Vietnam War, complete with helicopters and explosions. All of Anderson's movies feature this focus on the complexity of family relationships, and in movies like *Rushmore* and *Moonrise Kingdom*, they show a real sensitivity towards the emotional lives of children entering adolescence, which explains in part why his movies have become so popular with young people.

Anderson's sense of whimsy, his poignant humor, and his gently eccentric characters might at first make him seem the polar opposite of his contemporary Quentin Tarantino, whose films are famous for their graphic violence, but the two share a love and extensive knowledge of movie history, and both create screen experiences that constantly imitate and evoke the history of cinema. For fans of both directors, part of the pleasure of watching and discussing their movies involves recognizing and decoding these references. On the one hand, this constant invocation

Fig 8.27
Precocious prep school scholarship student Max Fischer (Jason Schwartzman) attempts to impress teacher Rosemary Cross (Olivia Williams) in Wes Anderson's quirky and endearing *Rushmore*.

of other movies and older styles of screen experiences – the use of sudden zoom-in close-ups and focus on young love reminiscent of the French New Wave movies of François Truffaut, along with deliberately "old-fashioned" special effects in *Moonrise Kingdom*, for example – can make Anderson's movies sound more like elaborate games rather than emotionally engaging films. But Anderson is equally known as a practitioner of what is sometimes called a "new sincerity," a desire to avoid cynicism and cliche and use his eccentric style to challenge his viewer's expectations enough to allow them to engage with his characters as individuals rather than stereotypes.

Like Tarantino, Wes Anderson aims to make movies that stand out from mainstream Hollywood screen experiences, even as they draw from and play with aspects of those experiences. This idea of the director as auteur/author of a movie, a model developed in the 1950s to argue for the cultural worth of the movies as an art form, today also functions in indie movies as a way to contrast corporate mass production with the individual and handmade. In reality, this distinction remains more theoretical than actual. Movies like Anderson's are still financed by and distributed through companies like Focus Features, which is a subsidiary of media giant Comcast. The "indie" model itself has become its own brand and created its own set of predictable storytelling patterns and styles, from a focus on emotional misfits to the use of a handheld camera to suggest "authenticity."

While Anderson's vision is intensely personal, there is also a kind of epic ambition to his movies as well, as characters travel the globe and become involved in old-fashioned intrigues modeled on older action movies. That Anderson has managed to survive and even flourish in this current screen age of rapid change and the disrupting of what we mean by "the movies" perhaps speaks to an enduring love and nostalgia for the idea of a kind of "classic" movie screen experience: two hours spent in the dark watching a collection of unforgettable characters who share larger-than-life imaginations.

Lena Dunham

At first glance, the writer, director, and actor Lena Dunham might seem an unusual choice to end a textbook on the screen ages of American movies. After all, as of 2014, she had made only one movie (although she did write, direct, and star in it), the semi-autobiographical DIY feature *Tiny Furniture* in 2010. While *Tiny Furniture* was critically well received, it was not widely seen; Dunham actually came to greater attention two years later with her cable television series *Girls*, a bittersweet and sometimes sardonic comedy about four young women in their mid-twenties searching – and often floundering – in their quest to find work and a purpose to their lives in contemporary Manhattan. The program has become a cultural touchstone, for its portrait of the so-called "millennial" generation, its witty and observant social satire, and for the unprecedented fact that a major cable network – HBO – signed a twenty-four-year-old woman to create her own series. But *Girls* is still a television series. Will Dunham go on to make more movies? Is she destined to remain an important voice in American cinema and culture? For both questions, it is still too soon to tell. So why end with Dunham? Precisely because Dunham's career is at a beginning, and that beginning exemplifies some of the trends in the digital age that we have been examining and that are likely to influence the future screen ages of American cinema:

Fig 8.28
Producer, director, writer, and actor Lena Dunham on the set of *Girls*. Source: Apatow Productions / The Kobal Collection.

The persistence of the indie ideal

Dunham's "discovery" represents one of the latest examples of the enduring meaning and practice of "indie" moviemaking, especially given the radically lowered production costs of the digital age. In spite of the many voices who argue, not without cause, that the term "indie" has become meaningless, especially in the increasingly interconnected global media economy, every year still brings exciting new experiments in low-budget, alternative screen experiences that speak to the life experiences of young people living in the early twenty-first century.

Tiny Furniture first caught the eye of critics and indie fans at the South by Southwest (SXSW) Film Festival in Austin. The SXSW festival began not long after the Sundance Festival, and in the first decade of the new century functioned as an even more accessible, more independent version of Sundance. Like Sundance, SXSW has had to contend with the downside of its success, including huge crowds, media attention, and an increasing corporate presence and influence. From one perspective, this inevitable take-over of influential indie venues by globalized media corporations demonstrates the difficulty if not futility of trying to maintain alternative spaces for the cultivation of new screen experiences and experiments; from another, the experience of the SXSW Festival also suggests we will always see the emergence of new outlets and new entry points for new moviemakers, especially as the online world creates almost endless possibilities for creators and viewers of screen experiences to find each other outside of mainstream commercial venues.

Fig 8.29
Aura (Lena Dunham) searches for direction in her life as she moves back in with her parents, including her photographer mother Siri (played by Dunham's real-life mother Laurie Simmons) in Dunham's semi-autobiographical *Tiny Furniture*.

Gender and the movies

Dunham's career likewise points to the continuing impact of gender demographics on the evolving screen ages of American cinema. "[W]omen are the only future in rock and roll," the late rock star Kurt Cobain wrote in his journal in the early 1990s; can the same be said for American cinema at the beginning of the twenty-first century?[2] As has been discussed throughout *Screen Ages*, the role of women in movie production has been a recurring sore spot in the history of American movies. In the twenty-first century, the impact of both continuing feminist activism for gender and sexual equality along with sheer demographics – women constitute not only slightly over half the population, they now are the clear majority in terms of those seeking college degrees – points to the possibility of moving beyond the "one step forward, two steps back" model of women behind as well as in front of the camera.

With *Girls*, Lena Dunham has become the youngest woman ever to head a major television program, and her example may point to a model of a creative "girl" wonder to counter the longstanding "boy wonder" gender genre of movie artists like Orson Welles or Steven Spielberg. We know a different gender future is possible because we can also see Dunham's career as pointing back to the beginnings of cinema, as Dunham in 2010 was following in the footsteps of pioneering women filmmakers such as Alice Guy-Blaché a century earlier.

Case study 8.1: Pick a "typical" movie

Throughout the book, we have seen how the simple term "movie" can encompass a wide and diverse range of screen experiences, from the hand-cranked actualities of early cinema to silent screen epics to drive-in movies to televisions, smart phones, and tablets. As a member of our current screen age and a student of the history of American screen ages, apply what you have learned and discovered to answer the question, "What would you describe as a 'typical' movie?" In thinking about this question, you might consider:

- the similarities and differences between how producers, distributors, exhibitors, and viewers describe the screen experiences they call "the movies"
- whether and to what extent "movie" refers to any artistic visual experience, to those experiences we understand as narrative or stories, to those experiences produced and marketed by "professionals," or to the work of amateurs and professionals alike
- how the term "movie" has evolved and changed over the history of American cinema
- whether it's even possible or worthwhile to try to describe a "typical" movie.

You should ground your discussion in the analysis of one or more particular examples of screen experiences that might be candidates for the "typical" movie. The point of your argument is not to settle the question once and for all but instead to further develop our understanding of the issues and ideas involved in understanding American movie history by looking closely at our own screen experiences.

Multiple screens/multiple "movies": Everything is cinema

Dunham's burgeoning career also exemplifies the blurring of lines between the categories of "movies" and "television," as our multiplying screen options and experiences begin to render some of these distinctions obsolete. The "television" program *Girls*, for example, follows the style, both in terms of visuals and narrative, of *Tiny Furniture*. In a way, *Girls* is a kind of indie movie television series. And Dunham preceded *Tiny Furniture* with her work on *Delusional Downtown Divas*, a web-based series about young, reality-challenged recent college graduates in the Manhattan fashion world. These three modes – web, movies, television – represent different aspects of cinematic screen experiences that form a continuum in Dunham's career, with the movie acting as a stepping stone between the relatively open accessibility of the web and the corporate-controlled accessibility of cable television.

Accessibility and unpredictability: Everyone's a moviemaker

Finally, Dunham's career points to both the unpredictability and insecurity of the contemporary media era – a theme of both *Tiny Furniture* and *Girls*, as the characters in both struggle to deal with a radically destabilized and downsized economy – but also the unprecedented accessibility and ability to create screen experiences. We are still really only just beginning to explore the possibilities and implications of the digital era in terms of making the tools of creating and sharing screen experiences accessible to millions around the world. In this way, our own screen age once again echoes the earliest days of cinema. Just as it would have been impossible for patrons peering into an early Kinetoscope to watch a few seconds of the bodybuilder Eugene Sandow flexing for the cameras to have imagined IMAX 3D movies, twenty-four hour cable news, and the home entertainment center, so too we are peering into a digital future that will likely hold equally dramatic changes and developments in the evolution of the screen ages of American movies. At the turn of the twentieth century, the very newness of the movies created opportunities for those – like Edwin S. Porter, D. W. Griffith, and Alice Guy-Blaché – with the interest and imagination to take advantage of them, to create new screen experiences that equally stirred the imaginations and emotions of early movie audiences. At the turn of the twenty-first century, we again find ourselves in a screen age of uncertainty and opportunity, of invention and accessibility. As the lines between moviemakers and movie watchers, between critics and creators, continues to blur, the future screen age is ours to make.

Case study 8.2: The future of the movies

The future is always unpredictable, and that is just as true for the future of movies. Pioneers like Thomas Edison, Edwin S. Porter, Alice Guy-Blaché, and D. W. Griffith were all inspired by the tremendous potential of cinema at the beginning of the twentieth century, but could any of them have foreseen the 3D IMAX movie, the Internet, YouTube?

As we have seen, moviemakers and movie fans (and the distinction between the two has only grown fuzzier over time) in our own screen age are just as interested – and just as unsure – about the future of the movies as those early experimenters in film. As you think about how your introduction to the serious study of American movie history is shaping and transforming your own understanding of how these screen experiences affect us and what they say about American culture, offer your own speculations and hypotheses about the possible future screen ages of American cinema. Explore as many connections as you can between these educated guesses and the specific information and historical developments you have begun to read about and study; in other words, describe what makes an educated guess "educated."

As a way of sparking thought and promoting discussion, explore other educated guesses from film scholars and moviemakers. As we mentioned in this last chapter, in 2013 both Steven Spielberg and George Lucas predicted what they call an "implosion" in the movie business that will result in a two-tier system of a few giant-budget megapictures every year (with mega ticket prices) and dozens of cheaper, smaller movies, both in theaters and on home screens. The same year, Steven Soderbergh, whose *Sex, Lies, and Videotape* helped kick off the contemporary cycle of "indie" movies, expressed pessimism about what he saw as the "State of the Cinema," drawing a distinction between movies and what he means by "cinema" – a more personal, artistically focused kind of screen experience than the tentpole franchise movie. While he sees a continuing market for spectacular special effects and action sequences, he worries that there will be less and less room in the movie industry for what he sees as more thoughtful, challenging movies.[3]

Who is correct? Only the future will tell us, a future that will be informed and influenced by what we think about it now. In your own statement, explain why you feel optimistic or pessimistic about the future of American movies and what specific trends and historical developments make you think this way – even if you think terms like optimism and pessimism are too simple or reductive to express your hopes and concerns about the future of our present screen age and those screen ages to come.

Notes

1   Bond, Paul, "Steven Spielberg Predicts 'Implosion' of Film Industry," *The Hollywood Reporter*, June 6, 2013, http://www.hollywoodreporter.com/news/steven-spielberg-predicts-implosion-film-567604

2   *Kurt Cobain: Journals*. New York: Penguin Group, 2003, p. 110.

3   "Steven Soderbergh's State of Cinema Talk," *Deadline.com*, April 30, 2013, http://www.deadline.com/2013/04/steven-soderbergh-state-of-cinema-address/

Explore further

Greven, David, *Manhood in Hollywood From Bush to Bush*. Austin: University of Texas Press, 2009.

Hills, Matt, *Fan Cultures*. London: Routledge, 2002.

Holmlund, Chris and Justin Wyatt (ed.), *Contemporary American Independent Film: From the Margins to the Mainstream*. London and New York: Routledge, 2005.

Jenkins, Henry, *Convergence Culture: Where Old and New Media Collide*. New York: New York University Press, 2006.

King, Geoff, *Spectacular Narratives: Hollywood in the Age of the Blockbuster*. London/New York: I.B.Tauris, 2000.

Levy, Emanuel, *Cinema of Outsiders: The Rise of American Independent Film*. New York: New York University Press, 1999.

Lewis, Jon (ed.), *The End of Cinema as We Know It: American Film in the Nineties*. New York: New York University Press, 2001.

Miller, Toby, Nitin Govil, John McMurria, Ting Wang, and Richard Maxwell, *Global Hollywood 2*. London: BFI Publishing, 2005.

Natoli, Joseph, *This is a Picture and Not the World: Movies and a Post-9/11 America*. Albany: State University of New York Press, 2007.

Neale, Steve (ed.), *Genre and Contemporary Hollywood*. London: BFI, 2002.

Neale, Steve and Murray Smith (eds.), *Contemporary Hollywood Cinema*. London/New York: Routledge, 1998.

Palmer, William J., *The Films of the Nineties: The Decade of Spin*. New York: Palgrave Macmillan, 2009.

Radner, Hilary and Rebecca Stringer (ed.), *Feminism at the Movies: Understanding Gender in Contemporary Popular Cinema*. London/New York: Routledge, 2011.

Shary, Timothy (ed.), *Millennial Masculinity: Men in Contemporary American Cinema*. Detroit: Wayne State University Press, 2013.

Tryon, Chuck, *Reinventing Cinema: Movies in the Age of Media Convergence*. New Brunswick, NJ: Rutgers University Press, 2009.

Zaniello, Tom, *The Cinema of Globalization: A Guide to Films about the New Economic Order*. Ithaca: ILR Press, 2007.

Glossary

Actuality – A non-narrative movie featuring "real-life" subject matter.

Auteur theory and auteurism – An influential theory of criticism and interpretation that views movies as the unique stylistic and thematic expression of their directors, the relationship of director to movie similar to that of author to book. Auteur theory developed among a group of rebellious young French film writers and directors in the 1950s and was popularized in the US by the movie critic Andrew Sarris in the early 1960s. Auteur theory has had a profound effect on how movies are studied and discussed and was influential in the rise of the New American Cinema.

"B" movie – The original use of the term "B" movie referred to the second, less heavily promoted part of a double feature, as opposed to the "A" movie, which was considered the main attraction. Over time, "B movie" came to indicate any lower budget movie, especially those associated with popular genres such as westerns, horror, crime movies, and teen pictures. Although the double feature disappeared as a regular part of mainstream movie exhibition in the late 1960s, the term "B movie" has persisted as a way of describing these movies.

Baby boom – Refers to the generation of people born in the 18 or so years after World War II, from 1946 to 1964. This period marked a dramatic uptick in population growth in the 1950s as soldiers returned from the war and the US entered a period of relative economic prosperity.

Big Five/Little Three – A reference to the eight major companies of the studios era. The Big Five – Metro Goldwyn Mayer (MGM), Paramount, 20th Century Fox, Warner Brothers, and RKO – all owned their own systems of production, distribution, and exhibition. By contrast, the Little Three – Universal, Columbia, and United Artists – did not own any theater chains, and United Artists did not even own a production facility. While their smaller holdings put them at a disadvantage during the studios era, the Little Three were much less affected by the results of the Paramount Decision than their Big Five counterparts.

Big Six – A reference to the small number of giant megacorporations that control the vast majority of media production – including movies – in the US and around the world. The actual number and composition of these megacorporations tends to vary from year to year as various mergers and acquisitions change their specific makeup, but the trend of increasing concentration of media ownership in a small group of powerful conglomerates continues. As of this book's writing, the "Big Six" consists of Comcast, the News Corporation, Disney, Viacom, Time Warner, and CBS.

Blaxploitation – A series of movies popular in the 1970s focused on the lives and experiences of working-class, urban, African American characters. Most movies labeled as Blaxploitation are lower-budget films, often though not exclusively crime movies focused on the drug trade. Blaxploitation movies arose in response to the surprising (to Hollywood executives) success of Melvin Van Peebles's independent *Sweet Sweetback's Baadasssss Song* and MGM's *Shaft* (Gordon Parks), both from 1971. Proponents of Blaxploitation cinema credit the movement with providing greater visibility and filmmaking opportunities for black actors and directors as well as creating innovative and exciting new approaches to action moviemaking; critics point out that many of these movies reinforce stereotypes about inner-city black life, especially the prevalence of crime and violence.

Bromance – A sub-genre of the romantic comedy popular in the early 2000s that features or focuses on the emotional relationship between two or more male characters as much if not more than the traditional heterosexual romance story. Examples include *The 40-Year-Old Virgin* (Judd Apatow 2005), *Wedding Crashers* (David Dobkin 2005), *Superbad* (Greg Mottola 2007), and *I Love You, Man* (John Hamburg 2009).

Cable television – A method of transmitting television programming that relies on cables connected to television sets rather than broadcasting through the air. Unlike broadcast television, which generates revenues by selling commercial advertising, cable television directly charges each viewer for subscribing. While cable television has been around since the 1950s, it became a major means of television transmission in the 1980s.

Cold War – Refers to the historical period of tension, conflict, and competition after World War II between the capitalist countries of the USA and western Europe and the Communist countries led by the USSR and its satellite countries in eastern Europe as well as by the People's Republic of China. While the USA never went to war directly with either the USSR or China, the period was marked by a series of proxy wars fought in smaller countries such as the Korean War in the 1950s and the Vietnam War in the 1960s. The Cold War largely came to an end with the break-up of the Soviet Union in 1991.

Computer-generated imagery (CGI) – Refers to a broad range of digital special effects that involves creating screen images solely using computer technology. These images range from static backgrounds to action sequences that can involve hundreds of completely computer-generated characters, as in the battle sequences in the three *The Lord of the Rings* movies directed by Peter Jackson. Computer animation, especially as pioneered by Pixar studios, involves animated movies completely generated using computer software.

Culture wars – Refers to a broad collection of controversies and debates around social issues and values that was part of defining various political divisions in the United States during the 1980s. These issues included reproductive and abortion rights, the growing multicultural identity of American society, the role of religion in politics, civil rights for gay and lesbian people, and the proper response to the AIDS epidemic. In terms of the movies, the culture wars represented an extension of long-standing arguments about the impact of cinema on American values and beliefs.

Disaster movies – A popular subgenre of movies in the 1970s, typically centered on an ensemble cast of characters each trying to survive a particular kind of disaster, from the man-made (a ship capsizing in *The Poseidon Adventure*, a skyscraper on fire in *The Towering Inferno*) to the natural (such as *Earthquake*).

Do-it-yourself (DIY) – A philosophy of artistic activity that emphasizes creative independence from corporate, academic, or other professional cultural institutions. A practice long associated with home improvement and arts and crafts, "DIY" was taken up by various radical and experimental artistic movements, especially punk rock, in the 1970s and 1980s as a counter to consumer marketing and corporate influence. The digital age has greatly expanded the opportunities for DIY activity, as digital technology has dramatically increased the means and lowered the costs of producing "homemade" music, videos, and movies.

Drive-in theater – An outdoor movie theater where patrons would watch movies from their cars. Drive-ins became especially popular in America after World War II as more people moved to the suburbs and away from the city centers where most traditional movie theaters were located. Drive-ins became especially associated with youth culture, as teenagers and young adults were attracted to the convenience, economy, and privacy of the drive-in theater.

Expressionism – An artistic movement strongly associated with Germany in the first decades of the twentieth century that experimented with using external visual details to express internal psychological conflict. In movies, the films of German directors such as F. W. Murnau and Fritz Lang, both of whom would immigrate to the United States, featured exaggerated, distorted sets and dramatic uses of deep shadows to create disturbing and powerful screen experiences. The large-scale immigration of German expressionist directors and cinematographers into Hollywood during the 1920s and 1930s, particularly after the rise of the Nazi Party, had a significant influence on American cinema, especially in genres such as the gangster movie and film noir (see Chapter 4).

Fan fiction – A kind of creative writing that involves stories based on characters and incidents from favorite books and movies. Fan fiction, especially understood as the retelling of popular stories, is as old as literature, but the accessibility of the Internet has created an extensive global network of fan fiction sites. The growth of fan fiction, a form of what is also known as "user-generated content," has played an extensive role in the increasingly interactive nature of what it means to be a fan and consumer of popular culture.

Fanediting – A form of interactive digital culture that consists of individuals re-editing existing movies into different versions, sometimes in an effort to improve the movie, sometimes to transform the movie in terms of genre or to combine it with other movies, a process also known as remixing or "mash up." The first significant instance of fanediting was *The Phantom Edit*, a revision of *Star Wars Episode I: The Phantom Menace*.

Feature film – A multiple reel movie that told an extended narrative beyond the fifteen-minute limitation of the single reel movies popular in the nickelodeons. This term has remained to this day to refer to the standard Hollywood movie.

Femme fatale – A genre of female performance most associated with film noir, the femme fatale refers to a beautiful and dangerous woman who uses her intelligence and sexual attraction to manipulate men in the pursuit of money and power. The femme fatale was both a negative stereotype and an intriguing figure in film noir. While femmes fatales were represented as heartless villains and usually met violent ends, they were also powerful and fascinating characters, symbols of both masculine anxiety and female assertiveness.

Film noir – Film noir, or "black film," refers to a series of American crime movies released primarily from the late 1940s through the early 1950s. Featuring gender genres such as the hardboiled male hero and the dangerous femme fatale, films noir were defined by a sense of pessimism, doom, and existential anxiety, telling stories of cynical, world-weary characters whose futile pursuit of sex, money, and power ends in defeat and tragedy. Film noir is equally known for its distinctive visual style and tone, featuring the dramatic use of shadows and fast-talking characters.

Franchise movie – A movie popular enough to spawn sequels as well as a wide range of cross-marketing opportunities, from soundtrack albums to toys to sponsor tie-ins. The most successful franchise movies, such as *Star Wars* or the *Indiana Jones* movies, have become cultural icons, almost a part of American folklore. Beginning in the 1970s, the major Hollywood studios have focused on creating franchise movies in order to ensure large and predictable sources of income.

Globalization – A catch-all term indicating a wide variety of economic, political, and cultural developments that stress the increasingly interconnected and interdependent nature of global activity, particularly in relation to the digital communications revolution. As money and capital is able to circulate around the world 24 hours a day, seven days a week, the lines between the global and local are becoming increasingly blurred. In terms of movies, the major production and distribution companies view the market for their screen experiences in terms of a broad global market, thus complicating our sense of what it means to describe a movie as "American."

Indie movie – Refers to movies made more or less independently of mainstream studio production. Independent movies are as old as the movie industry. The term "indie movie" became popular in the 1980s as the result of a wave of smaller, more personal filmmaking that developed in contrast to Hollywood's growing reliance on big-budget blockbuster movies. The indie movie movement is especially associated with the rise of various film festivals across the country, including the Sundance Festival in Park City, Utah and the South by Southwest Festival in Austin, Texas. Examples of early indie movies include Spike Lee's *She's Gotta Have It* (1986), Steven Soderbergh's *Sex, Lies, and Videotape* (1989), Quentin Tarantino's *Reservoir Dogs* (1992), and Kevin Smith's *Clerks* (1994).

Magic lantern/stereopticon – A device for projecting photographs using glass slides, a light source, and lenses that became a popular form of entertainment in the nineteenth century. Some skilled projectionists created the impression of movement by rapidly switching between slides.

McCarthyism/Red Scare – Refers to the period of investigations following World War II into what some claimed was widespread Communist influence and infiltration into American society. McCarthyism derives from the career of Republican US senator Joseph McCarthy, who rose to prominence with unfounded accusations that the government was riddled with Communist spies. The Red Scare led to a period of political fear and repression, particularly in the entertainment industries, where a series of "blacklists" ended the careers of many movie professionals suspected of subversive political beliefs.

Melodrama – A broad type of dramatic narrative that often involves placing characters in extreme peril, from the physical to the psychological, and that often seeks to provoke a strong emotional response from the audience. Many Hollywood melodramas have focused heavily on personal and romantic relationships and have featured strong women characters, leading to an association (and even a stereotype) of melodramas as "women's pictures."

Motion Picture Producers and Distributors of America (MPPDA) – A trade organization created by the Hollywood movie industry in 1922 to promote the image and interests of the movies, especially in the light of several major scandals, such as the Roscoe (Fatty) Arbuckle trial, which brought the threat of increased government censorship. Under founding MPPDA president Will Hays, the organization eventually developed the set of self-censoring guidelines that would form the motion picture Production Code. After World War II, the organization changed its name to the Motion Picture Association of America, which continues to this day.

Multiplex – A movie theater that features a number of smaller theaters all showing different movies. The multiplex arose as part of suburban mall culture in the late 1960s and has become the dominant kind of movie theater in the contemporary screen age. The first multiplexes had only two or three screens, although now multiplexes of twenty or more screens are common.

Mumblecore – Refers to a "DIY" group of American independent filmmakers in the early 2000s characterized by extremely low budgets, a focus on the everyday lives of college-educated 20-somethings, and a reliance on improvisation. Filmmakers associated with mumblecore include Andrew Bujalski, Mark and Jay Duplass, Joe Swanberg, Lynn Shelton, and Aaron Katz.

Mutoscope/Kinetoscope – Two of the main competing versions of individual viewing machines in the early ages of cinema. The Edison Company's Kinetoscope used the same technology as later movie projectors by shining a light source through a moving strip of film. The Mutoscope, marketed by the American Mutoscope Company (later American Biograph), used flipbook technology based on a series of photographs attached to a rotating drum.

Mutual case – Refers to the landmark 1915 legal case of *Mutual Film Corporation v. Industrial Commission of Ohio*, in which Mutual challenged the ability of the Industrial Commission to censor movies, claiming such censorship violated its First Amendment right of free speech. The US Supreme Court ruled, however, that movies were a business, not a form of speech, and thus could be regulated and censored by the government. The court later overruled its decision in 1952, granting movies free speech protections.

New American Cinema – Also called "New Hollywood," the "American New Wave," or the "Hollywood Renaissance," a period in American movie history from the late 1960s until the end of the 1970s that saw the emergence of a group of artistically ambitious filmmakers who were able to take advantage of Hollywood's interest in reaching a younger audience to create screen experiences that challenged older conventions of mainstream moviemaking and subject matter. The period is said to have started with *Bonnie and Clyde* (Arthur Penn 1967), a revisionist gangster movie influenced by French New Wave filmmaking. The New American Cinema includes directors such as Francis Ford Coppola, William Friedkin, Robert Altman, Martin Scorsese, Hal Ashby, Dennis Hopper, Alan Pakula, and others.

Nickelodeons – Small movie theaters popular from 1905 through 1915 that typically showed a rotating series of short films. The term "nickelodeon" refers to the common admission price of five cents.

Package/project system – Refers to a system of movie production that involves a producer or agent assembling a "package" of talent – writers, a director, actors, etc. – to work on a given movie "project," which may then be brought to a movie studio for financing. The package/project system largely replaced the studio system after World War II.

Paramount Decision – The 1949 US Supreme Court Decision that held the major studios in violation of antitrust law for their practice of trying to control the production, distribution, and exhibition of movies. As the result of the decision, officially known as *United States v. Paramount Pictures, Inc. et al.*, the studios had to begin the process of divesting themselves of the movie theaters they owned. The Paramount Decision was one key factor in the end of what was known as the studio system.

Poverty Row – A reference to the dozens of smaller studios that flourished in Hollywood during the studios era, including long-standing companies such as Monogram and Republic Pictures but also many smaller "studios" that were constantly appearing and disappearing. Many of these studios were located on Gower Street in Hollywood, and they were responsible for the hundreds of lower budget "B" movies – westerns, crime movies, melodramas, and action movies – that were a major part of the screen experiences of Americans in the studios era.

Product placement – A form of synergy and cross-marketing that involves companies paying moviemakers to include their products in the movies. While the practice actually spans the entire history of American cinema, product placement became especially widespread beginning in the 1980s. Prominent examples of product placement include references to Reese's Pieces in *E.T. the Extra-Terrestrial* (1982), and Calvin Klein underwear and Pepsi Cola in *Back to the Future* (1985).

Prohibition – The period in American history from the passage of the Eighteenth Amendment to the Constitution in 1919 forbidding the manufacture and sale of alcoholic beverages in the United States to its overturning by the Twenty-Third Amendment in 1933.

Reboot – The process of continuing a popular franchise series by starting over, introducing a new group of actors, new plotlines, and often a new style or approach to the series. Christopher Nolan's *Batman Begins* (2005) is considered a "reboot" of the Batman series begun by Tim Burton's *Batman* (1989). Other examples include *Spider-Man* (Sam Raimi 2002) and *The Amazing Spider-Man* (Marc Webb 2012), and *Superman* (Richard Donner 1978), *Superman Returns* (Bryan Singer 2006), and *Man of Steel* (Zack Snyder 2013).

Road show – Refers to a form of exhibition that involves premiering a movie through a series of exclusive theatrical engagements featuring advance sale tickets at major cities across the country before opening the film in wider release. While the practice is as old as American cinema, the road show became a distinctive feature of the 1950s screen age, when Hollywood was seeking to maintain a competitive edge with television. Road show pictures such as *The Ten Commandments, Around the World in Eighty Days*, and *Ben-Hur* were usually lavish productions of over two hours in length, and during their road show tours they would often feature a musical overture and a ten-minute intermission.

Runaway production – Refers to the practice of American movie production filming overseas to take advantage of lower labor costs in other countries, in effect "running away" from higher costs in the United States.

Slapstick – A form of movie and stage comedy that relies on physical mishaps and violence.

Studio system – The dominant organization of the American movie industry from the early 1920s until the Paramount decision of 1946 based on vertical integration and a factory-based model of production. Under the studio system, each of the major production companies tried to control all aspects of the movie business, from the development of movie projects through writing, planning, shooting, and post production to distribution and exhibition. Workers of all kinds, including actors, technicians, writers, directors, and designers, would be signed to long-term contracts, allowing studio executives to assign them to various projects.

Synergy – A business theory widely adopted by entertainment conglomerates in the 1980s that focused on creating cross-marketing opportunities connecting movies to the sale of related consumer products such as toys, video games, action figures, and clothing, and the promotion of other consumer goods such as fast food, soda, and automobiles.

Tentpole movie – The "tentpole" movie refers to a huge summer blockbuster whose profits will support a movie studio's overall operations for the year. Steven Spielberg's massive hit *Jaws* is usually credited – or blamed – as the first tentpole movie.

The independents – Any of a group of movie production companies not a part of the Motion Picture Patents Company. Some of these independents, such as the Independent Moving Pictures Company – later Universal Pictures – and Famous Players Film Company – later Paramount Pictures – eventually became some of the dominant companies in the studios age. The term "independent" has remained a part of the Hollywood lexicon to refer to various movie productions in some way outside "mainstream" Hollywood moviemaking.

The Motion Picture Patents Company – An organization founded by the Edison Company in 1908 in an effort to establish monopoly control over the American movie industry by controlling the patents for the technology involved in movie production. The MPPC eventually included all the major film production companies of the early years of American cinema but was increasingly challenged by the proliferation of independent movie companies in the nickelodeon era. A successful antitrust case against the MPPC led to its disintegration in 1918.

The Production Code – The Production Code was created in 1930 by the Motion Picture Producers and Distributors of America (MPPDA) as a form of self-censorship in order to forestall efforts at local and national government censorship. The Code was a list of what could and couldn't be included in movies, focusing in particular on issues related to sexuality, crime, religion, race, and ethnicity.

The Production Code Administration (PCA) – The Production Code Administration was instituted in 1934 under the leadership of Joseph Breen to more forcefully apply the Production Code. From 1934 until 1968, almost every Hollywood movie had to be approved by the PCA.

The Progressive Era – The period in American history between the 1890s and 1920s featuring efforts by politicians and social reformers to curb the power of increasingly large and monopolistic corporations. These reforms were also concerned with the impact of large-scale immigration and urbanization as well, featuring a mix of radical reform and condescending paternalism.

Uplift movement – An effort by movie studios in the early 1910s to appeal to more affluent audiences and avoid censorship pressures by trying to raise the cultural status and respectability of the movies, often by creating screen experiences based on prestigious literary or theatrical works, religious and historical stories, or other supposedly "uplifting" sources.

Vaudeville – A type of live variety show popular in the United States from the mid 1800s until the 1930s.

Vertical integration – The strategy of incorporating all aspects of the movie business, from production to distribution to exhibition, within a single company. Vertical integration was the central process in establishing the Hollywood studio system of the late 1920s through the end of World War II.

Videotape/VHS – A method of recording sound and images using magnetic tape. VHS, or "Video Home System," refers to a particular kind of video recording and playback using cassette tapes. While industry use of videotape goes back to the 1950s, the sale of consumer videotape cameras and recorders took off in the 1980s, allowing anyone to create their own sound movies, record programming from their television sets, and play prerecorded tapes at home.

Index

Page numbers in italic type refer to figures.